Contemporary Military Theory

The book aims to provide the reader with a state-of-the-art introduction to classic and modern military theory.

The text accounts for the most important theories within the field by developing and analyzing these theories, as well as problematizing both their normative and explanatory aims. While focusing on military theory, the book does not only reflect a single way of relating to knowledge of war and warfare, but furthers learning by introducing contrasting perspectives as well as constantly criticizing the theories.

There is a clear need for an introductory text for the entire field of military theory that focuses whole-heartedly on the theories – not on their context or how they are expressed in practice during war. This book covers questions such as how we should understand the changing character of war and the utility of force, and how the pursuit of political ends is achieved through military means. It draws upon and illustrates military thought through a wide-ranging number of examples from the Napoleonic Wars to the current war in Afghanistan.

This book will be of great interest for students of military theory, strategic studies, security studies, and defense studies.

Jan Angstrom is Professor of War Studies at the Swedish National Defence College, Sweden.

J. J. Widen is Associate Professor of War Studies at the Swedish National Defence College, Sweden.

Contemporary Military Theory

The dynamics of war

Jan Angstrom and J. J. Widen

 Routledge
Taylor & Francis Group

LONDON AND NEW YORK

First published 2015
by Routledge
2 Park Square, Milton Park, Abingdon, Oxon OX14 4RN

and by Routledge
711 Third Avenue, New York, NY 10017

Routledge is an imprint of the Taylor & Francis Group, an informa business

© 2015 Jan Angstrom and J. J. Widen

British Library Cataloguing in Publication Data
A catalogue record for this book is available from the British Library

Library of Congress Cataloging in Publication Data
Angstrom, Jan.
   Contemporary military theory : the dynamics of war /
   Jan Angstrom and J. J. Widen.
   pages cm
   Includes bibliographical references and index.
   1. Military art and science. 2. War (Philosophy)
   3. War. I. Widen, Jerker. II. Title.
   U102.A55 2014
   355.0201—dc23
   2014004058

ISBN: 978–0–415–64303–0 (hbk)
ISBN: 978–0–415–64304–7 (pbk)
ISBN: 978–0–203–08072–6 (ebk)

Typeset in Times New Roman
by Swales & Willis Ltd, Exeter, Devon

MIX
Paper from
responsible sources
FSC® C013604

Printed and bound by CPI Group (UK) Ltd, Croydon, CR0 4YY

Contents

Illustrations

Figures

Tables

Preface and acknowledgments

War has captured the imagination of countless people throughout history. Almost all humans – old and young, men, women, and children – have a relationship to war. War has changed the course of history, destroyed empires, changed forms of political order, and devastated countries' economies, and has killed, maimed, and traumatized millions of individuals. It has inspired societal change, economy, literature, art, and science in an often profound way. It is the tension between destruction and creativity, between grief and elation, as well as between sheer terror and hope of peace that gives war its special and indeed paramount importance for mankind. Since the advent of the nuclear age, war has even threatened to lay waste to the whole planet and make it inhabitable.

Even during peace, war and the shadow of future war permeate many, if not all, societies. In 2012, the Stockholm International Peace Research Institute (SIPRI) estimated that 1,753 billion USD was spent on military resources. Taken together, this represents a sum total of 2.5 percent of the global GDP. A fraction of this sum would rid the world of malaria, a disease currently responsible for more deaths than war. War and the threat of war do not only influence resource allocation, but are also highly visible in everyday life. We can see this in fiction, movies, news, and even in our language, where originally military terms such as strategy and tactics have spread to completely different contexts such as marketing, child care, and sports.

Given the immense importance of war, it is no surprise that there exists a wealth of knowledge about war. Given its importance, however, there is also surprisingly much that we have yet to discover about war. In this book, we focus on one particular form of knowledge about war. Namely theories of war and warfare. Military theory, in our understanding, does not imply impractical knowledge, since such theory is laden with practical guidance and can sometimes be read as a shorthand to achieving victory in war. We have avoided the temptation to try to capture only the most prominent of such advice and to portray the use of force in simplistic terms.

Instead, our primary pedagogical aim has been to focus on the complexities surrounding war in order to hopefully train the reader's ability to problematize and independently criticize the theories of war. It is our conviction that the ability to think critically about war and warfare will help to further our understanding of war in the future. War deserves to be understood in and of itself. It also deserves to be understood in order to improve decision-making on war and the use of force. Considering the enormous costs associated with war – for the defeated and victorious alike – improving the decision-making of the political elites and the military is of great importance. We are convinced that the ability to critically reflect upon the experience of war is a precondition for improving such decision-making, regardless of whether these decisions involve the use of force, limitations on the utility of force, or the creation of military capabilities.

Time and criticism have aided us in this endeavor. Indeed, they aptly captures the development of this book. We wrote the first version of the book in 2004 and since then it has been used in higher education in both civilian and military universities in – as far as we know – primarily Sweden and Norway. As such, we have been fortunate to receive feedback from hundreds of students over the last decade. In this much-revised and updated English-language version, we have been able to draw upon both our own development in terms of more experience as researchers and teachers, more and improved knowledge resulting from the vast increase of research on war following horrendous wars in the Congo, Afghanistan, Iraq, Libya, Syria and elsewhere, but also the countless hours of discussions with students about the book and its qualities. To begin with, we want to acknowledge the students' role in developing the book and its contents. Without careful and engaged readings of the book, making us aware of inconsistencies, providing advice on how to develop the book, and aiding us in our choice of military theoretical debates to review and evaluate, the book would not have been as strong.

We would also like to acknowledge the help of many colleagues and friends for fruitful, rich, and rewarding discussions. The list is too long to name, but includes current and former colleagues at, amongst others, King's College, London – host to the primary institution of war studies in the world – and Uppsala University – home of one of the foremost institutions of peace research in the world – as well as the Swedish National Defence College in Stockholm. Again, without challenging our ideas, forcing us to refine them, and encouraging us along the way, the book would not have been as strong. We also would like to acknowledge and single out individuals who have helped us with editing and translating bits and pieces of the text. Christoffer Hägg of Uppsala University aided us with double-checking quotes and editing the list of references, while Guy Skingsley and Charles Sulocki of the Swedish National Defence College helped us with raw translations of Chapters 6 and 7.

Finally, we would also like to express our gratitude to the three anonymous reviewers at Routledge for their valuable comments on earlier drafts of the book, and also to our very patient publisher, Andrew Humphrys, and his equally patient, professional, and knowledgeable staff at Routledge, Hannah Ferguson and Annabelle Harris. We also thank Julie Willis and Michelle Herbert at Swales & Willis for their professional, careful, and thorough production of the book.

The remaining flaws are our own.

Jan Angstrom and J. J. Widen
Stockholm, 3 June 2014

1   Military theory

An introduction

Introduction

This is not a book about war. It is a book about *ideas* about war. Such ideas have probably existed at least as long as war itself but, in the early history of mankind, they were seldom set down in writing in an enduring and comprehensible manner for posterity. It is, therefore, difficult to know to what extent military theorizing has occurred in other contexts than in the modern Western world. Like similar texts therefore, this book is biased towards Western thought from the Age of Enlightenment onwards, when ideas about war began in earnest to be formalized in writing. Military thought at large was for a long time intended exclusively for officers' training. It was not until during the Cold War that strategy started to be taught at a few civilian universities in the Western world (Freedman 1985; Betts 1997). However, towards the end of the Cold War, strategy in particular was hardly taught at defense colleges either. The near-frozen strategic situation and the superpowers' mutual assured destruction, had not lent itself to creative theorizing regarding conventional use of force. Instead, increasingly during the Cold War, waging war began to be thought of in terms of following manuals and staff procedures (Kelly & Brennan 2009).

Arguably, this was detrimental, and as soon as the Cold War ended it was followed by a renewed interest in theories of war. This interest was further fuelled by the outbreak of war and an increase in the number of armed conflicts immediately after the end of the Cold War (e.g. Themnér & Wallensteen 2011). Moreover, the wars appeared different from before, even spurring some to talk of "new wars" and others to talk of a revolution in military affairs (e.g. Kaldor 2006). Accordingly, the literature on strategy and military theory grew rapidly. Existing introductions to military theory are plentiful and, in many respects, good and authored by leading scholars. However, it is difficult to find any individual introductory work covering the entire field with a coherent and applied pedagogical idea, as well as one with an analytical and a problematizing approach. The existing literature can be divided into four general categories: (a) field-specific texts, (b) texts on the history of ideas, (c) individual-centred texts, and (d) texts on the art of war.

The first category of literature, *field-specific texts*, is very extensive and tends to provide both varied and detailed analyses of a specific sub-field of military theory (e.g. Till 2013; Beckett 2001; Stone 2011). The problem is that these texts, despite often being of good quality, only introduce a certain segment of military theory. This may, for example, concern books dealing with specific sub-fields, such as sea power, strategy, logistics, or guerrilla warfare. Nor is it unusual for these texts to have aims that go significantly beyond the introductory, and which may therefore provide important contributions to the state of our knowledge, primarily as a syntheses of their respective sub-fields.

The second category, *texts on the history of ideas*, has the advantage of capturing the development of military theory and the intellectual context within which it is formalized. A history of ideas perspective can partly explain the content of the theories – and thereby often provides an original contribution – at the same time as introducing the field (e.g. van Creveld 2000; Heuser 2010; Gat 2001). The problem with these texts is that they often tend to be narrative rather than problematizing and analytical. The theories described, moreover, are seldom developed conceptually. The explanatory aims of these texts sometimes mean they are more suitable for someone who is already familiar with the field.

The third category, *individual-centered texts*, where thinkers rather than their ideas are at the core, is often closely related to the texts on the history of ideas but has a clearer bio-graphical and individual-centred perspective (e.g. Paret 1986; Baylis & Garnett 1991; Heuser 2002). The focus of this literature on the individual theorists leads to a deeper understanding of the individual theorists' works and often an analysis of their intellectual development. This means that it often provides important contributions on how we should understand specific thinkers' military theories and why they formulated their ideas in a certain way. The problem with this category as an introductory text is that it tends to give a rather fragmentary picture of the field and often goes too deep, which makes it less suitable for beginners. The individual theorists in and of themselves are often at the centre of attention instead of com-prehensive and conceptual analyses of the actual theories.

The fourth and final category, *texts on the art of war*, is characterized by its aim of discuss-ing and problematizing the relationship between military theory and warfare. These texts (e.g. Lider 1983; Jones 1987; Baylis et al. 2010; Kassimeris & Buckley 2010; Gray 2007; Jordan, et al. 2008) contribute to analyses of how military theory has influenced doctrines, training and warfare and therefore provide an important contribution to the field. There are, however, problems with this category, in so far as it rarely develops the theories the texts discuss. Instead, military theory is introduced indirectly through its practical starting point in warfare or doctrine development. Establishing how military theory influences warfare is, however, problematic, as it is often difficult to decide whether it is the idea in and of itself or the actor putting it forward (and thereby a power structure) that has influenced the conduct of war (cf. Goldstein & Keohane 1993). This also means that this category of literature is more suitable for readers who are already familiar with the main features of military theory.

From our perspective, the existing introductory literature on military theory therefore appears too ambitious toward details, too specialized or too practically oriented to intro-duce the field optimally. This means that the current literature is often more suitable as in-depth literature. There is, consequently, a need for a comprehensive, accessible intro-ductory text for the entire field of military theory that focuses whole-heartedly on the theories – not on their context, their practical expressions in warfare or their advocates. Our approach is to systematically discuss military theory on the basis of its qualities as *theory* and – more precisely – as social science theory. By developing and systematizing military theory, this book can thus be said to complement and improve the existing litera-ture. It is important to point out, however, that this book is primarily a textbook with only limited aims as regards originality. For example, we do not claim that our interpretation of, for example, Clausewitz's reasoning on the nature of war is ground-breaking, but as an introductory book, its pedagogical approach, structure, analytical framework, and parts of its analysis have original features.

The book aims to provide the reader with a state-of-the-art introduction to classic and modern military theory. It will account for the most important theories within the field by developing and analyzing these theories, as well as problematizing both their normative and explanatory aims. It is a book about military theory that does not reflect a *single* way of relating to knowledge of war and warfare, but many alternative ways. Indeed, it is precisely by introducing contrasting perspectives, as well as constantly criticizing the theories, that learning is furthered. This approach will obviously cause certain problems. An introductory book that focuses on the actual theories and the concepts they have been built on will, by definition, lack large elements of the historical background that puts theories and theorists into context. This could lead to a limited understanding of the origin and aims of the theories and to the discussions in the book becoming more abstract than would otherwise have been the case. However, this approach has a proven pedagogical merit within political theory and there are no reasons to believe that it would be less advantageous for learning military theory.

Before we move on to a discussion of what military theory is, we would like to make the reader aware of two things that clarify, define and justify elements of the discussion to come: the relevance of exact and well-defined concepts and the question of how the views of large and small states differ. Concepts are key components within science and, thus, also within military theory. Rigorously formulated concepts will lead to boundaries being created where some elements of reality are excluded and some are included. This feature provides us with an analytical instrument and a tool for analyzing reality. Such tools are essential prerequisites for a systematic search for knowledge. Only precise and well-defined concepts allow valid generalizations and an effective exchange of knowledge between individuals.

Concepts also have other merits, e.g. the ability to make visible what we have previously only been able to perceive intuitively (or not even known). When, for example, the Prussian general and military theorist Carl von Clausewitz (1780–1831) formulated the concept of "friction" in order to capture the random elements in war, misunderstandings, bad weather, and technical problems etc. were not new phenomena per se. His concept made these problems visible, however, and served to categorize them as variables that those participating in war cannot avoid (Clausewitz 1993: 138–40; cf. Cimbala 2001). In this manner, concepts have a dramatic effect on how we perceive and categorize the world around us. They tend to simplify an efficient exchange of ideas between individuals, granting the possibility for criticism, which, in turn, is one of the strongest driving forces behind the search for new and better knowledge (Lakatos & Musgrave 1970). Concepts do not necessarily reflect an objective reality, but serve also partly to shape the manner in which we perceive this reality. Concepts are thus not only the end result of research, but also a prerequisite for this activity (Vasquez 1993: 14–40). The latter fact, in particular, has made it necessary in this book to discuss relevant concepts within military theory and their relationship to each other.

The majority of key military theorists in the Western world belongs to, or is closely associated with, the great powers of the world. Moreover, most of the empirical studies focus on cases where at least one side in the contest is a great power. This begs the question to what extent there is a great power bias in the field that renders generalizations to smaller powers invalid? There are obviously research results and theoretical arguments, generated from studies of great powers that only partly can be transferred to other countries and areas. An obvious case in point is nuclear strategy, since it is only a select few states that have acquired nuclear weapons. Samples that the results are based on may contain a bias towards the great powers' conduct of war and use of force more broadly. Without supplementary investigations into how small states act, it is not clear what generalizations can be transferred. But assuming that military theory is influenced by great powers and their interests is not the same as stating that these theories lack validity for smaller powers. These theories may have to be supplemented or modified, but we cannot be certain until research has actually demonstrated this. Such investigations, to the extent that they are necessary and scientifically possible, require careful and extensive studies and are, by necessity, outside the scope of this book. The theories presented in the book are, therefore, in many respects, a reflection of the existing theory within the different areas of military theory, and not an attempt to select or interpret these theories through the lenses of a particular nation.

Defining military theory

It appears reasonable to begin a textbook of this kind by attempting to answer the question: what is military theory? This question can best be answered by deciding on whether all ideas or theories about military matters constitute military theory. In the discussion below, the concept of military theory will be exactly defined by distinguishing it from (a) military thought, (b) military doctrine, (c) military history, and (d) other research fields concerned with military activities.

First, we should distinguish between military thought in general and military theory. The relationship between them can, perhaps, be most easily expressed as follows: while all theories constitute thought, not all thought amounts to theory. Theory is therefore a sub-set of thought. The boundary, however, is far from clear-cut and requires further clarification. A theory is more systematic than an idea and is consequently a more complex thought pattern that expresses links between different ideas. A comparison with political theory is fruitful here. Political theory deals with what politics is, how society should be governed and how human communities should be organized. This makes interpretations of concepts such as justice, power, equality and freedom key areas within political theory (e.g. Goodin & Klinge-mann 1996). This also means that, as not all political opinions constitute political theory, not all ideas or opinions that concern military matters are military theory. Both political theory and military theory are attempts at systematically organizing evidence of the empirical world to a varying degree of universal validity. Theories are thereby of a generalizing nature, which not all ideas need to be.

The word theory comes from the Greek *theoria*, literally meaning "contemplation." From the linguistic meaning of the word, we can also deduce a key feature of theories. They are abstractions and thereby not something we can "touch." Although this observation is hardly controversial, the concept of theory, as indicated above, is far from uniform. It is used in different ways by different individuals, but can also be interpreted differently in different academic and professional disciplines. A minimalist interpretation of the concept may contain elements where theories organize our observations through categorization and formulation of concepts, while theories with a higher aim can express a causal link between several quantities (cf. Parsons & Shils 1951). In this way, theory can include both statements that are not yet entirely proven and those that, through a great number of experiments and/or observations, have proven to be valid.

Naturally, there is a greater tendency to rely on a theory that is verified by empirical results (or at least not yet falsified), rather than an unproven or even improvable theory (cf. Popper 2002; Williams & May 1996). What is, instead, of vital importance for the value of the theory is how it is formulated, its logical consistency and its ability to correspond to systematic experiences (empirical data). But it is often difficult to determine how far a theory is in agreement with systematic experiences. This is sometimes due to the fact that there is, quite simply, not a sufficiently great amount of data or when that data is available, it is difficult to interpret. Of course, the theory's value also depends on whether its assertions have any practical application. When applying theories, it is important to establish in which situations the theories can and cannot be applied, and when a theory can or cannot explain various phenomena. A major part of the scientific process consists, therefore, of various attempts at identifying the scope of a theory. How many and what observations can the theory explain? What is the theory's explanatory power i.e. how detailed are the explanations of the observations in question? We can also state that, even with a minimalist interpretation of the concept of theory, the concept of thought is wider as it may contain claims of the kind that cannot be generalized, such as elements from doctrines, opinions and vague ideas. Our aim in this book is to concentrate as far as possible on military theories rather than on military thought.

Second, we should distinguish between military theory and military doctrines. Although both theory and doctrine could be said to constitute knowledge (and the terms thereby overlap to some extent) it is important to differentiate between them (cf. Hoiback 2013). Even with a rudimentary understanding of theory as being a systematized abstraction of reality with a view to establishing the link between two or more quantities, major differences emerge, compared with the concept of doctrine. Military doctrine is institutionalized knowledge of how, for what and why military resources should be utilized (Posen 1984: 13–14). It is thus considerably more specific in terms of time and space than theory. While doctrine should be regarded as an actor's decision on how something *should* be carried out in a specific context, theories are more general and need not necessarily have normative aims. Geoffrey Till (2013: 51), a leading sea power scholar, described the difference as being that, while theories deal with "the art of cookery, doctrine is concerned with today's menus." Both are important, but also different. For obvious reasons, it seems natural for this book to focus on military theory rather than on military doctrine.

Third, we should separate military theory from military history. Somewhat simplified, military theory, unlike military history, deals with the general rather than the specific, the abstract rather than the tangible, and the timeless rather than the contextual. In military history, researchers tend to see their specific object of study as meaningful in and of itself, while, in military theory, they view the subject of research as a case of a large universe of comparable phenomena. This does not, however, mean that military historians never theorize or that military theorists never investigate the unique (Gaddis 2002: 62–70; Carr 1964). On the contrary, it is common for social scientists and historians, who study the same object, for example war, to have more in common with each other than with other representatives of their respective disciplines. The difference between their approaches has, however, consequences with regard to the extent that generalizations can be regarded as valid and relevant. The perspective that the object of study is unique per se is, if we take it to its logical conclusion, not compatible with generalizing one's conclusions to other cases (Elman & Elman 2001; Kaufman 2001). By definition, military theory has, therefore, generalizing aims and it is something "more" than just a description of war and warfare (Eccles 1965: 26–8). As far as this book is concerned, this means that texts of a purely military historical nature will not be discussed. They are simply not theory.

Fourth, we can distinguish between military theory and *all* research that concerns military matters. This can be done, like Julian Lider (1980: 1–18, 377–407) and Martin van Creveld (2000: 15; cf. Betts 1997; Mahnken 2003; Freedman 1985), by describing the field and its development in accordance with its key issues. The two issues that we find at the core of military theory are the question of what war is (its nature and form) and how victory is achieved in war. Military theory can, in this way, be set apart from, for example, international law, anthropology, international relations, political science, security studies, peace research and sociology – even if the object of study, broadly defined as armed conflict, is partly overlapping (cf. Buzan & Hansen 2009). The choice of issues has several consequences with regard to the selection of the theories that we discuss. If, for example, we were to include the question of "how war can be avoided" in our discussion, the amount of literature would grow and become almost unmanageable. This would, of course, mean that thinkers such as Abbé St Pierre or Immanuel Kant in the eighteenth century were devoting themselves to military theory when they presented their peace plans and that we must, consequently, discuss these texts as well (Hemleben 1943). This means that studies on the causes of war are not of interest to military theory, while the causal relationships *within* war certainly are. As this book focuses on questions about the nature of war and how to win wars, this means, for example, that operational planning and preparations, logistics, military command, concepts of warfare, the development of doctrines and much more would have to be included, as these components can be regarded as variables (or principles) for how wars can be won. Consequently, even a narrow definition of military theory leads to a wide variety of disciplines and related subject fields.

Without preceding the discussion in Chapter 2 on what war is, we would like to emphasize that Clausewitz's (1993: 731–7) understanding of war as "a continuation of policy by other means" implies that military theory has close links to the study of politics, or more specifically, the study of the use of force or the threat of the use of force. It is, however, just as important for military theory to be able to deal with military operations in its analysis as they are an inescapable element of war. Moreover, it is often difficult to achieve a satisfactory answer to the question of how to win wars without taking account of the internal variables, such as operational art, the commander's skill, how technology and materiels are used, etc. An obvious consequence of this is that military theory is multi-disciplinary. The field's second key question, concerning how wars are won, is somewhat ambiguous. This ambiguity in particular has given rise to extensive literature in this field. It is, for example, by no means certain that a tactical victory in battle will lead to victory in war. In a corresponding manner, the way in which war is conducted at the strategic level may differ dramatically from how it should be conducted – and won – at the operational or tactical level.

The character of these central questions also means that we can interpret military theory as both normative and explanatory by nature. One of its aims is to identify guidelines for how a party *ought* to wage war in order to win. Here, the field again resembles political theory, which has a normative emphasis, e.g. concerning how a society *ought* to be organized in order to maximize certain interpretations of justice, democracy etc. The other aim of military theory is to explain the dynamics and outcome of war. Here, the field is concerned with identifying variables that can explain victory and defeat in war rather than being an intellectual tool to wage war more successfully. As we will see, the tension between these two approaches is a crucial driving force in the development of military theory.

The problem with defining the subject based on these two questions is that other disciplines also study them. The question of "how war is best won" is not unique to military theory and the results produced on the basis of the aforementioned question are not automatically military theory. A historian who tries to explain the outcome of a war but who has no ambitions of generalizing his observations cannot be said to be involved in military theorizing. It is also difficult to assert that historians and political scientists devoting themselves to this question have not understood that they are, in actual fact, military theorists. There are, therefore, some problems involved in any analytical division or understanding of the subject (cf. Schmidt 1994). It is worth noting that originality is one of the most important driving forces within science. Since individual researchers are continuously encouraged to question the existing boundaries of knowledge, the subject boundaries can never be regarded as fixed but rather as permeable interfaces. Definitions are still of some value, however, as they at least indicate where the emphasis is placed within a field.

What further makes an unambiguous definition of military theory difficult is that the field has been institutionalized differently. In Britain alone, the study of the conduct of war does not only take place at military educational institutions, but under the academic belonging of war studies, international relations, strategic studies, and security studies at civilian universities. To add further confusion, security studies, for example, tends to be understood differently at different universities. Partly due to the inherent qualities of modern research and modern academic structures, therefore, the way research and education is organized has an impact on how this knowledge is related to other fields and sub-fields. This has created a situation where borders between fields of study are very porous. In our understanding, military theory is wider than strategic studies, but narrower than security studies, war studies, and peace and conflict research respectively (Betts 1997). It was tempting to use the term "strategic studies" in this book too, but in the interest of clarity, we avoid this common term, since it is sometimes used for strategy only, while sometimes for all military-related research. Consequently, we find military theory to be a term better suited for our enquiry.

In conclusion, we suggest that military theory is a critical and systematic reflection on war and warfare, not the waging of war. Military theorists attempt to find patterns that can be generalized in actions during war, not to study individual cases per se. Military theory is a subject field consisting of several theories, not one individual theory. Military theory is primarily concerned with the nature and character of war as well as the successful conduct of war. Its theories are therefore both normative and explanatory, although, strictly speaking, it is more doubtful whether they can be descriptive. Military theory is multi-disciplinary in so far as one needs to have an understanding of the political, strategic, operational and tactical processes in war, but the subject mainly deals with the military aspects of war – not everything that concerns war. Military theory can be regarded as a sub-field within war studies, broadly conceived, just as political theory is a sub-field of political science. This also makes military theory relevant for other disciplines dealing with the causes, dynamics and resolution of armed conflicts, such as peace and conflict research, as well as security studies. Below, we will concentrate our effort on the field's two core questions i.e. what war is and how it can be won, as it is these two questions that make the subject unique.

The central themes of military theory

As argued above, military theory consists of a number of problem areas and themes that are worth emphasizing further. For the purposes of this book, four of these are of special interest, as an understanding of them also increases the possibility of understanding military theory. For this reason, they are also central themes running through this book.

The first theme is the notion of *levels of warfare*. In order to analyze war and warfare, a division into levels is often used as an instrument of clarification. The specific division into levels varies, however, depending on the context – theoretically or in terms of doctrine – and, sometimes, two, and up to five, levels are applied. The levels of warfare as an analytical instrument are, to a great extent, dependent on the nature of war and, among military theorists, the interpretations of the concepts vary, but also the division into levels per se. For example, the difference between the strategic and tactical levels has a rather long history, while the addition of the operational level is from a more recent date and is usually associated with the Napoleonic Wars in the early nineteenth century (e.g. Naveh 1997; Olsen & van Creveld 2011). The advantage of levels of warfare is that they increase the stringency of the military theoretical arguments. Victory at, for example, the tactical level does not necessarily mean victory at the strategic level. Moreover, an analysis of the nature of war will, perhaps, also have different consequences at the tactical and strategic level. War and warfare are complex phenomena that must be categorized and carved up to be made intellectually comprehensible. However, the levels of warfare – just like other military theory – also have practical features. It is certainly possible to interpret the levels of warfare as decision-making or command levels. In this way, the levels of warfare are not just a method of analyzing war, but also a tool for waging war.

The second central theme of military theory is the *exercise of military power* or use of force. Just as exercising military power is only part of a state's overall exercising of power, war and warfare are just parts of a state's overall exercising of military power. The question of how to win wars is, of course, just another way of putting the question of how to use military force most effectively. This means that military theory deals with the exercise of military power, but not the exercising of *all* military power. For example, the rule of a military dictator can be a form of use of force without being counted as military theory. Within military theory, the use of force covers everything from being able to indirectly influence an opponent to behave in a way that promotes our own interests, to persuasion or attraction (Nye 2004), and to crushing an opponent by means of military power, i.e. brute force. Between these extremes, there is also the capacity for deterrence, which is of a more latent nature and aims to persuade someone to refrain from doing something they would otherwise have wanted to do. Finally, there is coercion, which involves the ability to persuade someone to actively do something they would not otherwise have wanted to do through the threat of, or use of, force (e.g. Schelling 1966; George & Smoke 1974; Byman & Waxman 2002; Ring 2005). Military force and armed combat, or the threat of these, are often assumed to be means for achieving military and, ultimately, political aims. It is important for military theory to relate to the wider question of the exercising of military force as the subject field has ambitions of generalizing i.e. where the object of study is a case of something bigger. This also means that issues related to how force is translated into organized armed forces is an integral part of strategy and therefore also of military theory.

The third central theme of military theory is how military affairs should be studied and to what extent this, in turn, shapes the field (Soeters et al. 2014; Hoglund & Oberg 2010). As we have seen, it is not easy to define a field like military theory. Besides the modern division into scientific disciplines, reflecting the state of knowledge and the normative concerns when the disciplines were established on a broad front at universities during the end of the nineteenth century and beginning of the twentieth century (Barkawi & Brighton 2011), there are intra-disciplinary factors that mean the subject boundaries cannot be regarded as watertight bulkheads. If anything, they should be regarded as permeable interfaces, which makes attempts to unequivocally define military theory (or other scientific subject fields) even more difficult. Two of the most highly valued norms within the scientific community are originality and organized skepticism. These norms encourage individual researchers to search for hitherto untried avenues of thought, to combine not yet combined quantities, to stretch the limits of what knowledge is and to question existing interpretations of that knowledge and its limits. In practical terms, this means that fields change as research develops. This also means that questions of methods – *how* we know what we think we know – are a key part of military theory and its development.

The fourth and final central theme within military theory is, somewhat simplified, whether it should be interpreted as theory or practice. Is military theory explanatory and can it establish causal relationships that could explain why one side wins in battles, campaigns or wars or is it normative and can constitute guidance as to how to wage war? We do not believe that military theory is warfare. Instead, military theory balances between having practical aims (being an aid to practitioners) and having theoretical aims (being able to contribute towards increased knowledge and understanding of one's object of study). One of many expressions of this dualism within military theory are the so-called principles of war. Should we interpret these principles as a crib sheet for the practitioner with whose help the latter can formulate and implement plans for combat? Or should we understand concentration of force, surprise etc. as factors that could explain the outcome of a battle, campaign, or war?

It is possible to interpret these two alternative aims of military theory as rivals. Such an interpretation argues that explanatory theory searches for knowledge of war and warfare independently of any practical benefit. A better understanding of war is, therefore, a goal in and of itself. In this way, we can distinguish the explanatory aspect from military theory's normative aspect, in which it is more a case of military theory being able to produce guidelines as to how war should be waged and won. As a result, it is possible to regard military theory as facing a choice between practical and explanatory utility. The tension between these two approaches can be regarded as a considerable driving force in the development of the subject, a factor we touch on throughout. Although military theory's dual aims can be difficult to distinguish between in practice, we can separate them analytically in order thereby to make it easier to problematize various theories within the field.

Outline of the book

This book consists of ten chapters that, together, cover key aspects of military theory. The book is structured according to the two fundamental questions of military theory. While the introductory chapter forms the framework for the scope and relationship of military theory to other fields of study, the chapters that follow, Chapters 2–9, can be regarded as a presentation of the contents of military theory. We present here a great deal of those theories that answer military theory's main questions – what war is, broadly speaking, and how to win wars. Chapters 2–4 can be regarded as mainly conceptual analyses in which we discuss various interpretations of certain key concepts, such as war, victory, strategy, and operational art. In Chapters 5–9, we account for some theories that could be said to lay claim to filling the aforementioned concepts with substance. In the concluding Chapter 10, we will return to the four themes described above and further problematize them on the basis of the discussions made in the chapters and outline two rivaling dynamics of war. The outline of the book is thus a reflection of the content of the field.

The discussions in the individual chapters are permeated by the central themes of military theory. These constitute a latent structural logic and are thereby an important reason for the overall outline of the book. On the basis of the theme of levels of warfare, the book's structure can be regarded as going from Chapter 2 and its argument that war is a political phenomenon, on to Chapter 3 and Chapter 4, which deal with victory, strategy and operational art respectively. Operational art constitutes the conceptual basis for how the tactical level can be bound together with the strategic level. Chapters 5–9 accordingly discuss theories that fill the concept of operational art with substance and thereby deal with the different levels of warfare. On the basis of the theme of the exercising of military power, we can once again regard Chapter 2, with its argument that war is a battle of wills (where it is vital to impose one's will on the adversary) and Chapter 3 on strategy, defining victory as a springboard for discussing different theories about the use and utility of force, its effectiveness and its means in Chapters 4–9. On the basis of the theme of how military theoretical studies can be carried out, we can deduce a considerable element of the criticism of the explanatory aims of military theory. Finally, on the basis of the discussion in Chapters 2–4 that war takes place *between* actors with their own and opposing wills, we can deduce a considerable element of the criticism of the normative aims of military theory. The outline of the book is thus also a reflection of the central themes of the field.

In Chapter 2 (War) we discuss issues about the nature and character of war. We also elaborate on attempts to classify war. An introductory discussion regarding this question is of great importance, as we require an in-depth understanding of war and its nature before we can move on to introducing theories about how to win wars. One of the most fundamental assumptions made, rather often implicitly, in a great deal of the military theories discussed in the following chapters is that war is a rational political phenomenon. Amongst other things, this assumption is problematized in this chapter.

Chapter 3 (Strategy) introduces the discussion on how military theory has approached the question of how to win wars. It begins with outlining an understanding of the concept of victory. The chapter describes the fundamental ideas of strategy and its function in military theoretical thinking. Here, it is asserted that strategy as theory is characterized by three things: a systematic analysis of ends and means, finding solutions with scarce resources, and a peculiar logic that gives it a dynamic and often paradoxical character. Strategy thereby expresses a conscious manifestation of will with regard to how wars should be won and the political ends of the war being achieved.

In Chapter 4 (Operational art), we describe principles and ideas within military theory concerning operational art. The chapter mainly deals with operational art and related concepts at a conceptual level. As operational art expresses how tactical victories should lead to the strategic goals of a war being achieved, it is natural to continue the book with five chapters that, in a more tangible fashion, account for various solutions to the problems of operational art. In Chapters 5–9, we give operational art substance and show the diversity of ideas that have emerged in order to solve the problem of how tactical victories can be converted into strategic goals and ultimately into political victories.

In Chapter 5 (The principles of war), we introduce the principles of warfare, their inherent logic, their mutual relationships and the method behind their creation. As the principles can be regarded as an attempt to generate cumulative knowledge of how to win wars, they can be interpreted as both guidelines for the formation of strategy, operations and tactics and as an explanation of the outcome of various wars. It appears natural, therefore, for the chapter to begin with the more tangible part of military theory. In Chapter 6 (Joint operations), theories concerning joint operations, rather than those specific to the different branches of the armed forces, are introduced. Theories of the latter will, instead, be presented in Chapters 7–9.

In Chapter 7 (Land operations), the theories that exist regarding the exercise of military power on land are discussed. The aim of the chapter is to provide a general introduction to the study of ground warfare and its assumptions. The aim of Chapter 8 (Sea operations) is to introduce theories about sea power and its use in war and peace. In Chapter 9 (Air operations) modern airpower theory and its assumptions are introduced by discussing the effectiveness of airpower as an instrument of force.

The concluding chapter (Conclusions: the dynamics of war) discusses the question of the future relevance of military theory and its choice of paths between practical utility and explanatory social science theory. The chapter refers to the central themes of military theory and problematizes them on the basis of the discussions in the previous chapters. As such, it outlines the two dominant dynamics of war as either escalation or emulation. Are war and the use of force best characterized as cycles of violent actions and reactions or is it best characterized as a dynamic learning process?

Conclusions

Initially, we emphasized that this book deals with ideas about war rather than war as such. In this chapter, we have given a more detailed account of the structure of the book and the themes that permeate it. The reasons for our approach and our selection of theories can be derived from both what we regard military theory to be and also earlier attempts made to introduce the subject field. By examining earlier books introducing military theory, we can avoid rewriting books that other people have already written. For example, we do not discuss the influence of military theory on warfare and do not attempt to explain why theories are formulated in a certain way. We have criticized earlier introductory literature for being, to various degrees, far too deep, practical, or specialized to be able to function optimally as a reader's first encounter with military theory. Instead, parts of the earlier literature appear more designed for someone already familiar with the main features of the subject field. In this way, this book and its approach complement the existing literature.

By defining what military theory is and discussing its boundaries with other related forms of thinking on military phenomena, we can give further reasons for the structure of the book. As military theory has both normative and explanatory aims, we have chosen to problematize military theory on the basis of these aspects. As military theory attempts to identify generalizations about war, discussing the scope of these theories and degree of empirical verification is a considerable element in this book. As military theory inevitably deals with a form of exercising of military power, we will discuss opportunities and limitations concerning the use of military power.

Now that we have acquired a better understanding of what military theory is, we will move on in the next chapter to introducing our discussion on what war is. We therefore leave a discussion about the field so that we can, instead, concentrate on the contents of the field. Although the boundaries of military theory cannot be said to be clear-cut and the emphasis on the two core questions in this book may appear narrow, military theory is not, as already indicated, one uniform theory. On the contrary, it consists of a wealth of theories or approaches to its object of study.

Questions for discussion

1. Are all ideas about military phenomena military theory?
2. To what extent does military theory assist in attempts to study war or wage war?
3. What separates and unites military theory and military history?
4. To what extent are military doctrines influenced by military theory?
5. How is military theory related to other fields of study, e.g. strategic studies, peace and conflict studies, security studies and international relations?

Further reading

John Baylis, James Wirtz, & Colin S. Gray (eds.), *Strategy in the Contemporary World: An Introduction to Strategic Studies*, 3rd edn. (Oxford: Oxford University Press, 2010).
Carl von Clausewitz, *On War*, translation Michael Howard & Peter Paret (London: Everyman's Library, 1993).

Azar Gat, *A History of Military Thought: From the Enlightenment to the Cold War* (Oxford: Oxford University Press, 2001).

Harald Hoiback *Understanding Military Doctrine: A Multidisciplinary Approach* (London: Routledge, 2013).

David Jordan, James D. Kiras, David J. Lonsdale, Ian Speller, Christopher Tuck, & C. Dale Walton *Understanding Modern Warfare* (Cambridge: Cambridge University Press, 2008).

Julian Lider, *Military Theory: Concept, Structure, Problems* (Aldershot: Gower, 1983).

Thomas Mahnken & Joseph A. Maiolo (eds), *Strategic Studies – A Reader* (Abingdon: Routledge, 2008).

Peter Paret (ed.), *Makers of Modern Strategy: From Machiavelli to the Nuclear Age* (Princeton, NJ: Princeton University Press, 1986).

Michael Walzer, *Just and Unjust Wars: A Moral Argument with Historical Illustrations*, rev. edn. (New York: Basic Books, 2006).

2 War

Introduction

The terrorist attacks against Washington DC and New York on September 11, 2001 was a dramatic and horrifying experience. Suddenly, what for long had appeared a low-key, low-priority threat to the West became very tangible. Perhaps more subtly, however, the terrorist attacks also challenged the concept of war deeply embedded in security studies, military theory, international law and international relations. Were the September 11 attacks acts of war or crime on a grand scale? This is just one example of a broader category of questions about the nature of war. Are price wars the same phenomenon as war against terrorism, civil war, *Blitzkrieg* or world war? How are war and peace related to each other? Should all acts of violence – e.g. football hooliganism, organized crime, rioting, so-called structural violence (Galtung 1985) i.e. injustice, discrimination, and oppression – be understood as war?

The purpose of this chapter is to introduce different approaches to how war can be understood and categorized. This includes questions of to what extent our current categorizations are contextually bound. How should we, for example, understand the US Civil War? It was fought mainly in a manner consistent with contemporary interstate war, in which the parties unilaterally, before the war broke out, declared that they would respect the laws of war and treat any prisoners of war as if they were soldiers belonging to a foreign power (which is unique in the history of intrastate conflict). Meanwhile, a bitter guerrilla war was also waged in Kansas and Missouri (Brownlee 1986), which included the expulsion of, and atrocities against, civilians (what we today would regard as "ethnic cleansing"), and unconventional methods – e.g. long-range raids – were used on all fronts. Were there several wars going on in parallel with each other? Is it misleading to call it a "civil war"? The chapter contains two main parts. The first deals with conceptualizations of war while the second deals with different ways to categorize wars and armed conflict.

How we understand war is important since it helps us to limit generalizations of victory and defeat in war. It is therefore crucial for analytical purposes. It is also a central issue in policy discourse, if an operation is termed as war or does not have far-reaching legal and political implications. During the past decade, a number of small northern European states, such as Norway and Sweden, for example, avoided the term war when describing operations in Afghanistan. Former US president George W. Bush avoided the term "prisoner of war" in order to detain and interrogate suspected al-Qaeda operatives in Guantanamo Bay for longer than the laws of war would allow. To name a phenomenon as war is therefore an intensely *political* decision in and of itself (Mansfield 2008). How to understand war is also central for strategy, the pursuit of war, and efforts to stop war on behalf of the international community. Clausewitz (1993: 100) captured the logic behind this argument aptly:

[T]he first, the supreme, the most far-reaching act of judgment that the statesman and commander have to make is to establish . . . the kind of war on which they are embarking; neither mistaking it for, nor trying to turn it into, something that is alien to its nature.

Nearly 150 years later, and in a completely different context, Mao Tse-tung (1966: 96) expressed similar thoughts: "Unless you understand the actual circumstances of war, its nature and its relations to other things, you will not know the laws of war, or know how to direct war, or be able to win victory." Thus, it is important to understand war in order to wage it successfully or in order to intervene and stop bloodshed. Inability to understand war and properly analyze the nature and character of war, according to Harry G. Summers (1982), was the major reason why the US ultimately lost the Vietnam War. It is by understanding the war you are about to embark upon that you can identify correctly your comparative strategic and operational advantages, which, in turn, is necessary in order to construct an optimized strategy.

Conceptualizations of war

Perhaps the most common conception of war and peace is that they are different conditions that can exist between states. The distinction is often perceived as binary i.e. states are either at war or in peace. War and peace are, in this interpretation, opposites. During peace, individuals, groups and states can realize (or at least seek to attain) goals through dialogue, the rule of law and, typically, unarmed competition and conflicts are solved with peaceful means. During war, however, force, violence, and bloodshed are the vehicles with which the actors seek to realize their goals (Wight 1966: 33; Kalyvas 2005: 89). The understanding of war and peace as a dichotomy underpins (and is reproduced in) international law and Western policies. It is also fundamental to most of the academic discourse in strategic studies, international relations, and peace and conflict studies (cf. Coker 2010). In this interpretation, peace is understood to be the absence of war (cf. Samaddar 2004; Hoglund & Soderberg-Kovacs 2010). Following this dichotomous understanding, moreover, war is considered a break from normal peaceful relations where alternative laws take over "ordinary" laws and states seek to mobilize their armed forces and shift their economies to "war production." The dichotomous understanding of war and peace also presupposes that we can differentiate between war and peace chronologically. However, as Coker (1997) and Afflerbach & Strachan (2012) have demonstrated it can sometimes be difficult to identify war onsets and war terminations. Even momentous war experiences such as World War II can be tricky in this regard. Did it, for example, end in May 1945 or in August 1945? In addition to the binary interpretation of war, there are other ways to comprehend war.

In this part, three approaches to the understanding of war will be discussed. They give three slightly different answers to the question of what war is. The first approach seeks to identify the functional significance of war, the second assumes a distinction between war's nature and character, and the third seeks to understand war as an empirical phenomenon through identifying a measurable definition of war. Although the three approaches are closely related, there are also some differences. Above all, the three approaches have different points of departure for how they answer the question of what war is. This means that although the three approaches are similar (which is quite natural since they attempt to answer the same question, and are partly based on the same empirical evidence from the history of warfare), they hold slightly different answers to the question and at different levels of abstraction. By bringing together these different ways of how war should be understood, we can conjure a more comprehensive answer. On the one hand, without a measurable definition of war, we would find it difficult to test theories of war empirically. On the other hand, a measurable definition of war would not be possible without an assumption of the functional significance of war. In this way, these approaches complement each other.

What is the meaning of war?

The first approach to making sense of war tries to identify its functional significance. This approach highlights that before we can properly analyze a phenomenon, we have to attach a meaning to the event. For example, before we can, like Clausewitz (1993), argue that war is politically instrumental and rational, we must be able to "see" the possibility that war can be a tool to achieve certain ends. Within this approach to conceptualize war, one usually does not attempt to formulate operational definitions of war, instead focusing on making war comprehensible by identifying its meanings in different contexts. Below we identify seven different frames of reference that have been attached to war: war as a tool, war as armed violence, war as conflict management, war as bargaining, war as policing, war as art, and war as self-realization.

The first meaning – war as a *tool* – can be derived from Clausewitz's understanding of war as a political and rational phenomenon. This is probably the most influential understanding of war and it has proven to resonate well with large parts of later rationalist theory (e.g. Schelling 1966; Pillar 1983; Wagner 2000; Reiter 2003; Smith & Stam 2004). In arguing that war is "a continuation of policy by other means," Clausewitz (1993: 99) suggested that war was a means to achieve political goals: "The political object is the goal, war is the means of reaching it." Clearly, he also understood war as a means of exercising power for political purposes (1993: 83): "War is thus an act of force to compel our enemy to do our will." Other scholars have emphasized other purposes of war, but they join Clausewitz in understanding war primarily as a tool. David Keen (2000), for example, paraphrased Clausewitz and suggested that war is a continuation of economy by other means. What Keen referred to is that war can be used as a means of achieving economic objectives. This interpretation of war gained ground in particular during the 1990s, fuelled by the so-called greed or grievance debate and is common in several strands of research, especially research on African civil wars (e.g. Ballentine & Sherman 2003; Collier et al. 2009). Economic incentives are not only restricted to African warlords and elites, though. Furthermore, and according to Marxist theory, it is not possible to make a meaningful difference between politics and economics, as war is understood to be a tool for both these purposes (Heuser 2002: 138–42; Doyle 1997: 315–80). Others have stressed that wars are waged for honor or reputation (e.g. Lebow 2008, 2010), still maintaining the essential understanding that the meaning of war is a tool.

A second understanding of war implies that war means intense *violence* or mass killings. Martin Shaw (2003) has pointed out that the word "*Schlacht*" – which Clausewitz employs – is used for two purposes in the German language. It means both battle and slaughter. Shaw suggests that Clausewitz may have had this duality in mind when he used the term. In some sections of his masterpiece, *On War*, Clausewitz (1993: 145) places great importance on combat and fighting: "Essentially war is fighting, for fighting is the only effective principle in the manifold activities generally designated as war." The tension in Clausewitz's ideas is recognized by Beatrice Heuser (2002: 24–43, 186–90), in her distinction between the "young idealist" and "older realist" Clausewitz. Heuser argues that while the elder Clausewitz emphasizes the primacy of politics over war, the younger Clausewitz suggests that war has its own internal logic – an interaction between rivals – that drives its development to logical and violent extremes. The relationship between conflict, killing and war, therefore, may not be as clear in Clausewitz's thought as it is sometimes portrayed. Military historian Azar Gat (2001: 201–2) suggests that Clausewitz's premature death from cholera before he could finish revising *On War* has led to a fierce debate over the last two centuries regarding interpretations.

The third meaning of war highlights the basic antagonism within war and suggests that war is a method to manage conflicts. Here, war is likened to a *duel* between at least two parties. This meaning can also be derived from Clausewitz, who used the metaphor of a duel to provide war with a meaning. If we follow Clausewitz's line of thought a little further we can see that he meant that war – like eighteenth century duels – was a social institution. The duel can be interpreted as a social ritual with more or less formal rules and norms surrounding it that could be used to resolve a dispute between two individuals without resulting in unnecessary escalation (Vasquez 1993: 31–2, 39). War, in light of this, is an instrument to manage conflict, rather than synonymous with conflict itself. War is, to put it another way, a conflict management instrument with its own particular standards of right and wrong that have developed over the years and continue to do so (Holsti 2004). Furthermore, understanding war as a duel also implies that war is a social act. It is characterized by reciprocity i.e. both parties are trying to earn their way through waging war against each other. Interpreting war as a social act also means – as, among others, sociologists Georg Simmel (Ritzer 2008) and Lewis Coser (1956) have argued – that conflict is a sign of cohesion rather than collapse in a relation. From this perspective, war and peace are different, but not opposites; while peace could imply indifference, war cannot since it implies interaction.

The fourth meaning of war – war as *bargaining* – assumes that war is a form of communication. This interpretation follows from, among others, historian Geoffrey Blainey's (1988) argument that war arises when (at least) two parties have different perceptions of relative strength and Thomas Schelling's (1960, 1966) famous dictum that war is the diplomacy of violence. A number of scholars have followed suit and so-called bargaining theory has emerged as a comprehensive theory of war – explaining its causes, dynamics, duration and resolution (e.g. Slantchev 2011; Reiter 2009). According to this frame of reference, war is the means through which the parties collectively try to decide on a new allocation of the values at stake in the conflict. It is through war that the parties can signal their commitment to achieving certain aims, and information which otherwise would have been kept secret is shared by the opponents. In the end, communication through violence allows for the opponents to understand their respective bargaining positions and their structures of preferences converge around a new settlement. Unsurprisingly, war is not the most elegant of languages and communicating through violence certainly has its shortcomings (Mitchell 1981: 143–62). War thus resolves conflict and it operates as the mechanism for making collective decisions about who gets what, when and how. War is thus a way of reaching decisions, just as flipping a coin or voting – albeit through violence. Understanding war as bargaining, as Wagner (2000) points out, unites modern rationalist scholars such as Schelling and Slantchev with classical military theorists such as Clausewitz, who also held that war did not replace politics – but politics continued via the war. Clausewitz (1993: 731) argued that "war is only a branch of political activity; that it is in no sense autonomous." It also means that war as bargaining is an influential understanding which underpins much of strategic thought.

Rather than understanding war through the metaphor of a duel, Caroline Holmqvist-Jonsater (2014) has suggested that the relevant frame of reference is policing. In our fifth interpretation, it can be seen as an act of *policing*. She argues that Western policy makers and modern social thought has begun to witness the demise of instrumental war (war as a tool), as war to a larger extent is motivated and legitimized not as serving state interests, but rather serving international order. Hence, war is about creating and maintaining order – much like police forces create and maintain domestic order. This has far-reaching consequences for both the practice and theory of war. Understanding war as policing implies that war becomes perpetual, rather than short and decisive since fighting crime is a constant process. Moreover, it implies that war is normal rather than a break from normality.

The sixth frame of reference for war is *art*. At first, it may sound surprising that something as destructive as war can be understood on the same premises as the epitome of creativity – art. However, when one considers the obvious linguistic similarities, it is obvious that art and war are interlinked and that the language used to describe war tells us something about how contemporaries conceive of the phenomenon. We think, for example, of an *art* of war occurring in a *theatre* of operations, carried out by *actors*, *conducting* its operations that are *directed* by generals and their political masters. Armed forces even *rehearse* upcoming battles through maneuvers and training exercises. Moreover, there are several more synonyms which show how extremely close the language of war is to the language of art; one only has to think of operations and drama. This frame of reference, furthermore, is one that has been used consistently throughout history. It is believed that Chinese theorist Sun Tzu (1994) wrote his *Art of War* nearly 2,500 years ago. The fifteenth-century Italian Renaissance theorist Niccolo Machiavelli, French-Swiss military theorist Antoine Henri Jomini, and current British General Sir Rupert Smith (2005) all titled their major work on war: *The Art of War*. It seems that art mirrors life and since war historically has been a major part of life, the language of art has entered the realm of war. Approaching war as art implies that analyses of war are hampered by non-rational esthetic features that are difficult to capture in analytical instruments as well as difficult to replicate for practitioners.

The seventh and final frame of reference for war has its origins in a radically different position than rationalism. It is proposed that war is not instrumental, but an end in itself. War is *self-realization*. It is an integral part of human identity and through it, humans are allowed to confirm and re-confirm this identity. Within this understanding of war it is assumed that individuals – regardless of position in a decision-making hierarchy – are not rational, but act also upon emotions, righteousness, and identity. There are different schools of thought when it comes to how this identity is created. First, Israeli military historian Martin van Creveld (1991) relies on an assumption of human nature. Inspired by the Dutch philosopher Johan Huizinga, van Creveld suggests that human nature is to play. War, van Creveld advances, is the most interesting game of all, since the stakes are so high. This suggests that mankind will wage war as long as it is not predictable. Creveld uses this logic to explain the lack of nuclear war. Second, there are several scholars that suggest that identity is created in social interaction with others (e.g. Keegan 1994; Lynn 2008). This school of thought is more inspired by so-called social constructivism and it suggests that individuals' goals, as well as ideas of how to reach those goals, are shaped by culture (e.g. Hollis & Smith 1991). Keegan, for example, stresses the role of warrior communities such as the Zulus, the Spartans and the Cossacks and suggests that organized use of force in these societies cannot be understood as the result of political rational considerations, but is more akin to a lifestyle. In his 2008 book *The Culture of War*, Martin van Creveld also follows this line of thought, suggesting that norms of warfare play a central role in legitimizing ways to conduct operations and these norms are therefore critical when trying to understand the dynamics of war.

What is the nature of war?

The second approach to understanding war follows from Clausewitz's classic separation of war into its *nature* and *character*. Clausewitz's importance for our understanding of war cannot be understated and his theory is peerless when it comes to the intellectual interest it has received (e.g. Paret 1976; Howard 1983a; Aron 1985; Handel 1986; Strachan & Herberg-Rothe 2007; Herberg-Rothe 2007; Strachan 2007; Echevarria 2007; Herberg-Rothe et al. 2011). He argued, in short, that while the nature of war was constant, its character varied due to its political and social context. War thus continuously took different forms, but its logic was timeless. This approach is less focused on identifying operational criteria for war, which of course can be problematic for analytical purposes. Among those trying to identify the true nature of war, there are those who believe that war can be understood as a rational phenomenon and those who believe that war is irrational.

The clearest exponent, and probably the most-cited among those who believe that war is inherently rational, is Clausewitz. In *On War* (first published in 1832), Clausewitz faced two intellectual challenges: first, to explain why some wars escalated and others did not, and, second, to formulate theories – generalizations – on war despite the fact that war took on so many different faces. His solution to the first puzzle was to construct the conceptual pairing "absolute war" and "real war." In this way, Clausewitz was able to distinguish between an "ideal type" of war – a logically pure form – and war as it appeared in reality throughout history. Absolute war was characterized by an interaction among the combatants that continually pushed violence towards "its utmost boundaries." The interaction had this unfortunate dynamic since neither of the parties could fully control the other's actions. Because each of the parties involved in the war, moreover, knew this, it did not make sense to gradually escalate violence. Making the enemy defenseless as quickly and ruthlessly as possible was the aim of war. In the absolute war, there is no limit to the use of violence. The goal must be to defeat the enemy forces, conquer his country and break his will to continue the fight (Clausewitz 1993: 83–6). It is this reasoning that sometimes has led to Clausewitz being accused of advocating total war.

According to both Michael Handel (2001: 329–30) and Jan Willem Honig (1997: 109–21), Clausewitz believed that the Napoleonic wars had come close to absolute war, i.e. the logically pure form. However, he also realized that most wars did not escalate to the same degree as the Napoleonic wars; neither did they conform to "absolute war." Instead, "real war" displayed great variety in pace, duration, and intensity. Clausewitz deduced that friction and politics were inhibiting factors that prevented real war from becoming absolute war. By creating a theoretical construct of absolute war, he was able to explain deviation from this model and thus able to explain why some wars escalated while others did not. A central concept in Clausewitz's conception of the real war is "friction." What Clausewitz meant by the term is that friction, i.e. accidents, technical failures, misunderstandings, coincidences, weather problems, etc. that occur when different individuals are involved in one and the same project, is what distinguishes real war from war in theory. "Friction is the only concept," he (1993: 138) argued, "that more or less corresponds to the factors that distinguish real war from war on paper." His concept of politics is more ambiguous, prompting several scholars to investigate it (Herberg-Rothe 2007; Herberg-Rothe et al. 2011). French sociologist Raymond Aron (1985: 61–87) notes that Clausewitz identified and balanced in his argument two forms of "real" war – total and limited war – each associated with political objectives. In total war the aim is to put the opponent in such a situation that you can dictate the terms of peace, while in limited war using the military results in order to obtain success in the forthcoming negotiations on the basis of more limited ambitions.

Clausewitz's solution to the second problem, to create theory while recognizing the wide variety of war, was to argue that war had an inner essence, a nature (*Wesen*) which was common to all wars. The "character" of war thus became the practical and unique expression of individual wars. That way he could afford to generalize while avoiding self-contradictions. The nature of war, according to Clausewitz, consisted of two elements: the "duel," the basic antagonism which ultimately implied that war is violent, dynamic, and changing, as well as the so-called "triad," which ultimately meant that war is politically instrumental (cf. Waldman 2013).

First, the inherent antagonism in war meant that the intensity and duration of war varied. That variation can be constant may seem paradoxical, but need not be. What Clausewitz referred to is that, since war takes place between two parties, each of which do not control events individually, but are partially dependent upon the other party's actions, a dynamic evolves that is unique to every war. Clausewitz (1993: 101) thus claimed that, as one party attempts to impose its will upon the other, an interaction is created in which the parties dictate the conditions for the conquest on equal terms. Thus, the result is that the war is "a true chameleon that slightly adapts its characteristics to the given case." Therefore, variation can be said to be a part of the nature of war. That "war is nothing but a duel on a larger scale" between (at least) two actors also means, according to Clausewitz (1993: 83), that uncertainty and insecurity – the so-called *fog of war* – is a permanent feature of war. Since neither party can control their situation completely, neither of them can accurately predict the other's actions. Hence, uncertainty is a result of the reciprocal nature of war.

The second part of the nature of war, according to Clausewitz, was the so-called triad, i.e. that war ultimately is "a continuation of politics by other means." War should be understood as an instrument for achieving political goals:

> [W]e maintain . . . that war is simply a continuation of political intercourse, with the addition of other means. We deliberately use the phrase 'with the addition of other means' because we also want to make it clear that war in itself does not suspend political intercourse or change it into something entirely different.
>
> (Clausewitz 1993: 731)

War is not fought in a vacuum, but in a political context that sets the scene and makes war understandable. What distinguishes war from other forms of politics, however, are the means and methods employed; armed forces and violence. Thus, according to Clausewitz, we can understand war in terms of the political objectives that is pursued, thereby characterizing war as rational and instrumental. As an analytical model he suggested (1993: 101) that war balanced between the three independent forces, which form the so-called "triad":

> [A]s a total phenomenon its dominant tendencies always make war a paradoxical trinity – composed of primordial violence, hatred and enmity, which are to be regarded as a blind natural force; of the play of chance and probability within which the creative spirit is free to roam; and of its element of subordination, as an instrument of policy, which makes it subject to reason alone.

The three forces are commonly associated, perhaps too crudely, with the people (emotional forces), the commander (creative forces) and the political leadership (rational forces).

Sun Tzu (1994) understood the nature of war slightly different from Clausewitz. Like Clausewitz, Sun Tzu emphasized the political primacy over the military, the importance of rationality in war, and that change permeates the nature of war. This is clearly noticeable when one considers the length at which the latter treats war planning. However, there are also differences. Sun Tzu stressed cunning, surprise, and intelligence far more than Clausewitz.

His understanding of the nature of war thus is seemingly less focused on violence and more similar to the prevailing logic of strategy in limited war, where maneuver is more important than seeking a series of decisive battles (Handel 2001; cf. Lewis 2010).

The first step in outlining the alternative of rationalist war was to identify its alleged shortcomings. In particular, the trinity has received criticism (Angstrom 2005). On the one hand, it has been pointed out that the three poles of the trinity are all non-material and thus seemingly not taking into account the influence of economic or technological conditions. On the other hand, Clausewitz's operationalization of the trinity has received criticism. Creveld (1991), for example, believes that the fact that civil wars by far outnumber interstate war renders Clausewitz's triad in terms of government, armed forces, and people obsolete. Keegan (1994) maintains that war cannot simply be tied to politics and to the state because war existed prior to the state. Hence, although valid in a modern Western context, Clausewitz's generalization is simply not relevant everywhere. Furthermore, van Creveld (2008) criticizes Clausewitz's view of man as a rational being. Creveld also points out that war for purposes of survival is a challenge to the Clausewitzian understanding of war as a distinction between means and ends is pointless in such contexts.

Just pointing out potential flaws in the rationalist armor was not enough, however. At least two alternatives, both drawing upon versions of social constructivism, have taken shape over the last decades. First, one school of thought stresses the impact of norms, identity, and culture of armed forces and strategic elites on the conduct of war. Creveld (2008) criticizes Clausewitz's lack of analysis of legal and normative variables in the explanation for why some wars escalate while others do not. Instead, he suggests that war throughout history has always been surrounded by legal and normative regulations. Thus we can understand the variation in the course of events also by putting the war into its legal and ethical context, and not only – as Clausewitz does – into its political and military context. Instead, there are rules and norms that seem to underpin when war legitimately can be fought, how it is waged, and when it stops. For example, the act of declaring war can be understood as resulting from the norm (and need) to regulate and legitimize some forms of violence (while banning others). This norm was evidently so strong that even Hitler saw fit to declare war before launching his invasion of Poland in 1939 (van Creveld 2008; cf. Hallett 1998).

A version of the identity-based school of thought stresses in particular war and gender. The issue of women and war has traditionally received scant scholarly attention. Rapid progress, however, has been made on several accounts. We know, for example, that gender equality is positively correlated with intrastate peace (Melander 2005). Following an increasing amount of research of horrific atrocities against women in current war (e.g. Stern & Eriksson Baaz 2013), there has also been a wave of historical research highlighting, for example, mass rapes in eastern Germany in the end of World War II in which up to two million women were raped, many repeatedly (Beevor 2007), and forced prostitution in Asia by the Imperial Japanese of hundreds of thousands of women (e.g. Hicks 1997). We know that despite female soldiers in the front line being a hotly debated issue (e.g. van Creveld 2002), the number of female soldiers in the armed forces in the West is increasing. Following this development, there is also recognition of women's experience in combat (e.g. Wise 2011). Arguably more important than merely improving our empirical knowledge, however, is the introduction of feminist theory in the study of war. By highlighting the construction of a militarized masculinity in strategic discourse and basic training (e.g. Elshtain 1995; Tickner 2001; Goldstein 2001; Higate 2003; Wilcox 2009; Stern & Zalewski 2009; Hudson 2012; Sjoberg 2013), rationalist accounts of the nature of war is challenged. The argument, in short, suggests that a violent masculine identity is created and maintained through a set of practices in military organizations. Death and destruction, thus, does not come easier for men. The problem is the militarized masculinity.

The second school of thought suggests that war has turned into a postmodern phenomenon. These critics argue that Clausewitz was right for much of the nineteenth and twentieth centuries, but the nature of war has changed in recent decades. Instead, for much of the Western world, war has become something of a "spectator sport," as less of a state's resources and fewer people are directly affected by it. War, therefore, unfolds in the media, in a virtual social media. Michael Ignatieff (2000: 191) summarizes the argument as follows:

> [W]ar thus becomes virtual, not simply because it appears to take place on screen, but because it enlists societies only in virtual ways. Due to nuclear weapons, it is no longer a struggle for national survival; with the end of conscription, it no longer requires the actual participation of citizens; because of the bypassing of representative institutions, it no longer requires democratic consent; and as a result of the exceptional growth of the modern economy, it no longer draws on the entire economic system. These conditions transform war into something like a spectator sport.

Advocates of this theory (e.g. McInnes 2002; Coker 2001; Der Derian 2001; Ignatieff 2000; Hables Gray 1997; Bousquet 2008) point mainly to three factors that have driven the postmodern war: changes in technology, the West's reluctance to get involved militarily, and the high reliance on the use of air power to achieve their goals. Through the technological advances that enabled precision-guided bombs, the West has been able to increase its military efficiency, but also drastically reduce the danger of collateral damage to civilians. Together with increasing media attention, this has led to the West not only becoming sensitive to its own losses, but also, somewhat paradoxically, to the opponent's losses. Fewer losses and increasingly smaller force structures also imply that the armed forces have become more and more detached from the rest of the population. Through these processes, warfare is becoming increasingly divorced from the state and from politics. In its logical extension, this development seems incompatible with the Clausewitzian notion of war. It is also clear that the postmodern war thesis draws upon the Revolution in Military Affairs (RMA) debate. One of the more scintillating, but perhaps ultimately futile, notions is the development of non-lethal weapons. Surely, the removal of death from wars would represent a change in the nature of war but the postmodern war advocates also maintain that there is a danger that wars would become more, rather than less, frequent as society becomes more and more disconnected from the decisions, conduct, and suffering of war.

What does war look like?

The third approach to define war emphasizes the importance of formulating operational or measurable definitions of war. Rather than try to answer what war is based on an abstract, inherent nature of war, this approach is more "practical" and answers the question of what war is through its empirical manifestations. The great benefit of this approach is that we can distinguish different empirical patterns of war. For example, we know that major war is becoming a less frequent phenomenon in world politics (Vasquez 2012; Themnér & Wallensteen 2011; Väyrynen 2006) and maybe even that violence in general is declining (Pinker 2011; Goldstein 2011; Gat 2013), even if it may be too early to call it "obsolete" (Mueller 2004). Moreover, we also know that the number of intrastate armed conflicts by far has outnumbered interstate armed conflict since 1945 (see Figure 2.1) and that most armed conflicts occur in Africa, Asia and the Middle East. There is also an emerging consensus in this literature that the character of war (or at least the way we conceptualize this) is changing into something more complex and more heterogeneous (e.g. Strachan & Scheipers 2011; Bobbitt 2008). It has even been described as "war amongst the people" (Smith 2005) with a mixture of civil and military actors involved in the use of force raising questions about legitimacy, mercenaries, and accountability (e.g. Shearer 1998; Avant 2005; Mandel 2002; Singer 2004).

The most common definition of war within this approach is that war is "organized large-scale violent conflict." One of the key elements in this definition is that war is "organized," i.e. it is a collective and planned phenomenon, rather than random, arbitrary acts of violence. This of course says nothing about how *well* planned it is, but only that war is not a blood-thirsty, random, or stupid act (cf. Cramer 2006). "Organization" rather suggests that the violence in war is characterized by calculation, moderation, and control. The idea that violence in war is organized is closely related to Clausewitz's conception of war as an instrument. The organization of war also implies that war encompasses collective violence, rather than individual. Collective violence involves social structures and processes, thus reinforcing the degree of organization. "Large-scale" by this definition is often used to distinguish different forms of violent armed conflict. Several quantitatively oriented data collection projects such as the correlates-of-war project at University of Michigan (www.correlatesofwar.org, accessed April 7, 2014) and the Uppsala Conflict Data Programme at Uppsala University (www.pcr.uu.se/research/ucdp, accessed April 7, 2014) understand war to consist of at least 1,000 battle-related deaths per year, while other "minor" forms of armed conflicts contain fewer casualties. Equally central to the definition is how we understand the term "conflict." Peter Wallensteen (2011) defines conflict as a social situation in which at least two parties are committed to acquiring the same set of scarce resources at the same time. Adding "armed" only means that the parties have resorted to armed violence to resolve the conflict.

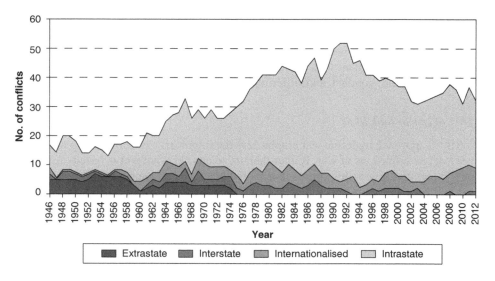

Figure 2.1 Armed conflict by type, 1946–2012 (Themnér & Wallensteen 2013).

This approach teaches us two important things. First, it is important to have a measurable concept of war. Indeed, it is the most important contribution to research on war that this approach provides, because it is only when there is a measurable definition of war that we can conduct systematical empirical studies. Moreover, the importance of being able to examine armed conflicts empirically cannot be overemphasized. The operationalization of "large-scale violence" can of course be criticized for being arbitrary, but it provides a tool by which one can compare wars across space and time. Second, this approach contributes to the realization that conflict in itself is not necessarily the same thing as war, but the conflict is still a prerequisite for war. This distinction is important because it indicates that war is only the result of a context in which there is a conflict.

Categorizations of war

It is common to try to distinguish between different forms of war. Categorizing war is important since it allows for more precise generalizations. It is also important for policy purposes. If there are different logics attached to different forms of war, uncovering valid categories can allow for more optimized policy responses. So how should we classify the phenomenon of war? This part of the chapter will therefore look at ways to understand conventional and non-conventional war, symmetric and asymmetric war, interstate and intrastate war, and high-intensity and low-intensity war. To be fruitful, categorizations must be mutually exclusive, neutral, logically exhaustive, and semantically consistent. If classifications are not made on a uniform basis, it may result in classifications such as when a ancient Chinese philosopher identified the following categories of animals: animals belonging to the emperor, embalmed animals, tame animals, piglets, mythical animals, wild dogs, animals that have just broken a pot, and animals that from a distance look like flies (Rosing 1994: 93). The problems with this classification hardly need further consideration. But how well do categorizations of war meet the standard criteria of fruitful categorizations?

Before attempting to categorize war, it is appropriate to ask whether all organized violence is the same phenomenon. We have already seen how Clausewitz distinguishes between the nature and character of war. This indirectly implies that war can change and thus be categorized, while at the same time remain the same phenomenon. Mike Smith (2005: 52) suggests that Clausewitz's logic is still valid – even in modern so-called low-intensity conflicts in the Third World: "Call it what you will – new war, ethnic war, guerrilla war, low-intensity war, terrorism, or the war on terrorism – in the end, there is only one meaningful category of war, and that is war itself." Charles Tilly (2003: 12–20), similarly, argues that all forms of collective violence, whether it expresses itself as war, as hooliganism, or as organized crime, may well be regarded as *one* phenomenon. Even if we understand war as one phenomenon, we should recognize that it takes different shapes and forms and is experienced differently by different individuals. A good indicator of the difficulties of classifying war is the rich flora of concepts that have been introduced to qualify the concept of war. One of the main problems obstructing categorizations of war is unavailability and unreliability of data. The warring parties have incentives to manipulate information about war and their operations, which also has an impact on how we can properly understand war. Moreover, since the character of war is changing as it is being fought; it is difficult to categorize a moving object (Lider 1980).

Categorizing war according to actors

Perhaps the most common classification is to distinguish between interstate and intrastate wars. The fact that this distinction is sometimes expressed as "war" and "civil war" shows how deeply entrenched and near-symbiotic war and interstate war are in the literature. There is, in short, a bias in much of military theory in favor of treating interstate war as more important than civil wars. This is also reflected in what is perceived as a military professionalism. Despite being an anomaly for the past 60 years or so, Western armed forces still largely cling on to an image of war as fought between large-scale regular armies. The fact that "small wars" only recently became part of the major Western powers' doctrinal hierarchies also show that the armed forces of the West have not really paid too much attention to them (Fishel 1995). Another sign of this more general tendency is that the British Army's newly established school for irregular warfare in 1940 was nicknamed "the school for ungentlemanly warfare" by its contemporaries (Beckett 2001: 21).

Interstate wars occur between states, while intrastate wars occur within them. The state, in turn, can be defined by two different perspectives: as an actor or as a phenomenon. Max Weber argued in the early twentieth century that the state is the actor who holds a monopoly on the legitimate use of violence within a given territory. It is based on an understanding of the state as an actor. We can, for example, as individual citizens, complain about the level of taxation the state enforces upon us or that the state exercises its power by its exclusive legislative and judicial powers. Its legitimate monopoly of violence refers to police, courts, and the military. Another way to define the state assumes the state to be a public legal person. It emphasizes that a state consists of a population, a given territory, and a government with control, and also that the government has interaction capabilities with other states (Hall & Ikenberry 1989; Giddens 1985; Hobson 2000). Both these ways of understanding the state can be criticized for being somewhat vague. For example, what is legitimacy? Is it reasonable to term power exercised by regimes in authoritarian states as legitimate when it violates human rights? Further, we can ask ourselves what "control" means? How much control, for example, should a government have to be called a state? One could, for example, claim that crime levels are a measure of state control. It therefore becomes clear that the difference between London and Kabul may be one of degrees of control, rather than absolute measures.

There are innumerable definitions of civil war, but they seem to share several traits. Perhaps the most obvious is that at least one of the actors in the conflict is not a state but rather some other social entity, such as an ethnic group, ideological faction, or other type of community. The counterpart to the rebel side is usually understood to be the government. Only lately, it has been recognized that a number of civil wars are conducted between different rebel groups – without the government taking an active role in the conflict. A further criterion commonly used to define internal conflicts is that they mainly take place within a state's borders or at least between neighboring peoples. The last criterion is important because it allows us to distinguish civil wars from the so-called "wars of national liberation," i.e. the colonial wars of the 1950s–70s, which are not usually understood as internal conflicts (cf. Brown 1996; Licklider 1993; Sambanis 2004).

Difficulties in defining the concept of "state" does, of course, imply that the binary division between interstate and intrastate wars has problems. If one cannot distinguish what is a state, it is hardly fruitful to try to separate war within and between states. Moreover, even in interstate wars, it may be difficult to clearly identify the sides, since the states may employ irregular forces or paramilitaries in addition to their regular armed forces. Despite these difficulties, this ground for classification is very common and permeates huge parts of the discourse. It also has some advantages which suggest that it is fruitful to distinguish between inter- and intrastate conflicts. Most importantly, there are several bodies of literature suggesting that the dynamics of the two categories of war are empirically different, which suggest that although they seem to be part of the same species – war – they should be separated.

It may also be pointed out that categorizations of war and armed conflict according to its actors both has its merits and its problems. Problems arise, for example, when the wars in and of themselves are about state-building or if there is a war that has both an internal and an external dimension. The reason is that then it is difficult to know whether what we observe can be placed into the usually binary division between the interstate war or civil war. How are we, for example, to understand the war in the Democratic Republic of Congo – what Prunier (2009) aptly has called "Africa's World War" – that over the last decade and a half has had an interstate dimension (Uganda, Rwanda, Burundi, Zimbabwe, Sudan, Chad, Angola, and France all had regular soldiers on the ground who took part in combat inside the Congo), a sub-national dimension (at least three major rebel groups, Rally for Congolese Democracy (RCD)/Goma, RCD/Movement for Liberation (ML), Movement for the Liberation of the Congo (MLC), and a series of splinter groups have been struggling for power with government forces), and an international dimension insofar as the UN has intervened in the country. The classification is also problematic when it comes to understanding the conflict between a state and one (or more) non-state actor who are not resident in the vicinity of the state such as US campaigns against al-Qaeda or its off-shoots (cf. Kilcullen 2009; Mackinlay 2010).

Categorizing war according to its purposes

Using the political purpose of war as the basis of classification is also very common. Here, we may think of wars of conquest as opposed to wars of territorial defense, or total war as opposed to limited war. The latter distinction is probably the most common and it separates those wars fought for absolutist ends (such as unconditional surrender or ethnic homogeneity in a defined territory) from those fought for negotiable ends (such as wars lacking an existential threat). It is important to recognize that this basis of categorization does not depend on an initial division of interstate and intrastate war. Hence, one could conceive of wars of conquest both within and between states. However, in the literature, it is common to make the distinction between different forms of civil wars according to its political purposes. Two categories stand out: ideological civil war and ethnic civil war (Kaufmann 1996a; Angstrom 2001; Sambanis 2001).

Ideological internal conflicts are the result of rival conceptions of how the state should be governed. At the center of this type of conflict are thus grievances about issues of power and resources within the state. It may, for example, be a demand for greater democracy (of any sort), increased opportunities for some economic classes, or smaller income gaps. In ideological conflicts loyalty is a variable, because consent and support for the "cause" must be created continuously and individuals can relatively easily change sides. The parties must constantly recruit new members while maintaining the already established support. This has implications for how war is conducted in these conflicts; there is, for example, no real value in committing atrocities against the population if it is support one seeks. This does not mean that atrocities do not happen in ideological civil wars. As Stathis Kalyvas (2006) has demonstrated, selective, intentional punishment can also be used to control the population (cf. Downes 2008).

While ideological civil war centers on state government, ethnic conflict centers on the relationship between the state, its borders, and its population. The ethnic conflict therefore questions the state's existence, not its rule. The objective of at least one of the parties involved is therefore either secession, i.e. to break out of the existing state and establish its own state, or irredentism, i.e. to break out of the existing state and join another existing state. In the short run, loyalty is not variable in ethnic conflicts. Even if we understand ethnic identity as essentially socially constructed and not primordial (Anderson 1991), individuals cannot choose their ethnic identity independently of context (as they can political position). The reason of course is not only that conflicts tend to harden identities (Kaufmann 1996b), but also that being accepted as belonging to a group depends on the other group members. Once large-scale violence has been initiated between the groups, it means that hardly anyone will want to shift groups or be allowed to change groups for fear of infiltrators. That the parties need to care less about building support also has implications for warfare, as we will see in Chapter 7.

However, there are also problems with the two-part categorization of internal conflicts. Most importantly, it does not seem to capture all forms of internal conflict. For example, it is difficult to understand the war in Liberia in the 1990s as either an ethnic or ideological conflict. At stake in Liberia, it seems, was not ethnicity, nor competing ideas of how the country should be ruled. Instead, it seemed to be more about *who* should rule the country. Similarly, the dynamics of ethnic or ideological conflicts cannot explain why warfare in some cases appears to be most intense in areas that are rich in natural resources. Furthermore, one can question categorizing wars based on the actors' goals and purposes. The problem with this is that actors may have an interest in manipulating information about their real objectives in war. Bob de Graaff (2005) suggests that was the case in the former Yugoslavia, where Serb leader Slobodan Milosevic hid his agenda during the war in the 1990s, partly to prevent the Western powers from intervening more forcefully (cf. Gow 1997, 2003), and partly because the war was not popular among the Serbian population. Furthermore, considering that the political objectives with the war may change as the war progresses, it is also difficult to categorize the war according to the parties' interests.

Categorizing war according to intensity

Another common criterion used to qualify the concept of war is its intensity. The idea to classify war or armed conflict along these lines emerged in the 1950s in the US where, under the threat of a nuclear war, the notion that armed conflict could be placed into a spectrum from nuclear war to terrorism took hold. Categorizing war according to its intensity presumes that relevant generalizations can be made between wars waged with high and low degrees of violence. Although it seems reasonable to assume that the dynamics involved in, and the features of, nuclear war are different from that of low-scale terrorism, problems of categorizing war according to intensity still emerge when "intensity" is measured. One common way to measure and operationalize "intensity" is the number of deaths per year in a conflict. As we have already mentioned, it is used in the quantitatively focused research of armed conflicts. Many use the 1,000 battle-related deaths per year as a line to separate war from other forms of organized violence. Following such an understanding of war, it is also common to draw another distinction between minor armed conflicts (1–25 battle deaths annually) and major armed conflict (using 25–999 deaths per year due to battle-related causes).

However, there are a number of problems related to using deaths as an indicator of the intensity of war. Securing data on the number of dead is difficult to obtain for outsiders because the conflicting parties have incentives to both hide and exaggerate the loss figures from battles. A further difficulty for outsiders in the collection of reliable and consistent data in many armed conflicts is that the warring parties can sometimes be difficult to distinguish from civilians, although the evidence suggests that the warring parties with local knowledge have no problems identifying each other (Duyvesteyn 2004, 2005). Moreover, the violence may be carried out in remote areas and the organizations may not have centralized knowledge of the personnel involved. Furthermore, it is often difficult to discern what is "battle-related." For example, there is overwhelming evidence that the Sudanese government used starvation as a weapon in its civil war in the south (Brosché & Rothbart 2012). How should this be understood? Is it still war or has it become genocide (cf. Prunier 2005)? Is it reasonable to distinguish between those fallen in battle and those starved to death when famine is a deliberate strategy? Establishing thresholds in number of deaths also display a degree of randomness. A war in which 950 are killed may not be that different a phenomenon from one in which 1,000 are killed. Indeed, there are several empirical cases that illustrate the difficulties further. For example, the 1982 Falklands War between the UK and Argentina appears to be just below the 1,000 battle-related deaths threshold (casualty figures vary between 910 and 972 deaths), resulting in its exclusion from some databases of war. Similarly, the "war" between Ecuador and Peru in 1941 is usually not included in data collections even though Ecuador lost about 40 percent of its territory, which can reasonably be regarded as a significant case of organized violence, even if the casualty figures were low (Holsti 1996: 154–5). As a consequence of these weaknesses a lot of effort in modern data collection strives instead to disaggregate data. The more fine-grained data is the better answers we can get in terms of patterns of violence. This relatively recent trend has much promise, but it still suffers from a few problems (Eck 2012).

Another approach is to assume the "classical" conflict spectrum. Rod Paschall (1990) suggests three categories of armed conflict. High-intensity conflict involves regular forces as well as nuclear weapons in a war between states. Mid-intensity conflicts involve only conventional forces, but the war is still being fought among states. Finally, low-intensity conflicts involve actors other than states, where the main armament consists of small arms. Paschall thus seems to suggest that "intensity" is related to access to particular weapon systems. Implicit here is probably the assumption that small arms can do less damage than nuclear weapons and that conflicts involving nuclear weapons are more intensive. Creveld (1991: 20) argues for a similar understanding of low-intensity conflict, but adds that they usually take place in the former Third World. Apparently, there is often an unspoken geographical dimension to the concept of low-intensity conflict.

Yet another criticism against distinguishing wars according to intensity relates to from whose perspective the armed conflict is of low or high intensity. For the individual soldier, it may not really matter if he or she will be fired upon in a world war or a protracted, low-intensity conflict. The experience is probably equally intense and war-like in both cases. Moreover, the experience of war for civilians differs in all likelihood very much in terms of intensity. Also on the societal level, the experiences of war can vary greatly. Howard Lee Dixon (1989:2), for example, suggests that it is only from a US perspective that a number of conflicts can be termed "low-intensity conflicts." For the parties involved in the rebellion, the experience is in all likelihood very intensive.

Categorizing war according to methods of warfare

If categorizations of war are permeated with problems if we use intensity, the nature of the actors, or objectives of war as basis for our categories, what about the method of warfare? There are an abundance of dichotomies that use methods of warfare to differentiate between wars: conventional and unconventional war, symmetric and asymmetric war, as well as regular and irregular war. The common denominator of these attempts is that the way war is conducted – the warfare – separates the categories. This way of classifying wars suffers from similar shortcomings as categorizations of war according to purpose of war, since modes of warfare can change during conflict.

Arguably the most widespread of these categorizations is the distinction between conventional and unconventional war. Conventional war is usually understood to be war conducted by large-scale organized, uniformed armed forces pitted against each other by their governments, abiding by the laws of war, and using high-technological weapons systems. Meanwhile, unconventional war is usually understood as its direct opposite: wars conducted by non-state actors, rag-tag units without discipline, armed with a mixture of sticks, stones, and small arms, not recognizing the laws of war (e.g. Harkavy & Neumann 2001: 16–24). However, there are good reasons to probe further into this distinction. First, the word "convention" has its origin in Latin and literally means "to come together," "agree upon," or "common." This suggests that conventional war should be understood as war where the parties agree upon a certain set of norms that set the boundaries for the means and methods employed in the war. In turn, this means that conventional war can involve far more modes of warfare than the standard understanding entails. Second, our usual conception reveals a Eurocentric world view. If we think of conventional war as the mode of warfare that is most common, it would be downright wrong to claim that mass-armies waging large-scale warfare empirically are the most common form of war. Globally, guerrilla warfare is certainly far more common. We can therefore with some justification argue that it is time to recognize that the concept of conventional war should actually correspond to the low-intensity internal conflict. And just because war can look differently, it does not mean that some versions of it are less rational (Duyvesteyn 2005; Reno 2011). Third, it is also slightly awkward that nuclear war – arguably the most cost-intensive weapons system known to mankind – is bunched together with Special Forces operations, terrorism, and guerrilla warfare in the category of unconventional war.

Instead of conventional and unconventional, some suggest that the dichotomy of symmetric and asymmetric war is a more fruitful approach to grasp modern war. The dichotomy resonates well with the biblical story of David and Goliath – weak against strong, guile against power, and innovation against reliability. It is widely acknowledged that warfare in general has changed its face since the end of the Cold War (e.g. van Creveld 2000; Strachan & Scheipers 2011). Two contrasting developments stand out. On the one hand, the great powers and the Western world have transformed, or are in the process of transforming, their armed forces from nationally oriented, large, often conscripts-based armies with high firepower, to expeditionary oriented, small, professional armed forces with high mobility and precision-guided munitions. This transformation has arguably produced the greatest military supremacy in modern history in favor of the West in general, and the US in particular (Berkowitz 2003; King 2011; Farrell et al. 2013). On the other hand, war is not fought among the great powers, but has pre-dominantly become an activity located in the weak powers of the world and most often become a matter *within* these states. These wars are fought with strategies of starvation, expulsion, and atrocities against civilians and by seemingly unorganized, small bands of militia and armed thugs, equipped pre-dominantly with small arms (van Creveld 1991; Ellis 1999; Kaplan 2000; Angstrom & Duyvesteyn 2005; Kalyvas 2006; Weinstein 2007). Both these, rather contrasting, developments can be accounted for by the concept of asymmetric war and asymmetric warfare in some interpretations. This is most apparent when it comes to violence conducted between the transformed forces of the strong and the irregulars in the midst of the weak. It should be noted, however, that these struggles – as has become evident in, for example, Afghanistan and Iraq – do not necessarily have the predicted outcome (e.g. Angstrom & Duyvesteyn 2007). From this perspective, it is hardly surprising that "asymmetry" has surfaced as one of the current buzzwords among the military and scholarly communities.

There are four schools of thought on asymmetric war emphasizing power distribution, organizational status of the actor, method of warfare, and norms respectively (Angstrom 2011). Arguably, the term "asymmetric war" and its modern usage are intimately connected to the Cold War (during which the emergence of superpowers made the distribution of power globally even more unequal than before) and the sudden increase of violent conflict in the Third World at the end of the Cold War. These two, only partly, related developments seemingly led to different understandings of the term asymmetric war. First, in light of uneven distribution of power, it made sense to understand asymmetric in terms of *power distribution* (e.g. Arreguin-Toft 2005; Paul 1994; Mack 1975). Second, in light of the growth of armed conflict between the state-run, organized, high-tech equipped armed forces of the West and the allegedly disorganized bands of armed groups in the Third World, it made sense to talk of asymmetry in terms of *organizational status* of the actor. Third, in light of the actual dynamics of warfare conducted by these actors, with the entire bandwidth of operational and tactical measures thrown at each other (with the exception of nuclear weapons), it made sense to talk of the asymmetric *use* of military power (Thornton 2007). If one, as Osinga (2002: 275) for example, claims that asymmetric war (understood to be "finding, creating, and exploiting asymmetries") "is the essence of strategy," it becomes very difficult, as Lawrence Freedman (2002: 84) has pointed out, to separate it from strategic thought and war in general. Finally, in light of the apparently separate value systems inherent in warfare in the Third World and the core liberal democratic values and their relationship to the use of force as perceived by the West, it made sense to talk of asymmetry in terms of *norms*. As Christopher Coker (2002: 319) points out:

> [I]n its use of force, however, it [the West] is attempting to make war both more humane and less 'risk averse'. Its enemies, by comparison, are trying to do the opposite: to make it more inhumane and make it more unpredictable.

Is terrorism war or crime? The concept of terrorism is very similar to the concept of asymmetric conflict, in the sense that terrorism is used both to denote a form of war and to describe a form of warfare. This ambiguity, together with the notion that terrorism has been politicized, i.e. rather than being a neutral expression; it has become an emotionally and politically charged word that can be exploited for political purposes, suggests that the concept of terrorism has lost much of its value as an analytical tool. The existence of rival views of how terrorism should be understood is also evident by the presence of over 80 definitions of the phenomenon (Thackrah 2004: 66–79). From the strict horizon of military theory, one can conceive of terrorism both as strategy and as tactics. First, terrorism is a tactic in which violence is used to instill fear for political purposes. As such, it is a mode of warfare that often coincides with and is used in revolutionary wars or by the party who is significantly weaker in an asymmetric conflict. Second, terrorism could also be understood as strategy. According to this school of thought (e.g. Neumann & Smith 2007; Duyvesteyn 2005; Pape 2005; Merari 1993; Crenshaw 1990; Byman 2005), terrorism operates along several lines. Through creating fear among civilians, it puts pressure on the state to react. Bombs provoke a reaction. Since this reaction most often entails repression in a variety of ways and since further bombings only reinforce the impression that the state cannot protect its citizens, the state continues to repress. These repressions, moreover, further create new grievances among the civilians, thus facilitating recruitment. It should be noted that understanding terrorism as strategy or tactic does not say anything about the actor that is using it. Accordingly, states can engage in terrorism. This interpretation is very unusual among states' official definitions of terrorism in which it is regularly implied that terrorism is conducted by non-state actors. Here, the political nature of naming something terrorism is obvious.

The current debate on the nature of terrorism also leads into the so-called "war on terrorism." The obvious problem with this concept is, as Lawrence Freedman (2002: 63) has suggested, that "wars are fought between opposing political entities and not against tactics." There are at least two alternative solutions to this conceptual problem. One can, on the one hand, understand the concept of war as an expression of its declaratory meaning. Since the concept of war evokes great national sacrifices and an event that is of utmost importance, it can sometimes be used to signal that a particular policy is important. This way the "war on terror" is not actually a real war, but the term is primarily used to mobilize domestic opinion in support of the war. On the other hand, one might argue that the "war on terror" is a war, but the current military theoretical concepts have problems handling it. According to this interpretation, the war on terror represents a new kind of war.

Categorizing war according to generations

A final and commonly used ground for classifying war is its temporal dimensions. Considering that the experience of war in human history is as long as it is hotly debated (e.g. Gat 2006; Kagan 1997; Ferrill 1985; Keegan 1994), it is not surprising that chronological categorizations are abundant. Some scholars suggest that war progresses through a series of different developments – generations of warfare, new and old wars (e.g. Rice 1988; Holsti 1996; Hammes 2006; Kaldor 2006; Münkler 2004). The problem with these endeavors in terms of categorization is that several of the developments are ongoing at the same time. Most notably, guerrilla warfare is hardly a new phenomenon and it is therefore difficult to squeeze it in as a development logically following from a certain state of interstate war. This suggests that there is a different dynamic attached to the development of warfare than a clear linear logic. The advantage of these attempts, however, is that by using a temporal dimension to war one focuses the attention on long-term trends in warfare.

First, modern warfare, from the peace of Westphalia in 1648, can be understood as a tripartite categorization consisting of institutionalized war, total war, and the third kind of war (Holsti 1996). Institutionalized war implies a form of war that gradually emerged as the state centralized its coercive powers. This was partly a result of the increased costs of war as was evident in the Thirty Years' War. With a growing bureaucracy, the state was more effective in collecting taxes and had a wider tax base and could thus afford war. Charles Tilly (1992) expressed this symbiotic relationship as "war made the state and the state makes war" (cf. van Creveld 2001; Porter 1994; Davis & Pereira 2003). Institutionalized war also made civilians redundant in war. The Thirty Years' War had entailed widespread atrocities against the civilian population as marauding armies scampered across Central Europe to find supplies. As the process of centralizing armies under state control progressed, civilians came to be understood mainly as a home front supporting the army. The Napoleonic wars started the development towards total war, which reached its peak with World War II. In total war, the relevant political actor gradually shifted from the state (the monarch) to the state (understood as the nation). This gradual shift also made civilians a part of the war effort as well as part of the enemy. Total war, in theory, implied that the entire resources of the state were devoted to war. While the great powers prepared for yet another major interstate war in Central Europe, however, the development of warfare took a radical shift in another direction than was expected in the West. The "third kind of war" emerged in the former Third World and consisted of guerrilla warfare tactics and civilians being deliberately targeted, and the organization of violence regularly consisted of rag-tag bands of irregulars, child soldiers, and criminals, rather than organized, centralized, uniformed personnel (Holsti 1996).

Second, it has been suggested that warfare throughout history can be categorized in different generations (e.g. Hammes 2006). The first generation encompasses war as it was conducted in Western Europe in the latter part of the seventeenth and early eighteenth century. It centered on the prevalent tactics of massed manpower in firing lines, where the aim of maneuver was to enable volleys of gunfire towards the opposing lines. The second generation introduced indirect fire, e.g. artillery, and focused on massing firepower against the opponents. The second generation started with the end of the Napoleonic Wars and reached its point of culmination towards the end of World War I. The third generation, which roughly translates to maneuver warfare, began at the end of World War I when German forces used infiltration tactics to unravel the allied lines in early 1918, but failed to exploit tactical advances into operational depth. Combining maneuver and firepower in this novel manner paved the way for the later German successes on the battlefields of World War II. It also became the chosen strategy for the Israeli Defense Forces in its wars against Arab opposition in 1967 and 1973. Fourth generation warfare, many suggest, is related to an "evolved form of insurgency." Classifications according to generations have, however, received fierce criticism and Echevarria (2011a: 51) suggests that there is a lack of systematic evidence in favor of the theory, with its advocates cherry-picking only cases which seemingly fit their argument, that the theory obscures the complexities surrounding developments of warfare, and that the categorization lacks rigor.

Third, it has been suggested that war after the end of the Cold War has transformed into something inherently "new" (Kaldor 2006; Münkler 2005). The central themes in this literature are that while old wars were about power politics, new wars are about identity politics. Moreover, while old wars were fought by large-scale, organized, uniformed armed forces in pitch battles, new wars are characterized by a deliberate attacks on civilians by rag-tag groups of warlords, criminals, militias, and rebel fractions, not centrally or hierarchically led and commanded. The final aspect that separates old and new is that the new wars are influenced by a globalized world economy, while in old wars economy was centralized. Despite receiving fierce criticism for flawed evidence, over-generalizing from one case study (e.g. Kalyvas 2001; Melander et al. 2009; Maao 2011), the so-called new wars thesis has gained grounds in the scholarly and policy debate. As a categorization, however, it shares the problems of the other temporal based classifications.

Conclusions

War is an extremely multi-faceted and complex phenomenon. By describing three different approaches to make war understandable in the first part of the chapter, it is possible to reach a more comprehensive answer to the question of what war is. The first approach – to try to understand what war is by identifying its functional relevance – contributes to the understanding of war by giving us insights into the meaning of war in a larger social context. By focusing on the nature of war, the second approach contains proposals on how wars should be understood, both in the abstract and real form, thus highlighting the problems to be solved in order to theorize about war. This issue has also been driven to extremes in the debate about whether one can consider war as a rational phenomenon or not. Seeking a measurable definition of war, the third approach finally contributes to the study of war by enabling systematic empirical investigation.

The second part of the chapter has dealt with various ways of classifying war and armed conflict. The discussion has centered around whether it is fruitful to distinguish between war based on its actors and their warring institutions, its intensity, or its methods. By continuously stressing both advantages and disadvantages of these attempts, the discussion provides a critical analysis of war and how it should be approached. Understanding war should not be taken lightly, since the consequences of failing to understand its dynamics correctly can be dire.

The chapter can also be seen as a springboard for several other issues related to military theory. By separating battle and war, we can more easily project and analyze war according to levels of warfare. That war, according to Clausewitz, is about influencing the opponent's will makes it natural to think of war in terms of military power. Based on the fact that the war takes place between the parties, we can easily understand many of the problems that occur on military theory's normative side. Many military theorists comprehend war as a rational instrument used for political purposes. Military operations can thus be understood with the help of their political context. With this view in mind, it is natural to continue the book with a chapter on strategy – the link between military operations and the political objectives in war.

Questions for discussion

1. When does war occur?
2. Is the nature of war timeless?
3. What distinguishes war from other forms of violence?
4. Why is it important to categorize war?
5. What is friction and why it is an important concept in understanding the nature of war?
6. How can one know whether war is a rational or irrational phenomenon?

Further reading

Jan Angstrom & Isabelle Duyvesteyn (eds.), *Rethinking the Nature of War* (London: Frank Cass, 2005).

Carl von Clausewitz, *On War*, translation Peter Paret & Michael Howard (Princeton: Princeton University Press, 1993).

Hew Strachan & Sibylle Scheipers (eds.), *The Changing Character of War* (Oxford: Oxford University Press, 2011).

Martin van Creveld, *The Transformation of War* (New York: The Free Press, 1991).

Azar Gat, *War in Human Civilization* (Oxford: Oxford University Press, 2006).

Valerie Hudson, *Sex and World Peace* (New York: Columbia University Press, 2012).

Karl Erik Haug & Ole Jorgen Maao (eds.), *Conceptualising Modern War* (London: Hurst, 2011).

Colin McInnes, *Spectator Sport War: The West and Contemporary Conflict* (Boulder, CO: Lynne Rienner, 2002).

Laura Sjoberg, *Gendering Global Conflict: Towards a Feminist Theory of War* (New York: Columbia University Press, 2013).

John A. Vasquez (ed.) *What Do We Know About War?*, 2nd edn. (Lanham, MD: Rowman & Littlefield, 2012).

3 Strategy

Introduction

While the last chapter dealt with how we should approach and understand war, this chapter deals with strategy. If war is an organized, politically instrumental phenomenon, as perhaps the dominant interpretation posits, then strategy is the rationalist process that tries to create coherence between the political aims *of* war and the military aims *in* war. In its most rudimentary form, strategy can be said to be as old as human civilization, whereas strategy in its modern form emerged during the latter part of the Enlightenment. Strategy and strategic thought presume that war and the use of force is a political tool. If war were to be ontologically irrational, emotional, and primordial, the concept of strategy would be rendered devoid of meaningful content. This is important to bear in mind. We should also remember, however, that even if strategy presumes that we can approach war and organized violence as a rationalist phenomenon, it does not exclude the possibility of miscalculations, decisions made on the basis of flawed information, cultural biases, or indeed that strategic decisions are made under pressure leading to cognitive distortions. Indeed, large parts of the literature advance such deviations from the ideal model.

This short introduction begs a series of questions. How should we understand the concept of strategy and what influences how we think about it? What organizational interfaces are there between the political leadership and the military organization, i.e. who conducts strategy, who shapes it, and how is the strategic process – planning, implementation, and evaluation – institutionalized? Why do actors pursue the strategies they do? Are states' strategic considerations different from non-state actors? How are ideas about the use of force institutionalized into armed forces? In what context – civil or military – is strategy conducted? To what extent do ends influence the creation of means or is it the available means that shape nations' goals? How do norms of expected behavior and rationalist calculations interact in the shaping of strategy and its processes?

The aim of this chapter is to introduce the assumptions underpinning strategy and its role in military theory. The chapter is divided into four sections dealing with (1) different understandings of strategy, (2) the strategic context, (3) the concept of victory, and (4) the logic of strategy. The first section analyzes the development of the concept of strategy since the Enlightenment. In the second section, we elaborate on various general factors that influence the contents of strategies as well as condition the theory and practice of strategic thought. In the third section, we discuss the remarkably oft-forgotten concept of victory. In the context of political ends and military means, it is necessary to clearly understand what constitutes victory. In the final section, we elaborate on the three components of strategy and in particular on the interaction between ends and means. Pursuing political ends with scarce military means against another opponent is the essence of strategy and the inherent logic involved is analyzed.

The development of the concept of strategy

The term strategy is derived from the ancient Greek words *stratos* and *a'gein*. It literally meant to lead an army and *strategos* was the word for General in ancient Greece. The origin of the concept is therefore inextricably linked to military affairs and denotes the commander or the art of commanding an army. Considering the wide modern usage of "strategy" in business, marketing, sports, and politics, however, it is clear that strategy is one of those words whose meaning and use has transcended its original domain. Indeed, some would extend the meaning of strategy to all realms of life itself (Dixit & Nalebuff 2008; Chwe 2013) or for non-violent political action (Chenoweth & Stephan 2012). In this more general sense, strategic behavior is usually understood to be shorthand for thinking rationally and coherently about means and ends in situations of choice. In order to situate "strategy" in the military context some have chosen to add the prefix "military strategy." In this book, we will still use "strategy" – partly for the sake of readability, partly because the concept was originally linked to military affairs. In the context of this book, it would still appear obvious that what we are talking about is the use of force – not strategies for marriages, selling consumer-products, or winning elections.

Partly forgotten in medieval military thought (although certainly practiced for centuries), the concept of strategy was rediscovered during the latter part of the Enlightenment. It grew from the practical need to distinguish tactics from the practice of creating, organizing, and maintaining armed forces during long campaigns. The French officer and theorist Paul Gedeon Joly de Maizeroy described in 1777 how tactics was mechanical (and therefore depended on mathematics) by nature, and included the composition and maintenance of troops and the way to march, maneuver, and fight, while strategy consisted of the overall war effort and relied upon intuition (van Creveld 2000: 94; Wedin 2007: 37–8). In 1799 the Prussian General Adam Heinrich Dietrich von Bülow put forward similar ideas and suggested that tactics ought to be understood as the art of troop movements *within* range of enemy weapons, while strategy was the art of armies' movements out of sight of each other and *outside* the weapons range (Gat 2001: 43–4). In 1837, Swiss military theorist Antoine Henri Jomini argued that strategy was the art of waging war on the map and that the term included the entire military theatre of operations (Jomini 1987: 460).

Clausewitz, however, broke with this practice-oriented use of the term strategy and suggested in his seminal book, *On War*, that tactics should be understood as "the use of armed forces in the engagement" and strategy as "the use of engagements for the object of the war" (Clausewitz 1993: 146). According to Clausewitz, whose military theorizing was informed more by abstract and philosophical reasoning than practice, all warfare should be impregnated with the overall political end of the war. War and politics were part of the same phenomenon, he claimed, which also is reflected in his concept of strategy. In his understanding he thus separated the objective *in* war, i.e. victory in battle, from the objective *of* war, i.e. to meet the political end of war. As a definition, it is laudably clear in terms of specifying a causal logic as to how tactics and strategy is related. However, by narrowing the meaning of the term to war, one could argue that it neglects the use of force in peacetime, i.e. deterrence, as well as the use of force short of war.

One soldier-scholar that has remedied this shortcoming is British strategist Basil H. Liddell Hart (1895–1970). In 1929, he defined strategy as "the art of distributing and applying military means to fulfill the ends of policy" (Liddell Hart 1991: 321). This understanding does not presuppose a state of war (although it certainly includes war), while stressing that the use of force sometimes is best understood as a deterrent. In all likelihood, Clausewitz did not deliberately exclude the use of force in peace. Instead, given the context – the turmoil of the Napoleonic Wars – in which he developed his theory of war, he probably understood also the latent side of strategy, i.e. deterrence and through the weakness of Prussia also the importance of organization and creation of military capabilities as inherently strategic. In addition, Liddell Hart (1991: 322) introduced the concept of "grand strategy" to denote the joint coordination and direction of "all the resources of a nation, or a band of nations, toward the attainment of the political object of the war." In this understanding, grand strategy goes beyond what we identified as military theory in the introductory chapter. And even though Liddell Hart's concept certainly is understood as one expression of policy of the state, it is not all policies of the state. This illustrates the difficulties involved in different conceptualizations of the levels of warfare.

In another conceptualization, French general and strategist André Beaufre (1902–75) defined strategy as the "art of understanding and mastering an interaction of wills that use force to determine the outcome of a conflict" (Beaufre 1963: 21–22). The strength of Beaufre's definition is that it stresses the dynamics and interaction that characterizes strategic thought. Strategy is not directed against an object, but it is rather a dynamic game between two opposite wills. One problem with Beaufre's definition is that it does not take the political aim of the hostilities as its starting point, but rather "conflict" in a broader sense. This seemingly makes the concept devoid of agency and most other definitions of the concept emphasize that strategy involves agency. Paret (1986: 3), for example, suggested that strategy "is the use of armed force to achieve military objectives and, by extension, the political purpose of the war." Drawing upon Clausewitz, Schelling, and Liddell Hart, British strategist Colin S. Gray (1999: 1) describes strategy as "the theory and practice of the use, and threat of use, organized force for political purposes." Gray makes a telling contribution to the development of the concept by explicitly including the threat of using military power. Several military organizations also pledge to similar understandings of strategy. For example, the US Army's doctrine for military operations, *FM 100-5, Operations* (1986: 9) describes strategy as "the art and science of employing the armed forces of a nation or alliance to secure policy objectives by the application, or threat of, force."

It is clear that the definitions of strategy have developed over the past 200 years and that this development partly can be explained by the conduct of war and general technological development. For example, as the range of weapons increased dramatically, it had consequences for how strategy should be related to tactics and thus also influenced the way we think about the concept. What most scholars now agree upon is that military strategy is (1) subordinate to politics serving as a political tool, (2) characterized by a dynamic interactive relationship, and (3) operates through the use of force both during war and peace. Due to its instrumental nature, strategy can also fruitfully be understood as a plan for how an actor employs and concentrates limited resources. A strategy, therefore, is an expression of an actor's management of scarce resources and how these are directed and used to punch above its weight. The threat of using military power is thus as important in strategizing as the actual use of military force.

One problem, closely related to the debate on how the concept of strategy is defined, is whether we should approach strategy as an art or science. Those stressing that strategy is an art usually refer to conduct of particular strategies or the exercise of them, while others stress that strategy should be studied, evaluated, and indeed implemented with scientific precision and associated methods. From this perspective, therefore, it is possible to make a distinction between the practice of strategizing and the study of strategy. The distinction may appear self-evident, but it carries important repercussions. Taking Sweden as an example, if we assume that strategy is an art, a small state wedged between great powers – in the east Russia, in the south Germany, and in the west either Britain or the US – will not be able to emulate strategies from other states. Swedish strategies will differ since they are drawn from particularities of the Swedish case. In this sense, strategy as an art is reductionist. If we, however, understand strategy from the perspective of science and theory, then Sweden (as other states) would be able to draw upon the strategies of other states living under the same conditions. Hence, much of the reasoning in the following sections relies upon an assumption that it is possible to approach strategy as a theory – and thus that strategy operates as widely and relevantly as our theoretical and methodological tools allow. The basic components of strategy – managing scarce resources, sorting out means and ends, and dealing with its inter-active nature – is important regardless of whether the actors are great powers, small powers, guerrilla groups, or terrorist bands.

The strategic context

Before proceeding with a discussion on victory and the logic of strategy, it is necessary to elaborate on the context in which strategy operates. The obvious answer is that it involves politics. Strategy is the interface between battlefield tactics – destruction, death, and demolition – and politics. It is about how politics is turned into military tasks and targets. Politics is, however, a remarkably elusive concept and can be approached from a number of different perspectives. In this section, we suggest that, in particular, six dimensions of politics are important for the strategic context and influence both the contents and pursuit of strategy as well as how strategic thought has developed: geography, history, ideology, economy, technology, and political system. There are, of course, other intangible and tangible factors involved and the formation of strategy, how the pursuit of strategy is organized, and how strategic thought is conceptualized is highly complex. For our introductory purposes, however, these six factors serve us well to introduce how we can approach strategy. In the section on the logic of strategy, we will also deal with its interactive nature, thus adding the complexity of two political wills opposed to each other (cf. Murray & Grimsley 1994; Gray 1999; Byman & Waxman 2002; Stone 2011; Betts 2012).

Geography is an important intermediary for politics and strategy in several ways. Indeed, some (cf. Dalby et al. 2006) have even suggested that geographical factors determine the extent to which a state is exposed to threats or is a target for surrounding powers.[1] In this sense, geography can also determine opportunities and limit strategic behavior, including influencing the formulation of military doctrine. Examples of such geographical factors are location, size, climate, topography, demography, and natural resources. These factors some-times influence the physical and material conditions for the use or threat of military force. The relevance of specific geographical factors is seemingly highly contextual and will vary over time and place. Undoubtedly, some geographical factors have been reduced in rele-vance due to technological developments, but to completely eliminate spatial considerations in strategy is nigh-impossible.

For example, location and size can influence the strategic process. When it comes to loca-tion, it mainly relates to proximity in relation to other actors or a secure access to strategic assets and resources. The latter is often understood to involve access to the high seas and glo-bal trade regimes. Britain and France, to take but two examples, have a largely similar size, population, material wealth, and technological sophistication, but have completely different military experiences. While the surrounding seas for centuries largely protected Britain from the ravages of war, France was forced to spill much blood in defense, and in some cases expansion, of a series of contested borders with other European powers. During the 1930s, Britain's geographical position provided food for thought for some, most notably Liddell Hart, who claimed that there was a particular "British way in war." His argument, which has been subject to criticism, was that Britain historically had been most successful, militarily and politically, while avoiding major commitments on the continent and instead opted for a peripheral strategy that maximized the Royal Navy's ability to project power against the enemy's weak points. The victory over Napoleon in 1815 and Hitler in 1945 are historical examples usually cited by Liddell Hart's critics as contrary evidence to this thesis (Liddell Hart 1932; Bond 1977: 65–87). France, according to this logic and exposed due to a long land border, developed a defensive strategy (Doughty 1994).

A state's size is also considered an important geographical determinant of strategy. Murray and Grimsley (1994: 9) argue that large territorial areas have the advantage that enemy attacks can be more easily absorbed. The physical wear and tear, with ever increasing and stretched logistical lines, delays and weakens enemy offensive capabilities, thus making the opponent easy prey for counter-offensives. Russian and Israeli strategies and strategic history are often presented as "evidence" for this thesis. The former government has on several occasions during the past used its large territory to gain time and slowly wear down enemy offensives. This geographical factor was also a great asset during the Cold War when the threat of a massive attack with atomic weapons characterized the military doctrines. Russia's extensive territory has given the country a strategic margin that few other countries enjoy. As such, it seemingly has an influence on the country's strategic doctrine. The reversed logic, still stressing geography, occurs for Israel. Here, it is the lack of strategic depth due to its limited size that has led Israeli strategists to favor pre-emptive strikes, movement, speed, and a dominant offensive to avoid a costly war of attrition on their own soil. Indeed, this mindset seems to have influenced policymakers and war planning in Israel from the 1948 war to the Second Lebanon War in 2006.

While geographical conditions appear to provide a reasonable explanation for the contents of strategy it should also be noted that there are shortcomings of their explanatory power. The logic seems to be that states with limited geographical depth use offensive strategies that emphasize mobility, speed, and firepower, while states with large geographic depth design strategies that emphasize strategic defensive in combination with war of attrition. Although intuitive, this cannot explain why the main exponent of offensive and mobile warfare in Europe has been Germany, rather than states such as Luxembourg or the Baltic states. Using geography as a single-variable explanation therefore entails significant problems.

Instead, to use geography in combination with technological and demographic conditions has gained more analytical leverage. This approach has, for example, given rise to the so-called "offensive-defensive balance" (e.g. Brown, et al. 2004). This latter concept tries to – on the basis of technological developments and demographic and geographic conditions – determine whether the offensive or the defensive has an advantage. In conditions where the offensive is more conducive to victory, it is then suggested that not only will states construe strategies that are more offensive, but that wars will also occur more frequently and last for less time. Meanwhile, in conditions where the defense has the advantage, wars will occur more rarely and states will favor defensive strategies and longevity in supplies. Hence, contexts where military exploits are best sought after through attack thus tend to have a higher degree of suspicion and more acute security dilemmas and preventive attacks than contexts where the defense has advantages over the offensive (cf. J. Snyder 1984; Strachan 2003).

Historical experiences are another factor that shapes a state's perceptions of threat and by extension its military strategy. Collective and individual experiences of war and terror, hunger and poverty, injustice and oppression, and military victories and losses create expectations and preconceptions about the nature of war, as well as potential adversaries. These experiences, whether they rest on a rational coherent evidentiary basis or not, can in turn generate more or less tension between actors. Britain and France during the interwar period can again serve as an example.

When Britain and France began to prepare their strategies to counter the threat from Hitler's Germany, the experiences of World War I were highly influential. The war of attrition on the Western Front had seemingly shown that an aggressive strategy, with attempts at rapid breakthrough of the enemy lines with the help of infantry, produced poor results and had been costly both in lives and in material terms. In Britain, it was concluded that strategic bombers as well as mechanized armored units would be successful in future war. Meanwhile, in France, it was emphasized instead that a defensive strategy with extensive fortifications and a strengthening of the Maginot Line would deter an attack. In hindsight, historical experience provided poor counsel. First, the initial assessment, that Hitler due to the dreadful experiences of World War I would not risk war to support his political ambitions in Europe, was proven wrong. Second, even as the German attack on France was imminent in 1940, the military leadership in both countries was convinced that the Germans would try to repeat the failed version of the Schlieffen Plan – a large-scale attack through the Netherlands and Belgium into northern France. This resulted in serious miscalculations with far-reaching consequences (Murray 1994; Doughty 1994). In this context it should be mentioned that the historical experiences as exemplified above were by no means the only factors that pointed in this direction, but only one of several contributing factors to the development of strategies in the interwar period in Britain and France.

Again, it would seem that historical experience is a reasonable explanation for states' strategies. However, this is not entirely unproblematic. The main criticism of this school of thought is that "historical experience" is not a natural phenomenon. Historical events can be interpreted differently by different individuals, they can be completely misunderstood, and a selective use of history can rather generate myths instead of dismantling and uncovering them. Research on the role of analogies and metaphors in decision-making also suggests that the interpretation of historical experience is an inherently political process and often takes place in a context not only of rivaling interpretations of a particular event, but also in a context of competing analogies (Vertzberger 1990; Khong 1992; Paris 2002; Angstrom 2011). The images of events that we constantly construct need therefore not necessarily reflect an objective reality of the very same events. It can therefore be difficult to explain the contents and implementation of strategies with historical experience directly. For example, Jonathan Mercer (1996) has shown that negative "reputation" in international politics tends to be tenacious but good "reputation" can be quickly changed to a negative. This process, according to Mercer, is often based on irrational factors and misunderstandings rather than an objective reality. This suggests that psychological factors, rather than objective "historical experience," explains some states' strategy. It should also be pointed out that experimental studies have shown that past experience of interaction with an opponent has an impact on how people interact in the future. Robert Axelrod (1984) has described this as the parties interact in the "shadow of the future," i.e. in their interaction partners are taking account of past and coming interaction and this may in turn have a dampening effect on short-term profit-interest and instead foster cooperation (cf. Jervis 1978; Oye 1985).

A third political factor that has been put forward as an explanation of states' strategies is *ideology*. By ideology we mean beliefs about how reality is constituted and beliefs about political order (distribution of power and resources). These beliefs can be both religious and secular in nature and take the form of cultural phenomena and concepts. Ideology and its cultural expression affect the decision-makers and the communities where they operate on a conscious as well as unconscious way. Ideological beliefs can also generate threats that other people from other cultures and societies would not even recognize as threats. During the Cold War, for example, ideology had a major impact on superpowers' strategic thought. The US, for its part, claimed to be defending the "free world," based on a value system underpinned by a set of beliefs giving primacy to individual freedom, rule of law, and democracy. These values were considered to be diametrically opposed to those of the Soviet regime. Many US strategists even believed that a conflict between these powers was almost inevitable. The communist leadership in the Kremlin was, for its part influenced by Lenin's interpretation of Marx and Engels, and viewed the capitalist world with great suspicion. The communist ideology with its materialist worldview, perception of science, emphasis on class struggle, and dialectics also had an impact on the strategic thinking and the formulation of military doctrine in the Soviet Union. It generated a particular understanding of the nature of war, the organization of the armed forces, and even operational planning. In the Soviet Union, too, many strategists viewed conflict between the superpowers as inevitable (e.g. Glantz 1991b: 64–6; Vigor 1975).

Ideology can thus operate as a grid through which the strategic situation as well as "historical experience" is filtered. As an explanation of the contents of states' strategies, it also has some shortcomings. The main analytical problem is the difficulty involved in distinguishing the idea from the actor that holds the idea. This means that it is difficult to identify the correct causal relationship – what comes first: the idea or the actor that holds the idea? A second line of criticism is that it is difficult to accurately pinpoint at what level of analysis that ideology, identity, or belief system operate. For example, the US conducted a continuous containment policy (e.g. Kennan 1947; Spykman 1942) against the Soviet Union regardless of whether the presidency was held by republicans or democrats (Gaddis 2005). Similarly, it seems that ethnic and religious identity has an impact in some cases, but not in others.

The fourth, inherently political, issue that we deal with here as important for strategy is *economic factors*. These include raw materials as well as the capability to process them, the ability to produce important industrial and military equipment, fuel, and food. Some of the economic factors are closely intertwined with the geographical factors such as natural resources such as oil, iron ore, uranium, and water. Economic factors create both opportunities and limitations on the use of military means. The most obvious problem for rulers throughout history has been how to pay for war. Indeed, for a long time in European history, it was thought that one could let "war pay for war" by allowing spoils to be shared between the victorious armies and preferably wage war on others' territories. This became, however, increasingly difficult as armies grew and borrowing money – issuing war bonds – became more common. War became funded by debt (Slantchev 2012). Even if Liberman (1996) demonstrates that in some cases military conquest can be financially rewarding, it has become exceedingly rare with occupations and conquests. Instead, military power seems to be used for other purposes and war then rarely pays off in economic terms. Even when waging limited wars (as opposed to existential wars), it devours immense financial resources. For example, it has been estimated that by May 2013, the cost of the Iraq War for the US has been over two trillion US dollars. In the developing world, moreover, international aid is an important source of revenue for warring parties (Duffield 2007).

There are plenty of cases in which economic factors were crucial to strategic thought and contents of a particular state's strategy. During the run-up to war in the Pacific between Japan and the US in 1941–45, Japanese aggression in Korea, Manchuria, and China induced US economic sanctions, culminating in a total embargo on oil and fuel. This forced Japan to further expand in Asia and eventually led to the ill-fated Japanese attack on Pearl Harbor (Murray & Grimsley 1994: 17–18). The shortage of oil and fuel, together with being relatively inferior to the US industrial capacity, were ultimately important causes of Japanese defeat. Furthermore, economy naturally becomes part of the equation when it comes to the creation of military capabilities. The logic is straightforward. Unless you can finance certain military technologies such as tanks, air forces, or navies, it does not make sense to form strategies that utilize such equipment. Although it seems obvious that strategies and strategy are influenced by economic factors, it is not as straightforward as one might think at first glance. Most importantly, economy cannot easily explain variation in state strategies. Even with the same economic system and similar sized economies, states do not necessarily pursue the same strategy. And, conversely, states with different economic systems or different degrees of wealth may pursue similar strategies. Economy, it seems, is therefore important, but it needs to be qualified with political judgment to make sense as a variable to explain strategy.

Technology is another factor of importance in this context and it has, arguably, become increasingly important in modern warfare. Here, we refer to technology that contributes to military capabilities directly and not technology that boosts the economy and thus the potential of increasing military power indirectly. There is a vast literature (e.g. Buzan 1987; Gray 2002; O'Hanlon 2000) suggesting that technological developments have had a major impact on the conduct of warfare and the strategies that states pursue. From improved techniques for building fortifications to the introduction of stirrups or new weapons such as breech loaded rifles, and new communications such as the telegraph or early warning systems such as radar, technology has made a difference in war. Gradually, these developments have not only increased the firepower of military units, but also their ability to maneuver and to protect themselves. The introduction of tanks on the Western Front during World War I even famously led to such quick and unexpected early breakthroughs of enemy lines that follow-on forces did not manage to react in time and gaps were not exploited.

Yet another obvious case where technology had a huge impact on the strategic development is the superpower rivalry during the Cold War. Nuclear missiles, their reach, size, explosive capacity, precision, carriers (e.g. bombers, missiles, artillery), operational readiness, early warning systems, and radar system capabilities were all a vital part of the strategies pursued and clearly the result of the development of either weapons technology or dual-use technology. Any technological errors or omissions were understood to have potentially grave consequences, especially during periods when relations between the superpowers were tense. Perceived technological differences and disparities were sometimes even driving strategy. For example, in the late 1950s and early 1960s, the US – mistakenly, as it was proved later – thought it had slipped back in the arms race against the Soviet Union and the so-called "missile gap" was a major reason for an expansion of the nuclear program (e.g. Gaddis 1998). In the 1980s, moreover, then US president Ronald Reagan's program for early warning and destruction of Soviet intercontinental ballistic missiles while in flight – the so-called strategic defense initiative or "star wars" program – put huge constraints on the Soviet defense budget (in order to "catch up") that inadvertently weakened the already fragile Soviet economy and contributed to the collapse of the Soviet Union (e.g. Payne 1986; Westad 2000).

Correlating with the development of increasingly high-technological armed forces, however, are increasing costs of war. In explanatory terms, this means that it is difficult to separate whether or not it is technology or economic factors that should explain the conduct of strategy as well as the development of strategic thought. It goes without saying that there is hardly a need to either theorize on or conduct war planning for a strategic bombing fleet if one cannot afford to build such a capability. A further problem for technology as an explanation is that some states have the technological know-how to pursue some strategies, but choose not to. Technology therefore seems inadequate as an explanation for an actor's strategy in isolation from other variables. The technology that allowed mechanization and large-scale introduction of tanks into the armed forces was available not only for Germany but also for Britain and France during the interwar period. If there were only technology that drove strategy we should have had similar interwar doctrines in the three states. But it was only the former that developed the *Blitzkrieg* concept, while the two latter states developed largely defensive strategies. Similarly, Sweden had the technological capacity to develop nuclear weapons during the 1950s, which undoubtedly was a strategic decision, but ultimately chose not to proceed (e.g. Agrell 2002). Furthermore, it is also difficult to isolate whether technology drives strategy or strategic needs that govern the development of technology (Mahnken 2008).

Finally, the *political system* – practices, procedures, and norms – in a country is claimed to be of great importance for determining the contents of strategy (e.g. Murray & Grimsley 1994). Advocates of this set of explanations tend to hypothesize that the political system can be linked to strategy and overall war performance in three ways. First, the political system sets the organizational and procedural boundaries for how strategic analysis is conducted. This, in turn, can explain the speed with which actors react and are able to counter threats or seize opportunities that arise (Brooks 2008; Gartner 1997). As an explanation, this draws heavily upon the existence and kind of so-called standard operating procedures within the bureaucracies of war or problems of organizational in-fighting (cf. Allison 1971; Vertzberger 1990). For example, Murray and Grimsley (1994) note that in authoritarian political systems "bad news" is often buried along the chain of command. This means that decision-makers are forced to sometimes make decisions on life and death with imperfect information. Although it is common in many cases for officials or military personnel to provide decision-makers with the information they want or expect, rather than information that provides the most accurate reflection of reality, this problem is particularly acute in authoritarian states, as bringers of unpleasant truths risk more in dictatorships than in democracies. Furthermore, political systems can sometimes encourage bureaucracies to pursue their particular interests at first hand. As such, empirical cases of in-fighting between the branches of the armed forces in budget or acquisition issues are plentiful (e.g. Karlsson 2002).

Second, the political system in question largely sets the conditions for civil-military relations, which in turn influences both the conduct of war as well as decision-making to go to war. Civil-military relations theory is usually associated with the sub-field military sociology (e.g. Huntington 1957; Janowitz 1960; Abrahamsson 1972; Moskos 1976; Feaver 2003; Barany 2012), but the focus of study is intimately related to the formation of strategy and creation of armed forces and their internal dynamics, as well as the conduct of war (e.g. Egnell 2009). In particular, the field highlights that the way an actor organizes and relates the political sphere to the military also informs a large part of the decision-making procedures, but also which domains of strategic decision-making belong to civilian or military control. One can, for example, easily hypothesize that a political system that allows for the acquisition of military equipment solely under military control would purchase possibly different

equipment than one under the control of civilians. It is as easy to hypothesize that the education and organization of the officers' corps will be different in societies with different civil-
military relations. On a more fundamental level, what we understand as civil and military
also influence what targets in war we think are legitimate (Angstrom 2013). Creveld (2008:
158) even suggests that the entire institution of war is dependent upon separating civilians
from the military, because we would not be able to separate war (as legitimate killing) from
murder if we did not come up with a separate category of the population, i.e. the military,
that is authorized to kill.

Third, the political system can also influence the political ends that states pursue in their
strategies and the means and methods with which the actors pursue the aforementioned political ends. There are mainly two versions of this argument. The first school of thought stresses
that differences in political system directly influence whether or not states are aggressive,
war-prone, or prone to conduct their wars in a particular way. The perhaps biggest empirical
claim of this school of thought is the finding that established democracies do not fight each
other. They may very well fight against authoritarian states, but not against other democracies (e.g. Russett 1994; Snyder 2000; Mansfield & Snyder 2005). Another important finding
is that democracies appear to be successful in war (e.g. Brown, et al. 2011). Reiter and Stam
(2002) show that, contrary to belief of a better coordination of war efforts of authoritarian
states, democracies tend to win their wars far more often than other states. They explain this
finding by two inherent traits of democracy. On the one hand, democracies are more likely to
have less obstruction of correct information being channeled to decision-makers and on the
other hand, by promoting individuality and freedom in society in general, even the military
in democracies tend to promote individuals that are creative and seize the initiative. It goes
without saying that in war, initiative and creativity are important characteristics for the decision-making elites. The second school of thought emphasizes norms that are promoted and
conditioned by a particular political system. Here, it is hypothesized that democracies are
more likely than authoritarian states to go to war for liberal, humanitarian reasons and that
democracies are more likely to conduct their wars according to the standards set by international humanitarian law.

Before summarizing this section, we should also draw attention to a school of thought
advocating that so-called strategic culture has a major influence on shaping and conducting
strategy (e.g. Johnston 1995; Katzenstein 1996; Sondhaus 2006; Angstrom & Honig 2012).
Instead of suggesting that the above factors influence strategy directly, this school of thought
suggests that, among others, ideology, politics, historical experiences, collective memories,
identity, norms on the use of force, and understandings of how military force operates, influence the conduct of strategy only indirectly. Together, they form actors' strategic culture,
and it is this unique strategic culture that influences how actors behave strategically. Strategic culture operates in two ways: it influences how actors understand the strategic situation
as well as shaping the actors' understanding of which political ends that should be pursued
and with what means and methods the political end should be reached. Hence, variation
in strategic culture can explain why the US almost immediately after the September 11,
2001 attacks understood the challenge to be – and required a response – of military kind.
Conversely, Britain, far more accustomed to terrorist attacks after the conflict in Northern
Ireland, interpreted and responded to the July 7, 2005 bombings in London with police rather
than military forces.

In sum, there have been plenty of attempts to elucidate how the strategic context, in particular the politics, is important for the pursuit of strategy. We have also seen how all of these
attempts suffer in terms of explanatory power. First, there are serious problems if we think

of them as mono-causal relationships. Instead, and this is where it becomes tricky, it seems that there are different combinations of factors that influence strategies in certain cases. The "right" combination, however, has yet to be discovered. Second, a major scholarly debate among those putting forward strategic context as important seems to be between those who rely on material factors and those who suggest that strategy relies on intangible factors. How do we design studies that separate the effects of a nuclear deterrence from the perceptions of a nuclear threat? Third, drawing upon so-called path dependency, some scholars stress that strategy is not shaped in a vacuum. Instead, the contents of a strategy are determined not only by the political goals, but also by available means. And since military equipment sometimes takes up to 10–15 years to develop, introduce in training, and get operational, one could argue that strategy is not a process of translating political ends into military targets, but rather a process of finding a political goal that fits with the existing military hardware (Gray & Johnson: 2009: 378).

The role of victory in strategic thought

Despite the obvious importance of the concept of victory in strategic thought (Bond 1998), it is remarkably underdeveloped. That the concept is linked to war endings as well as issues of surrender (cf. Afflerbach and Strachan 2012; Wagner-Pacifici 2005) is hardly controversial, but beyond such basic observations, the concept is less developed. Considering that war decides, at least partly, the fate of individuals, groups, states, and alliances globally, as well as influencing patterns of conflict and cooperation among and within states for generations to come, it is even more surprising that victory as a concept has not received more attention. David Baldwin, for example, has suggested that: "Despite the voluminous literature on war, very little attention has been devoted to the concept of success." Surprising as this seems, it is even more baffling when one considers that the "idea that 'every war has a winner' is deeply embedded in the literature on military force" (Baldwin 2002: 187). There has, however, been some progress in the research since then (e.g. Mandel 2006; Johnson & Tierney 2006; Angstrom & Duyvesteyn 2007; Martel 2007) and four different conceptualizations have emerged. Two of them – end-state and cost-benefit calculus – essentially rely upon a traditional rationalist framework, while the remaining two – match-fixing and shared norms – rely upon perceptions and a constructivist framework.

First, probably the most common understanding of victory is to think of it as a desired end-state (Mandel 2006). If the end-state is reached, one can declare victory, and if the end-state is not reached it constitutes defeat. This is an essentially rationalist notion that implies that before military action ensues, a political end-state has been formed and the progress of the war can be measured against this political end-state. It is important to recognize that an end-state understanding of victory and defeat does not take into account the costs involved. Hence, victory can be declared regardless of the costs of war – in either casualties or economic costs. If we take a strict end-state position, in short, it would be victory if the German Army in the spring of 1940 had lost 20 armored divisions and tied another 20 to drawn out counter-insurgency operations when occupying Norway, despite the fact that such a development would have postponed or made impossible a campaign against France and the Low Countries later the same spring. This is also the nucleus of the criticism against end-state interpretations. They tend not to regard other plans or alternative use of power that an actor can wield, and in most situations regarding life or death, peace and war, there is more than one objective. Measuring victory as war aims vs. war outcomes, moreover, does not take into consideration that end-states are inherently ambiguous and fluctuating. Political end-states tend to be vague in order to create freedom of maneuver for the decision-makers, thus leading to difficulties in creating a clear-cut "score-keeping" with which to evaluate the military operations. As war progresses, furthermore, end-states can be modified and changed, leading to what is usually called "mission creep."

Second, victory can be understood in terms of a cost-benefit calculus (Mandel 2006). Here, it becomes important to evaluate reaching the political end-state relative to the costs associated with reaching it. Hence, we can have situations where the political end-state was reached, but the costs were so over-bearing that it would constitute strategic defeat anyway. The critical question is not if we achieved what we set out to do, but rather whether it was worth it? Although this has the advantage of taking into account spent resources, and therefore enables a far more nuanced understanding of victory, it also entails some problems. The most significant of these is that creating an analytical framework to measure victory is as politically laden as end-states are ambiguous. It involves, by necessity, making estimations as to whether one's post-war benefits in inherently difficult areas to measure such as political reputation, resolve, or power, has improved compared to pre-war estimates and the costs of war. Furthermore, these estimates must be addressed either in absolute terms or in relative terms towards the opponent. In a zero-sum, absolute game, these estimates may be straightforward. In retrospect, one can argue that Finland, for example, won the Winter War against the Soviet Union in 1939–40, since even though it lost territories in the east, it still hindered an occupation of the entire country and thereby also avoided a later enforced membership in the Warsaw Pact and Soviet domination. At the time, though, these obvious post-World War II benefits were not clear. In relative terms, it is even more difficult to determine whether or not one state is better off after a war in comparison with the opponent. For example, should we understand the US and its allies as victorious in Afghanistan considering the enormous costs associated with the war? On the one hand, allied forces removed the Taliban from power in 2001, instead supporting the early installation of a new interim (later elected) government in Kabul. From this perspective, Western powers can be understood as successful. On the other hand, Taliban insurgents are still able to launch attacks more or less nationwide in Afghanistan, which suggests that they hardly have been defeated. Hence, although intuitively attractive, understanding victory and defeat in terms of a cost-benefit calculus encounters problems of conflicting values.

Third, Johnson and Tierney (2006) suggest that instead of versions of score-keeping, victory should be understood as "match-fixing." Here, they try to solve the inherent problem of fluctuating, ambiguous end-states or conflicting metrics in cost-benefit ratios by suggesting that victory is socially constructed. Victory, in short, is what we make of it. By focusing on how perceptions of victory are created, it is possible to uncover how events during war should not be understood in terms of score-keeping, but are rather influenced by a series of preconceptions of what war is, what it is worth, what the expectations on military action are, and how information are processed and spread. Drawing, among others, upon the cases of the failed rescue attempt during the Mayaguez incident in 1975 (which was heralded as a success) and the largely successful aid relief operation in Somalia 1992–4 (which was heralded as a major failure), Johnson & Tierney (2006, 2007) are able to show that events during war are influenced by, for example, the expectations upon military action and the way events are communicated. In the Mayaguez case, after the Vietnam War, the US public had low expectations on what military power could achieve and when the 39 imprisoned US sailors returned home (although they had already been released when the US marines initiated its rescue operation that in itself involved the death of 41 US soldiers), it seemed that US military action had rescued the sailors and the operation was heralded a success. Meanwhile, in Somalia, expectations of the utility of US military force were high after the Gulf War and the end of the Cold War. In such circumstances the loss of 43 US soldiers – despite the successful protection of the aid relief program that saved up to 1,000,000 Somalis from starvation – was deemed a failure. The match-fixing understanding thus highlights that actor-specific characteristics and perceptions influence the process of analyzing and determining victory and defeat. It can, however, be criticized for focusing only on the characteristics of one actor. Simply put, from this perspective a conflict can have two winners.

Fourth, victory has also been understood to be socially constructed between the two opponents (Honig, forthcoming). This understanding stresses that, as the parties fight, they reveal information not only about their resolve and preferences, but also about their norms. The way military force is organized and utilized, in short, both reveals how the actor understands itself and what it considers to be legitimate military behavior. Through the war, the opponents can learn their respective norm structure, and through the violence they can start to share this norm structure. Once the norm structure is shared – effectively when one jointly has decided upon the definition of victory – then military power can bear fruit. In sports terms: when the parties have agreed what should count as a "goal," then we can start to play to have a winner. The problem, of course, and this is also highlighted in the sports metaphor, is that this "coming together" of norms can take a long time. Imagine the dilemmas facing both teams when one team playing ice hockey is facing another playing cricket and they are supposed to – while playing – agree upon the nature of the game they are playing and its rules. In war, of course, the stakes are also much higher than in sports and this adds further complications to the formation of a joint norm structure. One of the advantages of this understanding of victory is that it can help us to understand why some wars are longer than others. Furthermore, this understanding also suggest that in order to be victorious in war, there must be a plan not only how to defeat the opponent, but also how to play the game to your advantage. In short, rather than merely count body bags, you also need to make the opponent think that counting body bags is the way victory and defeat should be measured and determined.

Although we can think of four different understandings of the concept of victory, we may also approach it as a case of conceptual change. Martel (2007), for example, convincingly shows that victory has been understood differently in different contexts and at different levels of war. It is even one of the more intensely politically laden concepts that we can think of. The reason, of course, is that if we think of victory in the sense of match-fixing, then the parties involved in the conflict have an interest to declare themselves winners and thereby shape public perception of what counts in war. The drivers for conceptual change can also be exogenous to the fighting. During the Cold War and the advent of nuclear balance and the dangers of nuclear holocaust, for example, it simply did not make much sense to talk of a winner in war (Baylis & Garnett 1991: 1; Hobbs 1979). Moreover, and especially in interventions in civil war during the last two decades, Western powers and their organizations have mainly been dealt the hand of creating peace. Victory has become peace – and not only peace understood as absence of violence, but also peace in terms of creating rule of law, just governance, and a fully operating market economy. Regardless of how we approach victory and defeat, however, it is important both for policy or practical purposes and in terms of democratic accountability to be precise by what we mean by victory. For analytical purposes, naturally, such precision is also a necessity. Victory is also a key component in the formation of political ends, and in the next section we will elaborate more on the logic of strategy and how means and ends meet.

The logic of strategy

As the interface between politics and war, strategy is underpinned by three elements. First, it relies upon distinguishing between political ends and military ends. This means that military action is made understandable and accountable in relation to the political ends it is meant to serve. It is the differentiation between means and ends that makes strategy instrumental. Second, strategy would be rendered meaningless if the actor had unlimited resources. In short, it is scarce resources that force actors to choose among different means that all potentially could be effective in reaching the political end. Strategy therefore depends on carefully managing these limited resources. Third, strategy is a dynamic concept trying to capture an interactive element between actors with opposing wills. This means that strategy can be assessed primarily in relation to other actors. Whether or not something is clever and successful, simply put, depends on how your opponent acts. Below we will elaborate on these three elements of strategy. For analytical purposes, we separate the discussion, but it should be recognized that the three are dependent upon each other. It is because strategy is conducted towards others that actors can never focus only on one relationship in isolation. This means that even the US is stretched for resources and needs to carefully consider its means and ends.

The goal of strategy is to, within a specific normative and political setting, influence one's counterpart in a direction that favors one's interests. This can involve everything from the total destruction of the opponent's military capabilities to make him defenseless, to threats, or just the use of latent military force. There has been plenty of evidence over the last decade in Iraq and Afghanistan suggesting that death and destruction are not always the optimal and most efficient method of wielding military power. In this section, we will therefore in parallel to the more common direct approaches of brute force and coercion also highlight indirect approaches and deterrence. Considering that the most efficient use of military means almost always are preferable to costly options, it is ideal if strategy can force the opponent into a position where he sees his interests better served to end the war on our terms than to continue the resistance. In more formal terms: the aim of the use of force is to influence the opponent's structure of preferences in a direction that you prefer. This reasoning makes clear the intimate relationship between strategy and the assumption of rationality.

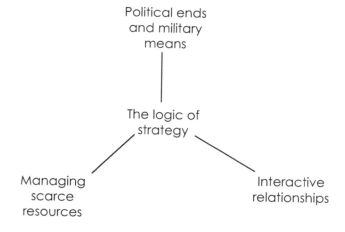

Figure 3.1 The logic of strategy.

Military means and political ends

The first element of strategy refers to a distinction between political ends and military means. The distinction between ends and means provide strategic analysis with part of its explanatory and normative conceptual powers. It makes it possible to deconstruct a particular behavior and either point to flawed, overambitious political ends or underestimated means. The distinction between means and ends also makes clear the link to strategy being conducted under conditions of scarce resources. If an actor possessed unlimited resources, there would be no need to carefully choose among different means and ways to use these. Some think of political ends as important a priori such as survival, or as a result of political values such as freedom or sovereignty. Others think of political ends as a result of a pre-existing identity. Ringmar (1996), for example, suggests that the Swedish entry in the Thirty Years' War should be understood as a reflection of King Gustavus Adolphus' understanding of statehood and the expectations on contemporary monarchs as well as Sweden's self-appointed role as the leading remaining Protestant state, rather than the standard explanation of fear of an impending Catholic invasion and Swedish trade interests being threatened when the armies of the imperial league began roaming the German Baltic Sea ports. In the formation of strategy and explanations of particular strategies, the political ends sometimes seem to take a backseat to a focus on the means. Often this preoccupation with the means of war is a result of researchers being too concerned with what we can observe. Still, separating ends and means is valuable since it underpins the crucial Clausewitzian distinction between ends sought *through* war and ends *within* war.

Using strategy as an analytical lens means that the line between peace and war – so central in much current theorizing, international law, and diplomatic practice –becomes less important. Strategy, in short, is conducted both during peace and during war. This may seem paradoxical, but, for example, deterrence can operate both during peace (i.e. preventing war) and war (preventing further escalation of war). Hence, by its very existence, military power can influence policy-making. In practice, the political ends during peace are identical to those of wartime, i.e. to influence the opponent in a direction that favors one's interests – to induce the opponent to do what you want. Moreover, the threat of violence also operates and transcends any border between war and peace. Even in war, the threat of further escalation is still prevalent. It is the "power to hurt" more – the danger of continued future death and destruction – in Schelling's (1966: 3) words, that makes an opponent comply.

How then should military means be used to achieve political ends? How does force operate? In principle, there is a host of different ways to use force for political purposes, but they can fruitfully be differentiated in three broad categories. First, deterrence is central in strategic theory. The gist of deterrence theory is that the opponent will refrain from doing something he wants to because the costs of doing it will be higher than the expected gains (e.g. Schelling 1966; George & Smoke 1974; Jervis et al. 1985; Morgan 2003; Freedman 2004; Paul et al. 2009). Deterrence therefore works through discouraging certain courses of action that the opponent otherwise could have pursued. There are several assumptions that underpin the logic of deterrence. The most fundamental of these is that the actors need to perceive the latent "power to hurt" in a similar way. Otherwise, deterrence will fail. For example, if a particular air defense system is intended to work as a deterrent, but the opponent fails to either be aware of its existence (keeping stuff secret may not always be the most efficient idea), fails to recognize its importance (since this deals with the opponent's capability to correctly interpret information, it is something that is partly out of one's hands), or mistakenly believes that the air defense system will not be used against it (i.e. the deterrent is not credible), then deterrence will not have the intended effect. This suggests that there are a number of potential dilemmas involved in pursuing political ends through deterrence. Deception can, for example, be self-defeating, insofar as if one manages to keep a particular weapon system a secret (because it is beneficial for the purposes of surprise on the battle-field), the weapon system will not contribute to building a credible deterrent that would have discouraged the war altogether. Traditional deterrence theory, furthermore, used to stress that the actors were understood to be states. It was the state that best approximated a unitary actor. Lately, however, there has been an increase in interest in deterrence against non-state actors and in particular deterrence against terrorist organizations (e.g. Wenger & Wilner 2012). This research has been a natural development from the fact that we now know that non-state actors also act in an organized way and that they resemble state bureaucracies (e.g. Shapiro & Siegel 2012).

Second, coercion is an equally central part of strategic theory. Coercion relies upon actors calculating and planning their courses of action on the basis of cost-benefit analyses (e.g. Schelling 1966; Byman & Waxman 2002; Stone 2011). From such an angle, the use of force (or threats thereof) is about convincing the opponent to choose a course of action that you prefer. Already here, it is necessary to identify a further central component of coercion. It relies upon the adversary having a choice. If you remove the opportunity to choose, we are not talking about coercion, but brute force (see below). Coercion is thus about using force to alter the opponent's calculations about costs and benefits of certain actions. It is about making him choose what you want. Schelling (1966: 34) explains:

> [M]ilitary strategy can no longer be thought of, as it could in some countries in some eras, as the science of military victory. It is now equally, if not more, the art of coercion, of intimidation and deterrence. The instruments of war are more punitive than acquisitive. Military strategy, whether we like it or not, has become the diplomacy of violence.

Coercion becomes central in this context since it depends upon convincing the opponent that if he does not choose what we want, the costs will be unbearable. Again, it is not the ongoing death and destruction that necessarily operate as the causal mechanism, but rather the expectation of future death and destruction. "Stripped down to its chassis, so to speak, almost any war emerges as an exercise in coercion. The application of force is combined with a conditional intention to stop once a desired set of political objectives is achieved" (Stone 2011: 639). Hence, for coercion, so-called "escalation dominance" becomes critical. Being able to escalate more than your opponent offers you the opportunity to incur future costs on the opponent. And here enter, of course, the practical difficulties of choosing and pursuing strategy. How do you make someone amenable to your will by incurring death and destruction? Under what conditions does that lead to success and under what conditions do death and destruction instead lead to a more determined resistance? How do you alter the opponent's structure of preferences when these are secret?

Third, brute force is yet another central way of reaching political ends. The key difference between brute force and coercion is not necessarily the use of force or the level of force that is applied. Instead, brute force relies upon removing or negating the bargaining situation through destruction. Hence, rather than coercing Iraq in 1981 to stop its nuclear program through threats or the use of force against other targets, Israel carried out a surprise air attack on the nuclear facility in Osirak itself. This effectively removed the Iraqi regime's choice. Similarly, the Clausewitzian idea of destroying your opponent's armed forces – making the enemy defenseless – and then dictating the terms of the peace, is essentially an exercise in brute force as it removes the ability to choose.

It is precisely the distinction between ends and means that makes clear that in war, one should never lose sight of its political end and never succumb to the temptation of understanding war as an exercise of military techniques (Stone 2011). Death and destruction, to some extent, will probably remain an integral part of the conduct of war, but through strategic analysis we are able to attribute a meaning to violence. The distinction between means and ends – force as an instrument to achieve a goal – also highlights the ethical dimension of war. The distinction between political ends and military means mirrors the distinction between a legitimate or just cause to go to war and the necessity of waging the war in a just way.

Scarcity of resources

The second element of strategy is that it is formed and pursued under the pressure of scarce resources (e.g. Gow 2003; Brodie 1949; Betts 1997). As elaborated upon above, the necessity of distinguishing between means and ends comes from the fact that all actors have to carefully manage resources. While moderation and restraint are key parts of strategy, in order not to jeopardize the political end of the war by making the opponent more determined to resist, there is also a second reason why restraint is an inevitable part of strategy: scarcity of resources. Indeed, James Gow (2003) suggests that restraint is not always the result of prudence on behalf of the decision-makers. Rather, it is the result of actors having limited resources. In the face of uncertainty about others' intentions, future developments, and scarce resources, it is strategically unwise to commit all your forces to one theatre of operations. Once engaged, it is difficult to adjust to suddenly emerging threats in other areas.

As an element of strategy, scarcity of resources has both absolute and relative dimensions. On the one hand, shortage of resources implies that there is only a certain set of military capabilities that one can acquire. On the other hand, it also means that even if you cannot acquire all potential military capabilities, you may still possess more military capabilities if your opponent is weaker. On top of the more general cut-backs on defense spending resulting from the end of the Cold War (King 2011), the financial crisis that has swept the global economy during the last five years has made scarcity of resources even more acute. The time of austerity, as it has become known, has also put a strain on the number and kind of international interventions states appear to be interested in. Training missions, education of officers, air power, special operations forces, and liaison officers seem to be the new way of conducting the diplomacy of violence (e.g. Engelbrekt et al. 2013). Austerity has also led to a problem of escalation dominance. After over a decade of war in Iraq and Afghanistan, Western armed forces are stripped to the bare essentials and struggle to sustain troop sizes. Following from the scarcity of resources, the immediate dilemma the strategist faces is that it is not possible a priori to determine what capabilities that will be necessary in order to wage a successful war. Unpredictable events still occur and unpredictable effects of actions are plentiful in war.

How, then, do states deal with scarcity? First, forming coalitions and alliances is probably the key solution to problems of scarcity. Freedman (2013) even elevates coalition building as being one of the central components of strategy. We treat it here as a solution to the problem of limited resources. The scarcity that strategists deal with are not only of material kind, such as acquiring more bullets, tanks, and soldiers, but also of immaterial kind, such as gaining legitimacy and political freedom of maneuver for military action. Alliances and coalitions can, aptly put together, contribute to solving both of these scarcities. In order to solve problems of limited material resources, alliances are an age-old solution, as the shifting patterns of alliances in European history over the last 200 years can testify. However, acquiring optimal levels of material resources through alliances are not necessarily always a perfect solution. There is plenty of evidence that states, when involved in alliances, try to "pass the buck" to other alliance partners to free-ride on the security and military capabilities their partners have acquired. Even within NATO, at the height of the Cold War and a serious threat from the Soviet Union, there was constant bargaining among the member states about how to share the burden of defense spending (e.g. Snyder 1984, 2007). That all actors – regardless of level of absolute powers – share the problem of scarce resources is also evident in the current US policies of coalition building and alliances. Since the end of the Cold War, NATO has – instead of dissolving – increased in member states from Eastern Europe, while also signing collaborative treaties with another 41 countries around the Mediterranean, in the Middle East, in Central Asia, in East Asia, and in the former Soviet Union (Edstrom et al. 2011).

Forming alliances and building coalitions are also central in gaining legitimacy to act in a certain region. And since military action requires political support, building a coalition can be central for the success of the operation (Kreps 2011). In this sense, alliances are an integral part of a strategy. Coalitions, collaborations, and alliances not only enable action, but can also bring about success of a strategy. French Cold War strategist André Beaufre, for example, maintained that alliances were a part of what he understood as the "external maneuver." Beaufre (1963: 102–4) understood strategy very much in terms of a competition for freedom of action. He argued that nuclear weapons curtailed the freedom of action, since the overhanging threat of nuclear escalation made the great powers apprehensive to use force. To gain freedom of action, the external maneuver consists of, for example, building coalitions to acquire political support of a particular course of action before it occurs. The "internal maneuver," according to Beaufre, is related to the more direct use of force to reach the political end in the theatre of operations. This also means that, in the continuous interaction with potential future opponents, the maneuvering has to simultaneously limit the opponent's freedom of action, while creating the setting for, and immediate plans of, one's military action.

Second, scarce resources can also be eased with a better use of existing resources. In order to do so, most Western armed forces have over the past centuries developed ever more elaborate planning procedures as well as command and control hierarchies. Accordingly, military units grew larger staffs and the French Revolutionary Wars also witnessed the emergence of a new category of officer that specialized in planning: the staff officer. In a simultaneous development, cabinets and governments grew too, thus reinforcing the need to coordinate efforts more efficiently. This also created more intricate systems of governance in civil-military relations. The process itself was nothing short of revolutionary. Until the mid-eighteenth century, the king himself, with his fellow marshals and generals, planned and conducted wars. Two hundred years later, thousands of individuals were involved in the planning and decision-making process. War had acquired its bureaucracy (e.g. van Creveld 1985; Cohen 2002; Imlay & Duffy Toft 2006). The key assumption behind the claim that more elaborate and detailed planning can alleviate problems of scarcity is that, by optimizing resources, one could mitigate shortage in military capabilities. There is, however, a shortage of actual empirical studies that test the extent to which war's bureaucracy leads to a better use of resources or if the cost of the bureaucracy is higher than the cost of a previous "slack" management.

Third, the problem of scarce resources can also be dealt with through avoiding costly showdowns. There is a long-standing strand of strategic theory stressing that cunning – *mētis*

– is far superior as a strategy than violence and brute strength – *biē* (Freedman 2013: 22–53). The dichotomy between being clever and deceiving your opponent, thus winning without the costs usually attributed to war and achieving victory openly through overwhelming force, also represents two different ways of managing the problem of scarce resources. If you wage the war with large-scale force, your resources will be tied down and your strategic freedom of maneuver curtailed. Meanwhile, if you wage the war by being shrewd and deceitful, you may still be able to use your reserves elsewhere, thus maintaining freedom of action. The latter way is, of course, not only a way of preserving your forces, but also signifies how a nominally weaker part can punch above its weight. When Odysseus convinces the Greek army outside the besieged city of Troy, with its impenetrable walls, to pretend to abandon the battlefield leaving only a small unit inside a wooden horse behind, to fool the Trojans into their doom or when Norse Viking chieftain Hastein pretends to be dead and, under the pretense of wanting a Christian funeral, is given leave to enter into the medieval city of Luna (in modern Italy), only to quickly arise from the dead and slaughter its citizens, they display *mētis*. In ancient China, Sun Tzu (1994: 177) also voiced similar preferences. In stating that supreme strategic skills are not found in "attaining one hundred victories in one hundred battles," but rather to subdue "the enemy without fighting," he clearly positions himself in favor of *mētis*.

The dichotomy between cunning and raw power is also visible in modern strategic thought. Liddell Hart (1991), for example, distinguished between what he understood as direct and indirect methods. While the former was about concentrating your own forces directly against the strongest defenses, the latter was all about avoiding the strongest enemy positions, instead striking at the weaker elements of the opposition. However, the indirect strategy is no guarantee of victory. Consider Saddam Hussein's attempt to draw Israel into the Persian Gulf War in 1991 to break the alliance between the Arab Gulf states and the US. This is a clear-cut example of an indirect strategy. The Iraqi regime recognized that the alliance made US and British forward basing possible. The forward basing – Operation Desert Shield – was a precondition for the later assault. In order to stop the counter-offensive after the invasion of Kuwait, Hussein therefore needed to break the alliance rather than attacking the US and Western military build-up. The easiest way to do so was to try to lure Israel into joining the war. The plan, however, was thwarted when Israel was given the Patriot Missile System to defend itself from the threat of Iraqi Scud-missiles. The choice between cunning and power is, moreover, not necessarily just a rational choice, but also dependent upon normative context. For example, when Homer's story about Odysseus travelled to become Virgil's Ulysses in Rome, it was treachery and deceit that was the message, rather than anticipation and intelligence. *Mētis* was not honorable (Freedman 2013: 42). Similarly, when we think of norms of war from medieval chivalry to modern laws of war and the use of, for example, human shields when confronted with Western airpower (which in a way is the cunning way – *mētis* – to avoid the disadvantage of having to face the overwhelming superiority of the West), it is often construed as illegitimate or cheating.

The dynamics of strategy

The third element of strategy is its interactive nature. Whatever decision we make regarding means and ends, it is dependent upon how our opponent acts for its degree of success. Getting the strategy "right," therefore, is partly out of one's hands. The dynamic nature of strategy is a long-standing theme in strategic theory. Clausewitz (1993), for example, emphasized it when describing war as a struggle between two living forces against each other. This creates an interaction in which my opponent dictates terms to the same extent that I dictate his. Beaufre (1963) also noted that strategy involved an abstract interplay between opposing wills. The key to success in strategy thus lay in mastering the problems of dialectical struggle. Schelling (1966), too, noted that strategy was about interdependent decision-making. As John Stone (2011: 5) succinctly puts it: "our optimum course of action depends on what we anticipate our adversary's response will be – a response that will in turn be conditioned by his expectation of how we shall respond to him."

One seminal strand of thought in strategic theory has developed so-called game theory to better analyze the interdependency of strategies where multiple actors compete for the same resources. There is a host of social dilemmas that are used to explain everything from economic behavior, to arms races, ecological disasters, and conflict (e.g. Kollock 1998; Oye 1985; Ostrom 1990; Posen 2003). One of the more common games – the tragedy of the common – can be used to illustrate how the strategies of the parties are interdependent. In the game – and there are versions of it stemming back to Aristotle – four farmers live next to a common in the middle of a village. Each of the farmers is dependent on their two cows to produce milk and butter for the market every day for their livelihood. The problem arises when one of the farmers manages to save enough money to buy a further two cows. Suddenly the common cannot sustain the grazing livestock. Realizing that their cows will gradually weaken due to the shortage of grass and stop producing milk, the farmers are left with a dilemma. What should they do? The rational strategy for each of farmers is to let their cows out onto the common to eat earlier in the morning so that they can have the most of what little grass there is left. The problem of course is that when all of the farmers try to pre-empt the others, the grass on the common does not have enough time to grow back and gradually the green common is turned into a brown patch of dirt. Hence, when all of the farmers act rationally individually, it results in an irrational collective outcome.

The game allows us to identify a few key aspects of the interdependency of strategy. First, it is clear that strategists attempt to anticipate what others will do. Schelling (1960) expressed this as strategic behavior influencing the others' expectations of your own behavior. The farmers ponder the situation, put themselves in others' shoes and decide individually that it is preferable to try to pre-empt the others, since if any of the others succeed, the others will be left without a secure livelihood. Second, the game is construed as a zero-sum game where all the farmers stand to lose and compete for the same resources. It is "pure competition" in Schelling's (1960) words. This is done in order to simplify and bring out the logic of interdependent decision-making more clearly. In real-life, strategy is most often pursued in situations where there are multiple stakes involved. In real-life, therefore, the farmers would have had the opportunity to sell the cows and follow a different career path, in which the common is not the essential resource. Third, the game also highlights that strategy is being pursued not only in pure competition, but that there are also common interests shared among antagonists. Hence, even if each of the farmers wants their cows to be fat and healthy, they also share a common interest that the common should continue to be a green pasture. This makes it clear that neither of the farmers actually gain from pre-emption. The stakes are so high – mutual starvation and death – that negotiations about a schedule are far more likely. Following from this, it is evident that communication can mitigate the worries of the future. This form of communication, however, must overcome problems of credible commitment (e.g. Fearon 1995). If the farmers agree – without a system of punishment for defection – to honor a schedule, each of the farmers would still be in a position of potential harm. If they were to agree on a schedule and create an institution for punishment of defection, however, the costs of reneging would rise and expectations of future cooperation would be shared. It is easy to see why game theory became such an important analytical tool during the Cold War, when the nuclear arsenals threatened global devastation and there were incentives for pre-emptive strikes had the leaders acted in a short-sighted manner. Finally, understanding strategic interaction as one game has further problems, since in real-life situations there are repeated games (e.g. Williams 1991; Axelrod 1984). This means that there are opportunities for actors to learn how to deal with each other and past histories of interaction can add to information about future expected behavior.

Although game theory stresses rational choice, Schelling (1960) also pointed out that irrational behavior could be rational in competitive contexts. This was an important – and dangerous – realization. Being unpredictable, in short, improved one's bargaining situation. This can be seen in situations such as crises, where "brinkmanship-strategies" can be advantageous, although they increase the risk that the situation can spin out of control (Lebow 1981; Boin et al. 2006) The problem, of course, is that unpredictability could also heighten tensions and incur further escalation and potential reckless decisions. The very practical problem facing strategic decision-makers is that, when trying to anticipate the opponent's future behavior, including breaking points of resistance, it is impossible to know this with any degree of certainty. Again in sports terms: you are involved in a game where it is obvious only *after* the game if 1–0 was sufficient for victory or if you needed to win 9–0 to achieve victory.

This brings us to what many analysts consider to be the paradoxical logic that character-izes strategy. Luttwak (1987: 4) argues that the "entire realm of strategy is pervaded by a paradoxical logic of its own, standing against the ordinary linear logic by which we live in all other spheres of life." Illustrating his point, he suggests that a military force heading towards its operational target reaches a crossroads. The general knows that it is possible to reach the target through both routes. The first is wide, open, straight, and smooth, while the second is narrow, curvy, and uneven, practically inviting ambushes. Only in strategic affairs, Luttwak claims, would it at all be an issue which path to take. In ordinary life, it is obvious that the first route should be chosen – everything else being equal. In strategy, however, the second route may prove to be the shrewd choice. The bad road could be a good choice because due to its poor quality, it is probably less guarded, because the opponent does not expect us to take the poor road. The good road, conversely, could be the bad choice, because its quality has probably attracted the attention of the enemy as the most likely road that the general will take. This means that the good road will have better prepared defenses around it. Adding to the dilemma, of course, is the probability that the opponent also realizes that the general understands that the poor road is the good choice. So along which way should he proceed?

The only way to temporarily suspend the paradoxical logic, according to Luttwak, is to use surprise. Surprise, which in turn requires secrecy and deception, is thus not only a useful tool among many in war but of fundamental importance to outmaneuver one's opponent and gain an advantage. To temporarily suspend the paradoxical logic by surprise, however, also involves risks. Trying to maintain a high level of secrecy in the operational planning could endanger an optimized solution to the coordination of major operations, since commanders may not receive relevant information from their own subordinates if the subordinates do not know the full range of the strategic plan. Naturally, attempts to deceive and keep secret one's plans entail a risk of secrets being detected by the enemy. Moreover, attempts to deceive, for example by feigning an attack in one direction, by definition involve using military assets in the deception and these are resources that could have instead been allocated to the main effort. Unexpected, out-of-the-box solutions, finally, can also be problematic since it is more demanding for the armed forces to do things that they have not trained for. Indeed, attempting daring new tactics in the middle of a campaign can easily lead to calamity. Clausewitz (1993: 138) went even further stating that: "everything in war is very simple, but the simplest thing is difficult." Rather than trying to do "new" things, it is unexpected things that should be the aim to achieve surprise. Here again, the interactive element of strategy is evident. It is effectively the opponent that decides whether or not a particular action is "unexpected."

Cunning and force – *mētis* and *biē* – are thus still relevant in the discussion. Considering that the aim is to influence the will of the opponent in a direction that is favorable, deception has been a long-standing theme in strategy. Sun Tzu (1994: 168) even claimed that all warfare can be boiled down to trickery and deception: "Warfare is the way (Tao) of deception." This line of thought is relevant in other contexts than interstate conventional warfare. Mao Tse-tung (1961: 46) stressed surprise and deception in his analysis of successful guerrilla campaigns in a much-quoted passage:

> [I]n guerrilla warfare, select the tactic of seeming to come from the east and attacking from the west; avoid the solid, attack the hollow; attack; withdraw; deliver a lightning blow, seek a lightning decision. When guerrillas engage a stronger enemy, they withdraw when he advances; harass him when he stops, strike him when he is weary; pursue him, when he withdraws. In guerrilla strategy, the enemy's rear, flanks, and other vulnerable spots are his vital points, and there he must be harassed, attacked, dispersed, exhausted, and annihilated.

From understanding war as a duel of opposing wills, it follows that we can characterize strategy as a dynamic and interdependent phenomenon. The actions of one side in the conflict have consequences for the other side's activities and vice versa. Strategy, thus, is not directed at an inanimate object, but against an intelligent subject, himself trying to outmaneuver you. The dynamic nature of strategy makes it different to a lot of other human undertakings. The engineer who plans the construction of a bridge does not have to worry about the building material trying to destroy the plan. A boxer practicing against a sandbag does not have to worry about the sandbag trying to hit back. However, when faced with another boxer, the number of variables to consider before launching a combination dramatically increases. Planning to hit the sandbag, in turn, does not require too much imagination or elaborate planning procedures. The action is one-sided and therefore the calculation is simple.

Conclusions

The purpose of this chapter has been to outline the elements of military strategy. We have discussed the question of how strategy is defined, what strategy is, in what context it operates, and what logic it has according to military thought. Strategy has been described as the rational process that tries to create a connection between, and coherence of, military means and political ends. Strategy is what provides war with a political reference and thus provides a rationale for war. In our description, we have characterized strategy and strategic thought as relying upon three elements: a systematic analysis of ends and means, management of limited resources, and a paradoxical logic resulting from strategy's dynamic nature.

Although the contents of particular strategies vary over time and place, the inherent interactive element provides strategy with its particular logic. It is because strategy is shaped and pursued against several opponents – in peace as well as in war – that actors have scarce resources. And it is precisely because of the scarce resources that strategy is about tough choices. In the chapter, we have also described how the meaning of strategy changes over time. The contents of the term has varied between what we now would consider operational art and what some now describe as grand strategy, i.e. the state's combined means utilized to reach political ends. Furthermore, the creation of strategy occurs within a context consisting of geographic, political, economic, ideological, normative, and technological factors.

Because strategy can be understood as, and relies on, the ability to plan ahead and cognitively separate several potential futures from each other, strategy has often not only been understood as brute force, but also as deception, coercion, and cunning. Both strategists and theorists need to bear the multi-faceted nature of strategy in mind in their practices.

Questions for discussion

1. Is interpreting war as a rational phenomenon a prerequisite for strategic thought?
2. To what extent has the concept of strategy changed and evolved over time? How should such variation be understood?
3. How does the strategic context influence the formation of contemporary states' strategies?
4. How are honor, cunning, and force related in contemporary strategy? Why is there variation in how these concepts are understood to be related?
5. To what extent does the small state strategy differ from that of a great power, in theory and practice?
6. Is strategy an art requiring judgment when navigating uncertainties and ambiguity, or a science requiring precision and rigor in analysis?

Note

1 It should be noted that we do not refer to so-called *geopolitics*, i.e. the belief that geography directly determines the contents of policy and strategy (cf. Dalby et al. 2006). Geopolitics had a long intellectual pedigree during the twentieth century with Mackinder, Spykman, and others. The school of thought, however, was severely discredited by being associated with the Nazi concept of *lebensraum*. Today, geopolitics is still regarded as a prominent school of thought mainly in Russia and China. (e.g. Cohen 2008).

Further reading

Holger Afflerbach & Hew Strachan (eds.), *How Fighting Ends: A History of Surrender* (Oxford: Oxford University Press, 2012).

Lawrence Freedman, *Strategy: A History* (Oxford: Oxford University Press, 2013).

Colin S. Gray, *The Strategy Bridge: Theory for Practice* (Oxford: Oxford University Press, 2010).

Michael Howard, *War and the Liberal Conscience* (London: Hurst, 2008).

Patrick Morgan, *Deterrence Now* (Cambridge: Cambridge University Press, 2003).

Peter Paret (ed.), *Makers of Modern Strategy: From Machiavelli to the Nuclear Age* (Princeton, NJ: Princeton University Press, 1986).

Thomas C. Schelling, *Arms and Influence* (New Haven, CT: Yale University Press, 1966).

Rupert Smith, *The Utility of Force: The Art of War in the Modern World* (London: Allen Lane, 2005).

Glenn Snyder, *Alliance Politics* (Ithaca, NY: Cornell University Press, 2007).

4   Operational art

Introduction

In the spring of 1973 the last American soldier formally left Vietnam, an event that brought an end to a nearly twenty year US military engagement. During the war, US forces arguably had not lost a single major battle, they had acquired both air superiority and command of sea, greatly weakened the opponent's infrastructure and economy, killed far more opponents, and shot down many more of the opponent's fighter aircrafts than they themselves had lost. Yet, it was considered a lost war. How could this be? How was it possible that this large accumulation of tactical victories on all fronts and in all domains could not be translated into strategic and political gains for the US government and its allies?

Over the subsequent decade many strategists in the US and elsewhere thought hard about this paradox. Gradually, many of them reached similar conclusions. First, in war tactical victories do not automatically result in strategic victory. Thus, it was crucial to win the right tactical victories, and only strive to win those battles that it was possible to translate into strategic effect. Second, it was believed necessary to establish a level of war between the strategic and tactical level. At the so-called operational level, military command could concentrate on implementing the chosen strategy. It was in this context that "operational art" came to be understood as the optimal coordination of strategic goals and tactical means. Operational art, however, is far from a modern phenomenon and the idea has been around, both consciously and unconsciously, in one form or another, for a long time. The purpose of this chapter is to describe the principles and ideas that exist regarding operational art, and to discuss the explanatory and normative value of these theories. What is operational art and what does it do? What are the key concepts necessary to understand operational art, and what factors are necessary conditions for the implementation of military and naval operations?

The discussion in this chapter is almost exclusively kept on a conceptual level. The chapter deals with concepts and phenomena that are common to all operations, whether carried out jointly or by single services, in the air or on the ground, at sea or below the sea. The chapters that follow (Chapters 5–9) fill the concept of operational art with different content based on different theories. The present chapter, therefore, deals with definitions of operational art, center of gravity, command, logistics, and intelligence, while Chapters 5–9 deal with theories of, for example, the principles of war, combined arms, maneuver and attrition warfare, blockade and decapitation.

Operational art: historical development and definitions

Operational art emerged primarily as a result of changes in the conduct of war during the French Revolutionary Wars and technological developments during the early nineteenth century. The introduction of large national armies, increasingly based on conscription, as was the case in France in the 1790s, had a major impact on the conduct of war. Contributing factors were also the establishment of railways, the telegraph, and the mass production of armaments that began in the middle of the nineteenth century. The sheer volume of forces involved in this new kind of warfare forced fresh approaches to command in battle, since it became virtually impossible for commanders to personally lead their troops on horseback. Troops were now divided into smaller units (divisions, corps, and armies) and spread across the surface. This necessitated a new form of command with novel organizational solutions and associated staff, planning procedures, and command structures (English 1996; Vego 2009; Olsen & van Creveld 2011; Naveh 1997; Newell 1991).

Capitalizing on the industrial revolution, arms, ammunition, and explosives were increasingly mass produced in the middle of the nineteenth century onwards. Together with the growing size of armies, this created a greater need for supply lines from base areas where munitions and supplies were manufactured or stored. New forms of transportation, with the introduction of railways and motor vehicles, also tended to revolutionize military logistics. The introduction of the telegraph, and new, effective methods of communications and sharing of information, also affected the manner in which military intelligence was conducted (van Creveld 1977: 231–7; Herman 1996: 16–17). These changes quickly created a need for an operational level between the strategic and tactical level, since the distance between the two latter levels became too great. Wars tended less often to be settled in a single decisive blow. Instead, longer military campaigns, with a series of battles, were often needed to defeat an enemy. This put new demands on endurance, logistics, planning, and the ability to coordinate tactical actions to meet strategic objectives.

The introduction of nuclear weapons from 1945, furthermore, meant that military staff and individual military thinkers became less interested in the best ways to command large armies. The possession of nuclear weapons turned large concentrations of troops and munitions into attractive targets for nuclear attack and the need for operational art seemed increasingly outdated. In the 1960s and 1970s, however, developments occurred in operational thinking in both the Soviet Union and the US, in which alternatives to massive nuclear warfare between the two blocs began once more to be seriously discussed.

Three factors influenced American thinking during the 1970s in this regard. First, US operations in the Vietnam War seemed to prove that tactical victories did not automatically result in desired strategic effects. Second, technological developments were expected to have great impact on the future conduct of conventional warfare, the lessons from the Yom Kippur War in 1973 being a crucial example. Third, there was widespread dissatisfaction with the new American doctrine that appeared in the mid-1970s (Menning 1997: 42–3). Thus, the US Armed Forces came to realize that future wars could be both conventional and nuclear, which inspired new thinking concerning conventional military operations. This meant that the introduction of nuclear weapons on the international stage resulted both in the demise and rebirth of operational art.

The publication of the US Army *FM 100-5, Operations* in July 1976 was an important first step on the American side. This led to a renewal of interest in classic military thought and doctrine development. A radically revised version of *FM 100-5, Operations* came out in the summer of 1982, introducing the concept of "AirLand Battle." This innovative doctrine introduced, among other things, the idea of the "extended battlefield." Emphasis was put on initiative, greater speed and mobility, deep-strike attacks with smaller self-sufficient units, and the importance of coordinated air and ground operations throughout the theater of war (see Chapter 6). This AirLand Battle doctrine introduced many of the concepts that is today associated with maneuver warfare (see Chapter 7), and it proved a first step towards a new American form of operational art (Starry 1981; Echevarria 2011b: 154–6; Swain 1996: 157–61; Leonhard 1991; Lock-Pullan 2006).

The understanding and definition of operational art (as well as related concepts), presented by the US Army during this time, have been revised several times and have also influenced NATO doctrine. Due to its importance, it deserves to be quoted in full:

> [O]perational art is the skillful employment of military forces to attain strategic and/or operational objectives within a theater through the design, organisation, integration, and conduct of theater strategies, campaigns, major operations, and battles. Operational art translates theater strategy and design into operational design which links and integrates the tactical battles and engagements that, when fought and won, achieve the strategic aim. Tactical battles and engagements are fought and won to achieve operational results. No specific level of command is solely concerned with operational art. In its simplest expression, operational art determines when, where, and for what purpose major forces will fight. It governs the deployment of those forces, their commitments to or withdrawal from battle, and the sequencing of successive battles and major operations to attain major objectives. Operational art seeks to ensure that commanders use soldiers, materiel, and time effectively to achieve strategic aims through campaign design.
>
> (*FM 100-5, Operations*, 6–2, 1993)

According to this definition, the purpose of operational art is to use military forces in an efficient way to achieve strategic objectives. These often abstract objectives must be transformed, by the actor exercising operational art, into concrete operational activities and plans to link it to more concrete actions at the tactical level, thus giving the latter strategic meaning. Tactical actions – battles and combat with the enemy or avoidance of such activities – are the means to achieving operational results. Operational art must also decide where, when, and how battles should be conducted in order to optimally serve the strategic objectives. Such art thus controls the deployment and employment of military forces, and how individual battles, or avoidance thereof, should serve the higher purpose of the operation. Operational art also requires the military commander to use available resources – troops, armaments, and time – in the best way possible given the strategic objectives.

New developments with regard to conventional military operations and operational art also occurred on the Soviet side in the 1960s and 1970s. The main reason for this was the assumption that NATO's use of nuclear weapons in a future conflict could be delayed, and it was important therefore to promptly win the war on the ground before a political decision on using nuclear weapons was possible. During this period they had also observed the development of new weapons technology that had occurred in the West, based on advanced electronics and computers. These were considered to be a key factor for the outcome of any future war between the superpowers (see discussion regarding the Revolution in Military Affairs (RMA) in Chapter 6). These factors in turn led to a renaissance for conventional operational concepts and operational art (Glantz 1996: 134–9; Kipp 2011: 88–9).

Soviet operational art has a relatively long history and the first thoughts on the subject surfaced in the 1920s with different concepts concerning "deep battle," later developed as "deep operations" by Vladimir K. Triandafillov (1894–1931) and Mikhail N. Tukhachevsky (1893–1937). The inventor of modern operational art, however, is Alexander A. Svechin (1868–1938). In Svechin's work *Strategija* (Strategy) from 1927, he introduced operational art as a bridge between tactics and strategy, describing it as a means by which the senior commander could transform tactical successes into strategic success in a given theater of military operations. More specifically, he described it as the "totality of maneuvers and battles in a given part of a theater of military action directed toward the achievement of the common goal, set as final in the given period of the campaign" (Kipp 1992: 38). These ideas influenced the American definition of operational art (cf. Triandafillov 1994; Stoecker 1998; Glantz 1991; Harrison 2001; Kokoshin 1998).

Soviet Major General S. N. Kozlov's *The Officer's Handbook* (1977), moreover, defined the term as: "that part of military art concerned with the fundamentals of preparing and conducting operations involving operational formation of the armed forces on land, at sea, and in the air in accordance with overall strategic design and plans" (Kozlov 1977: 58). Here, it seems that operational art aims at using the preparation and execution of joint military operations to achieve the overall strategic objectives. In this way, the term has been associated with thoughts on joint operations in modern times. Another definition of operational art has been presented by the Soviet General and former Defense Minister, Andrei Grechko, in which the difference between strategy, operational art, and tactics are described as follows:

> [W]hile strategy encompasses questions dealing with the preparation and use of the Armed Forces in war, operational art involves resolution of problems of preparing for and waging joint and independent operations and combat actions by operational formations and Services of the Armed Forces in individual theaters of military operations. With regard to tactics, operational art occupies a dominant position. It determines tactical missions, and the role and place of tactical operations by units and formations in achieving operational goals.
>
> (Grechko 1975: 281–2)

Again, similarities are apparent with American definitions of operational art. The main difference is that Soviet versions explicitly emphasize that operational art takes place within an operational area, while American definitions emphasize the role of the commander performing operational art at the operational level of war. One problem with the definitions of operational art considered so far is that they assume an ideal world where the ends-means hierarchy is controlled from the top, from the strategic level via the operational down to the tactical level, where thus the lower levels are expected to support the higher levels. In practice, however, it is common that the very opposite occurs, i.e. situations in which, for example, tactical successes guide operational behavior rather than vice versa. If the latter occurs, these objectives will become fuzzy and difficult to achieve, creating a conflict among goals at different levels. Although in practice an interaction always takes place between the tactical and operational level, on the one hand, and between the operational and the strategic level, on the other, it is certainly risky if tactical events are allowed to affect the strategic objectives without an operational "filter" (Lind 1985: 24).

If "good" operational art ought to be something more than just a definition of successful campaigns, it requires a certain rigor in definitions and clear causal links. For instance, German General Erwin Rommel's campaign in North Africa from 1941 to 1943 cannot be described as good operational art because his tactical victories strongly influenced his strategic ambitions and ultimately these goals became impossible to implement. A victory like the one King Pyrrhus of Epirus won during Roman times ("one more such victory and we shall be utterly ruined": freely translated) is something good operational art must avoid since a tactical victory only becomes a real victory when it pays off in strategic effects and ultimately in political effects.

While the operational art that emerged during the nineteenth century primarily emanated from the challenges of commanding and handling growing armies, new technology, and logistical difficulties, there were relatively few discussions about how military operations should be conducted and how military doctrines ought to be formulated. The attrition warfare on the Western front 1914–18, and the many operational failures to preserve mobility during the war, served as an alarm bell for many military thinkers during the interwar period. This led to new thinking on operational concepts and doctrines trying to correct these deficiencies. The ensuing interwar years were a creative period in military thinking, especially concerning mechanized warfare and strategic air bombing. Military theorists in Britain, France, Italy, the Soviet Union, and Germany all provided valuable contributions. In Britain, two individuals particularly stood out in this regard – J. F. C. Fuller and Basil H. Liddell Hart. Both had experience of trench warfare during World War I and were critical of the methods used by the Western powers. Both were staunch supporters of mechanized warfare and argued for operational concepts that would increase mobility on the battlefield (Strachan 2011: 111–15).

Liddell Hart, especially, left lasting contributions to what would later be called "maneuver warfare" (see Chapter 7). His concept of an "indirect approach" shows many similarities with the German *Blitzkrieg* during World War II, the Israeli war in 1967 and the operational thinking that later arose in the US. In *Decisive Wars of History* (1929), Liddell Hart presented his ideas of an indirect approach that may be viewed as a philosophy of war rather than as an actual doctrine for how to win wars. In this book, he noted that the direct way of attacking the opponent at his strongest point, as Clausewitz argued, had rarely given good results, and that it was better instead to attack the enemy where he was weakest, and where he could offer least resistance. The best way to achieve victory in operational terms was by surprise and rapid movement. The latter would be made possible using motor vehicles and the former by searching for points where the opponent least expected to be attacked. The purpose of strategy was to put the opponent off balance, both physically and mentally (Liddell Hart 1929; Strachan 2011: 115; Danchev 1998: 155–64).

It is important to note that the concepts of direct and indirect methods of warfare as developed by Liddell Hart had the character of ideal types and logical constructs rather than as empirical descriptions. The distinction between direct and indirect method lies primarily in what constitutes the objective *in* (rather than *with*) a military operation – the opponent's strengths or his weaknesses. In both theory and practice, it is not always easy to determine what an opponent's strengths and weaknesses are, as opponents often are complex entities. If one directs the blow at the weakest points of the enemy's strongest military units, something the vast majority of military leaders in history have probably attempted, is one using a direct or an indirect method of warfare? Today, most military theorists would probably argue that they had attacked the "critical vulnerabilities" of the opponent's strongest units, i.e. an indirect method (see section on the center of gravity). Hence, this becomes almost a question of semantics, since the results are often determined afterwards. A deliberate attack on the enemy's weak points, which instead results in failure, attrition, and heavy losses, would likely be viewed by these thinkers as a direct method, despite the original intent. Thus it is very important to be rigorous with the use of these two terms. We now turn to an analysis of a concept usually referred to as center of gravity, a concept closely associated with direct and indirect methods of warfare.

Center of gravity

Determining ends and means in strategy is closely associated with a concept called center of gravity. In military planning and the execution of a military operation, designed to quickly and effectively defeat the enemy, it is crucial to determine the strengths and weaknesses of both the opponent and one's own forces. To neutralize, decimate, or destroy important capabilities of the opponent, in order to influence his will to fight, is usually described as attacking the enemy's center of gravity. But this concept is, according to many, far more complicated than that and it has often created misunderstanding and confusion in, for example, military doctrine. The purpose of this section is to deepen the discussion of the concept referred to as center of gravity. In so doing we will try to sort out the existing misunderstandings, and how the concept has been used and interpreted in military theory.

Clausewitz is usually associated with the term center of gravity or *Schwerpunkt* as he called it in German. In Book 6, Chapter 27, of his famous work *On War*, he discussed the concept at the operational and tactical level of war. He drew parallels to the mechanical sciences and noted:

[A] center of gravity is always found where the mass is concentrated most densely. It presents the most effective target for a blow; furthermore, the heaviest blow is that struck by the center of gravity. The same holds true in war. The fighting forces of each belligerent – whether a single state or an alliance of states – have a certain unity and therefore some cohesion. . . . these forces will possess certain centers of gravity, which, by their movement and direction, govern the rest; and those centers of gravity will be found wherever the forces are most concentrated. But in war as in the world of inanimate matter the effect produced on a center of gravity is determined and limited by the cohesion of the parts.

(Clausewitz 1993: 587)

Here it is obvious that Clausewitz meant a center of power of a physical nature that has to do with military forces. This center of power, if attacked, affects other parts of the military organization. Finally, the concept is only relevant in relation to the opponent and cannot be understood in isolation (Schneider & Izzo 1987: 46–57; Strange & Iron 2005; Echevarria 2003a, 2003b; Eikmeier 2007; Rueschhoff & Dunne 2011: 120–5; Wood 2008). This operational and tactical definition of the concept must be set against the wider strategic version, presented in Book 8, Chapter 4 in *On War*, where military forces are only one of many possible centers of gravity. Concerning the war aim of destroying the enemy, Clausewitz (1993: 720) notes that

one must keep the dominant characteristics of both belligerents in mind. Out of these characteristics a certain center of gravity develops, the hub of all power and movement, on which everything depends. That is the point against which all our energies should be directed.

In giving examples of such centers of gravity, he mentions not only factors of a physical nature, such as a country's army or capital, but also moral factors such as the personality of individual leaders and public opinion.

As apparent, this definition differs slightly from the one previously mentioned. It is also here that we find one of the reasons for the misunderstandings that have existed as to what Clausewitz actually meant by his concept of center of gravity. While the first definition relates to the opposing military forces in a physical sense, and at the operational and tactical levels, the second definition is somewhat broader and is situated at the strategic level, incorporating both moral and psychological aspects. These differences between the two definitions are accentuated further by some creative wording in the various translations of the original German text. Joe Strange and Richard Iron (2004: 15; cf. Schneider & Izzo 1987: 49) argue that Clausewitz in both his definitions meant that a center of gravity was "a center of power and movement." They argue furthermore that centers of gravity were created, according to Clausewitz, within the relationship between the two opponents, and that centers of gravity do not exist in isolation. Finally, such centers of gravity are not "characteristics, capabilities or locations" *per se*, but rather "dynamic and powerful physical or moral agents of action or influence that *possess* certain characteristics, capabilities, and *benefit from* a given location or terrain."

There is thus a close link between operational art and the center of gravity concept. To attack the opponent's centers of gravity in the most effective way possible, guided by the needs that the strategic objectives creates, is one of the most important aspects of operational art. Strange and Iron (2004: 3) assert that centers of gravity exists at all levels of war and that Clausewitz meant his concept to signify a center of power and strength. This understanding of center of gravity has had the effect of supporters of the maneuver warfare theory observing a contradiction, since they believe the focus of operational art should be on enemy weaknesses, not strengths. Maneuver warfare theorist Robert Leonhard, for example, claims (1991: 20) that the enemy centers of gravity are not its "source of strength" but rather its "critical vulnerability". This is certainly consistent with his maneuver warfare concept, but not with Clausewitz's original concept.

One way to overcome this contradiction, Strange and Iron (2004) claim, is to recognize that elements of strength also have weaknesses, something they describe as "critical vulnerabilities." In operational art it is therefore important not only to determine centers of gravity, i.e. enemy strengths, but also the critical vulnerabilities that are closely connected with the former. Through concentration of one's own forces it is possible to create superiority *vis-à-vis* the enemy and to exploit these weaknesses, forcing the enemy to give battle at a time and place where it is at a disadvantage and thereby create success. At Stalingrad, for example, in the autumn and winter of 1942, the German Army's most effective and best armored divisions were dependent on rather poorly equipped Romanian, Italian, and Hungarian divisions to protect its flanks. The Soviet army took advantage of this fact, successfully encircling the German divisions through a pincer movement (Strange & Iron 2004: 8).

According to Strange and Iron (2004: 6–8), it is important to search for critical vulnerabilities and these may be technical, geographical, and psychological in nature and almost infinite in number. Over time, sources of strength may also be turned into weaknesses, due to the warring parties' interaction with one another. Time is therefore a crucial factor to take into consideration. Strange and Iron also choose to distinguish the center of gravity concept from specific capabilities that the center of gravity possesses (critical capabilities) and certain conditions and resources that are important for a center of gravity to become a critical capability (critical requirements). Furthermore, an enemy may in fact have a center of gravity without having critical vulnerabilities. In this manner, they solve, to some extent, the dilemmas caused by Clausewitz different definitions of center of gravity.

Milan Vego also claims that the center of gravity concept has often been confused with terms such as objectives, decisive points, or critical vulnerabilities and that these are wholly different. Vego (2000: 23) argues that any attempt to find an enemy's center of gravity must begin with an identification and analysis of the "critical factors" in a military or civil source of power, factors which can be both "critical strengths" and "critical weaknesses." Critical factors exist at all levels of war and can be more or less specific in form. At the strategic and operational level, they might be geographic functions, such as key base areas of operations, lines of operations, and communications, but also military functions, such as army units or specific branches within the armed forces. More abstract factors may be morale, the cohesion of an alliance or public opinion. These critical factors are "relative and subject to change over time," which commanders and staff officers must be mindful of in their planning and execution of operations (Vego 2000: 23). Vego (2000: 23) further argues that critical strengths are "capabilities vital for accomplishing a given or assumed military objective" and that critical weaknesses are "those sources of power . . . whose deficiencies adversely affect the accomplishment of a given or assumed military objective." Some critical weaknesses can be exploited and become critical vulnerabilities. Also critical strengths can become crucial vulnerabilities if they lack adequate protection and are open to enemy fire. Unlike Strange and Iron, Vego differentiates between critical weaknesses and critical vulnerabilities, and suggests that weaknesses do not necessarily mean vulnerabilities.

What, then, is a center of gravity, Vego asks? Centers of gravity can be found among critical strengths, but never among critical weaknesses or vulnerabilities. A center of gravity is not a target on the ground that one can destroy, nor is it synonymous with the military objective. Instead it is: "that source of leverage or massed strength – physical or moral – whose serious degradation, dislocation, neutralization or destruction will have the most decisive impact on the enemy's or one's own ability to accomplish a given military objective" (Vego 2000: 24). The more abstract elements of a center of gravity, on all levels of war, include the military leadership, doctrine, morale, and discipline. These are difficult to quantify and therefore difficult to assess and calculate. The higher up one proceeds in the levels of war, says Vego (2000: 25), the more elusive a center of gravity becomes. In the 1991 Gulf War the Iraqi leadership saw the cohesion of the US-led coalition as the alliance's strategic center of gravity, while the international coalition concluded that Saddam Hussein and his inner circle were a comparable phenomenon. Vego notes that centers of gravity at the operational and tactical levels regularly consist of the main concentration of enemy forces, and more specifically those with the highest degree of mobility and combat effectiveness. British commanders considered, for example, Rommel's main armored units, rather than his entire African corps, as his operational center of gravity. In large-scale, conventional wars, the more elusive elements connected to a center of gravity are usually found at the political and strategic level, while in irregular wars they are found mainly at the tactical level. Rarely do guerrillas concentrate their forces in such a way as to constitute an operational center of gravity (Vego 2000: 25).

As stated above, an assessment of different centers of gravity is of great importance to all military planning and operational activity. Such analyses determine the priorities made, sort out primary and secondary objectives, and decide how limited resources should be allocated to be used as efficiently as possible. The center of gravity concept may, however, be said to have limited explanatory value as a theory, i.e. as a means to explain victory and defeat in war, since it cannot be scientifically falsified. If State A attacks State B, where the charismatic leader of the latter is considered to be the center of gravity, but the war still continues despite the fact that the center of gravity has been successfully eliminated by State A, it is rarely concluded that the concept itself is wrong and ought to be disregarded, but rather that the attacking state's estimation of the center of gravity was wrong. Without careful theoretical development and empirical testing, therefore, the concept should be approached with some caution. It must also be noted that the center of gravity concept has metaphysical features that do not facilitate scientific analysis. Those who deal with the subject, including classical theorists such as Clausewitz, are in agreement that centers of gravity cannot be reduced to something materially tangible such as a building, a combat unit, or a person, but the concept is rather understood as a non-material force, a being, or an element that relies on such material things. This is usually the classic characteristic of metaphysical reasoning, something that the Western scientific tradition, from the Enlightenment onwards, has regularly been critical of.

As the discussion above has shown, there are still differences of opinion regarding center of gravity and how it should be interpreted. This includes questions of at which level of war the concept is most useful, whether the concept signifies strength or weakness, if it is material or immaterial, or whether any centers of gravity "exist" at all. No doubt these problems will continue to haunt those engaged in such deliberation. That the concept has been considered useful in military planning and operations is beyond question. If the center of gravity concept is an important factor to consider in the planning and execution of military operations, this is also the case with command in war. The need to coordinate and lead military operations is still an important part of any military theoretical discussion. We therefore continue this chapter with a description of the problems that are associated with command in war.

Command in military operations

According to an old Arabic proverb, an army of sheep led by a lion will defeat an army of lions led by a sheep. If anything, this saying is an indication of the importance given throughout history to command in war. Such command (a term which here also includes control and communications) is commonly defined as the functions that collectively guide military activities, but it can also be understood as the planning and implementation process needed to achieve military objectives (Smedberg 2001: 15–16; Shamir 2011; van Creveld 1985; Laver & Matthews 2008; Samuels 1995). Important factors that influence command in war are the characteristics of individual commanders, doctrines, staff organization, and various forms of communication technology. Command is also influenced by certain external factors such as the characteristics of the military-political context in which it takes place, time, and the opponent and his actions. Differences in these external factors may have different implications for command in wars on land, at sea, and in the air. Finally, there is a close link between command and doctrine as the latter constitutes a means for how wars are commanded and conducted.

The character of command is influenced by the level at which it has to operate. At the strategic level, more long-term decisions are made on how to translate political goals into military aims and thus how to direct and create military force. At the operational level, meanwhile, the concern is primarily to coordinate various forces towards the common strategic objectives. On the tactical level, finally, command mainly focuses on how to use available resources in the battle space. It follows that the closer one gets to the tactical level, the shorter the time perspective.

Perhaps the most important task for military command is to manage confusion and uncertainty on the battlefield, something Clausewitz (1993: 119–20) aptly caught in his metaphor "the fog of war." This can in principle be achieved in two ways – by trying to control the chaos that occurs or by accepting this uncertainty and if possible trying to use it to one's own advantage, relative to the opponent. These two philosophies of command have resulted in two current practices: a) so-called mission-directed tactics (*Auftragstaktik* in German) delegating more responsibility and leaving more room for initiative to subordinate commanders; and b) order-directed tactics (*Befehlstaktik*) trying to increase control at higher levels of command and by emphasizing instead the role of planning and the implementation of these orders by subordinate commanders (Smedberg 2001: 282–3; Leonhard 1991: 117–18). The two philosophies of command, and in fact even the two practical approaches, should be understood as ideal types, because in many cases mission-directed tactics include phases or elements of order-directed tactics, and vice versa.

Both of these ideal types of command in war have advantages and disadvantages depending on the level of command, the military domain, and general context in which they take place. Leonhard (1991: 117–18) argues that in an operational context mission-directed tactics tries to find openings in the enemy lines, while orders-directed tactics attempts to create them. Where the former exploits the opportunities created on the battlefield, the latter utilizes joint strength through concentration. While mission-directed tactics emphasize speed and movement, he continues, order-directed tactics emphasize the momentum generated by relentless attack in a concerted direction. The form and character of mission-directed and order-directed tactics may of course differ from country to country. Orders-directed tactics in the Soviet Union and Britain thus have a lot in common but also much that differs. The same applies to mission-directed tactics in countries such as the US and Israel.

An important factor in all military command is technology and the impact that new inventions create. The telegraph, radio, computer, and satellite are examples of inventions that have had major implications for the conduct of military operations over the last 150 years. In times of rapid technological development, it easily happens that technology creates overconfidence in the ability of military organizations to solve problems of command, since new technologies often solve old problems, but also tend to create new ones. Thus there are always limits to how much information a person can absorb and manage, and technological means may only remedy this problem to a certain degree (Smedberg 2001: 284).

In his book, *Command in War*, Martin van Creveld argues that command cannot be understood in isolation but must be viewed in the larger context in which it appears. It is not possible, van Creveld (1985: 261) claims, to formulate principles of what should guide a command structure or its use: "no single communications or data processing technology, no single system of organization, no single procedure or method, is in itself sufficient to guarantee the successful or even adequate conduct of command in war." Military history has shown many examples, he suggests, of very disparate command systems that have led to equally good results. Since the beginning of time, van Creveld holds, military command has been focused on one thing, namely, a desire for certainty – certainty about the enemy's state of readiness, his plans and intentions, the environment in which he operates, but especially certainty about the condition and activities of one's own troops. Certainty, van Creveld argues, "is best understood as the product of two factors, the amount of information available for decision-making and the nature of the task to be performed." The history of military command can thus be explained as "a race between the demand for information and the ability of command systems to meet it." This contest is eternal and it unfolds continuously within every military organization regardless of the level of command. It cannot be overcome with the help of new technologies or greater resources. Undoubtedly, present-day command systems have better capacity to manage, process, and transmit information but their ability to provide the certainty commanders crave has not markedly improved (van Creveld 1985: 264–6).

Why, then, do modern command systems, despite their relative sophistication, not create much greater certainty than their predecessors did? Creveld (1985: 266–7) provides three arguments. First, and along Clausewitzian lines, there are elements in the nature of war that cause strong emotions in people, such as fear, anger, revenge, and hatred. This means that humans often act irrationally and based on emotions. Second, and again congruent with Clausewitz, war consists of at least two divergent and hostile wills that contradict each other, and since each belligerent is free (and certain) to deceive the other, the struggle between them is difficult or impossible to predict. Certainty is therefore by definition hard to bring about. Third, the more information that is made available, the more time is needed to assess it, and the greater the difficulty of distinguishing between what is relevant and irrelevant, important and unimportant, reliable and unreliable, and true and false.

Creveld believes that this quest for certainty has tended to determine the design of command systems, where the degree of human element in a system is also proportional to the degree of uncertainty. The more human element in relation to technical elements in a command structure, the more uncertainty is generated. History shows, van Creveld argues, that those armies that avoided to turn their troops into automatic machines and did not try to control everything from the top, but gave the subordinate commanders considerable latitude, proved to be the most successful ones tactically. Examples of such leadership are Napoleon's marshals in the early nineteenth century, Ludendorff's storm detachments at the end of World War I, German army commanders during World War II, and Israeli divisional commanders during the Six-Day War in 1967 (van Creveld 1985: 268–70).

In order to explain this relationship, van Creveld (1985: 269–70) claims that certainty is not only a result of information, but also of time. Less of the first can save more of the latter. He emphasizes certain key ingredients in what the Germans traditionally called *Auftragstaktik*, or a mission-directed command philosophy. This includes the ability of superior headquarters to determine minimalist goals rather than maximalist ones, to allow lower-level commanders the freedom to choose their own way to reach the objective and in accordance with the current situation on the battlefield. Such an approach, van Creveld argues, also reduces the amount of information to manage and increases the will of superior commanders to avoid giving orders to the "subordinates' subordinates." A prerequisite for this command philosophy is an acceptance of the fact that both confusion and profusion are inevitable in war and that this apparent chaos does not rule out a successful outcome. On the contrary, it might even be a necessary requirement for achieving decisive results on the battlefield.

Finally, van Creveld (1985: 274) emphasizes that the two ways to deal with uncertainty, namely centralization and decentralization of command, may not necessarily be viewed as opposites, but rather as intertwined. A higher degree of certainty at the top of the chain of command can only be obtained at the expense of a lower degree of certainty further down in the hierarchy. Conversely, certainty at the lower tactical levels can only occur if senior commanders and superior staffs are willing to accept a higher degree of uncertainty. Thus, military command is reduced to a distribution of uncertainty between the different levels of command within the military hierarchy. In a centralized command structure, security is ensured for the different parts by certainty for the whole, while in a decentralized command structure the opposite is true. In a time of radically improved opportunities to use modern technology and computers to acquire a better picture of the battlefield, the temptation may be even greater for superior headquarters to centralize military command in order to achieve certainty. There may for that reason be a conflict between mission-directed tactics and the modern idea of network-centric warfare, since technology enables centralized command to a greater extent than in previous eras of military history.

Logistics in military operations

To conduct military operations requires armed forces, but also the resources to support and maintain these forces on the battlefield. The term logistics comes in all probability from the ancient Greek word *logisteuein*, meaning "to administer," but in modern times, and in a military context, the term is understood as "the supply and movement of armed forces" (Corvisier 1994: 460; Gray 1999: 32). In principle, the art of logistics comes down to acquiring the right things and bringing them to the right place, at the right time, and in the right quantity. As such, logistics has aptly been described as the "arbiter of opportunity" and as such is both a critical part of strategy as well as a potential key target in war (Kane 2001). The history of warfare has shown that this is a rather difficult task which requires a lot of time, plenty of thought, and vast resources from any military organization (van Creveld 1977; Sinclair 1992; Lynn 1993).

Lots of books have been written about tactics and strategy, but very few on logistics. Nor do basic textbooks and introductions to the art of war or military theory include more than fragments concerning logistics (e.g. Kassimeris & Buckley 2010; Sloan 2012; Baylis et al. 2010; van Creveld 2000). Yet, several famous commanders and prominent military theorists emphasize the importance of logistics for a successful outcome in warfare. The British Field Marshal Bernard Montgomery noted for example that 80 percent of the problems he had to deal with during World War II were of a logistical nature (Thomson 1991: 4). British military historian Michael Howard (1983b: 102) stated that "no campaign can be understood, and no valid conclusions drawn from it, unless its logistical problems are studied as thoroughly as the course of operations." Why this relative absence of studies concerning logistics, and why this fixation on the more operational aspects of warfare? The simple reason is probably that logistics is a far less glamorous subject, and as a vocation it leaves less to the imagination and demands harder routine work and quantitative calculations (van Creveld 1977: 1; Thomson 1991: 3).

Clausewitz's contemporary, General Antoine Henri Jomini, was the first to define logistics as part of the art of war. He related it to the concept of strategy and tactics, and noted (Jomini 1987: 460) that "strategy decides where to act; logistics brings the troops to this point; . . . [and] tactics decides the manner of execution and the employment of the troops." However, in his analysis of logistics, he expanded the concept beyond current understandings of the term and also included general staff work in connection with military operations (Thomson 1991: 5; Jomini 1987: 528–42). Inspired by Jomini's definition of logistics and its relationship to strategy and tactics, the French military historian Eric Muraise defines logistics as "the art of moving and servicing troops in accordance with the tactical and strategic requirements" (Corvisier 1994: 460). Here, logistics appears as a means of tactics and strategy, and the latter two shall govern the former. In practice the inverse relationship may certainly exist from time to time. Muraise argues that logistics involves three things:

- maintenance and transportation – ensuring the supply of munitions and to make sure that both troops and equipment are in good condition;
- selection and evacuation – evaluation, withdrawal, and replacement of personnel and equipment that emanate from the battle;
- restoration – repair of equipment and medical care for the injured, which requires bases and depots, both protected and unprotected.

Muraise's description is similar to that suggested by British logistics expert P. D. Foxton. The latter suggests five functions of logistics, namely to supply the troops with provisions, transportation and movements, maintenance and repair, medical care, and minor functions such as mail handling, food, and beverages, as well as to provide the military organization with personnel (Foxton 1994: 11). However, logistics may not only be divided into functions but also categorized based on the different ways to accomplish it. The Israeli logistics expert Moshe Kress claims that there are three different methods of providing armed forces with maintenance: securing resources on the battlefield, troops carrying their own resources, and finally transporting resources from the rear, via maintenance lines, and distributing them to troops in the combat zone. Historically, the choice between these three methods has been guided by the character of war, logistical needs, and the existing capability of the troops. In pre-modern times, food and water were more or less the only things that were needed. Such resources could fairly easy be obtained when on the move, for example from looting civilians or from the spoils of the enemy. "Fuel" for draft animals was obtained in a similar way. Since food and water at one location were often limited, armies were forced to move in order to survive. Often enough they stayed close to fertile areas and trade routes. The entry of motor vehicles as an important means of transportation in modern warfare changed these conditions in a radical way (Kress 2002: 10–11).

When the resources needed for military operations became more varied and specialized, and when transportation became increasingly important, armed forces began to carry with them the logistical support needed for military campaigns. One of the first to use this method was Alexander the Great during his campaigns in the Middle East and the sub-continent 300 BC. During the seventeenth and eighteenth centuries, when the amount of ammunition consumed during battle was limited, such munitions could be carried on wagons drawn by horses. This ammunition was not instantly usable on the battlefield but was used as storage. The ammunition that would be used in battle had to be carried by the soldiers themselves. In general, this method of logistics caused problems for the troops, because it created a logistical "tail" which hindered mobility (Kress 2002: 11).

If the two methods just mentioned were the primary ways to maintain troops until the middle of the nineteenth century, the industrial revolution created opportunities for a third way, namely to send the resources forward to the front. The expansion of railway systems all over the world, and in Europe in particular, was an important factor. Logistical support could now be sent from the rear to the front, over longer distances and at speeds that had previously been unthinkable. When operational art developed based on this new method of transportation, armies quickly became dependent on this form of logistics. This became even more noticeable when the motor vehicle and transport aircraft were introduced, where the former demanded huge amounts of fuel in order to operate, which multiplied the total amount of resources that must reach the troops (Kress 2002: 11).

Kress argues that the concept of logistics is best divided into strategic logistics, operational logistics, and tactical logistics. These three levels are not strictly separated, but sometimes tend to blend into one another. Moreover, many argue that new information technology will be likely to integrate these three levels into a single unit. Strategic logistics includes the construction and maintenance of military or military-related infrastructure. This comprises the technological infrastructure needed to develop, improve, and maintain different weapons systems, industrial infrastructure for production and maintenance of equipment and materials, the stock of ammunition, fuel, spare parts, medicine, food, and other things needed for the military operations, facilities to store these things, as well as various transport functions, both static and dynamic components. The static components consist of railroads, canals, airports, and seaports, etc. and the dynamic components of transport aircraft, ships, trains, trucks, etc. An important factor in logistics at the strategic level is efficiency, since resources are often limited and must be used as efficiently as possible. Decisions at this level are stable and relatively insensitive to the changing requirements from lower levels. The plans are robust and long-term (Kress 2002: 19–26).

On the other end of the spectrum, we find tactical logistics, which, according to Kress, are meant to be used in actual battle. At this level, changes are greater and the situation often confused due to hostile activities. Maintaining forces at this level is a difficult task and here the emphasis is on bringing forward ammunition, food, water, fuel, repairs, evacuation, and care for the injured, as well as dealing with prisoners of war. If the main goal at the strategic level is to achieve cost-effectiveness, the aim at the tactical level is rather efficiency in the allocation and optimal maintenance of the fighting forces. As stated above, the right things must arrive in proper quantities, at the right place, and at the right time (Kress 2002: 26–8). The connecting link between the strategic and tactical levels is operational logistics. Kress defines this concept as

> a collection of means, resources, organizations and process that share the common goal of sustaining campaigns and large-scale military operations. This collection, which is derived from the strategic logistics level, is utilized by the campaign leaders as input for the tactical logistics. Op[erational] Log[istics] is designated to sustain battles that are distributed in time and space.
>
> (Kress 2002: 37)

On this level, the cost-effectiveness at the strategic level is converted into combat effectiveness at the tactical level, and the goal is to support activities in the area of operations and to assist tactical logistics.

After this slightly abstract analysis of logistical ends and means it is useful to present a more practical model of how logistics can work in an actual military operation. Based on British experiences and heavily influenced by the demands of large-scale conventional warfare in industrialized states, Foxton describes how logistics can be conducted, detailing three logistical zones of activity: the rear area, forward area, and combat area. The rear logistical area serves as an access and exit point for the area of operations, and it is here that reinforcements of troops, munitions, and supplies are unloaded from ships or transport aircraft, then collected and organized, and finally brought forward to the combat zone. In this area there are also stores, depots, workshops, and hospitals. An example of such a zone would be the South Korean city of Pusan and the ports used by US and United Nations (UN) forces at the beginning of the Korean War (Foxton 1994: 6–7).

The boundaries of the forward logistical area are fluid but it usually extends from the railhead to the farthest reach of enemy artillery or missiles. At the point where heavy transportation is not possible, either through enemy activities or because the train tracks do not run, a base is established and the unloading and transfer of supplies and equipment to trucks etc. takes place. In this area, munitions and supplies are kept that are too precious to be stored in the combat zone or with the troops themselves. Here, supplies and equipment are divided into smaller units that will then be passed on to the various forces in the combat area (Foxton 1994: 7).

The last one, the combat logistical area, extends from the boundary of the extreme range of the enemy's artillery or missiles and up to the front line. In this area, the logistical support is tied directly to the combat units and is meant to serve them in their activities. For safety reasons, some things are divided up, for example warheads and charges, in order to avoid unnecessary explosions if hit by enemy fire. Here, ammunition and supplies are also sorted and rationed out to accommodate the needs of the different fighting units. In this zone, ammunition and supplies are usually stored on trucks and other motor vehicles to quickly be able to move them when units are advancing and retreating. The commander may in this case weigh the risk of hostile fire against the need to place the supplies and equipment as close to the fighting forces as possible (Foxton 1994: 7).

It might be concluded that logistics is a crucial part of all warfare and that it has become even more important as armed forces have become larger and more mechanized. The huge amount of equipment and supplies needed to conduct the US-led alliance's war against Iraq in 2003 is an example of this. These conditions apply, however, to a lesser degree for actors in small wars and insurgencies who still use logistical methods similar to the ones employed in the eighteenth and nineteenth century. The similarities in military geography and logistics contribute to explaining similarities in tactics and operations. For example, even if 150 years of technological development separate the first Anglo-Afghan War and the current Afghan War, the fighting still follows regular fighting seasons (Johnson 2012; Guistozzi 2009; Sinno 2008). These actors can manage their logistics with the help of locals in areas where they operate, or by looting. Since the vast majority of wars in our time consist of such small wars (see Chapter 2), it is reasonable to think that the logistical problems of the great powers are undoubtedly the most complex, but perhaps not always the most appropriate ones when trying to understand the logistics of a non-state actor.

Intelligence in military operations

As mentioned in the section on command in military operations, the history of command can be described as a race between the need for information and the command system's ability to meet this need. Certainty regarding the enemy's state of readiness and his plans, but also knowledge of one's own organization, requires intelligence. As with effective methods of command and logistical resources, intelligence is thus an important prerequisite for conducting military operations. But intelligence is a vast and complex phenomenon, which covers not only military aspects but also political and economic ones, as well as matters related to policing (cf. Shulsky & Schmitt 2002; Herman 1996; Lowenthal 2011; Clark 2004; Johnson & Wirtz 2010; Laqueur 1985; Keegan 2003). As such, intelligence in war is about reducing uncertainty and thus improving the decision-making (Handel 1990: 7–11).

The need for intelligence in war is as old as war itself. As early as 500 BC, Sun Tzu argued that:

> [O]ne who knows the enemy and knows himself will not be endangered in a hundred engagements. One who does not know the enemy but knows himself will sometimes be victorious, sometimes meet with defeat. One who knows neither the enemy nor himself will invariably be defeated in every engagement.
>
> (Sun Tzu 1994: 179)

Sun Tzu also emphasized the importance of informers and spies, something that today would be described as human intelligence. He concluded (1994: 231) that "advance knowledge cannot be gained from ghosts and spirits, inferred from phenomena, or projected from the measures of Heaven, but must be gained from men for it is the knowledge of the enemy's true situation." In the contemporary world, there are of course other and often more technologically sophisticated methods by which to obtain such information, for example signals intelligence, satellite surveillance, photo reconnaissance, and computer hacking. Clausewitz (1993: 136), for his part, held a skeptical view of the value of intelligence. He defined it as "every sort of information about the enemy and his country – the basis, in short, of our own plans and operations." He argued that the intelligence acquired in war was often contradictory, false, or marred with uncertainty. In general, most individuals tended to believe bad news rather than good news and it was a natural human weakness, Clausewitz argued, to exaggerate the former. In a modern context, people talk of a tendency for planning for "worst-case scenarios." Obviously, a lot has happened in terms of technology and the ability to collect, sort out, evaluate, and distribute intelligence since Sun Tzu's and Clausewitz's times, but so has the ability to protect one's own information. Many of the problems that the classical military theorists wrestled with still seem to persist.

Although the collection and use of intelligence has been part of war for a very long time, such activities were not institutionalized and properly organized until the second half of the nineteenth century. During that time, technological advances resulted in armies receiving improved weaponry and they could now use railroads for transportation and movement, and the telegraph in order to communicate. Meanwhile, navies acquired ships made of iron and powered by steam, with bigger guns, grenades, and thicker armor protection, and later also equipped with wireless radio. Wars also came to include larger armies, spread over larger areas, which created more opportunities for surprise and victory through quick movement and mobilization. This forced a new approach to military command which resulted in the creation of permanent staffs and headquarters tasked with issues concerning mobilization, war planning, and other forms of support for the commanders. Such work also included the need to obtain information concerning the enemy and one's own forces, terrain conditions, communications, and other things relevant to the conduct of military operations (Herman 1996: 16).

In its broadest sense, intelligence consists of collecting and compiling information and, based on this information, making different kinds of assessments. In a military context, these activities focus primarily on the intentions and capabilities of the enemy, and attempt to predict future events and developments. With such a general definition, intelligence has much in common with regular research and investigative work in the civilian domain. Intelligence, however, involves a few important dimensions that are usually lacking in scientific work. First, intelligence work, as done by armed forces, is characterized by extensive secrecy, both regarding one's own operations and concerning the information dealt with. Second, intelligence work is characterized by a struggle between at least two wills, where the aim of the operation is to obtain information that the adversary regularly tries to protect and keep secret. As a consequence, it is not surprising that, in the intelligence community, one is trying to use deception and disinformation to obstruct and undermine the operations of the opponent. (Shulsky & Schmitt 2002: 171–2) As can be noted, intelligence is similar to strategy where two subjects fight each other in something resembling a duel (see Chapter 3). In this case the objective is access to crucial information of a secret nature. In regular science, the researcher regularly tries to collect and assess information about a static object that lacks its own will and which is not actively trying to undermine or obstruct the research. Ultimately, intelligence work thus tries to acquire information that an adversary is trying to conceal.

To obtain this kind of information often requires specific means and methods that can penetrate the security measures being set up by the adversary in the hope of protecting the information. In the military context, this includes the interception of communications between armed units, aerial and satellite reconnaissance, detection of ship movements through sonar, analysis of captured materials and documentation, or questioning of prisoners of war. Important information can also be obtained indirectly through deductive logic and analysis of the open sources and data available (Shulsky & Schmitt 2002: 172). In the military domain, intelligence often serves as a "force multiplier" and "optimizer." The American military theorist Michael Handel argues for example that:

> [G]ood intelligence will act as a force multiplier by facilitating a more focused and economical use of force. On the other hand, when all other things are equal, poor intelligence acts as a force divider by wasting and eroding strength. In the long run, therefore, the side with better intelligence will not only use its power more profitable but will also more effectively conserve it.
>
> (Herman 1996: 138)

Another expert in the field, R. V. Jones, claims that:

> [T]he ultimate object of intelligence is to enable action to be optimized. The individual or body which has to decide on action needs information about its opponent as an ingredient likely to be vital in determining its decision; and this information may suggest that action should be taken on a larger or smaller scale than that which otherwise would be taken, or even that a different course of action would be better.
>
> (Herman 1996: 138–9)

Thus, superiority in intelligence does not win wars on its own but can serve to optimize the military organization's activities and make them more efficient. This is no doubt a weighty factor in all warfare. The need for information about the enemy and his activities is important in connection with the often difficult decisions that the military commander has to make.

Trying to determine the effect of intelligence in various war situations is a complicated task. War is ultimately determined by the fighting forces and intelligence is only one of many means that these forces employ. The British intelligence expert Michael Herman argues that intelligence in military operations must be evaluated in two ways: first, the accuracy of the intelligence in relation to reality, and second, the quality of the intelligence compared with that of the opponent. It is possible that both sides can have both good and bad intelligence on each other. During World War II, the Germans tended to underestimate the total resources of the Soviet Union, while they were inclined to overestimate the resources of the American and British side. As a result, the Germans largely built their planning and preparations, including the defense of France and southern Europe, on a faulty evaluation of the combined Allied military strength (Herman 1996: 145–7).

It is important to point out that intelligence takes place at all levels of warfare and not just on the operational level. At the strategic level, intelligence serves as an "alarm bell" in order to receive early notice of a planned military attack. During the Cold War, Scandinavian military intelligence services had largely this function, i.e. to warn of a possible military build-up and an attack from the Soviet Union and the Warsaw Pact. On the tactical level, intelligence is primarily concerned with determining and assessing hostile activity. Information used directly in battle is slightly different from the one described above, since the collection of information is part of the battle and the interaction with the enemy. At the tactical level, in addition to various forms of reconnaissance and surveillance, the interrogation of prisoners of war and analysis of captured equipment and documents act as vital intelligence sources. In peacekeeping operations, finally, the intelligence received from conversations with the local population is of great value (Herman 1996: 79–80, 121–4, 139).

In sum, it can be concluded that knowledge about the enemy and one's own activities requires intelligence and that this is an important prerequisite for the implementation of military operations. Intelligence work consists primarily of the collection of information, on the basis of which different types of assessments are produced, mainly concerning the evaluation of enemy capabilities, plans, and activities. What often distinguishes intelligence from ordinary research and investigation work is mainly the high degree of secrecy, and that operations are based on procuring such information as the opponent tries to protect and keep confidential. The consequence of this will be a situation similar to a dual and a tendency to use deception and disinformation. In the military operational context intelligence often serves as a force multiplier and as an optimizer for one's own operations. Finally, intelligence work takes place at all levels of warfare.

Conclusions

The purpose of this chapter has been to describe the principles and ideas that exist in military theory regarding operational art. The concept of operational art was described as the art of translating tactical actions to strategic effect. Operational art can thus be said to connect the tactical battles with the strategic goals by means of military operations, decided at the operational level. The problem with operational art, as defined in this chapter, is that the theory presupposes an ends-means hierarchy that is controlled from the top down, where the lower level is supposed to serve the higher level. In practice, tactical actions are often allowed to determine the operational and strategic objectives, rather than vice versa. This is unsatisfactory from a military theoretical perspective since the causal relationships become invalidated and reversed. As a consequence the operational level becomes a kind of filter for the flow of ideas between the strategic and tactical level, a filter that is more or less arbitrary in nature.

As mentioned above, operational art is also dependent on a number of important concepts, factors, and functions to be explained theoretically and converted into practice. The center of gravity concept was introduced and described as something difficult to interpret and to define. Despite this, it is considered a crucial focal point in operational activities. Analyses of both one's own and enemy centers of gravity guides the priorities that must be made between primary and secondary objectives, which improves the ability to use limited resources in the best way possible. Military command was described as a means to manage uncertainty and confusion on the battlefield, i.e. to gain knowledge about the enemy, his plans and state of readiness, and the operational environment. To conduct military operations requires not only armed forces, but also the resources to maintain and move them. This is the task of logistics. Finally, intelligence was described as a necessary precondition for the military command's quest for certainty and information about the opponent. In this manner, this chapter has been a discussion of different means of military power.

As described above, operational art is an old phenomenon that has seen a revival in the modern era and been formalized in various theories. It is also obvious that operational art, understood in its broadest sense, is a necessity in many military domains. Transforming tactical successes into strategic success is a timeless problem that requires attention in many different contexts. In Chapters 5–9, the discussion will therefore be further deepened with an emphasis on the principles of war and specific theories of employing military power in joint operations as well as operations on land, at sea, and in the air.

Questions for discussion

1. To what extent does the operational art of a small state differ from that of a great power?
2. What are the operational advantages and disadvantages of indirect and direct methods?
3. Why is center of gravity a meaningful concept in operational planning and execution?
4. What are the strengths and weaknesses of decentralized and centralized command and control?
5. Is logistics a function of operational implementation or is it a prerequisite for such activity?
6. How do intelligence needs and practices compare in conventional wars and small wars, or between strategic and tactical levels?

Further reading

Martin van Creveld, *Supplying War: Logistics from Wallenstein to Patton* (Cambridge: Cambridge University Press, 1977).

Martin van Creveld, *Command in War* (Cambridge MA and London: Harvard University Press, 1985).

Michael Herman, *Intelligence Power in Peace and War* (Cambridge: Cambridge University Press, 1996).

Moshe Kress, *Operational Logistics: The Art and Science of Sustaining Military Operations* (Boston: Kluwer Academic Publishers, 2002).

B. J. C. McKercher & Michael A. Hennessy (eds.) *The Operational Art – Developments in the Theories of War* (Westport, CT: Praeger, 1996).

John Andreas Olsen & Martin van Creveld (eds.), *The Evolution of Operational Art: From Napoleon to the Present* (Oxford: Oxford University Press, 2011).

Abram N. Shulsky & Gary J. Schmitt, *Silent Warfare: Understanding the World of Intelligence*, 3rd edn. (Washington DC: Brassey's, 2002).

Milan Vego, *Joint Operational Warfare: Theory and Practice* (Newport, RI: US Naval War College, 2008).

5   The principles of war

Introduction

Nineteenth century French military theorist Charles Ardant de Picq (1987: 69) argued that "man does not enter battle to fight, but for victory. He does everything that he can to avoid the first and obtain the second." For natural reasons, a great deal of military thought focuses on how to attain victory in war. One of the clearest expressions of this has been the so-called principles of war. These principles have not been formulated by any individual thinker, but should be regarded more as a form of collective wisdom. From a practitioner's point of view, it is entirely understandable to attempt to identify guidelines for winning a war. It is equally understandable that the scientific enquiry into how to explain the outcome of war begins by attempting to identify variables that could explain victory and defeat. These two partly separate aspirations – though concurrent in military theory – have resulted in various versions of so-called principles of war. Concepts such as the concentration of force, surprise, economy of force, morale, initiative, flexibility, and simplicity have been regarded as universal and timeless principles through which war can be won. But how should we interpret these principles? What problems are inherent within the aspiration, both in practical and theoretical terms, to search for and apply these principles?

The purpose of this chapter is to introduce the principles of war, their inherent logic, their mutual relationship, and the method behind their creation. The principles are contested among both theorists and practitioners, which is evident from the varying institutionalization of the principles in doctrines. The American military historian John Alger (1982) even suggests that those who stress the importance of the principles of war are often unaware of the fact that they only recently were regarded as "timeless" truths. The apparent universality and immutability of the principles may therefore lead to notions that they have an obvious place in both doctrine and military theory. In actual fact, they have been frequently contested and criticized for being, among other things, imprecise, contradictory, and invalid. The great debate regarding the principles of war applies therefore to their existence, but there has also at times been acrimonious debate, among those who accept their existence, about what the principles are and how many there should be.

The chapter has two main parts. The first one constitutes a general introduction to the principles of war. This part discusses various theorists' views of the principles of war and their different interpretations. Here, we also investigate how the principles have emerged, the military debates the principles have given rise to, and examples of how the individual principles may be interpreted. In the second part of the chapter, which is more analytical, we present two different approaches to the understanding of this phenomenon, namely the principles of war as military practice and the principles of war as explanatory theory.

The principles of war: an overview

This first part and general introduction to the principles of war consists of three sections. The first will discuss conceptual aspects. How should the principles be interpreted? Within which frameworks do they occur? For natural reasons, this section will primarily reflect the debate between those who have already accepted the existence of the principles. The next section will serve as a history of ideas and describe the intellectual development of the principles from the beginning and into the present day. This section will primarily illustrate the debate about the existence of the principles. In the third section, a number of principles, their inherent logic and their mutual relationships will be introduced and discussed. Here, it is important to point out that the primary purpose is not to attempt to select the most important and most applicable principles or to establish a ranking order among them, but rather to provide better methodological and epistemological understanding of the principles.

The principles of war: conceptual issues

The purpose of creating the principles of war, according to some, lies in the aim of accumulating experience and knowledge for the education of future generations. Each soldier or officer should not have to begin from scratch, but should receive a certain modicum of established knowledge. In a similar manner, science seeks to gradually build knowledge so that the wheel need not be reinvented. There is no great debate about these objectives, but that is where unanimity ends. Several debates in military theory converge around the principles of war, which is one of the reasons why they are so contested. What is perhaps most obvious is that the debate regarding whether war can be regarded as science or art is brought to a head in the discussion of the principles of war.

First, opinion is divided on the nature of the principles. Throughout history, the principles of war have either been interpreted as "rules and regulations" or as variables for explaining the outcome of war. These two notions are closely related but there are slight differences in meaning. If we interpret the principles as rules and regulations, they should be followed by practitioners. Interpreting the principles as rules and regulations also means that they can be interpreted as variables for explaining the outcome of war. It would seem reasonable for the principles to include both these elements since they, as rules and regulations, probably reflect a causal relationship. Admiral Alfred Thayer Mahan (1999: 64), for example, was of the opinion that, historically, naval battles are won by those who adhere to the principles of war. It would, of course, be odd if someone advocated that generals should follow rules and regulations that did not lead to victory. If, on the one hand, they are to be interpreted as variables, they should be measurable, precise, and logically consistent. If, on the other hand, we interpret them as slightly more flexible guidelines – which is the most common interpretation – deviations from the principles can be acceptable and even encouraged by some under certain circumstances. Swedish military historian Alf W. Johansson (1988: 66) seems to adopt the attitude that the principles are "guidelines," as he believes that the principles cannot be regarded as scientific laws based on military historical experience, but as "a number of aspects of warfare." Using this approach, they could be regarded as variables that can be used to categorize military experience, and abstractions from it, but not as causal theories. The art of war will then be a matter of effectively combining these principles, but also knowing when the principles can be ignored in a real-life situation.

Second, opinions are divided concerning to which level of warfare the principles apply. On the one hand, there are those who believe that the principles of war are universal regardless of level. Paul Katz (1987: 37) believes, for example, that they are "a collection of concise rules for warfare" that "are independent of time, place and situation," which is why the principles are relevant for all "battle leaders, from the low-ranking officer to the general." In a similar manner, John M. Collins (2002: 81) argues that the principles of war apply to both the strategic and tactical level but that they are primarily applicable at the operational level. On the other hand, the British major general and military thinker J. F. C. Fuller (1878–1966) put together one list of principles for the strategic level and another for the tactical level (Fuller's tactical principles were demoralization, endurance, and shock), which suggests he believed it was essential to adapt the principles, their content, and their form according to levels of war (Alger 1982: 232–3). How we relate to this question influences, in turn, the scope of the theoretical claim of the principles. For example, it is obviously not the case that strategic surprise necessarily involves tactical surprise and that tactical flexibility does not necessarily lead to strategic flexibility. If it is possible to adapt the principles of war to different levels, this raises the question on which level they are most preferably used. For example, what type of surprise, tactical or strategic, is it that decides the outcome of war?

Third, there is debate regarding what types of war the principles apply to. Some people believe that the principles are the same regardless of the type of conflict, while others believe that there are different sets of principles for different conflicts. This question again refers to the scope of the theory. If the principles are only valid in certain types of war, their scope will obviously decrease. Russell Glenn (1998: 56) points out, for instance, that during the 1990s the US Army had different sets of principles depending on whether they were dealing with warfare or operations other than war. In the latter, legitimacy is included instead of concentration of force, restraint instead of economy of force, and perseverance rather than offence. Charles E. Callwell (1859–1928) also argued, at the pinnacle of British colonialism, that so-called small wars had a unique set of principles. He suggested, for example, that combat was more important than maneuver which was controversial around the turn of the century – and that concentration of force was not essential for success when it came to small wars (Callwell 1996: 85–96, 108–14). John Keegan (1961: 61–72) asserted that the principles of war imply the aspiration for unconditional surrender, which, according to him, meant that they were not suitable in the nuclear age or for thinking with regard to wars between nuclear states.

Fourth, it is often asserted that the principles are universal for warfare in all types of environments or arenas. But this is also contested. Jomini believed that the "fundamental principles upon which rest all good combinations of war have always existed" and that they "are unchangeable; they are independent of the arms employed, of times, and of places" (Fallwell 1955: 50). However, Mahan, otherwise a great admirer of Jomini, formulated his principles in a different way. He included, for example, the setting up of logistics bases, the maintenance of sea-lines of communication, and the disruption of commercial shipping, in addition to Jomini's principles of objectives and concentration of force (Mahan 1999: 63). Swedish military historian Marco Smedberg (1998: 160–2) suggests that air warfare has different principles from ground warfare. For a period, the US Air Force had a different set of principles from the Army, in which they included "timing and tempo," "logistics," and "cohesion" (Glenn 1998: 52). The last two examples indicate that it is not entirely obvious that the principles are valid for all forms of warfare at sea, in the air, and on the ground without further definition and enquiry.

Fifth, there is extensive debate regarding how many principles there are and what they are, which is illustrated in Table 5.1 (adapted from Bellamy 1990: 14; Alger 1982: 193–270).

Sixth, opinions are divided on exactly what the principles should be able to explain, i.e. what the dependent variable is. In fact, we could imagine several different alternatives. Are

Table 5.1 The principles of war according to a limited selection of key military thinkers

Jomini (1816)	Foch (1906)	Fuller (1923)	Montgomery (1945)	Savkin (1953)	Mao (1954)
Concentration of force against a decisive point.	Economy of force	Concentration of force	Concentration of force	Concentration of force	Local concentration of force
	Freedom of action	Surprise	Surprise	Surprise	Surprise
	Freedom to deploy forces	Decisiveness	Initiative	Mobility	Mobile combat
	Security, etc.	Offensive Mobility Economy of force	Morale Leadership Air power	Tempo Initiative Recovery	Offensive Continual attack Destruction
		Objectives Endurance Security	Simplicity Coordination	Objectives Coordination	Objectives Autonomy Uniform leadership Morale

the principles valid for individual battles, for campaigns, for war, for all military activity, or are they a path to success for all human activity in a general sense? Mahan, for example, was of the opinion that the principles were valid as a path to success in everything from ship-building and the composition of fleets, to planning and conducting naval operations (Alger 1982: 91). For his part, Fuller argued in 1920 that the principles were "eternal, universal and fundamental" and applied to everything from boxing matches to battle (Alger 1982: 123). Without a more detailed definition of exactly what the principles are intended to explain, it is by no means obvious that they can be used as an explanation.

The content and number of principles vary from author to author and from doctrine to doctrine. The number of principles has varied from Jomini's original single principle to Wilhelm Friedrich von Rüstow's (1821–78) 27 principles. Within this interval we can, for example, find the British Field Marshall Bernard Montgomery and Vasilii Savkin, who mention eight (and the latter an additional four "laws"), Mao mentions ten, Fuller decided – after a great deal of contemplation – on nine fundamental principles, and the French General Ferdinand Foch (1851–1929) named four principles, but kept the door open for there being more when he concluded his list with a famous "etc." In his initial formulation in 1816, Jomini believed that concentration of force against the decisive point was the only principle, but that there were up to twelve different ways of achieving this concentration of force. He gradually revised his view and varied the number of methods for achieving concentration of force. Some of these methods were later developed into being regarded as principles in their own right, e.g., maneuver and surprise. (Alger 1982: 204–8) Other thinkers also developed their views. Liddell Hart (1932: 301–3) initially adhered to Jomini's original idea and applied only one principle, "concentration of strength against weakness." (However, he did not, strictly speaking, term it "principle," but instead "practical guides.") He subsequently developed eight maxims in the form of "do's and don'ts" (Liddell Hart (1932: 301–3).

The number, content, and form of the principles also vary in doctrines, something that is made clear from Table 5.2. (Adapted from Alger 1982: 193–270) What is perhaps important is not which principles the different doctrines deal with, but that they vary, which suggests that the principles of war – even in their institutionalized form – are not one theory, but

Table 5.2 The principles of war according to the Great Powers' army doctrines, or joint ones for the different branches of the armed forces

USA (1921)	Great Britain (1920)	France (1936)	West Germany (1962)	The Soviet Union (1942)	China (1955)
Concentration of force	Concentration of force	Concentration of force	Concentration of force	Concentration of force	Concentration of force
Surprise	Surprise	Surprise	Simplicity	Surprise	Surprise
Economy of force	Economy of force	Freedom of action	Uniform leadership	Economy of force	Freedom of action
Objectives	Objectives		Objectives	Following-up	Objectives
Offensive	Offensive		Legitimacy	Superiority	Offensive
Uniform leadership	Coordination			Coordination	Coordination
Mobility	Flexibility			Mobility, tempo, and initiative	Mobility, initiative, and flexibility
Security	Security				Security
Simplicity	Morale				Morale
					Political mobilization

several. The second thing that emerges from the table is that the principles of war were institutionalized at roughly the same time in Western Europe, with the exception of Germany, in the aftermath of World War I and during the interwar period. This shows that the institutionalization of the principles into doctrine is primarily a modern phenomenon.

We can conclude that the number, form, and content of the principles of war vary to a great extent in both doctrine and theory. So far, this section has dealt with the conceptual discussion on how the principles of war should be interpreted. Now it is time to discuss the development of the principles.

The principles of war: the history of ideas

As shown previously, to present the principles of war as a concise list of concepts is a modern phenomenon. It could reasonably be said that the principles of war as we understand them today did not begin to emerge until the 1920s. The principles – and the questions they are an expression of – can, however, be traced further back in the military history of ideas. The first person to express something similar to the principles of war was probably Sun Tzu (1994), who stressed, for instance, the importance of surprise and careful planning. We should, however, note that he also argued that there are no fixed rules for success in all warfare. The latter suggests that Sun Tzu should be regarded as a predecessor of those who argue that the circumstances of war vary so much that it is not possible to establish any timeless principles. During antiquity and in medieval Europe, much thought was given to identifying guidelines for maintaining discipline, organization, fortification, and administration. This was a natural thing to do as, first and foremost, logistical challenges in medieval warfare often led to armies plundering rural areas, both to keep their own army on its feet and also to make logistics more difficult for the opponent. The warring parties also attempted to sack, or demand ransoms from, towns in order to support their armies. The principal way of protecting oneself from being plundered was improving one's own fortifications (Alger 1982: 92–213).

The scientific revolution and Age of Enlightenment not only influenced society in general, but also the development of military thought. It is actually here that the principles, as they are interpreted today, have their origins. By representing war, like other phenomena, as scientific, the foundation was laid for the belief that there were also principles that governed war. The origin of the principles was also influenced by the study of warfare at the first military schools that were founded during this period to train future generations of officers. Within this context, alongside the study of artillery and more technical aspects, the need to study military history and learn lessons through the systematic study of war grew rapidly. This meant, by extension, more books about the art of war being written by teachers at the colleges than by generals in the field. This favored the notion that it was possible to uncover timeless principles of war, as those who were teachers were more receptive than generals to scientific ideals. In this manner, the foundation for the search for principles was laid – fundamental truths expressed as guidelines for action. During the seventeenth and eithteenth centuries, in France in particular – through, among others, Antoine Manassés de Pas (1648–1711), Jean Charles (1669–1752), and Maurice of Saxony (1696–1750) – textbooks on the art of war emerged, expressing lessons believed to be timeless. The notion that there are principles of war thereby began to be established, although their number, form, and content had not yet been defined (Alger 1982: 7–14).

In contrast to what is sometimes asserted, Jomini was not the first to write down a list of the principles of war. It was the Marquis de Silva in France and Henry Lloyd (1718–83) in Britain, at the end of the eighteenth century, who with their numbered lists of principles pioneered this practice. Despite this, Jomini made a big contribution to the principles of war with his strong argument at the beginning of his career that there were principles of war and that they were immutable and universal. Clausewitz (1993) also presented lessons in the form of principles but was, at the same time, very careful to point out that they were intended as aids for personal reflection prior to fighting breaking out, rather than guidelines for how war should be conducted. We should, however, note that Jomini, as time passed, also appears to have been increasingly caught in two minds with regard to the principles. He believed that the principles required the commander utilizing them to use his talents. According to Jomini (1987: 437–8), the core problem was that

> nothing is better calculated to kill natural genius and to cause error to triumph, than those pedantic theories, based upon the false idea that war is a positive science, all the operations of which can be reduced to infallible calculations.

Even today the debate between advocates and critics of the existence and usefulness of the principles pertains to these two positions – war as a science and thereby based on general principles or war as an art based on creativity.

In the nineteenth century, Jomini's teachings gradually served as guidance in the European Great Powers' military staff colleges, with the possible exception of Germany. In France, a great deal of thinking was devoted to identifying the *right* principles. In Great Britain and the US, a lengthy debate was started regarding whether principles existed and, if so, what they were. Patrick Leonard MacDougall (1819–94), Commandant of the Royal Military College and a great admirer of Jomini's ideas, virtually copied these principles for use in the British Army. MacDougall's teachings were, however, always disputed and, among others, Wellington, who finally proved to be Napoleon's match, considered military education to be "nonsense" (Alger 1982: 38). In the US, Jomini's ideas on concentration of force appeared to have been verified through the North's victory over the South in the Civil War (1861–5). The received wisdom at the end of the war was that the Confederacy's able generals, Robert E. Lee, Nathan Bedford Forest, and Thomas "Stonewall" Jackson, had lost the war against the Union's greater resources. In Prussia there were a few advocates of general principles of war – e.g., Rüstow, who identified 27 "fundamental laws" for warfare – but the mainstream of Prussian military thinkers consisted of critics. Georg Heinrich von Berenhorst (1733–1814), Clausewitz and, later, Moltke the Elder rejected the ideas and, instead, stressed that each situation was unique, which is why it was not possible to establish any general principles. Berenhorst was, above all, critical of the principles being riddled with exceptions; "What is the use of rules when one is covered up to one's ears with exceptions?" he asked rhetorically at the beginning of the nineteenth century (Gat 2001: 156). Moltke went further and claimed that: "In War, as in the arts, there is no general standard, in neither can talent be replaced by a rule" (Alger 1982: 57).

Around the turn of the century, there was a fierce debate in both the US and between the European Great Powers. Two positions had gradually formed, inspired by Clausewitz and Jomini: either all rules and principles were rejected or else they were embraced whole-heartedly. Regardless of the approach that dominated, each military thinker was forced to adopt a position on the question concerning the existence of the principles. At that time, Mahan, for example, believed that the principles were valid for all social relations and Moltke totally rejected them. Friedrich von Bernhardi (1849–1930) attempted to maintain a compromise policy and argued that there certainly were principles, but one should refrain from regarding them as laws or binding rules, as they could then limit the commander's freedom of action (Alger 1982: 98). The principles had not yet been officially codified in the doctrines or regulations of the Great Powers at the start of World War I, although the *British Field Service Regulations* from 1909 mentioned the existence of similar principles, but without naming any of them (Alger 1982: 102).

With World War I, this changed, however. First, the war created the need to train greater numbers of soldiers and officers than ever before, which required finding a few simple rules according to which war was to be conducted. Second, the principles of war, as we know them today, were created by Fuller, who Alger (1982: 106) considers to be, "unquestionably the most influential contributor to the modern concept of 'principles of war' in the twentieth century." Fuller's first list of eight principles in an article from 1916 mainly emerged as the result of his combat experience on the Western Front. When he later began to study military history more systematically, he developed his argument to contain nine principles in 1923. Fuller succeeded, more than any of his contemporaries, in capturing the principles and, at least initially, making his voice heard in the British defense establishment.

During the interwar period, the principles of war were institutionalized and codified in the Great Powers' doctrines and regulations. We should, however, note that they were still contested. In what would come to be the US Army's doctrine or regulations, *FM-100, Operations*, the principles were, for example, included in 1921, disappeared in 1928, returned in 1939, disappeared again in 1941, returned in 1949, and disappeared yet again in 1976, to finally return in 1978. In a similar manner, some of Fuller's original ideas were codified in the British Army's *Field Service Regulations* in 1920, only to then disappear in the 1935 version and return, after World War II. In France, the principles were initially rejected by the working group on doctrines set up after the war and led by Petáin (and after Foch had left the army). It was not until 1936 that the principles made their entry into the French Army doctrine. In Germany, they resisted the temptation to follow the victorious powers from World War I and introduce principles. Despite this, the emergence of the principles of war was eagerly discussed in interwar Germany (Citino 2004: 32–5). In the newly-formed Soviet Union, the principles were also rejected after a heated debate, mainly between Mikhail Frunze (1885–1925) and Leon Trotsky (1879–1940), where the latter asserted that the principles were a "bourgeois" invention and that there were no eternal laws in warfare (Alger 1982: 135).

At the outset of World War II, the principles of war were more or less established and much discussed within military theory, although they had by and large disappeared from the Great Powers' doctrines. For understandable reasons, during the war more time was devoted to conducting operations than philosophizing about war, which is why the debate on the principles of war was rather low-key, with the exception of Field Marshal Bernard Montgomery, who distributed a text on his view of the principles of war to his subordinates. After the war, the principles consequently returned in the British doctrines, although their existence was also debated from then on. For example, the military historian John Keegan (1961) argued that they were not valid since no systematic testing had been carried out. In the US, the principles also remained controversial. Peter Paret, the well-known Clausewitz expert, suggested, for example, that the principles of war were nothing but "a catalogue of commonplaces that . . . has served generations of soldiers as an excuse not to think things through for themselves" (Alger 1982: 164).

Despite often-bitter criticism, the principles have remained in American doctrines. After the war, the concept was developed in France from 1936 and, in 1973, three principles and five "laws" were included, which were a means of adhering to the principles. In Germany, and later West Germany, the principles were still dismissed in doctrine, despite the regular debate after the war. It was not until the release of the 1962 field manual *Truppenführung* that a list of 35 principles for conventional warfare and nuclear warfare were included, but, even then, it was strongly pointed out that they were not generally valid. These warnings also returned in the 1973 version, where the tactical principles resembled those used in Great Britain and the US, although there were still a significantly greater number of them. It was stated that war cannot be reduced to a formula and that success is, instead, the result of the commander's critical thinking and also free and creative action within the confines of the mission (Alger 1982: 154). It was not until the 1990s that the number of principles was limited in German doctrines and their collection resembled the few principles of the other countries. In the Soviet Union, the principles were not codified until 1942, following an order from Stalin, although they had previously been used in practice. During the reform period that followed Stalin's death in 1953, "the permanent operational factors" gradually disappeared, to be replaced by the identical "principles of the art of war," which were traced back to Lenin. Today, and throughout history, the principles have thus been subject to extensive debate. But what do the principles involve? What is the logic behind them and what is their mutual relationship?

A selection of the principles of war: logic and mutual relationship

As previously mentioned, the number of principles varies from theorist to theorist, which also applies to the mutual relationships and definitions. In this section, we intend to describe a number of principles that frequently occur in textbooks and doctrines (e.g. Collins 2002: 81–5). However, it is important to point out that the primary aim is not to attempt to select the theoretically most important or most useable principles in practice or to establish a ranking between them, but to analyze the principles' inner logic and their mutual relationship. In order to illustrate our reasoning, we have chosen twelve principles that frequently occur in current Western doctrines.

The principle of purpose. Military endeavors should be aimed at clear and achievable objectives – political as well as military. These should, in turn, be based on established security interests, which form the basis for all strategic concepts and military operations. The objectives should be logically consistent, clearly worded, and optimally concentrated on the enemy's centers of gravity. Plans and operations at each level – strategic, operational, and tactical – should help achieve the overall political objective without ending up in opposition to each other. Objectives established at the beginning of a military operation often tend to become blurred and unclear as the operation proceeds and unexpected events occur. An experienced decision-maker or commander should regularly review his objectives, Collins asserts, so as to assure himself that they are tenable and rationally based. According to him, during the Korean War, the objective of the military operations was changed four times during the first year, where the aim was initially to withstand the North Korean attack (June–August 1950), then to unite North and South Korea (September–November 1950), then to survive the Chinese counter-attack (December 1950–March 1951), and finally to aim for a status quo and a truce (April 1951–July 1953) (Collins 2002: 82). This event is not unique in military history, but shows the difficulty of clarifying and adhering to an objective. In peacekeeping operations too, "mission creep," i.e., where the objective of the operation changes as the operation goes on, is regarded with some skepticism and as a recipe for disaster (cf. Fearon & Laitin 2004).

The principle of initiative. Offensive and effective action makes it possible to act rather than react to the enemy and at a time and place of one's own choosing. Collins (2002: 82) believes that this is the best way of gaining and maintaining the initiative, at the same time as withholding it from the enemy. Success with this principle provides increased room for maneuver, which will inspire your own troops and demoralize the enemy, as well as create opportunities for exploiting the enemy's vulnerabilities. The party with the initiative will also control the course of events on the battlefield. The German attack westwards in May 1940 could be said to be an example of a military operation where one party, in this case Germany, succeeded, right from the outset, in taking the initiative and retaining it during the entire campaign. In this way, it was difficult for the French troops and their allies to launch effective counter-attacks. Collins (2002: 82) suggests that any skilful strategist will only adopt a defensive position and remain passive until the opportunity arises to act and take the initiative. The Russian/Soviet retreats eastwards in 1812 and 1941–2 had the aim of, among other things, gaining time until sufficient forces had been assembled to begin well-aimed counter-attacks against the then stretched out invader. This is also what happened outside Moscow in the winter of 1812–13 and at Stalingrad in the winter of 1942–3 (Collins 2002: 82).

The principle of flexibility. Maintaining flexibility and freedom of action is often highly valued in the execution of military operations. To believe that it is possible to conduct planning based on definite and certain factors is perhaps the most serious of all military mistakes, as no one can foresee how different events will develop in the long run. Political and military objectives can change totally unexpectedly, both one's own and the opponent's. The plans that have been drawn up and the resources produced may prove insufficient in light of the development of events. That is why good margins and alternative plans that have already been developed are necessary in order to maintain one's own freedom of action in the event of the opponent sabotaging or rendering impossible the execution of the original plan. Collins (2002: 82) believes that the best way of avoiding these risks is to create a spectrum of both short- and long-term strategies. A general who often provided evidence of the value of the principle of flexibility was the German General Erwin Rommel, who, in North Africa in 1941, despite being numerically inferior, succeeded in forcing back and, in many cases, defeating his British opponents through flexible use of the weapons systems and units available to him.

The principle of concentration. One of the most important principles in warfare is the ability to concentrate one's resources in time and space to create local superiority over the opponent. Sometimes this is expressed as the principle of concentration of force. This applies to all levels of warfare, and in all contexts. Military forces that are inferior in terms of quantity and even quality may gain the upper hand against an opponent who is, overall, superior if they are able to concentrate their resources and the opponent fails to do the same. The principle of concentration is also connected to the principle of initiative. Already Sun Tzu (1994: 192) seemingly argued in favor of the value of concentration, when suggesting that if the enemy prepares himself in all areas, he will be weak overall. Jomini (1987: 461–3) was also careful to point out the value of this principle and believed that the entire art of war could be reduced to the ability to concentrate one's own forces against the decisive point. Based on this reasoning, he argued that it was important to take and retain the initiative. The Russian counter-attacks north and south of Stalingrad in November 1942 are good examples of concentrating existing resources against an opponent whose troops have become too divided and dispersed. Today, this principle has been much debated in certain quarters, as there are some who believe that the development of new technology has moved towards focusing on effects (Morgan et al. 2003), instead of the older way of thinking, "git thar furst, with the mostest," as confederate general Nathan Bedford Forrest put it.

The principle of economy. Each state or state-like entity, including great powers, has limited resources, which means that the concentration of forces in time and space requires economy of resources in other places. The limited means that are available lead to the need to prioritize so that operations only receive as large a proportion of the available resources as the task requires. Here, we can also speak of an economy of force. This principle is thus closely connected with the notion that the use of military force is calculated and rational. The principle of economy is closely associated with the principle of concentration. The principle of economy can be illustrated by the US and British decision, during World War II, to first focus their efforts on defeating Nazi Germany and, only after this, defeating Japan (Collins 2002: 83). An example of where neglecting to stick to this principle resulted in an expensive mistake was Hitler's attempt to wage war on several fronts – in the east against the Soviet Union, in the south-east against Yugoslavia and Greece, in the south against the British in North Africa – at the same time as they had not yet concluded the war against Great Britain in the west. This proved a crucial mistake, which finally led to his ruin. Collins (2002: 83) argues that any sensible strategist would be wise not to take on several powerful enemies at the same time, as this makes it difficult to concentrate personnel and resources.

The principle of maneuver. Being mobile on the battlefield and flexible in one's strategic thought will contribute towards the ability to be able to quickly switch from one direction of attack to another or from a certain pattern of behavior to another. The principle of maneuver will also contribute towards the capacity to concentrate one's resources against the decisive point. Collins maintains that attacks on the flank, envelopments on the ground and from the air, relocating quickly, and infiltration of the enemy's lines with a view to avoiding the enemy's positions of strength are preferable to carrying out direct frontal attacks. Every skilful strategist, he continues, should, in the spirit of Liddell Hart, strive to maintain power and speed physically and intellectually and not allow the opponent to regain their balance. Then, one should target the opponent's weaknesses (lines of least resistance) right up until the ultimate objective has been achieved (Collins 2002: 83). The German General Heinz Guderian's rapid maneuvers and mobile operations during the campaign in the West in May–June 1940 is a good example of the advantages that may result from the principle of maneuver. Another more modern example is the US-led alliance's ground war against Iraq in February 1991 and March–April 2003.

The principle of surprise. As suggested in Chapter 3, surprise is usually an important principle in all warfare. This principle is particularly important as it tends to invalidate the logical paradox described earlier. Surprise is, however, no guarantee of success, although it undoubtedly increases the prospects of a successful result (Collins 2002: 83). A successful surprise can create effects and results that greatly exceed the value of the effort and the materiel used. An enemy, who is shocked, distracted, or ends up in a state of imbalance, being pressed for time, will also lose the initiative, which is one of the objectives of surprise. An example of a successful surprise at a strategic and operational level is the Japanese attack on Pearl Harbor in December 1941. Here, the Japanese armed forces succeeded in deceiving and misleading the American intelligence services, who were not able to discover the Japanese Navy's concentration of naval forces in the waters next to the US Pacific fleet's main base. The effect was dramatic and caused the US entry into World War II. Another similar example is al-Qaeda's attacks on the World Trade Center and the Pentagon in September 2001. There seems to have been limited advance warning in this case, and, to the extent that it existed, it did not result in any extensive measures to counteract the effects of the planned action. In a similar way, surprise also fulfils an important function at a tactical level and in combat.

The principle of security. Like a boxer in the ring, states and their armed forces must constantly protect themselves. Security is a means of countering surprise and serves to maintain the state's power and influence. It also aims to reduce the risk of foreign and domestic enemies spoiling one's own strategic and operational plans and threatening the state's population, infrastructure, resources, and armed forces. Some ways of achieving this are finding out, through intelligence activity, the enemy's capacity and intentions, with a view to countering the opponent's means of surprise. This also includes counterespionage and attempts to reveal enemy subversion (Collins 2002: 83). Armed combat requires the protection of flanks, lines of supply, and one's own bases. A certain safety margin in the operations plans and the amount of resources is important for managing unforeseen risks and ensuring success.

The principle of simplicity. In a military context, it is regarded as a virtue to strive for simplicity and thereby avoid altogether too complicated plans and operations since they often become increasingly complicated when they face reality. Clear and simple plans also reduce the risk of misunderstandings and confusion. In his famous work, *On War*, Clausewitz (1993: 80) described the friction that characterizes all warfare and compared this with movement in a resistant element, such as water, where even the most natural and simple movements are difficult. Just as there is a need for safety margins in military operations, simplicity is therefore required to counter this friction. According to Collins (2002: 84), a good example of a simple order is the one issued to General Eisenhower in February 1944 by the US-UK joint military command. In this order, it was stated, in a few brief words, that he was to go ashore on the European continent and, in consultation with the allies, carry out operations directed at the heart of Germany and destroying the German armed forces. This order applied right up to the end of the war.

The principle of unity. This principle is regarded to be of great importance because concerted and coordinated actions have better chances of succeeding. Collins (2002: 84) argues that a coordinated leadership "are better able to assign responsibility, promulgate policies, establish procedures, issue guidance, approve plans, set standards, supervise implementation, and settle disruptive disputes." An example of a lack of coordination is the American warfare in Vietnam, where the commander for the Pacific region, with its headquarters in Hawaii, was responsible for air warfare, another commander was responsible for ground operations, and diplomacy was dealt with by the American Ambassador in Saigon. At the same time, almost forty different organizations on the South Vietnamese side were involved in reform work in the rural areas. This lack of coordination, arguably, reduced the opportunities for the US and its allies to wage war effectively in Vietnam.

The principle of morale. The importance of morale for effective warfare has often been stressed by both ancient and contemporary generals and military thinkers. Napoleon, for example, believed that morale was three times as important as material strength (1985: 407–41). Clausewitz (1993: 216) argued that "moral elements are among the most important in war" and that war consisted equally of physical and moral causes and effects. Good morale is often considered important for countering the effects of the frictions that arise in war, but also the danger and physical pressures that soldiers and commanders are subjected to. Good morale in combat may be influenced by many things, including the perceived legitimacy of the actual war, opportunity for recovery and rest, the feasibility of the mission, the effectiveness of the equipment in relation to the opponent, the quality of leadership, and the level of training. The norm in many armed forces of not leaving a fallen comrade behind, or devoting a great deal of energy to saving pilots who have been shot down over enemy territory, are practical examples of how good morale is preserved in military organizations. Another example of the importance of good morale among the civilian population is the British people's resistance to the German bombings in the summer of 1940 (Collins 2002: 84–5).

The principle of time. Time is a factor that affects almost all activities in war. Wise strategists or commanders will, therefore, organize their activities in such a manner that the time factor favors their side and ensures that the opponent ends up pressed for time (Collins 2002: 85). Timing, i.e., knowing when something should be done or a decision made, is also related to this principle (e.g. Leonhard 1994). A modern day example is the Kosovo War, in which the sustained bombing of Serbia put pressure on the Serbian leader, Slobodan Milosevic, to conclude that time was against him and that a truce was the best way to avoid further losses (Gow 2003; Lambeth 2001; Hosmer 2001). Time may also be an important factor at an operational level when a counter-attack is to be launched at exactly the right time for the greatest possible effect.

The principles of war as theory or practice

In the first part of this chapter, we provided an account of the conceptual aspects of the principles of war. We also provided an introduction to the logic that is involved in the principles. The discussion showed that the principles are disputed and may vary based on their form, content, and number. Based on this, we will now turn to the chapter's second and analytical part, in which we tackle in greater detail the question of whether the principles should be interpreted as theory or practice. We begin in reverse order.

The principles of war as practice

In his final instructions to the Prussian Crown Prince Frederick William in 1812, in which Clausewitz briefly summarized warfare according to a few principles, he warned of adhering too strictly to the principles:

> [T]he principles of the art of war are in themselves extremely simple and quite within the reach of sound common sense. . . . Extensive knowledge and deep learning are by no means necessary, nor are extraordinary intellectual faculties. . . . The conduct of war itself is without doubt very difficult.

(Clausewitz 1987: 364)

These words have maintained their relevance in our time. Since then, the big question has actually been whether learning the principles of war, which are, in theory, simple and almost trivial, is of any practical use in the difficult art of waging war. Are the principles of war usable in practical action, or could using them even lead to problems?

Although Jomini and Clausewitz represent opposite poles in the question of whether the principles are of practical utility, they still have much that unites them. As the foremost interpreter of positive principles for how warfare should be conducted, Jomini believed that there were a number of fundamental principles in war that it would be dangerous to deviate from. Although Jomini was ambivalent in his relationship to the principles, he asserted that their use had, throughout the course of history, led to success. Jomini believed that the maxims that it was possible to extract from these principles were few in number. Despite the fact that these maxims sometimes changed character depending on the circumstances, they could generally serve as a compass for the commander in the execution of his difficult task of carrying out military operations in the chaos that war entailed. Individuals with an innate talent could certainly apply these principles as well as someone who had undertaken advanced studies in the subject, but Jomini believed that a simple and explicit theory that focused on causal relationships but was free of exaggerated exactitude could also create this talent. The theory could thereby increase the general ability and self-confidence of a military commander. A few simple principles based on studies of military history, with a great deal of space provided for natural talent, were thus the best way of educating officers (Jomini 1987: 437–8).

Clausewitz, on the other hand, was more critical of the possibility of being able to formulate positive principles for how warfare should be conducted. He (1993: 161–2) believed that it was simply not possible to construct a model for the art of war that can serve as a scaffolding on which the commander can rely for support at any time. Whenever he has to fall back on his innate talent, he will find himself outside the model and in conflict with it; no matter how versatile the code, the situation will always lead to the consequences we have already alluded to: talent and genius operate outside the rules, and theory conflicts with practice.

Three factors, according to Clausewitz, made a positive system consisting of the principles of war impossible. First, war largely consisted of moral and psychological factors (such as courage, fear, and ambition), which were not measurable. Second, war was characterized by human interaction, whose "very nature" is "bound to make it unpredictable." Third, war was characterized by great uncertainty where "all action takes place, so to speak, in a kind of twilight," usually described as the fog of war. Clausewitz (1993: 158–62) was of the opinion that these phenomena were insurmountable barriers for a theory formulated as a plan of action.

Instead of a positive doctrine, which the principles of war were an example of, he wanted attempts at theorizing to focus on the nature of war, as well as its ends and means. Clausewitz (1993: 163, 1987: 371; cf. Paret 1976: 198–9) believed that this theory would "educate the mind of the future commander, or, more accurately, to guide him in his self-education, not to accompany him to the battlefield." Thus, the principles of war were not the final product in an analysis of military history, but, on the contrary, a tool for the commander to understand and analyze the problems that the history of the war provided examples of. Talent and genius would take care of the rest.

The different perspectives that Jomini and Clausewitz represent capture the fundamental structural problems that many people believe exist in the application of the principles of war (cf. Brodie 1959: 21–7; Keegan 1961). The more detailed the principles become, like recommended courses of action for military commanders, the greater the risk that the practical activity on the battlefield will become routine, dogmatic, and, thereby, predictable. Predictable behavior will soon come into conflict with the dynamic nature of war and lead, in those cases where there is no great superiority, to significant advantages for the opponent who can, thereby, adapt and optimize his own behavior. As mentioned in Chapter 3, war is ultimately a contest between opposing wills. Consequently, strategic thought is not directed at a lifeless object, but at a living organism that in an intelligent manner seeks countermeasures to all attempts to create superiority or advantageous positions. This suggests that the most effective action is the unexpected action, i.e., surprise. If there is an altogether too rigid specification of the principles of war, including the principle of surprise, the very deviations from these principles will be the most unexpected thing that can be done. If, for example, an enemy expects a surprise from our own side in every situation, deviating from the principle of surprise would be an example of surprise. This is an example of the paradoxes inherent in the use of the principles of war.

If the principles, instead, are kept vague and imprecise in order to avoid this trap, the result will be that they provide a minimum of guidance for the commander when the fog and chaos of war ensue. The fact that the principles of war in this vague form then become so simple that they are virtually banal, while actual war is so complex and chaotic, could easily lead to the conclusion that the principles appear to have a relatively low value in helping the commander to win wars. We could also assert that the principles of war are knowledge at such an elementary level that advanced learning is more likely to consist of the ability to determine under which conditions one should deviate from the principles with a view to gaining advantages over the enemy. The conclusion to the argument above is, therefore, that the principles of war should never be used maximally, but, instead, *optimally*, i.e., in the most favorable manner in relation to the opponent. Using them maximally could, therefore, be almost as dangerous as minimal use.

Another practical problem with using the principles, if we assume that they are valid and will lead to victory in war, is that they should mainly work on an enemy who does not use them himself. This was asserted by the German military theorist Georg Heinrich von Berenhorst, who, despite considering Jomini's principles mainly valid, felt that participants fighting in the same manner would cancel each other out and thereby neutralize the effect of the principles. In a situation like this, factors such as the number of soldiers, their courage or lack of such qualities, or pure chance, would be decisive, which, paradoxically enough, were the factors that the principles had originally tried to overcome and find a replacement for. Berenhorst believed that this was the case in ancient history when the Greeks and Romans had been successful with their principles of war against "barbarous peoples," something that proved to be ineffective in internal conflicts where courage and talent tended to be decisive. He believed that this was also the case with Jomini's principles, which were primarily based on experiences from the Napoleonic Wars. As long as Napoleon was their sole exponent, he achieved success but the numerically superior enemies quickly learned his tricks, which ultimately meant him losing the upper hand (Gat 2001: 157; Paret 1976: 205). Certain battles on the Western Front during World War I also appear to support this, as both parties used similar tactics and never achieved a breakthrough.

How is it that lots of prominent generals and military theorists persist in their arguments regarding the value of the principles of war despite the problems demonstrated by Berenhorst and Clausewitz? The likely answer is probably that they are easy to understand. Moreover, they fill a moral and organizational function as a focal point for the military organization.

The use of the principles of war often takes the character of a self-fulfilling prophesy, where soldiers and their commanders believe that the principles produce results and they thereby act in a manner that leads to successful results – results that could equally be a result of chance, technical advantages, or numerical superiority.

The principles of war as explanatory social science theory

If the principles of war cannot be interpreted without difficulties in practical terms, should we then, instead, interpret the principles as variables for explaining the outcome of war? In order for the principles to be able to function as an explanatory theory, some fundamental requirements need to be fulfilled. First, there must be a definite connection between the principles (the independent variables) and the outcome of war (the dependent variable). If there is no connection between the assumed cause and effect we are attempting to explain, there will be good reasons for believing that the cause singled out (for example, that one side in the conflict concentrated its forces) is incorrect. Second, the principles must contain a logical link to the outcome of war since otherwise the connection may be random, even if it exists. For example, there are not many people today who still believe that the stork delivers babies, even if the arrival of the stork in the spring coincides with a great number of children being born. How well can the principles meet these requirements?

A clear-cut answer to the question of whether there is a definite connection between adherence to the principles of war and the outcome of war can only be obtained through a systematic empirical investigation. Oddly enough – as John Keegan (1961: 66) points out – this has never been done, which is why he draws the conclusion that the principles of war are perhaps not even valid. During the twentieth century at least, generations of officers have therefore been trained and placed their trust in something that, as far as we know, has not been systematically proved. It might be the case that the principles represent one of many views of how war should be conducted. Limited space and time do not allow us to carry out such an empirical systematical study here, but we can at least discuss certain preliminary questions regarding such an investigation.

In order to carry out an empirical investigation, it would be necessary for the principles to be measurable. This is where the prospective researcher encounters immediate problems regarding the principles of war. In the introduction to the chapter, we gave an account of the rather extensive debate that exists on the nature, content, number, and form of the principles. Based on this discussion, we can deal with problems concerning the conceptual precision of the principles. What, for example, does concentration of force mean? Is it concentration of force concerning effects, firepower, the number of soldiers, or the number of tanks, to name but a few alternatives, that is referred to? What should concentration of force be directed against? Jomini suggests "the decisive point." But what does the "decisive point" consist of? Is it perhaps the case that we can only know what the decisive point is until after the battle has been concluded? It is perhaps even the case that concentration of force *per se* creates a decisive point no matter where it is deployed. In this case, it is hardly an actual decisive point that the commander needs to look for in his planning or the theorist in his analysis, but something created by the battle. Without knowing exactly what type of concentration of force the principle refers to, it will obviously be difficult to test its empirical validity. Similar arguments can be presented regarding other principles, which is something observed by the American strategic theorist Bernard Brodie. He suggested (1959: 23) that the simplicity and alleged universality of the principles are either the result of "divine revelation or of a level of generality too broad to be operationally interesting." In their present state, the principles are quite simply so general that their universality cannot be tested, which makes them uninteresting as an explanation for the outcome of war.

Is it, then, even possible to argue for a connection between the principles of war and the outcome of war? Here, we should be able to observe that adherence to the principles should be accompanied by victory and avoidance should lead to defeat. In order for the connection to be definite, it is also necessary for the converse to apply, i.e., it should be impossible to achieve victory if we avoid using the principles, while strict application of the principles should not correlate with defeat. Both Keegan (1961) and Brodie (1959: 23–7) discuss in fact examples of the opposite. They believe that there are a number of examples when a military power has split their own resources (the opposite of concentration of force and local superiority) and nevertheless achieved victory. In addition, there are examples of commanders who have followed the principles but still lost the battle. Nevertheless, there are also cases where the principles have been adhered to and victory achieved. The fact that examples of the opposite occur means, however, that the connection between principles and outcome of war is not clear-cut. This spells problems for the principles of war as theory.

The principles' internal logic is also problematic. We have already mentioned that the principles of "objective" (read: set an objective and stick to it) and "flexibility" obviously are not entirely compatible. In the same way, it is difficult to reconcile the principle of "economy" with "concentration of force." For the principles of war to be able to function as an explanatory theory quite simply requires that the relationship between them is elucidated – not just logically but also empirically tested. A similar problem, where the burden of proof also lies with those advocating the principles, is defining which of all the possible combinations of the principles will lead to success.

The fact that the causal relationship between adherence to the principles and victory does not appear clear-cut also means that it is necessary to consider alternative explanations (cf. Biddle 2004: 14–77). One of the principles' fundamental qualities as an explanation is that they are based on how the general uses his units in combat. This is, however, not the only thing that influences the outcome of battles or campaigns. For example, the US-led coalition in 2003 would probably have defeated the Iraqi Army even if it had been employed differently. Somewhat in jest, we could assert that it does not really matter how much a platoon of infantry soldiers equipped with small fire arms concentrates its efforts when it meets a mechanized division with air support in open terrain. Resources, materiel, and technology therefore also play an important part in the outcome of war or individual battles. For example, Napoleon commented, laconically, that "God is on the side of the biggest battalions." There would, therefore, appear to be an abundance of rival explanations for the principles of war.

Conclusions

The attempts to identify a small number of guidelines that armed forces should adhere to in order to win all types of war, as well as the scientific search for a *single* variable, are not unlike endeavors to find a panacea that cures every illness. The principles of war are a typical example of the dual nature of military theory: both the prescriptive statements regarding how war should be waged and the explanatory aspirations. In this chapter, we have given an account of several important debates regarding the principles of war. The existence, content, form, and number of the principles have been, and continue to be, contested among theorists and practitioners. By discussing the principles' history of ideas, we have attempted to demonstrate how thinking about their existence has varied in time and space. Of course, this does not rule them out as timeless and universal. The fact that the content, form, and number of the principles vary may well mean that there has been an increase in knowledge, i.e. that the principles that have gradually disappeared were quite simply wrong. In order to test this, however, extensive and systematic empirical studies are necessary. It is also clear from the discussion that the criticism that they are imprecise has some validity. Perhaps it is this very lack of precision that has led to the enduring value of the principles – expressed in such universal form that they can be interpreted in whatever fashion one likes. This quality means, however, that there are great obstacles to testing their validity.

Through a discussion on how we should interpret the nature of the principles of war, as explanatory theory or military practice, we have demonstrated that the debate over their existence can be traced back to a wider discussion with regard to whether war should be regarded as science or art. It has been shown in the chapter that key military theorists, such as Sun Tzu, Jomini, and Clausewitz, were caught in two minds about the principles and, thereby, about the question of whether war is an art or a science. They waver between these positions and thereby struggle with the same intellectual problems, although their solutions are ultimately different.

Regardless of whether we interpret the principles of war as theory or practice, applying them is a problem. For the practitioner, the problem is particularly one of balancing the principles against each other (as some of them are in direct opposition to each other) to figure out the "winning combination" and avoid being predictable. Paradoxically, in a logical sense, we follow the principles of surprise and flexibility if we do not bother following the principles at all. For the theorist, the importance of the principles is unclear due to a lack of precision in the concepts. Moreover, their explanatory power can be questioned, as the connection between adherence to the principles and victory, and ignoring the principles and defeat, is far from clear-cut. There are also major challenges when it comes to operationalizing the principles to make a systematic investigation possible. In this way, theories about the principles of war are permeated by the four themes of military theory expressed in Chapter 1.

Perhaps the solution to the practical problem is to never allow the principles to be anything other than our servants. If we commit ourselves to them, we may quickly become a prisoner of the principles. For the theoretical challenges, extensive work will be required on defining the importance of the principles so that they become measurable. Until then, we cannot clearly investigate to what extent a connection exists between adherence to the principles and victory and defeat in war.

Questions for discussion

1. Is it meaningful to speak of the principles of war?
2. To what extent can the principles of war be said to constitute the collective wisdom of the art of war?
3. Are the principles of war common to all branches of the armed forces?
4. To what extent have the principles of war been influenced by the technological development?
5. Is there any difference between a small state's principles of war and a great power's?

Further reading

John I. Alger, *The Quest for Victory: The History of the Principles of War* (Westport, CT: Greenwood Press, 1982).

Carl von Clausewitz, "Principles of War," in *Roots of Strategy*, vol. 2 (Mechanicsburg, PA: Stackpole Books, 1987).

John M. Collins, *Military Strategy: Principles, Practices, and Historical Perspectives* (Washington DC: Brassey's, 2002).

Antoine Henri Jomini, "Summary of The Art of War," in *Roots of Strategy*, vol. 2 (Mechanicsburg, PA: Stackpole Books, 1987).

Robert R. Leonhard, *The Principles of War for the Information Age* (New York: Ballantine Books, 1998).

Anthony D. McIvor (ed.), *Rethinking the Principles of War* (Annapolis, MD: U.S. Naval Institute Press, 2007).

6   Joint operations

Introduction

Modern Western warfare has become synonymous with joint warfare. By this we mean warfare built on doctrinally coordinated and jointly-exercised forces from different services trying to achieve strategic aims through combat on the tactical level. Even if "jointness" is currently a buzzword, such operations are not a recent phenomenon (Beaumont 1993; Citino 2004). The American general, and subsequent president, Dwight D. Eisenhower proposed in 1946 that "separate ground, sea, and air warfare is gone forever" (Murray 2002: 36). Cooperation between land and sea forces goes back a long way, even if by definition joint operations did not occur until the sixteenth century, when several European states institutionalized their navy and army as separate services (Glete 2000). This last century has seen the creation of the Air Force, allowing now joint operations in four different combinations – land-sea, land-air, sea-air, and integrated air-land-sea.

Joint operations are often quoted as the most effective method of war-fighting. Using forces from many services permits greater freedom of action, while at the same time it presents the enemy with several threats to deal with simultaneously. However, joint operations also entail that different cultures, interests, and command structures must cooperate, which can lead to problems. Often, joint operations are easier to imagine (and to wish for) than to realize. Examples of both successful and unsuccessful joint operations can be found in history (Murray 2002: 32). In World War II, the Germans were particularly successful at linking land and air forces at the tactical level, but not so at the operational level between air and sea. Allied joint operations in the Pacific, and then later in Western Europe, were reportedly successful at the strategic level. At which level does operating jointly achieve most success? Which causal relationships are noteworthy in theories of joint operations? How should military operations be executed in order to achieve strategic objectives most effectively, jointly or in single service?

The aim of this chapter is to introduce theories of joint operations. While Chapter 4 dealt with operational art in conceptual terms, this chapter will fill operational art with more concrete substance. When Chapter 4 discussed the importance of winning the right tactical battle (i.e. those leading to useful strategic effects), this chapter will present the theories of how this happens. One important limitation is that we do not assess theories of single service operations. Instead, these will be found in Chapter 7 (Land operations), Chapter 8 (Sea operations), and Chapter 9 (Air operations). Thus, for example, theories on the use of airpower as an independent force are found in Chapter 9, whereas this chapter deals with theories of how air and land forces cooperate. The discussion of operational art and related terms will therefore continue in the subsequent chapters of the book.

This chapter opens with a discussion of the advantages and disadvantages of joint operations compared to single service ones. This is done in order to understand the logic behind joint operations. The following three parts discuss theories within joint operations in the combinations of land-sea, land-air, and sea-air. The chapter concludes by discussing joint operations with all three services cooperating, including Network-Centric Warfare (NCW) and the so-called RMA.

Joint or single service operations?

The dominating trend in the application of Western military force today seems to be joint operations. Considering the problems arising from differences in service culture, command hierarchies, and technological challenges, it may seem surprising that joint operations currently are the preferred option. Structural interoperability problems could result in delays in decision-making and effects, leading to disastrous consequences. Furthermore, it is far from certain that all military operations need to be joint efforts. Clausewitz stated that "Everything in war is very simple, but the simplest thing is difficult" (Clausewitz 1993: 138). Given such problems, why are joint operations often highlighted and deemed as important? What is the logic behind joint operations as being more effective than single service ones?

To answer such questions we must first define joint and single service operations. Single service operations refer to those executed by forces from the same service, whilst joint operations mean those executed by forces from more than one service. For a joint operation, the commander selects those capabilities from the respective services required to achieve the assigned objective and able to create multiple synergies. This in turn means being able to forge the individual forces' capabilities into a single combined one in order to achieve the joint objective. The main idea, then, is that the combined effect of the joint forces is greater than the sum of their individual ones. As a consequence, joint includes everything from the cooperation between services to the optimal use of services' strengths and weaknesses in order to achieve a strategic or operational level objective.

Some of the ideas underpinning the assumed advantages of joint operations are found within "combined arms theory." Although this theory was developed within a tactical context it has nevertheless been extrapolated into the rationale behind joint operations. Expressions of combined arms theory has occurred often throughout military history. The Swedish king and military commander, Gustavus Adolphus' (1594–1632) restructuring of his army, electing to combine infantry, cavalry, and artillery at the tactical level, is but one example (Rothenberg 1985: 45–55). The ideas were further developed in the eighteenth century and later implemented successfully by Napoleon, using maneuver, organization by divisions and corps, and combining different weapon systems in military campaigns (Paret 1986: 123–42). Jomini (1987: 543–52) elaborated the theory in his *Précis de l'art de la guerre* (1837–38), describing the use of different arms – infantry, cavalry, artillery – and how they could be combined to achieve the best possible effect on the battlefield.

The basic trend from the nineteenth century has been an ever-wider integration of arms, and at lower levels, within military units. Military commanders have increasingly been forced away from single service, and specific weapon-based, operations into greater cooperation and unified action, in order to maximize the effects of weapon systems. In modern times, with the introduction of advanced weapons and technology, this has become even more necessary, and led to increased specialization in training, exercise, and maintenance (House 1984: 1).

In *Combined Arms Warfare in the Twentieth Century*, US Army officer, Jonathan House (2001: 4), explains the term "combined arms" as an idea that different arms, weapon systems, or services must be used together to maximize "the survival and combat effectiveness of the others." The strength of one system will compensate for the weakness of another, providing an otherwise missing synergy. House argues that joint operations are thus a more effective method of achieving military objectives. However, the thinking on combined operations is wider than just joint operations, since its logic can be used also between weapon systems or arms. The advantages of combined arms theory include greater freedom of action for commanders and an increased threat to the enemy. If attacked in at least two ways, uncertainty will be created in the mind of the enemy as to how the attack will unfold, leading to difficulties for him in defending himself. It will also provide greater possibilities to counter his reaction to the attack, all of which gives more courses of action to fulfill the military task at hand (House 2001: 1–10; cf. Cedergren 2005).

The US Army officer, Robert Leonhard (1991: 93–4), proposes that combined arms theory may be best understood if divided into three different but related principles. The first principle is that each part of a joint operation has strengths and weaknesses which differ from the other parts. For example, infantry units have an advantage over armored units on covered or broken ground, whereas armor's advantage lies in open ground. The idea then is to combine arms and/or services into a unified force under unified command, in such a way that the weaknesses of one element can be compensated for by the strengths of another. Infantry can protect armor in battle over closed and broken ground, subsequently using armor to quickly penetrate enemy lines. The whole is thus greater than the sum of the parts.

The second principle builds on the proposition to create dilemmas for the enemy. When combined arms theory is correctly applied, the differing arms complement each other so as to create a dilemma for the enemy, in which defending against one element creates vulnerability to attack from another. If, for example, an enemy armored unit wishes to protect itself from air attack, the standard method is to disperse and dig in. However, if the air attack is combined with an armored assault on the ground, the enemy is forced to choose between dispersed positions (good defense against airpower, but easy targets for armored tank units) or massed positions (good defense against army units, but sitting ducks for opposition airpower) (Leonhard 1991: 94–5).

The third principle builds on the idea of forcing the enemy onto unfavorable ground. Instead of engaging enemy tanks with your own over open ground, you lead them into terrain that is to your advantage, such as where your infantry can engage and destroy these units. This works naturally in reverse as well, forcing the enemy infantry into the open where your armor can engage them. The aim is thus to match the enemy's weakness with your own strength (Leonhard 1991: 96–7). This can be seen also in air warfare when using missiles and Special Forces for sabotage in the first phase to destroy the enemy's air defense systems, and then, when his capacity to defend and protect his forces and infrastructure is diminished, deploy your air assets more freely. Efficiency, freedom of action, and flexibility appear to be the main arguments for using joint operations to achieve military objectives. However, this tells us relatively little about how land-, sea-, and airpower should be organized and deployed in more practical terms. The following sections will deal with theories on joint operations in the realms of land-sea, land-air, sea-air, and finally all three integrated.

Joint operations: land-sea

Using maritime forces for operations on land is as old as naval battles. The best example of the former is opposed landings on enemy shores (now called amphibious operations). Another use for naval power is engaging targets on the enemy coast, using airpower launched from aircraft carriers (which we will return to later), and naval gunfire and/or precision-guided munitions launched from surface and submarine platforms against enemy coastlines. These last ones can be used as part of naval diplomacy (see the discussion in Chapter 8) and in support of land operations (see further below).

Already around 500 BC, Greek city states used their fleet to land troops behind the Persian army and during the Punic Wars around 300 BC, between Rome and Carthage; several landing operations influenced the war's outcome. During World War I there were a handful of significant amphibious operations and the largest of these, the British-French led invasion at Gallipoli in 1915–16, which aimed to capture Constantinople (present-day Istanbul), ended in disaster. World War II, however, saw many hundreds of landing operations, mainly by the Allies with the US as chief among them. The best-known are the 1944 Normandy landings, in which hundreds of thousands of troops and thousands of ships (as well as thousands of aircraft) were involved (Bartlett 1983; Evans 1990; Lovering 2007). The aims of amphibious operations are many, including opening new fronts, tactical support to land operations, and forcing unfavorable moves on the enemy (see Chapter 8).

Rolling barrages from the sea against targets on enemy shores using naval gunfire is also known from history, and since the introduction of precision weapons this has taken on a new lease of life. One classic example is the coastal bombardment by the US battleship New Jersey against the Vietnamese coast in the late 1960s. Another is the use of ship-borne precision-guided missiles against land targets – Tomahawks – fired from American submarines during the two Gulf Wars in 1991 and 2003 (cf. Marolda & Schneller 2001). Of special interest in this section is the naval bombardment used in support of land operations. Those bombardments with strategic aims rather than directly linked to a military land operation are dealt with in Chapter 9, and those carried out in support of naval diplomacy in Chapter 8.

Two maritime thinkers who stand out in the sea-land field of combined arms theory are the British naval historian Julian S. Corbett (1854–1922) and the British major general Charles E. Callwell (1859–1928). In the early twentieth century, Corbett proposed that war at sea and war on land were closely linked, and that naval warfare rarely decided the war as a whole, which instead took place on land. It was the unique and thrifty combination of sea and land warfare which gave the British success in the war against continental powers in the eighteenth and nineteenth century, Corbett claimed. This kind of warfare permitted disproportional strategic gains with relatively limited resources. It also provided greater possibilities of waging limited wars, rather than costly total wars. According to Corbett, it was important to avoid friction between the different services when conducting joint operations with land and sea forces. The navy and army should act like "the two lobes of one brain, each self-contained and instinct with its own life and law, yet inseparable from the other; neither moving except by joint and unified impulse." Moreover, "without such sympathy of action," he argued, "there can be no true unity of counsel, and combined expeditions will remain . . . merely an army carried by a fleet" (Corbett 1988: 218–19; Widen 2012; Schurman 1981).

Like Corbett, Callwell agreed that there exists a mutual reliance between the exercise of sea power and military power on land. They also agreed on the importance of sea control to conduct and maintain operations on land. However, Callwell (1905: 444) differs in making explicit the reverse relationship, i.e. that naval forces are equally reliant on land forces to establish and maintain bases, or threaten enemy bases. In order to make this mutual reliance as effective as possible it requires "co-ordination of authority . . . harmony in the council chambers and in the theatre of operations." One modern example of Callwell's thesis is the difficulty that the advances along the Baltic coast and the Black Sea of the *Wehrmacht* created for the Soviet fleets regarding bases and maintenance during World War II. When the tide of war turned in 1943, it radically changed the conditions for Soviet sea power, which then was able to contribute to final victory. This means, maintains British naval theorist Geoffrey Till (2013: 107), that Mahan's thesis on sea power as the principal means of promoting a state's power and influence works exactly in reverse in the Russian/Soviet case – land power controls the power and influence at sea.

Callwell's book *Military Operations and Maritime Preponderance: Their Relations and Interdependence* (1905) has been described by British strategist Colin Gray (1996b: xv) as the only classical text on joint thinking and warfare. As the book contains much original thinking on amphibious operations it merits further attention here. One of the issues which Callwell deals with is that the different services (there were only two in his day) tend to drift apart in peacetime, leading to differing views of the other's role and tasks, causing ignorance of each other and occasionally rivalry, and finally resulting in frictions and misunderstandings in wartime, when cooperation is vital. "Mutual confidence in peace and mutual understanding of respective functions" are needed for harmony to exist in wartime between army and fleet, according to Callwell (1905: 21–2). In amphibious operations, Callwell argues (1905: 170), those countries with the necessary capabilities had many advantages. This however required certain preconditions for success and such operations were also accompanied by certain risks. First, he claims that "the ability of amphibious force to inflict grave injury upon the foe is usually immense. The capabilities of [a] purely naval force to cause the adversary damage is often very limited." By this he meant that war is seldom concluded at sea and amphibious forces are often required to threaten or defeat the enemy. Despite the technological advances since Callwell's book was published, and the exponential increase in power projection since the early twentieth century, this thesis still has relevance today. Second, Callwell notes that amphibious warfare enjoys advantages of operating on the interior lines (compare with Jomini's theories in Chapter 7) much more than pure land warfare does, but also of surprise and initiative over the opponent. This of course presupposes that the time and place of landing is held sufficiently secret (Callwell 1905: 263, 269, 283; Shy 1986: 169–70; Vego 2009: IV–68–69). The Gallipoli landings in 1915 are a good example of operations hampered by lack of strategic surprise even though tactically the Turkish defenders were deceived (Till 2013: 195; cf. Moorehead 2007; Carlyon 2003). Callwell was, as mentioned, also aware of the risks of amphibious operations. He concluded that delays due to the great distances to be covered by sea are often problematic, which causes challenges regarding resupply and maintenance of the landed troops. Guaranteeing the sustainability of a large landing operation requires considerable naval resources, both in absolute terms and relative to the enemy, and all this whilst the enemy is trying to delay and degrade the operation. Furthermore, the landing will be harder the better prepared the defenses are (Callwell 1905: 244).

Which kinds of amphibious operations are there, and what is required in modern times to execute such operations? Till (2013: 189–90) presents four basic types:

- *amphibious assault*, aiming to gain a foothold on enemy ground, hold it, build up forces, and open a new front;
- *amphibious raid*, to gain a temporary foothold in order to achieve a tactical or operational objective, thereafter making a planned withdrawal;
- *amphibious withdrawal*, together with naval forces withdraw and evacuate troops from a combat area in order to recover them;
- *amphibious feints and demonstrations*, aiming to deceive the enemy and commit his forces elsewhere.

These four types can be combined and form different phases within operations. Assault, raid, and withdrawal may be complemented with feint, and raid usually includes a variation on withdrawal in order to extract the raiding troops. Which type of operation is chosen will depend upon the overall aim and the resources available. The Allied raid on Dieppe in August 1942 aimed to probe the German defenses, using the intelligence gathered for the coming Normandy landings in 1944. At the time of the Dieppe raid (executed largely by Canadian forces) the Allies were not sufficiently strong for a full-scale invasion on the European continent and therefore a raid had to suffice. Part of the Normandy landings included a feint against Calais, which helped to commit a good deal of the German forces away from the real landing areas (Holmes 2001: 260, 649–55; cf. Zuehlke 2012; Beevor 2009).

Till (2013: 190–7) suggests that for a landing operation to succeed, certain operational prerequisites must be in place. First, local maritime superiority in the landing area is necessary and this will entail the navy being tasked to protect the operation as a whole from enemy interference. This includes all phases, from embarkation at one's own sea ports, through sea transport, the landing itself, support to the ongoing operation, and finally possibly the withdrawal. As the German operations in Norway 1940 and Crete in 1941 show, local maritime superiority may also be gained with the help of airpower. Second, careful and comprehensive preparation is required in order to succeed. Preparations for the Normandy landings began years before the June 1944 launch. Third, the landings must involve all services, i.e. a joint operation, while a fourth prerequisite is speed and surprise. Finally, it is important to remember that the defender has many advantages over an attacker coming from the sea (such as better protection, mobile defense, fixed installations, land-based resupply, etc). Thus, it is always good to have the technological edge, even an innovative edge, as well as surprise over one's opponent.

What conclusions, then, can be drawn from sea-land joint operations and the combined arms theories described so far? House's (2001) theories concerning the strengths of a particular system compensating for the weaknesses in another (also incorporated in Leonhard's [1991] first principle), means that joint sea-land operations tend to provide land forces with greater mobility and surprise. Furthermore, naval forces tend to be able to better threaten enemy bases of strategic value. Finally, land forces gain from naval gunfire support and precision-guided weapons, which are harder to achieve from land. Leonhard's (1991) second principle, i.e. that the complement of different elements creates a dilemma for the enemy, merits further study. In amphibious landing operations the landed forces gain advantage from the surprise and mobility afforded by sealift. The enemy is thus forced into a dilemma, unable to concentrate defenses without knowing where the assault will occur. A good example of this is when 30,000 British troops on the English side of the Channel could tie up 300,000 of Napoleon's troops, the latter being unsure where best to defend the French coastline (Corbett 1988: 69–70). Leonhard's third principle – forcing the enemy onto unfavorable ground – can be seen in sea-land joint operations, for instance in the choice of landing area, even though the defender seems to enjoy the advantage. Obviously one can improve the odds relatively, but still the best landing area is an undefended one, which is usually difficult to find in practice. Finally, it is worth noting that the advantages for joint operations presuppose that the separate services can happily and efficiently cooperate and complement each other. History, however, shows this to be rather difficult to achieve at times.

Joint operations: land-air

Large-scale air forces were first used during World War I. Germany bombed London in 1917 and in 1918 the German spring offensive *Operation Michael* was one of the first land-air joint operations. Unsurprisingly, this led to debate as to how this new service should best be used. The main sticking point, which remains to this day, is between those wanting to use airpower separately from land and naval forces in order to achieve strategic, war-winning results, and those wanting to use airpower primarily to support land operations. With very few exceptions the latter theory developed in headquarters dominated by army officers (e.g. Vennesson 1995: 36–67). Conversely, the theory of airpower working best independently grew from air force dominated thinking. It is worth mentioning that it is mainly proponents of maneuver warfare that favor airpower supporting land operations.

The idea that the new service (air force) would be best employed together with ground forces emerged in Europe in the interwar years. Even in nations where proponents of independent strategic bombing were strong, there were also those that favored the air force in a supporting role. Italy's General Amedeo Mecozzi (1892–1971) argued that airpower should be concentrated to support ground operations, rather than strategic bombing. Contrary to his more famous contemporary Guilio Douhet (see Chapter 9), Mecozzi stated that a relatively limited fighter capability could defend against bombers, thus freeing up the remainder of airpower to support ground forces (Corum 1997: 160). In Britain, Fuller and Liddell Hart developed propositions that mechanized units supported by air forces (see also Chapter 7) could be used to break through enemy lines and to exploit the enemy depth (Holden Reid 1998). This, they believed, could avoid the stalemates of the trenches.

It was in Germany, however, and later in the Soviet Union, that thoughts of airpower being used most effectively to support ground operations were codified into doctrine. Both countries had their proponents of strategic bombing, but the geopolitical position, technological problems, operational experience from World War I, joint military cooperation in the Soviet Union, Stalin's purges, as well as experiences from the Spanish Civil War, led to the repression of the idea of the air force operating independently. In the Soviet Union, two of the great advocates of strategic airpower – Alexander Lapchinskii and Vasili Chripin – were executed during the 1930s, together with 75 other senior members (of a total of 80) of the Soviet military high command (Stockwell 1956: 12). After World War I and according to the Treaty of Versailles, Germany was forbidden to hold air forces, but by promoting air force officers to the general staff they could keep both thinking and studies of the air war of World War I alive. This made joint thinking natural for the German general staff. In contrast to the other great powers, the role of the air force was comparatively strong in Germany, and in the closing moments of World War I, the German Air Force resisted the Allies most effectively. James S. Corum (1997: 169) claims that because the air force had such a strong position, the airpower theorists did not need to recommend strategic bombing to justify the air force's independence, which was the case in both the UK and US. This meant that institutional interests did not play into the development of airpower theory.

The development of airpower theory in interwar Germany was focused on the general staff rather than on any particular theorist. Studies under Helmut Wilberg (1880–1941) of air warfare during World War I re-evaluated German tactics and recommended a greater air offensive, as well as increasing the importance of air superiority. General Hans von Seeckt (1866–1936), one of the founders of the operational concept which came to be known as *Blitzkrieg*, ascribed it a central role in future war. Seeckt argued that, in order to avoid the stalemates of the Western Front during1914–18, small light mechanized units using maneuver – *Bewegung* – should encircle and defeat the enemy. He proposed in this context that airpower was central insofar as airpower could destroy or disrupt mobilization, force concentrations, and enable advances to the operation area. According to him, airpower also had a significant role in subsequent operations through indirect support (interdiction), i.e.

isolating troops from reinforcements and resupply, and limiting their freedom to maneuver (Corum 1992; Buckley 1999: 84–7). Von Seeckt initiated an exchange program with the Soviet Union in order to avoid the restrictions of the Treaty of Versailles. This meant that German pilots could cooperate and fly with the Soviet Air Force, giving them the chance to practically develop and test both new weaponry and operational concepts.

In the Soviet Union, whose air force was significantly influenced by its cooperation with Germany, the air force was linked to the idea of "deep battle" (see Chapter 4 and Chapter 7). Even though in 1923 General Michail Frunze (1885–1925) proposed that the main role of the air force was to support land operations, the Soviet Union had its proponents for strategic bombing. General Alexander N. Lapchinskii (1882–1938) suggested in the early 1920s that strategic bombing would decide the outcome of future war. When Frunze died in mysterious circumstances, after a minor operation in 1925, he was replaced by Tukhachevsky, who immediately began developing and refining the "deep battle" idea.

Tukhachevsky's key idea was that, through reconnaissance and bombardment, the air force would prepare the breakthrough of enemy lines for the ground forces. Thereafter, much like von Seeckt's thoughts, airpower would prevent mobilization of reserves against a mechanized assault, by simultaneously locking up the area of operations and landing air-borne units (a novelty at the time) deep behind enemy lines. (Corum 1997: 162–8; van Creveld 1994: 128–31) A deliberate feature of Soviet thinking was that airpower formed a central element of the principle of combined engagement at the operational level. It thus became the air force's primary task to achieve local air superiority, after which they could support ground operations unhindered. Tukhachevsky's theory on "deep operations," despite being codified into Red Army doctrine, had only a marginal influence at the start of World War II, probably because he was one of the casualties of Stalin's purges in the later 1930s, along with three in five Soviet marshals. Later in World War II, "deep battle" gained more credence but was then propagated (for political convenience) as coming from Stalin himself (Fast Scott & Scott 1982: 21–2).

During the Cold War, the Western Powers saw airpower as largely independent and mainly because it was the platform of choice for delivery of nuclear weapons. Nonetheless, discussions of airpower in a supporting role, such as close air support and battlefield interdiction, continued unabated. Experience from the Korean and Vietnam wars greatly influenced thinking concerning the development of airpower in relation to ground units.

The US Army experienced a crisis after the Vietnam War, which allowed fresh thinking to come through in a number of areas. One of these was how land and air forces could cooperate in military operations. Such thinking showed itself most clearly in the AirLand Battle doctrine of 1982 (see Chapter 4), which basically introduced the phrases "maneuver warfare" and "deep battle" into the army lexicon. This was followed in turn by a re-evaluation of the cooperation between air forces and ground forces, which largely followed von Seeckt's and Tukhachevsky's theories. In an expected European war, airpower would be used to assert air superiority, and to attack the Soviet Army's second and third echelons. Locking up the area of operations would allow American units to operate free from Soviet air attack or Soviet military reserves. One modern expression for the use of land forces and air forces together, to achieve best effect, is Robert Pape's (1998; 2004) "hammer and anvil" theory. This likens airpower to a hammer requiring a hard surface to base whatever is struck, the land units providing that unyielding surface. Pape's theory is largely a modern expression of the basic idea which von Seeckt and Tukhachevsky proposed in the interwar years. He suggests that airpower plays a significant role in mechanized warfare in two ways: both facilitating a breakthrough by direct engagement (battlefield interdiction) of enemy lines, or by attrition of enemy logistics; and once the breakthrough is achieved airpower can support the advance by ensuring that enemy reserves cannot attack the flanks (Pape 1996, 2004).

The novel feature in Pape's (2004) theory was not his logic, but rather that he noted airpower's capability to deliver precision-guided weapons against individual tanks, thus supporting an armored advance. Among other things, he claims that war-fighting in Afghanistan in 2001 shows that the roles played by air and land have changed, and that perhaps it is land supporting air rather than the reverse. Furthermore, the expanded use of Special Forces, together with airpower, achieved the greatest effect of the war in Afghanistan in 2001, which showed observers in the US that there are alternatives to large-scale ground invasions. Finally, in contrast to quite a number of other airpower theorists, Pape based his theoretical claims on empirical evidence, rather than deductions possible due to a particular form of technological development.

In summary, we may conclude that ideas on how airpower can be integrated with land forces into joint operations have not significantly progressed since the interwar years. However, technological and weapon development improvements have brought great change, from carpet bombing to precision-guided strikes. The dilemma for the enemy now is that combined engagements mean that whatever he does he will be open to attack. General Allen Peck, one of the main leaders of the planning and execution of the Iraq War in 2003, perhaps expressed it best when he said: "Ground troops forced the enemy's hand. If they massed, airpower could kill them. If they scattered they would get cut through by the ground forces" (Pape 2004: 128).

How then might we interpret joint air-land operations from the combined arms theories given above? Clearly there is synergy to be achieved through joint use of land- and airpower, since land units fix the enemy and control events on the ground, while airpower has maneuverability and firepower, as well as the capability to engage enemy concentrations in depth. Furthermore, air forces can lock up the area of operations and prevent enemy reinforcements in the area of a breakthrough. Their capability to operate jointly, to create dilemmas and an increased threat for the enemy, is best expressed by Peck in the quotation above – enemy concentrations are attacked from the air, and enemy dispersals result in easy breakthrough on the ground. No matter how the enemy acts he will be on the horns of a dilemma, forced onto unfavorable ground or difficult situations.

Joint operations: sea-air

In the previous section, we examined how new concepts and doctrines for the joint use of land and air forces developed in the 1920s and 1930s, mainly in Germany and the Soviet Union, and how they were implemented in the Spanish Civil War and during World War II. Developments in joint sea-air operational concepts and thinking paralleled this, which would greatly influence war at sea during World War II and the development of sea power thereafter (Hezlet 1970). The US Air Force General William Mitchell (1879–1936) had already declared by the mid-1920s that the time of the great battleships was past, as they were now too vulnerable to air and sub-surface threats. Ships could now operate only in open seas, leaving all sea control within range of aircraft to the latter (Mitchell 1999: 428). Many were skeptical of Mitchell's optimism, but the German operations against Norway in 1940 and Crete in 1941, as well as the Japanese attack on Pearl Harbor in 1941 and the American victory at Midway in 1942, made contemporary military thinkers appreciate that there had been a radical new change in war-fighting on, and in proximity to, the sea (Brodie 1943: 50–64, 175–214). How did airpower affect the war at sea? What consequences did this have in modern times?

During the 1920s and 1930s, airpower could not significantly alter wars at sea, having neither the range nor the performance required, nor the robustness or precision of bombing. Aircraft in the age before radar were initially configured for reconnaissance, as fighter escorts, and as forward observation platforms. It was not until aircraft became more robust, faster, and better-armed that land- and carrier-based aircraft became a serious threat to large surface warships. The tactical and operational use of airpower at sea changed and developed during the whole of World War II, which saw rather dramatic events. Aircraft carriers came to replace battleships as the dominant weapons platform for war in the open seas. This, however, required many escort vessels to protect it, such as light cruisers for air defense, destroyers for submarine defense, minesweepers, and submarines for reconnaissance and intelligence gathering (Hughes Jr. 2000: 90–5; Till 2013: 140–1; van Creveld 1989: 211–14).

The two main demonstrations of carriers' and naval aviation's effect, in power projection and sea war, came at Pearl Harbor in 1941 and Midway in 1942. At Pearl Harbor, a Japanese fleet of six carriers and two battleships (with escorts) managed in just a few hours to sink or damage eight American battleships and destroy 186 aircraft, most of them on the ground. The surprise attack was carried out by 350 Japanese aircraft, lifting from carriers some 400 kilometers from their targets. Japanese losses were 29 aircraft and six submarines, of which five were mini-subs. The Pearl Harbor attack proved the value of the combination of carriers and aircraft, projecting power from the sea against enemy coasts (Holmes 2001: 696).

The battle of Midway became the most famous sea battle of World War II and the turning point for the Japanese offensive in the Pacific. Despite being evenly matched in numbers, Japan lost four of its carriers against one American. It is worth noting that the warships of both sides avoided almost completely close contact with – and sight of – each other during the battle, and that it was principally fought between the (mainly carrier-based) naval aviation forces (Holmes 2001: 583–4). This example shows both the carrier's vulnerability and the potential of naval aviation to sink large warships at previously unthinkable ranges. From the battle of Midway to the present day the carrier has become the dominant platform for war-fighting at sea.

However, the role of the carrier has not been so obvious in littoral seas, where land-based air forces and missiles are not only cheaper and safer but also more effective. Many aircraft types are not suited for take-off and landing on carrier decks, and most land-based bombers can take considerably larger payloads. On the other hand, they are locked to their operating bases and therefore lack the flexibility of the carrier. It is the carrier's power projection capability which has made it so popular amongst the great powers with global interests (Grove 1990: 138–9; Till 2013: 125–8).

How have military thinkers assessed airpower's affect on war at sea? The Soviet Admiral Sergei G. Gorshkov (1979: 229) wrote in the 1970s that naval aviation from World War II onwards has been "converted into a most important means of armed struggle at sea." He further claimed that the advent of nuclear weapons and precision-guided weapons made the engagement of static targets more effective, freeing up naval aviation to direct attacks against surface warships, submarines, troop- and supply transport, and other more maneuverable targets at sea.

Grove claims that sea- and airpower have become indivisible and that sea-based platforms have become one of the most flexible and least vulnerable ways of using airpower, whether aircraft or missiles. While there are advantages with land-based naval aviation, operational problems have been created at times due to disputes concerning organizational and bureaucratic boundaries between the two air forces. Grove (1990: 138–139) states:

[T]he full potential of land-based airpower over the sea has often not been fully exploited. Navies have been limited in their abilities to operate aircraft. The situation is usually happiest when the sea/land boundary is used as the basic organizational divide, i.e. aircraft designed to operate over or from the sea being operated by the navy: those over land by the air force.

Historical accident, however, has often dictated otherwise.

Gray claims for his part that, in the same way as sea power has enabled more effective land forces, so airpower has enabled more effective naval forces. He sees Pearl Harbor as the clearest example of this, and this is how naval aviation should be viewed. Sea control and power projection in practice effectively mean the threat available from aircraft and cruise missiles. Naval gunfire and torpedoes are still effective, but the greatest threat comes from air. Therefore, Gray (1999: 235) concludes that air and sea power have become fused, and "the tactical, operational, and even strategic relationship between seapower and airpower is so close that to talk of joint air-sea, or sea-air, warfare is misleading. Seapower and airpower have become interdependent." Gray's argument has many parallels with those of Callwell and Corbett on land-sea warfare.

How then have the standard theoretical concepts of command of the sea and command of the air been affected by the integration of sea- and airpower? A deeper analysis of these two terms will be made in Chapters 8 and 9, while this part concerns itself with the theoretical relationship between the two. Whilst sea control can be understood as the capability to establish control of important sea-lines of communication (SLOC), air superiority can be understood as the capability to control the airspace. Thus a question arises as to how it is possible to establish and then maintain maritime communications without also controlling the airspace over these lines. Perhaps air superiority is all that is required in order to say one has sea control? Based on World War II experiences, many military theorists would say "no" to the former and "yes" to the latter.

The American naval thinker Milan Vego tackles such questions in his book on naval strategy in narrow seas, and states that since World War II air superiority has been the deciding factor of sea warfare. According to Vego (2003a: 7, 123–4), this has been especially so in narrow seas, i.e. waters that can be controlled from respective sides of land, such as the English Channel. Since modern military aircraft have ever-extended ranges, sustainability, and greater speeds, most seas and oceans are well suited for combined operations of naval and land-based air forces. Consequently, he claims, there are very few maritime areas which cannot be surveilled and attacked from the air. The struggle for air superiority in such areas is likened to that over coastal areas, where control of the airspace over narrow seas is needed to achieve sea control and a fleet can only sustain an operation in such waters if it has air superiority.

Vego uses the German attacks on Norway in 1940 and Crete in 1941 as examples of operations where local air superiority resulted in local sea control in the neighboring maritime areas. In the case of Norway, the Germans succeeded in transporting troops over the entire Skagerrak, landing them on several places on the Norwegian coast, despite the Royal Navy's command of the sea. He maintains, however, that this was compensated for on the German side by strategic surprise, air superiority, and mining the western straits of Skagerrak. Furthermore, Vego (2003a: 124, 188) cites Crete 1941 as a unique case in military history, as it was the first time an area only accessible by air and sea (an island) was taken by a power lacking local sea control. From this reasoning it can be concluded that sea control is usually dependent on air superiority and that the two terms have become wholly integrated. Speaking of sea control necessarily includes air superiority, and little separates the two concerning sea warfare and maritime operations.

Recently, there has been further debate on joint sea-air operations in the US. Drawing upon the AirLand Battle doctrine from the 1980s – and in anticipation of perceived long-term threats from China and Iran, the US Air Force and Navy have jointly developed an "AirSea Battle" doctrine. Aiming to secure access to the western Pacific Ocean and the Persian Gulf in a conflict situation, and to preserve US maritime power projection capabilities in these regions, the doctrine provides a basis for winning a salvo competition with guided munitions and for disrupting and destroying enemy systems. Success, it is projected, is accomplished by using both kinetic and non-kinetic means – by scouting enemy battle networks, by early long-range attacks, as well as through coordination of operations and firepower from geographically dispersed but temporally coordinated forces (van Tol et al. 2010).

Moving, then, to the theoretical aspects of combined operations, as described in the beginning of the chapter, it can be said that the joint use of sea- and airpower has the following advantages in the operational context. First, airpower increases not only naval firepower but also its mobility and range. Paradoxically, naval power increases the mobility and flexibility of airpower, since it is freed from fixed and vulnerable land bases. Second, airpower increases the threat for an enemy operating at sea, as he must then account for threats not only on the surface and sub-surface, but also from the air. Naval combat is thus three-dimensional. Finally, the threat from land-based aircraft often forces warships away from coastal operations, and in combination with surface vessels and hunter/killer submarines in open waters it provides a synergy.

The integrated battle space: RMA as joint operations

Joint operations have been discussed so far in binary terms: land-sea, land-air, and sea-air, focusing primarily on the historical context of their birth and breakthrough. Whilst the first has existed pretty much as long as warfare itself, the last two are a product of the developments of the first half of the twentieth century. Joint operations involving land, sea, and air forces together have existed for most of the twentieth century, but have become increasingly relevant as technology has developed in the last few decades. As mentioned in this chapter's introduction, modern Western warfare has more or less been equal to joint warfare. New weapon-, sensor-, computer-, and telecommunications technology has integrated the battle space and brought information up almost to parity with firepower and movement. As a consequence, the traditional boundaries between land, sea, and air are slowly but surely disappearing. The next section discusses this phenomenon – starting from the first advocates of the technological revolution in the early 1990s to the emergence of "cyber warfare."

In the early 1990s, the West and especially the US began speaking of a "Revolution in Military Affairs" (Toffler & Toffler 1993; Gray 2002; Adamsky 2010; Lomov 2002). The idea originated in Soviet military thought in the 1970s, claiming that a "revolution in modern warfare" brought about by new generations of precision-guided weapons linked to modern information technology and effective sensors could rival the introduction of mechanized units (*Blitzkrieg*), aircraft carriers, and nuclear weapons earlier in the 1900s. New technology would make it possible to find and accurately engage long-distance targets in almost real time. The empirical basis for these theories came from analyses of American war-fighting in Vietnam, the Yom Kippur War in 1973, and the Falklands conflict of 1982. The discussion was considerably boosted after the overwhelming success of the American-led coalition over

Iraq in the Gulf War of 1991 – Iraq being primarily equipped with Cold War Soviet weapons and trained in Soviet doctrine (O'Hanlon 2000: 7–9).

In the war for Kuwait, American airpower, according to its own figures, succeeded in destroying 2,000–3,000 Iraqi armored vehicles, despite normally flying higher than three thousand meters to avoid enemy ground fire. They claimed their precision-guided weapons had a 20–30 percent hit probability, which was considerably higher than was the previously accepted level for successful engagements. As a comparison, Tami Davies Biddle (2002) has demonstrated that even in the US daytime "precision" bombing during World War II, less than a few percent of the bombs hit within a kilometer of the intended targets (then often sizeable factory complexes, let alone armored vehicles), while the British nighttime area bombing fared even worse. Furthermore, in 1991 tanks and other vehicles could be found and engaged despite being dug in, and despite local Iraqi ground superiority for much of the war. The US-led coalition's mechanized units were equally successful. Iraqi tanks were knocked out at ranges of 2,000–3,000 meters and the hit probability was, according Americans statistics, around 85 percent, despite the fact that US tanks were on the move and frequently caught in sandstorms. The final 50:1 casualty tally in US favor was – according to Israeli figures – at least five times higher than the Israeli defense forces had achieved against their Arab neighbors (O'Hanlon 2000: 10). The popular conclusion, especially in the US, was that a revolution in modern warfare was imminent.

The target-rate of Coalition air forces against Iraqi armored vehicles in 1991 was later questioned, especially in the light of the Kosovo 1999 conflict, where the Serbs managed to hide and protect their tanks. Most importantly, it is difficult to verify numbers of targets destroyed by airpower without verification on the ground. The figures for destroyed Iraqi vehicles and the aerial hit probability compared to former Yugoslavia, is now reckoned to have been exaggerated (Nardulli 2002: 44–56). The increased caution regarding empirical evidence for impending revolution in military affairs has not, however, significantly affected optimism for RMA in the US and many Western countries.

From early on, there have been surprisingly few differing views in the US on how RMA should be defined and understood from within the military, but the Pentagon gave a fairly universal definition, incorporated in the forward-looking doctrines *Joint Vision 2010* (1996) and *Joint Vision 2020* (2000). The latter gave a series of operational concepts describing the future aims of the US armed forces, which could be interpreted as the basis of RMA. "Dominant maneuver" described the capability to gain the advantageous position through decisive speed and superior tempo on the battle space, based on joint operations. "Precision engagement" was the capability to find, monitor, and track enemy targets, select and use the most appropriate system for engagement, and use balanced weapon systems to achieve the desired effect. "Focused logistics" meant the capability to get the right forces and equipment into the joint force, and to ensure maintenance in the right place, time, and amount. "Full dimensional protection" was the capability to protect those troops and assets necessary for the execution of the operation (O'Hanlon 2000: 2; Joint Chiefs of Staff 2000). Added to this was "information superiority," meaning the capability to collect and process a constant stream of information whilst simultaneously preventing the enemy from doing so; and "decision superiority," depicting the capability of taking better decisions faster than the enemy, which was being increasingly highlighted in this context (Joint Chiefs of Staff 2000). These aims were predicated on a number of assumptions. First, computers and electronics would continue to enable significant advances in weapon systems and war-fighting methods. This concerned mainly the capability for information management, information networks, and communications technology, missiles, and other advanced munitions and equipment. Second, sensor capacity would radically improve leading to increased capability to monitor the battle space. Third, vehicles, vessels, missiles, and aircraft would become lighter, more fuel-efficient, faster, and harder to detect; allowing faster deployment of troops and greater combat effectiveness. Finally, new weapon types for use in and from space, lasers, and advanced biological agents would be developed and brought into service (O'Hanlon 2000: 2–3).

Criticism of the alleged change in the nature of war came mainly from the scholarly community. Michael O'Hanlon, an American defense expert, saw RMA as a few convincing hypotheses whose technological assumptions were uncertain and as yet unconfirmed for the US. Furthermore, he claimed that such a revolution, should it come about in the next decades, would take considerably longer to realize than the optimistic projections given and would be more like a rapid evolution. As an historic comparison, O'Hanlon cited that the development in the 1930s and 1940s of the operational concepts of mechanization, carrier groups, radar-guided air defense, and nuclear weapons were quicker and more sweeping than showed by the 1990s cases (O'Hanlon 2000: 192–3). Moreover, renowned military analyst Stephen Biddle added further criticism of the RMA concept. He suggested that the technological developments of the twentieth century had made war all the more complex; that certain states had been more successful than others in managing this complexity and thereby more skilful at protecting themselves against the improvements in firepower of the twentieth century. This development had led to great disparities in the battle space when a military power capable of handling such complexities (e.g. US) met an adversary less capable of such (e.g. Iraq in 1991). Biddle (1998:4) argued that the advantages would be far smaller given two antagonists more evenly matched in handling the complexities. Thus, he concluded, there had not been a revolutionary development of the nature of warfare. Although the most optimistic of the RMA proponents' projections has yet to be realized, there have unquestionably been a series of developments in Iraq and Afghanistan over the last decade that bear witness to the impact of technology on the conduct of war. Both the early advocates and the early opponents, therefore, may have overstated their cases. Perhaps most significantly, though, it is not certain that the effects on tactical and strategic level are as straight forward as predicted. For example, it is far from certain that the current US drone strike campaign along the North West Frontier in Afghanistan and Pakistan will just have the tactical (accumulated gradually to the strategic level) effect of wearing down the command and control hierarchy of the Taliban and al-Qaida. The way and the methods with which the campaign is conducted could possibly lead to other unanticipated effects insofar as the Taliban responding with other measures is concerned.

RMA has also been described by some as a passage from so-called platform-centered warfare over to so-called network-based warfare; the distinction is mainly concerned with where the information to base decisions upon comes from. In "platform-centered warfare," the information comes primarily from platforms such as aircraft, ships/boats, or vehicles. "Platform" should here be interpreted in the wider sense, not limited to vessels but also including humans and groups of soldiers. Also, it is the unit which takes the decision. In "network-based warfare," decisions are based not on the individual platform's sensors but on a network of interlinked platforms and sensors. Sensors feed the network, collecting data and feeding it on to differing users. Each platform has access to the network's information, meaning that each platform does not necessarily need its own sensors as it can rely on the network's collective sensors. In this way, the network-centric warrior will have "full battle-space awareness" and information can be shared by all simultaneously, in theory leading to more efficient maneuver and targeting (Arntzen & Grotan 2011).

It is worth noting that no country today has a completely network-based defense, but that many countries are looking to achieve this. Some posit that network-based defense is built on a series of hypotheses containing unanswered questions and problems to achieve the reality it claims – even describing it as a "management fad" (Arntzen & Grotan 2011: 257). Examples of such problems are how the differing elements of the system will share data, how different people will get this information, and how they will interpret it in the same way. Furthermore, how should the information be organized in the net in order to give meaning to the information, and how should a more developed network lead to an improved shared situational awareness simply because the separate nodes in the net have access to this information (Brehmer 2002: 85–6). Only the future will tell whether such problems can be solved.

How does RMA fit into military thought? Proponents of RMA tend to be critical of parts of Clausewitzian theory. Parting from Clausewitz's fog of war and friction, such critics point to the uncertainties and chaos of the battle space being radically reduced through new technology, and that winners of future conflict are those with information superiority or so-called "dominant battle space awareness" (O'Hanlon 2000: 8–9). One example of such a viewpoint was American admiral William A. Owens, who in his book *Lifting the Fog of War* (2001) claimed that new technology – the basis of RMA – would revolutionize warfare. According to him, future commanders would enjoy

> instant access to a live, three-dimensional image of the entire battlefield displayed on a computer screen, an image generated by a network of sensors, unmanned aerial vehicles, reconnaissance aircraft, and special operations soldiers on the ground. The commander will know the precise location and activity of enemy units – even those attempting to cloak their movements by operating at night, in poor weather, or hiding behind mountains or under trees.
>
> (Owens 2001: 14)

The question of how friction or the fog of war will be entirely or even partially eliminated from the battle space is currently unanswered. It may be hard to imagine a war that does not contain danger, fear, physical effort, and uncertainty that Clausewitz (1993: 138–40, 158–63) described as "the atmosphere of war." Hence, even if the debate on RMA has been ongoing for nearly two decades, there are still both opponents and proponents in this context (Cebrowski & Garstka 1998; Vego 2003b).

The increased interest in communications technology and computers in warfare has also spawned a debate on warfare in cyber space. Some want to elevate cyber space to a position equal to that of air, sea, and land domains and even imply that force structures ought to be changed and include cyber forces, while others dismiss the idea of warfare in cyber space altogether (e.g. Libicki 2012; Rid 2013; Stone 2013). The US armed forces created a new Cyber Command in 2009 under its Strategic Command, which can be understood as recognition of the growing importance of cyberspace. Cyber warfare involves destroying and disrupting the opponent's information management system in order to gain as much information about the opponent as possible, while, at the same time, denying the opponent the chance to learn about oneself and the state of the opponent's forces. The strategic logic of cyber warfare resembles that of the logic of decapitation in airpower theory (see Chapter 9). By disrupting the opponent's system for information management, you effectively make the opponent blind and therefore a sitting duck. The blindness does not have to include destroying or shutting down the opponent's computers and network, though. It can be equally effective to overload the opponent's systems and thus incur confusion and disorientation (Libicki

2007). Cyber warfare challenges a straightforward distinction between war and peace, since it may be difficult to determine whether or not a cyber attack on bank systems, power plants, water sanitation, and media and government agencies is an intentional attack by a foreign power or expensive pranks by underground hackers (Arquilla & Ronfeldt 2001; Betz 2012; Betz 2011). Strategic considerations in the face of increasing uncertainty about the nature and intentions of an opponent are therefore increasingly challenging (Libicki 2009).

How can the theory of an ever more integrated battle space be related to theories of combined arms? First, it is clear that joint operations are an almost inescapable part of the thinking around RMA and network-based defense. The whole point of the network is that each element works together within a larger system. The network consists therefore of parts, weaker or stronger depending on time and place, which combine to lend the network strength as a whole. Second, the integrated battle space creates expanded and multi-dimensional threats for an aggressor without information superiority, since intelligence on opposition activities and dispositions will be transmitted and acted upon near-instantly. Third, the advantage of maneuver, precision engagement, information handling, and protection and decision capabilities, affords great opportunities to choose the place to engage the opponent, thus putting the aggressor at a disadvantage in all situations. This in turn can result in the latter avoiding combat on symmetrical terms, turning instead to unconventional or asymmetric methods, making success and superiority come at a price.

Conclusions

The aim of this chapter has been to introduce various theories of joint operations. The discussion has presented the overarching theory of combined arms warfare, and this has been used in presenting the thinking on joint operations found in the land-sea, land-air, sea-air, and land-sea-air combinations. Combined arms theory is based on the principle that differing weapon systems, arms, and/or services should be used together in order to maximize the effects of each element and the whole. This applies across all levels of warfare: tactical, operational, and strategic. The theory consists mainly of three elements: first, that joint operations result in the weaknesses of one part being compensated by the strengths in another; second, that joint operations create more dilemmas and greater threats for the enemy since he must consider more functions and deal with greater risks; third, that joint operations allow greater opportunities to force the enemy into situations and onto ground disadvantageous to him and advantageous to one's own forces.

Combined arms theory permeates most thinking on joint operations and is essentially normative, and only indirectly explanatory. As such it gives assertions on which advantages accrue to joint operations (i.e. the three described above), and how to win wars. These assertions are underpinned with empirical examples rather than systematic analyses. The focus of combined arms theory is on the advantages of joint operations without discussing in depth the potential problems of such operations. This may seem remarkable given that joint operations always come with a raft of problems. The most serious is perhaps that joint operations can be counterproductive in that the time needed for coordination and planning of joint operations can outweigh the gain in efficiency. The risk is reduced if the different units of the joint operation are used to working together. Continuous joint training and exercising could therefore reduce the friction of cooperation, although perhaps not entirely eliminate it.

The combined arms theory is to some extent explanatory in its indirect attempt to show that a commander who directs his operations according to the three elements has a greater chance of winning the battle. However, there are problems involved in formulating concrete variables to demonstrate such reasoning, as the theory's form is relatively unspecific. This makes it difficult to analyze how the three elements interact and influence each other in theory. This would merit further study. Finally, it should be noted that although this chapter has considered the thinking on joint operations, and the opportunities and problems which arise when units from differing services jointly execute military operations, the next three chapters will complement this by looking at the theories of single service operations within land, sea, and air.

Questions for discussion

1. What advantages accrue from executing either joint or single service operations?
2. To what extent is it possible to reduce organisational friction between services in joint operations?
3. To what extent is the increased focus on joint operations due to technological advances?
4. How can operations in space and information operations be said to influence joint operations?
5. Is it more important for smaller rather than larger nations to consider joint operations?
6. Is cyber war a reality, fiction, or the future of warfare?

Further reading

Merrill L. Bartlett, (ed.) *Assault from the Sea: Essays on the History of Amphibious Warfare* (Annapolis, MD: Naval Institute Press, 1983).

Robert M. Citino, *Blitzkrieg to Desert Storm: The Evolution of Operational Warfare* (Lawrence: University Press of Kansas, 2004).

James S. Corum, *The Roots of Blitzkrieg: Hans von Seeckt and German Military Reform* (Lawrence, Kansas: University Press of Kansas, 1992).

Ellwood P. Hinman IV, Thomas E. Jahn, & James G. Jinnette, *AirLandBattle 21: Transformational Concepts for Integrating Twenty-First Century Air and Ground Forces* (Farnham: Ashgate, 2009).

Jonathan M. House, *Combined Arms Warfare in the Twentieth Century* (Lawrence, Kansas: University Press of Kansas, 2001).

William A. Owens with Edward Offley, *Lifting the Fog of War* (New York: Farrar, Straus and Giroux, 2000).

Thomas Rid, *Cyber War Will Not Take Place* (Oxford: Oxford University Press, 2013).

Geoffrey Till, *Seapower: A Guide for the Twenty-First Century*, 3rd edn. (London: Routledge, 2013).

Milan Vego, *Joint Operational Warfare* (Newport, RI: U.S. Naval War College, 2008).

7 Land operations

Introduction

There are many theories focusing on land operations. This is a natural consequence of the historical importance of land warfare in deciding the outcome of wars. Both Fuller and Liddell Hart, for example, argued that while air and naval forces were important to the war as a whole, they were still ultimately dependent on success on land (Holden Reid 1998: 209). Even the seapower theorist Corbett (1988: 15–16) recognized that since people lived on land, wars would be settled on land rather than at sea. Similarly, airpower theorist, Robert Pape (2004: 119), agrees that while air power is an important factor in war-fighting, wars are still settled on land. Propositions like these have given land operations a unique position in military theory. This position is not unproblematic, however, since theories concerning land operations are often equated with, or are treated as if they were, general theories of warfare. In the previous chapter (on joint operations), we saw that many theorists have considered sea and air power primarily as supporting elements to the land campaign. This is also indicative of the weight allotted to land operations by military theorists, consciously or subconsciously, in their studies of warfare.

In the last 20 years, warfare on land has manifested itself in large mechanized conflicts such as Iraq 1991 and 2003, as well as in low-intensity and guerrilla wars such as Somalia 1994 and Afghanistan 2001. What makes land warfare distinct in character, unlike air and naval warfare, is its intimate interaction with the terrain and the fact that such wars often take place amongst the people. This environment sets limits but also provides opportunities for those who can use it effectively. Closely related to this issue is the emphasis on time and movement as seen, for example, in maneuver warfare theories, and how this is to be combined with fire and protection. Theories of land warfare can thus be seen as different ways of relating to time, space, fire, movement, and protection (cf. Fuller 1931: 2–4; Kiras 2002; Leonhard 1994; Biddle 2004). What are the causal relationships between these elements? How and why, for example, can time be traded with space, and movement balanced against fire, etc.?

This chapter aims to introduce modern theories of land warfare. Since the military theory of land operations is so vast, it is important to note that the chapter will not capture every theory concerning the inherent challenge of finding the right balance between time, space, fire, movement, and protection. The chapter consists of three parts. The first part introduces the concept of ground operations and includes a comprehensive discussion about means and ends in land operations. It also introduces the conflict between the five basic aspects (or elements) just mentioned. The second part deals with theories of land operations in a state-to-state context. This part compares maneuver warfare and war of attrition as two different logical constructs, and introduces two practical applications of the maneuver warfare concept – the German and Soviet/Russian maneuver warfare schools of thought. One should note that the two practical concepts are applications and together they give an insight into the nuances of how maneuver warfare has been conducted. The third part of the chapter introduces theories of small wars and insurgencies. This part covers theories dealing with three different constellations of actors: national liberation movements and colonial powers, rebels and governments, and civil wars and international intervening forces.

Land operations: concepts, ends, and means

Land operations are designed to hold and control the terrain or possibly to take and defend terrain with the aim of defeating an opponent. The latter can be achieved either by attacking the enemy's will in a psychological sense, or his armed forces in a more physical sense. Controlling territory is of obvious importance. This is where a country's population lives and it is also where the majority of the infrastructure and capacity that supply and feed this population are found. Furthermore, the forces that operate in other arenas (e.g. navies and air forces) regularly depend on the land domain for basing and supply. Hence, control over a territory aims to protect one's own forces, critical infrastructure, or the civilian population. Control over a territory can also be said to be a prerequisite to ensure future successful land operations, since land forces are dependent on base areas for support. The means with which to establish land operational control are mainly land forces, i.e. the armed units that operate on land (Evans 2004: 3–6). It should be pointed out that there is a dearth of research on these problems and related concepts. This may seem odd, given the importance that has been attached to land warfare throughout history. A partial explanation for this may be that many who study war do so in general terms only and view land operations as an implicit part of general warfare. This view has resulted in little examination on a conceptual level of specific questions relating to land warfare. There is, however, a wealth of historical analysis on land war and its development throughout history (e.g. Tuck 2008; Bellamy 1990; Browning 2002; Chandler 2000).

Based on one of the themes presented in Chapter 1, land operations can be described as an exercise of military power related to the land domain (cf. Johnsen 2004: 5–9). It may include brute force, i.e. the physical capture or destruction of the enemy, or include coercion, i.e. forcing an opponent to vacate an area of land or to give up important military capabilities. It may also include deterrence, i.e. compelling the enemy to abstain from land operations aimed against one's own territory. Peacekeeping operations, for example, can be described as an attempt to discourage the parties involved in a conflict from occupying or violating a territorial area (e.g. Bellamy 1997; Parsons 1995; Crocker et al. 1996).

The importance of the elements of land warfare – time, space, fire, movement, and protection – can be further illustrated by a brief discussion of the relationship between offensive and defensive operations. Clausewitz (1993: 357–69; cf. Aron 1985: 146–53; Heuser 2002: 90–102), for example, notes that there is an interaction between offense and defense, where one man's attack becomes the other man's defense. He also claimed, controversially at the time and still in contrast to several other military theorists, that attack is the weaker form and defense the stronger form of war (Sumida 2008). The interaction between offense and defense is often dependent on technology and other factors such as better and faster means of transport (movement), more manageable and more efficient weapons (fire), better communications equipment (time), and stronger fortifications or thicker armor (protection).

The offensive has the advantage due to the morale of the attacker often thought to be positively affected by seizing the initiative and attacking. The attacker also has the discretion to choose the time and place of the battle. The defender, in turn, benefits from the fact that it is usually easier to maintain something than to conquer it. The defender can also take advantage of the terrain and fortifications. An indication that, historically, defense has been considered the stronger strategy is that to be successful, an attacker is said to require a superior force ratio of 3:1 or more. Furthermore, armies fight in an environment where topography, infrastructure, and climate conditions are important factors and create friction. Finally, movement and the maneuvering of armies and units also mean that time is an important factor. Clausewitz (1993: 528) pointed out that the attack has an inherent weakness in that its momentum starts to wane once the attack has commenced, i.e. the attack has a point of culmination after which its power wanes, and the attacking party becomes vulnerable to counter-attack. There are also trade-offs between the elements of land warfare in offense and defense. For example, it is possible to forego the advantage of covered terrain to benefit from the possibility of choosing the time and place of attack. Furthermore, firepower is generally greater in fixed positions than during movement. Maneuvers on the battlefield are thus an attempt to compensate for reduced firepower by concentration of force and increased movement. An attacking commander can thus hypothetically make the assessment, based on the mission, that space and fire are elements worth trading for time and movement in order to achieve a better effect at a point where the enemy is more vulnerable.

The analysis of land operations based on the five elements can also be compared with some of Jomini's (1987) military thought. His main thesis, which was presented at the beginning of the nineteenth century, was that warfare's overriding principle was to concentrate the bulk of the force against an enemy's flank, i.e. muster the troops against a weaker point. He further described a number of operational concepts, the most important one being the relationship between interior and exterior lines of operations. To get one's own army to operate on interior lines and to force the enemy to operate on their exterior lines was perhaps a commander's most important task, said Jomini. The advantage of operating on interior lines was that this (as opposed to the exterior lines) avoided a fragmentation of one's own forces. It also improved the ability to maintain and support these forces, increased speed of movement and achieved concentration of force at the decisive point. As a result, one could use a greater number of one's troops against an opponent's smaller and dispersed forces. Jomini (1987: 473) thus advocated a method that was diametrically opposed to the double envelopment of the enemy and that, instead, the commander, using clever strategic moves and with as little disruption as possible, would achieve local tactical superiority at the decisive point (or points), which often consisted of a flank. In other words, he argued that movement and time were worth more than space, firepower, and protection. Admittedly, this concentration of force against an enemy's weak point was also a way to compensate for the reduced firepower in the attacking units and the reduced protection of the terrain. These examples from Clausewitz and Jomini's military thought serve as an illustration of the function of the five elements in land operations. Hence, they are worth keeping in mind as we embark on theories of maneuver and attritional warfare, as well as theories of guerrilla warfare and counter-insurgency.

Theories of maneuver and attrition warfare

This section presents a number of modern theories on land operations and it begins with a discussion of maneuver and attrition warfare as ideal types, i.e. as logical constructs rather than reflections of reality. After this, we present two applications of maneuver theory – the German and Soviet/Russian maneuver warfare schools of thought – to demonstrate that there are differences in nuance within the theory.

Maneuver and attrition warfare as ideal types

Influenced by the divide between indirect and direct method (see Chapter 4), the second half of the 1970s and onwards saw an analogous distinction made between maneuver warfare and attrition warfare (e.g. Mearsheimer 1983; Lind 1985; Luttwak 1987; Leonhard 1991; Hooker Jr. 1993). As with the indirect and direct methods, maneuver warfare and attrition warfare should be understood as logical constructs as most battles, campaigns, and wars contain elements of both, though in a varying degree dependent on space and time. Furthermore, attritional warfare, sometimes referred to as "industrial warfare," was invented by supporters of maneuver warfare in the 1980s in order to create a counterpart to define their own theories. Attrition warfare thus has few, if any, self-proclaimed followers and is in many respects a caricature. This being said, German military historian Hans Delbrück's (1848–1929) *Ermattungsstrategie* (strategy of exhaustion) demonstrates that there are advocates of attrition (Craig 1986: 341–3) and so is the more current former US colonel Ralph Peters (e.g. Peters 2004). Nevertheless, the concepts have a value in aiding understanding of the aspirations of modern land warfare.

Attrition warfare is, in Luttwak's (1987: 92) words, "waged by industrial methods." The opponent is regarded primarily as a series of targets and success is achieved by "the cumulative effect of superior firepower and material strength." This ultimately leads to the elimination of the opponent's overall fighting capability, or the retreat or surrender of the opponent. The greater the element of attritional warfare, Luttwak maintains, the more routinized will be the techniques for identification of targets, fire, mobility, and supply. Furthermore, an attritional mindset tends to produce tactical decisions which are repetitive and mechanical, and the need for operational thinking becomes limited. Victory is certain if superior firepower can be placed within range of targets such as the opponent's defensive positions and cities, if the firepower possesses the necessary qualitative and quantitative properties, if the enemy is forced to concentrate his forces in order to achieve his objectives (which rarely occurs in, for example, guerrilla warfare), and if material superiority can be maintained. Implicit in this war-fighting concept is that the opponent's countermeasures are to be absorbed rather than avoided. Superior capacity for causing attrition of the opponent, Luttwak (1987: 92) suggests, is thus a condition for victory, and this method of warfare rarely results in easy victories in terms of loss of life and material, in relation to the adversary's strength.

Luttwak maintains that there has never been any pure form of attritional warfare which completely lacked elements of cunning or deception. Warfare has, therefore, never been reduced to a purely industrial process. However, there are examples of war, he argues, which are largely characterized by attrition. Here Luttwak (1987: 92–3) points mainly to the trench wars on the Western Front during World War I, where warfare was often dominated by relatively symmetrical concentrations of artillery. He also mentions the German Air Force, the *Luftwaffe*, which tried to gradually decimate the Royal Air Force (RAF), in the summer of 1940, by constantly seeking aerial combat. This showed a misjudgment by the German High Command concerning their material superiority and capability to reduce the RAF's fighting ability.

Luttwak also describes the anti-thesis of attritional warfare, a concept he calls "relational maneuver," more commonly known as *maneuver warfare*. In this type of warfare the actions are related to the target's character. Instead of destroying the enemy physically, the aim is to reduce the enemy's combat effectiveness by "systemic disruption." By understanding the adversary's war-fighting system as consisting of command structures, doctrine and training, force structure, troop dispositions, and technical aids, it becomes possible to conceive of war-fighting in other ways than decimating the opponent's armed forces. Instead of seeking out and attacking the opponent's strengths, a party using maneuver warfare seeks to avoid them and match its own strengths with the enemy's weaknesses, be they physical, psychological, technical, or organizational in nature (Luttwak 1987: 93–4).

Liddell Hart's discussion of the indirect approach (see Chapter 4) is thus an important basis for modern thinking on maneuver warfare. He argued that strikes in the enemy's rear and the indirect method could achieve dislocation or disruption of the opponent's mental preparation for upcoming operations. Thus the decisive battle has already been won before it has begun (Holden Reid 1998: 47). Luttwak (1987: 93–4) argues that war of attrition is essentially a physical process that guarantees results that are proportionate to the nature and quantity of the effort. Such operations will not yield results unless there is material superiority. Maneuver warfare relies instead (for successful results) on the accuracy by which the enemy's weaknesses have been identified, on the degree of surprise that is achieved, and the precision of the action.

It follows that maneuver warfare can give results that are proportionately greater than the resources deployed and that a nominally inferior party can retire with a win against a nominally stronger adversary. It also means that maneuver warfare can completely fail if the numerically weaker side does not behave in an appropriate manner or faces stronger resistance than anticipated. Hence, war of attrition tends to fail slowly, while success is cumulative. Failures of maneuver warfare, on the other hand, are quick and dramatic, as is the success that can be achieved with relatively limited means. A single mistake, however, can jeopardize the entire operation. Luttwak (1987: 94–5) notes, therefore, that the war of attrition is characterized by high costs and low risks, while maneuver warfare is characterized by low costs and high risks.

One consequence of this reasoning is that for maneuver warfare to succeed it requires accuracy in the identification of enemy's weaknesses, high tempo, and a high level of initiative and precision of action to exploit these weaknesses. Such warfare concepts cannot replace quality with quantity and an increase in troop levels can only be utilized if troops are well trained and combat effective. A significantly larger force would also infringe on the ability to achieve surprise and speed. At such places where contact is made with the enemy, and the accumulated force is applied, it is likely that the direct method will be applied at the tactical level, even if the opponent's strengths usually can be avoided at the operational level (Luttwak 1987: 94–5.) Just as is the case with attritional warfare, Luttwak argues that there is no such thing as pure maneuver warfare, as they both exist on a spectrum and the balance will shift from one to the other on a case by case basis. The more maneuver warfare is applied, he states, the more important becomes the operational level. Luttwak (1987: 95–6) provides some examples of war with a high degree of maneuver warfare and mentions the German *Blitzkrieg* operations against Poland, Norway, Denmark, France, and the Soviet Union (until 1942). The American General Douglas MacArthur's counter-offensive at Inchon in 1950, which cut off the invading North Korean troops, is also an example of such warfare.

Luttwak claims that countries that consider themselves – objectively or subjectively – materially stronger than their enemies tend to stick to attritional warfare. Those who, rightly or wrongly, believe themselves to be materially weaker will instead seek to focus on the enemy's weaknesses, i.e. maneuver warfare. There are exceptions, however, and it sometimes depends on individual personalities or circumstances, such as General George Patton in the summer of 1944 or General MacArthur in Korea 1950. Perceptions of relative strength, moreover, are contextual, since it partly depends on the opponent and the perception of the opponent's strength. Israel, for example, used maneuver warfare in the 1967 Six-Day War, but changed orientation after its success due to its perceived material superiority. The 1973 war is instead, at least initially, better characterized as attritional warfare (Luttwak 1987: 97–8; cf. Kesseli 2001). Choice of operational concept is therefore neither predetermined, nor constant. Even within the same army, it can vary.

Attrition and maneuver warfare, it should be pointed out, do not belong solely at the operational level. Luttwak (1987: 98–9, 108–9), on the one hand, considers the concepts most important at the operational level, because maneuver has the most significant impact on the operational level. This does not imply that attritional warfare is an inferior form of warfare, only that its focus on physical destruction is directly proportional to the task and that any gains will be costly. Clearly, it is beneficial if rapid and inexpensive victories can be obtained at a tactical and operational level through maneuver warfare, but it is dangerous if political and military leaders believe that maneuver warfare is a panacea. Victory in war is rarely easy to achieve and if the two fighting parties are relatively equal in strength and possess the will to defend themselves it can easily lead to attritional warfare. British military historian, Hew Strachan, on the other hand, has also evaluated the two war-fighting concepts and reaches different conclusions than Luttwak. Strachan argues that attritional warfare is rather a consequence of failed maneuver warfare (e.g., on the Western Front during World War I). He suggests that the two concepts do not belong at the same level of war. Attritional warfare is a method that belongs at the tactical level where physical destruction is the goal. Maneuver warfare, on the other hand, belongs at the operational level, where the idea is to be smarter than the opponent, striking against his will and cohesion, through the envelopments and movements on interior lines of operations. According to Strachan, wars of attrition and maneuver warfare are not opposites, but rather methods that exist in parallel and are closely associated (Strachan 2001: 80–99).

The dichotomy of maneuver and attrition is important, since ideal types sharpen our ability to reason but also have the ability to refine the causal links in the theoretical and abstract discussions of war and warfare. Furthermore, the concepts are tools with which to analyze and categorize the extensive empirical data that is available. There are also problems with the concepts of manoeuvre warfare and attritional warfare. First, it is far from certain at which level of war the dichotomy is relevant. Are they comparable or is attrition something that is inherently more important at the tactical and strategic level, while maneuver is inherently more important at the operational level? Second, the gap between the strategic and tactical level in the naval and air domains is narrower than for land warfare. The limited gap that exists at the operational level of the former will thus have consequences for the conduct of maneuver warfare. Therefore, it may not even be useful to talk about a distinction between maneuver warfare and attritional warfare for naval and air forces. Third, it can be problematic to distinguish between maneuver warfare and attritional warfare in wars other than traditional interstate wars. It is, for example, difficult to categorize guerrilla warfare and terrorism as either attritional or maneuver warfare, as they seem to contain elements of both. Guerrilla warfare is usually characterized by indirect method, which indicates that it is maneuver warfare, but at the same time the purpose of guerrilla warfare is commonly understood to be to gradually erode or wear out the regime's legitimacy by continuous attacks over time. The latter indicates that guerrilla war would rather qualify as war of attrition.

Maneuver warfare in practice

In this section we distinguish between two empirical manifestations of maneuver warfare. By demonstrating that there are versions of how maneuver warfare theory can be understood and empirically applied, we can illustrate that there are important nuances in the theory. It is also worth noting that both the German and the Soviet interpreters of maneuver warfare theory emphasize the importance of air power in their respective concepts (cf. Corum 1992; Citino 1999; Condell & Zabecki 2001; Lind 1985; Leonhard 1991; Fast Scott & Scott 1982; Harrison 2001; Glantz 1991a; Glantz 1991b; Simpkin 1985). Finally, it should also be noted that even though we focus on the German and Soviet/Russian interpretations of maneuver warfare, similar nuances can also be identified in the military debate in Britain and the US. The military debate in the US, in particular, has at times been heated and generated from the Gulf War in 1991 to present what could perhaps be said to be a further empirical adaptation (with its small peculiarities) of maneuver warfare (e.g. Ullman & Wade 1996).

Fuller (1926) and Liddell Hart (1932, 1929) argued for increased mechanization of the British Army and a greater degree of coordination between ground and air forces. These thoughts did not, however, have much impact on doctrine and organization. Fuller claimed that future war would be determined using small mechanized armies where separate tank units formed the core that created the breakthrough in the enemy lines. These units would then be able to conduct deep strikes behind enemy lines. Once the enemy's lines for resupply and reinforcements were cut off, the army would then focus its efforts against the trapped enemy forces and achieve victory. Liddell Hart, meanwhile, outlined his strategy of indirect approach to stress the importance of maneuver (cf. Holden Reid 1998; Bond & Alexander 1986; Gat 2001: 531–60, 664–95; Danchev 1998; Bond 1977; Holden Reid 1987). Fuller and Liddell Hart differed somewhat regarding their views on the purpose of mechanization. Fuller strove to create an army that was better prepared and more effective at achieving victory in decisive battle, while Liddell Hart argued that an army through the indirect method, mechanization, and movement could win the decisive battle before it even began (Holden Reid 1998: 13–32). As we can see, these thoughts are similar to modern day reasoning on maneuver warfare. The discussions in both Germany and the Soviet Union were similar but independent of the British debate, but, unlike in Britain, they resulted in widespread organizational changes.

The German maneuver warfare school – or what Stephen Biddle (2004) terms "the modern system" – continuous to be heavily influenced by German experiences of the world wars. Towards the end of World War I, both sides tried to come up with new ways to break the deadlock on the Western Front – the Allied side developed the tank, while the Germans tried its new infiltration and storm-troop tactics (Gudmundsson 1995; Childs 1999; Biddle 2004). Despite tactical success, the Germans failed to secure operational success with their new tactics. However, the seed was sown and two decades later the *Wehrmacht* was in a position to reap the benefits of its tactical innovation. After losing World War I, Germany began integrating these two solutions, and coupled with tactical aviation created *Bewegungskrieg* (literally a "war of movement" that posterity termed *Blitzkrieg* when its effects were witnessed in the war against Poland in 1939). The idea was, as described by Liddell Hart, that an attack would be like water running down a hill side passing over the adversary, where the highest parts of the surface (the strongest enemy positions) would be by-passed while the lowest parts of the surface (the weakest enemy positions) would be submerged and small islands formed. It was then thought that the attacking force would knock out vital hostile resistance nests and facilities, and that a second wave of attacking troops would eliminate the remaining pockets of resistance. Tanks were to be used as spearheads in order to penetrate the enemy lines while the tactical air wing served as mobile and forward artillery. This warfare concept celebrated, at least initially, great triumphs on both the Western and Eastern Fronts.

William S. Lind, one of several recent advocates of the German maneuver warfare school, notes that maneuver warfare is to be regarded as a kind of "military judo," i.e. a method to fight smart and to defeat an enemy through cunning rather than by brute force. For him, the term maneuver is more than just movement. It is a way to gain an advantage over the enemy by always being faster and eventually undermining his ability to remain organized in battle (Lind 1985: 2–6). To demonstrate this, Lind incorporated the US Air Force Colonel John Boyd's (1927–97) model of the Observe, Orient, Decide, and Act (OODA) loop into maneuver warfare theory. Boyd's model was based on his experiences as a fighter pilot during the Korean War. The problem that Boyd tried to solve with the help of his model was why US aircraft, although generally inferior in technical standard, could defeat the Chinese and North Korean MiG-fighters. He found that individuals' behavior in conflict and war could be seen as the repeated cycles of observe-orient-decide-act. The individual (or organization) that could undergo such a decision cycle faster than the opponent would have a decisive advantage, Boyd concluded. This had also been the case in air combat during the Korean war, in which the pilots of US aircrafts had better visibility from the cockpit and were able to switch from one maneuver to another faster than their opponents despite facing aircraft that were able to keep a higher speed, climb faster, and had a superior turning radius. By repeating the OODA loop, the pilot who could react faster would eventually force the opponent into ever more difficult situations in which his behavior became gradually obsolete. The margins between the players would steadily increase and eventually make the slower player increasingly desperate, something that in the end would most likely lead to his collapse (Lind 1985: 2–7; cf. Hammond 2001; Coram 2002; Osinga 2007). Lind (1985: 6–8) suggested that the aim of maneuver warfare is to get through Boyd's decision cycle faster than the opponent, and this places three fundamental requirements on a military organization wishing to conduct maneuver warfare. First, only a decentralized led military force could go through such a decision cycle sufficiently fast. Second, anyone who practices maneuver warfare must accept the confusion and disorder which prevails on the battlefield and use those factors to their relative advantage. Third, all "patterns, recipes, and formulas" must be avoided to prevent the enemy from predicting what we will do next. A principle is thus to have no fixed templates to follow and it can be fatal to study too much military history, according to Lind. Initiatives, variety, and constant innovation are of the utmost importance.

Tactics, therefore, consist of a mental process that includes three "filters" through which the master plan must pass after it has evolved. First, mission-type orders (or mission-directed tactics, see Chapter 4) is an important tool for the commander because it has the degree of decentralization required to rapidly implement Boyd's cycle. Mission-type orders mean that the subordinate is allocated resources and told *what* is to be achieved, but not *how* to achieve it. The latter is up to the subordinate commander to decide. This system is thought to foster subordinate commanders who are able to seize the initiative when possible. While conducting the mission the subordinate should act in accordance with the commander's intent and the stated end result. The subordinate has the discretion to decide what is needed and how he or she will conduct the mission to achieve these objectives. In such a system, the tolerance for errors has to be high. Punishing less successful initiatives will inhibit all initiative, Lind argues (1985: 13–17). The verification is done instead by the intent and aim. Second, it requires concentration of force (Lind uses the word *Schwerpunkt*). This can be a specific location in the terrain or lie with a unit, but may also relate to time. It can be a place where the commander believes a decisive outcome can be obtained. When a unit has been designated main effort, all other units should support it. This is especially important for a nominally outnumbered side, which then still can achieve local superiority (Lind 1985: 17–18). Third, strengths and weaknesses (Lind uses the terms "surfaces and gaps") have to be identified in order to know where to concentrate efforts. For a platoon, company, or battalion commander a likely enemy weakness is a gap in the enemy's deployed force. The way to identify this gap is through combat reconnaissance. The role of reconnaissance is to seek out the enemy's strengths and weaknesses and to determine the direction of the major attack. When troops have succeeded in widening the gap they should push forward and exploit the space behind enemy lines to attack the enemy in the rear. Concurrently, the combat reconnaissance force will continue seeking out the path of least resistance. This force leads "the main force around the enemy surfaces and ever more deeply into the enemy position" (Lind 1985: 18–19).

Meanwhile, the Soviet/Russian maneuver warfare school has its roots in the interwar period, when military theorists such as Tukhachevsky and Triandafillov formulated new concepts for mechanized warfare. Although the Soviet/Russian school has much in common with the German, there are differences (Leonhard 1991: 52–54). First, the Soviet/Russian school employed more detailed orders to subordinates, rather than mission-type orders. This may partly be explained by the political situation that existed in the former Soviet Union, but also by the relatively low educational level of the then Red Army. The legacy of the old Tsarist army, in which initiative and aggressive military commanders at lower levels were not rewarded, also meant that the Soviet/Russian maneuver warfare school did not embrace mission-directed tactics. Detailed orders had the effect of replacing individual initiative, and instead commanders were expected to execute their orders, regardless of the degree of enemy resistance. Second, it emphasized the importance of thorough preparation before an operation. The idea was that careful and detailed planning would ensure success even before the battle commenced, which was partly a by-product of the communist regime's "scientific" ambitions. As the Soviet commander was expected to execute the decisions and achieve the goals the Moscow leadership had set, regardless of the degree of resistance it was therefore important to make careful preparations. This included deep reconnaissance missions, exercises, and security and deception operations. It also meant that logistic support and fire support were deployed in accordance with the plan before the battle began. Any flexibility at the lower levels in executing the plan was not permitted, unlike in the German school. If Soviet military commanders were to demonstrate energy and initiative, this had to take place during the planning phase and before the plan was put into action. In this system, initiatives would occur at the operational level. Third, the Soviet/Russian maneuver warfare school strongly emphasized depth in the operation. This factor was probably a result of the country's geography and experience of warfare on the Russian steppes.

In this type of warfare, focus is mainly on the operational and strategic level rather than on the tactical, and the idea is to maximize each breakthrough by penetrating, with the highest possible speed, as deeply as possible behind enemy lines. This has been described as "deep battle" or "deep operations" (Leonhard 1991: 52–6). In order to facilitate deep operations, some suggested that the army should include a regular force, whose job it was to fix the enemy and create a breakthrough in his lines, and a special follow-on force whose function it was to take advantage of penetrations. This did require that the two forces were differently equipped, that they were organized in different ways and that their doctrines were different. The former should be equipped to handle what we previously termed attrition warfare while the follow-on force should be a unit that was capable of fast maneuvers in depth, i.e. maneuver warfare. The German maneuver warfare school, moreover, only treated momentum in a cursory manner. While the German school of thought also emphasized pace and speed to conduct maneuver warfare, the Soviet/Russian school spoke rather of physical momentum. In this way, the initiative could turn in one's own favor. In military terms, this meant that the mass could be defined as the combat power of a given formation. Speed is defined as the change in a formation's position over time (Leonhard 1991: 57–8; Simpkin 1985: 93–115).

Based on arguments from physics, and with the aim of improving momentum, British Brigadier Richard F. Simpkin concluded that it is better for modern armies to increase speed in the advance rather than to concentrate forces. He also tried to show that if a penetration of the enemy in depth is to be successful, the force that fixates the enemy should be capable of twice the speed of the enemy, while the follow-on force, which is to go deep, should achieve four times the speed of the enemy. This is said to be one of the reasons why Soviet commanders preferred to conduct counter-attacks, and thus exploit the advancing enemy force's movement to increase the relative velocity of the counter-attack. Finally, Simpkin conducts an analysis of "tempo" as an important element in maneuver warfare and notes that the physical speed of a military unit is only one component of what is often described as tempo. Another important factor to determine the operational combat effectiveness of a unit is how quickly the military headquarters can evaluate tasks, make decisions, and convert orders into action (Leonhard 1991: 57–8; Simpkin 1985: 93–115).

Theories of land operations in "small wars" and insurgencies

Guerrilla warfare is hardly a modern phenomenon. The German military historian Werner Hahlweg (1968: 25) tracks guerrilla warfare back to antiquity. Ian Beckett (2001: 1; cf. Asprey 1975; Moran 2001) suggests that the oldest documented record of this kind of warfare is a parchment from 1,500 BC. Since then, guerrilla warfare has played an important part in how various actors have tried to achieve their political and military aims in the land domain. The basic features of it seem to be enduring. By utilizing local knowledge, establishing base areas in remote and difficult terrain, and employing mobility and rapid assault as the main fighting style, the weaker actor could sometimes succeed against a nominally stronger and better equipped opponent. In this part of the chapter, we will leave theories on land operations in large-scale interstate war and turn to "small wars" in three constellations: (1) national liberations movements vs. their colonial masters, (2) rebels vs. governments, and (3) civil war parties vs. international interventions. This structure also roughly coincides with three schools of thought on small wars and insurgencies. The different constellations of actors, as well as differences in contextual normative framework, makes it problematic to automatically assume that a counter-insurgency theory developed from, for example, empirical cases of colonialism, which is easily transferable to the current context. As Stathis Kalyvas (2012: 202–19) argues, our concepts and practices for understanding or dealing with small wars are contingent upon context.

Central to all the three schools of theorizing small wars is the concept of legitimacy. In political science, legitimacy can best be described as an "essentially contested concept" (Holsti 1996: 82–98; Matheson 1987; Hurd 2007; Clark 2005; Lake 2009). This means that the interpretation of the concept, in and of itself, shapes our enquiries and our interpretation of the results. For example, should legitimacy be understood in a relational contractual sense (subjects grant a sovereign the right to rule if the latter provides essential services to the subordinates such as security, well-being, etc.) or should we understand it in other ways? Or should we approach the concept more qualitatively and create a spectrum from "acceptance," to "consent" and "support" in order to conceptualize legitimacy? Yet another issue of contention is what legitimacy is based on. Is it merely a rationalistic provider-beneficiary relationship or are ideational bonds (e.g. religion, nationalism, political ideologies) also important in creating group cohesion around which claims of legitimacy can be made? Or is it gender, family, and kinship bonds that matter as a claim for legitimacy? A final dimension of legitimacy obviously relates to the characteristics, cohesion, and level of the subjects in question. Is, in short, the "consent of the governed" conditioned upon different premises depending on whether the subjects are an ethnic group, a relatively homogenous social-economic group, or a more heterogeneous group? Is it more or less difficult to acquire legitimacy for an actor depending on whether the actor belongs to the same socio-political sphere or is an outsider to the political context? Are there trade-offs between different groups that should consent to a particular strategy? Can a UN Security Council resolution provide local legitimacy among a target population in an intervention or does the resolution impede such legitimacy (while it can of course provide the intervening army with its domestic support), since it is not locally decided?

In virtually all research on small wars and insurgencies, moreover, legitimacy is considered to be the currency in a zero-sum game for the same political space and power. In military planning-terms, small wars are distinguished from regular interstate war mainly by the fact that the parties involved in the small war share the same center of gravity, i.e. the support of the population. This common starting point has led to similar claims from across a wide range of theorists, where the "hearts and minds" of the population are critical and where insurgency and counter-insurgency are 90 percent political and 10 percent military, in comparison to regular war, which is understood to have the opposite share (Kilcullen 2009; Rich & Duyvesteyn 2012).

The zero-sum game occurs because the population cannot give its consent to several parties at the same time, but also because the armed violence contributes to polarizing society and forcing political allegiance from the population. The zero-sum understanding implies that if one party to the ideological conflict loses support, the other side wins that support. Committing atrocities against civilians, for example, therefore becomes problematic on several accounts. Besides the more obvious moral-legal-political implications, there are also apparent strategic disadvantages of massacring the civilians whose support you seek. Despite this, civilians are still targeted under certain conditions. Kalyvas (2006) most importantly suggests that civilian targeting is associated with loss of control over contested pieces of territory. When authorities or rebels move into a contested area, they target collaborators of the opponent. Sharing the same center of gravity also implies that it is relatively easy to disrupt or deny the opponent from gaining legitimacy. Consider, for example, a case where the right to rule is intimately linked to the state as the provider of security. If a rebel movement than carries out a few highly publicized attacks – even on the civilian population itself – it still undermines government legitimacy, since the state could not protect its citizens. The strategy of "bleeding Goliath with 1,000 small cuts," as the story goes, provokes government over-reaction with excessive coercive means, which in turn further pushes the population into the arms of the nominally weaker rebels. We now turn to how this logic plays out among various constellations of actors and the theories that have been developed to better grasp the dynamics of the wars.

Colonial small wars: the first school of small war theories

The first school of small war theories is intimately linked with colonialism and the wars of de-colonization. This has several implications. For example, it is not certain that practices developed by colonial administrative powers to maintain the colonial structures are nor-matively-politically acceptable today. Hence, even if a certain theory of victory in colonial counter-insurgency was bound to end up in success or failure, the opposite may be true today. Moreover, even if much of the theoretical discussion centers on the concept of legitimacy, it is slightly differently understood and the reference object of this legitimacy is different from how we now understand the term.

The word *guerrilla* comes from Spanish, and literally means "a small war." The term began to be used during the Spanish revolt against Napoleon's forces in Spain from 1808 to 1814. Beckett (2001: 12) notes that theories of guerrilla warfare did not become part of mainstream military theory until the early twentieth century. This resulted in little theoreti-cal development amongst classical theorists to better understand this form of warfare. For example, approximately 1 percent of Clausewitz's *On War* deals with guerrilla warfare or "the people in arms," as he called it (Clausewitz 1993: 578–84; Hahlweg 1986: 127–33; cf. Duyvesteyn 2004).

Instead, the first school of theorizing came from those with experience from the colonial wars and so-called "imperial policing" (Moreman 1997). To make its methods more under-standable, guerrilla warfare in so-called wars of national liberation should primarily be seen in the light of its political context. The key features in these conflicts were independence from overseas colonial powers, on the one hand, and on the other hand, maintaining a system of overseas rule. The political context thus meant that the right to rule over a certain geo-graphical space and its inhabitants was at the heart of the conflict. Only to a lesser degree was the claim of legitimacy related to ideological predispositions in terms of allocating resources within the country's economy. Simply put, independence of, for example, China from Japan, was not primarily related to agrarian reforms or the level of taxation, but fundamentally about the creation of an independent Chinese polity. The political context, therefore, made certain strategies of insurgency and counter-insurgency possible. And even if the immediate cause of a rebellion was related to allocation of resources, as soon as the rebels were able to frame the conflict in terms of national liberation/independence, it made certain counter-insurgency strategies less viable.

While Callwell's (1896) and Lawrence's (1922) works are heavily influenced by the colonial era and its values, they nevertheless still aptly captured early British counter-insurgency thought. Callwell underscored the importance of the terrain to the guerrillas and how a protracted conflict often benefits the native party. To defeat the guerrillas, he (1996: 85–96) stressed aggressive behavior and the need to maintain combat contact with the guerrillas, while at the same time denying them freedom of movement through a system of "secure" areas and fortifications. In this way, one could corner off their escape routes, denying the guerrillas advantages from superior mobility and local knowledge. Similarly Lawrence (1997), who is known to a wider audience as Lawrence of Arabia, claimed that the side in a guerrilla war that best utilized mobility, secure base areas, legitimacy, and time, would decide the war to their advantage. According to him, it was therefore just as important for the colonial power as it is for the guerrillas to have secure bases and enlist the support of the population. In this way, the colonial power should separate the population from the guerrillas, which in turn was a prerequisite in order to combat the guerrillas more effectively. During the Malayan emergency, the British furthered this approach and pre-vented the guerrillas from receiving support (through a system of newly built hamlets and through a strict blockade on the borders), while reaching a political solution of Malayan independence. Through this approach – strategic concessions and tactical maneuver – the support of the rebellion dried up and the guerrilla was eventually defeated (Thompson

1966; Mockaitis 1990; Mockaitis 1995; Nagl 2002; Record 2007; Corum 2008). Often, the British mode of counter-insurgency has been heralded as a "minimum-force" approach and positioned against repression (e.g. Kitson 1971). This has sometimes led to the assumption that the British mode of counter-insurgency hardly includes the use of force. Lately, several researchers have undermined this burgeoning myth and instead stressed that British colonial policing included repression, torture, and brutality (Bennett 2013; Mumford 2011).

The French, too, realized early on that political, economic, and military efforts must go hand-in-hand to successfully fight a guerrilla movement. For various reasons, however, they tended to emphasize the military dimension more than the early British theorists. During the 1840s, Thomas-Robert Bugeaud (1784–1849), who had witnessed first-hand Napoleon's failed campaign in Spain, developed the French colonial strategy of *tache d'huile* (literally "oil spots"). It was based on a gradual expansion of their empire from well-fortified and secure base areas. In frustration over the failed war in Algeria in the 1840s, despite French troops controlling the larger cities, Bugeaud made the raid a tool for success. In practice, the raid meant that French troops had free reins to carry out whatever atrocity against the Arabic population they wished: by destroying crops, slaughtering cows and goats, and through widespread looting, they meant to undermine public support for the guerrillas while at the same time preventing vital supplies from reaching the guerrilla. This hardline approach enjoyed initial success (Porch 1986), but also led to a series of renewed uprisings and instability in Algeria until its independence. When the French tried the same strategy in the war in Indochina 1947–54, their attempts to divide the population proved unsuccessful and they also failed to defeat the enemy militarily from their few strategic bases (Beckett 2001: 110–17). French failure in Indochina paved the way for the implementation of a new strategy – *guerre révolutionnaire* – in the war in Algeria from 1954 to 1962. The new strategy identified the initial stage of the uprising as the guerrilla's weakest point. As a consequence, *guerre révolutionnaire* emphasized that one of the key elements in combating guerrillas was to separate the population from the guerrillas to prevent recruitment and support. This was accomplished through a comprehensive program of relocation to robust "self-defense villages." Militarily, the new strategy still relied on patrols, attempts to restrict the guerrilla's freedom of movement, and intelligence gathering through systematic torture. Beckett (2001) states that *guerre révolutionnaire* was a military success, but ultimately the war in Algeria led to excessive political and economic costs for the French government. After a failed coup against the French President Charles de Gaulle, by French officers who were stationed in Algeria, negotiations began with the Algerian guerrillas and the French colonial rule in Algeria was soon dismantled (Horne 1977; Trinquier 1964; Galula 2006).

In theories on wars of national liberation, Mao Tse-tung's (1893–1976) theory on revolutionary warfare occupies a special position. We have already addressed certain elements of Mao's thought in Chapter 3, but there is reason to return to his reasoning. The three stages in Mao's theory of revolutionary warfare – strategic defensive, strategic equilibrium, and strategic offensive – reflected the different conditions of the revolutionary uprising that was based on variations in time, legitimacy, relationship of forces, and terrain conditions. Mao claimed that guerrilla warfare was an addition to, and a necessary step towards, the conventional force that was necessary to finally defeat the stronger party. The ultimate aim of defeating the opponent through strength implies shared views with, for example, Clausewitz's theories on large-scale conventional warfare (Peralta 1990). What have traditionally been termed guerrilla warfare tactics were thus, according to Mao, only a means, and not most important for winning the war. In his understanding, revolutionary warfare is not entirely synonymous with guerrilla warfare. Through retreats and continuous ambushes, without occupying terrain, Mao was able to withdraw gradually and avoid defeat. This tactic was designed for a protracted conflict in which the revolutionary side could mobilize and recruit new units. To encourage this, Mao emphasized the nationalistic aspect of the campaign (in the fight against Japan), and by formulating social and economic reform based on communist ideology. An important part in gaining people's trust was to offer a credible alternative to the sitting government. It was therefore important to build a functioning civic administration with schools and healthcare in the regions they controlled (e.g. Beckett 2001: 70–85; Kiras 2002; Taber 2002; Shy & Collier 1986). All this led the French Vietnam expert Bernard Fall (1998) to comment that: "When a country is being subverted it is not being outfought, it is being outadministered." In Vietnam, Vo Nguyen Giap developed his own version of revolutionary war that had much in common with Mao's theories. Giap (1962; 1970) was also a supporter of the idea that guerrilla warfare was only an addition to conventional warfare, the latter being initiated when the required strength had been reached. However, rather than a linear process, Giap aspired to wage all three stages of revolutionary warfare simultaneously (but in different regions of the operational theatre).

Internal insurgency and counter-insurgency: the second school of small war theories

The second school of small war theorists focuses on the seemingly perennial debate between legitimacy and brutality. In short, much of the debate during the colonial wars had revolved around the issue of how much violence was necessary to combat a rebellion. On the one hand, there were those who suggested that excessive force to deal with current troubles would deter future uprisings and therefore solve both short-term and long-term problems (e.g. Merom 2003). On the other hand, there were others who suggested that the hearts and minds of the population could only be won if the use of force was kept at a bare minimum and the rule of law strictly adhered to (e.g. Arreguin-Toft 2005). It is important to remember that both sides in the debate naturally understood the use of force to be part of the solution of how to subjugate the colonials. Instead, what changed for this generation of theorists was that they focused on a different actor constellation. These theories removed the colonial power from the analysis and understood the problem as inherently internal.

Heavily influenced by the theories of revolutionary war, post-colonial rebels seemingly followed strategies sharing several key elements when attempting to overthrow governments. First, the use of force against government facilities must not endanger recruitment opportunities. The rebels will, at least initially, be nominally weaker than the government and replacing casualties and increasing their forces will be imperative for the rebel side. Thus, the use of force should not undermine recruitment.

Second, when targeting government facilitates, the center of attention should be on disrupting the government's ability to provide public goods. It is when the government is perceived as incapable of providing basic services that rebels can step up their political agenda and set forth their version of an administrative system to tax the population (thus increasing revenue, which further increases the likelihood that they can increase their military power), and legitimately provide basic services to the population, thus earning its trust and loyalty. Attacks, in and of themselves, undermine governments' claims of being able to provide security. Hence, means and end coincide. This basic observation was used by Ernesto "Che" Guevara in his theory of the *Foco*, i.e. guerrillas should act as a vanguard in anticipation of the naturally ensuing mass revolution. In Guevara's interpretation (Beckett 2001: 169–79; Shy & Collier 1986: 815–62; Guevara 1969; Molloy 2001), it is important to point out that he relied less on existing public support than common insurgent strategy. Instead, his idea presupposed that the people would join the rebellion when "the true face and corrupt face" of the government showed itself through excessive force and repression as a response to the initial guerrilla attacks. Hence, support would follow violence, rather than violence being possible through existing support.

Third, rebel targeting should focus on government weak areas. Due to the nominally weaker nature of the rebel movement in comparison with the stronger government army, guerrillas should strike against weak spots and instead maximize their advantages of being agile, being able to choose the time and place for attack, and being able to escape. The kinship of insurgency theory to Liddell Hart's strategy of the indirect approach is obvious. For the government, this means that there are a number of dilemmas to deal with. On the one hand, it cannot necessarily strike out with excessive repression and brutality since that feeds into the story that the guerrillas try to provoke. On the other hand, if it remains passive, rebels can reinforce the claim that the government does not care about its people.

Fourth, creating legitimacy for the insurgency or the government is different under these conditions than under colonialism. Most importantly, it is not possible to earn loyalty by referring to claims of independence from a colonial power. Depending on political context – again – rebel fractions can still earn a following by appealing either to ideology or to ethnic identity (and possibly secession from an existing state for the ethnic group). Since ethnic conflict is a matter of the relationship between the state and its existing boundaries and population, and ideological internal conflicts are about how the country should be governed, warfare in conflict with ethnic overtones has a somewhat different dynamic than ideological civil wars. The main difference is that the parties do not share the same center of gravity. To that end, warfare in ethnic conflicts therefore resembles warfare between states more than the warfare conducted in ideological internal conflicts. Since popular support is not possible to influence to the same degree as it is in ideological conflicts, there is little need for the warring parties in an ethnic conflict to care about winning the "hearts and minds" of a neutral, undecided population. The reason for this of course is the difficulty of changing ethnic identity, as opposed to changing political views. This situation holds true even if we understand ethnic identity as changeable, because violence along ethnic lines polarizes society and suggests that you cannot as easily change identity (Kaufmann 1996a, 1996b).

If the strategy in an ethnic conflict aims to utilize military means to gain territory that coincides with a group's demographic and geographical spread, it is often logical (although morally reprehensible) that "ethnic cleansing" forms part of the operational art in an ethnic civil war. It is by dislodging the counterparty's ethnic kinsmen from their territory, whilst expanding one's own territory to include demographic "pockets" of its own population living in regions dominated by the counterparty's ethnic group, that tactical "victories" can lead to strategic success (Gow 2003: 172–98). While ideological conflicts concern the population's consent to the regime's policies, the legitimacy problems in ethnic conflict are characterized by a lack of what Holsti (1996: 82–98) describes as "horizontal legitimacy." This means that states are often composed of different political communities, and in states where these communities do not fit together in relation to the geographical boundaries they tend to have problems with horizontal legitimacy. In practice, therefore, the states where segments of the population (communities) do not give their consent are considered to have a low horizontal legitimacy.

Internationalized civil wars: the third school of small war theories

The third school of small wars-theorizing centers on cases of outside interventions in what is largely internal armed conflict, but – critically – where there is no colonial interest present. This presents new dimensions to the contest for legitimacy. Whereas insurgent groups are able to use nationalism in their claim for legitimacy, much like they could during colonial wars, incumbent governments relying on the presence of international forces face similar challenges as classic civil war uprisings, in so far as having to compete on unequal terms with rebels is concerned. The terms are unequal, as can be recalled, since the burden of proof in terms of providing public goods is on the government, while rebels simply have to disturb security, welfare, and trade in order to deny the government legitimacy. The international intervening forces, moreover, face the challenge of how to build legitimacy for the incumbent government and to a lesser extent, for themselves. Naturally, this means that for the international forces, the situation is not analogous to colonial uprisings, when the overall strategic aim was to maintain colonial rule. This seemingly puts the US war in Vietnam in the same overall category as the US war in Iraq or Afghanistan. Although there are striking similarities in US strategy in both these cases (e.g. phases of gradually transferring responsibility of security to local forces), it does not necessarily mean that the conflicts have similar incompatibilities, political purposes, or use similar means (Biddle 2006; Record & Terrill 2004; Brigham 2006; Gardner & Young 2007).

During the last few decades, internationalized civil wars have increasingly been understood as "complex," insofar as they contain a multitude of actors sometimes transgressing Western understandings of the boundaries between civil and military, or public and private. Regular intervening forces share the same operational space with private military companies, non-governmental organizations, international organizations, and national – possibly re-constituted – units. Add to this plethora of organizations the lack of unity of command and the difficulties of achieving strategic aims against insurgents, and the notion of "complexity" is understandable. The complexity is also seen in the very ambitious strategic aims of modern interventions. Rather than just separating two warring parties that already have agreed upon a peace treaty (i.e. peacekeeping), current interventions tend to have more far-reaching objectives of enforcing peace where there is none and building states where the necessary preconditions are more or less non-existent. Under these conditions, the relationship between tactics, operations, and strategy too becomes complex.

In order to make some of these complexities less daunting, Ivan Arreguin-Toft (2007) has suggested an analytical framework highlighting the diversity of actors and the potential trade-offs between them. Any intervening power, in short, needs to pay attention to five different target audiences – the domestic home opinion, its own forces, neutrals (both international and local), the opponent's forces, and the opponent's support base – for its strategy and tactics. Each strategy has a relative degree of utility for each of the target audiences, but no strategy can be optimal for all the target audiences. For example, a strategy intended to maximize the legitimacy of one's own forces would center on troop security. Such a strategy would imply tactics where the forces operated heavily armored, calling in air-strikes or artillery whenever one would be in doubt of the intentions of a group one encounters, and so on. Although such tactics would probably decrease the number of "blue" casualties and thereby be popular among one's own forces and possibly parts of one's own domestic support, it would in all likelihood also imply a higher number of civilian casualties. Hence, although popular among one's side, it would be increasingly unpopular among the other three target audiences. By using target audience analysis, it is possible to explain why strategies do not always get the intended results. One can, for example, understand the complexities facing an intervening force in state-building operations (e.g. Angstrom & Duyvesteyn 2010). On the one hand, the intervening force needs to create legitimacy for itself in order to gain the locals' trust and thereby better intelligence about the insurgents. On the other hand, by creating legitimacy for itself, it undermines the incumbent government's claim for legitimacy.

Using target audience analysis, it is also possible to outline the strategic logic of UN peace-keeping and peace enforcement. The three classical criteria for peacekeeping operations – consent from the parties, impartiality, and use of force for self-defense purposes – for example, can be understood as a strategy to maximize legitimacy from several of the target audiences. As a military strategy, peacekeeping is about deterring the formerly warring parties from re-starting hostilities by controlling the implementation of the peace agreement. By positioning themselves between the parties, peacekeepers can, using their right to self-defense, pose a credible threat against the warring parties for attempts to defect from the peace agreement. However, the principles are also about creating legitimacy. The domestic population of the intervener can support the operation since it seemingly is there to be a constructive force for peace. By insisting upon consent from the local parties before intervening, peacekeepers are also able to start from a position of strength. Still, even if most peacekeeping missions succeed (Fortna 2008; Daniel et al. 2008; Diehl & Druckman 2010), there are also failures. The degree of success has so far been explained by lack of political mandate and committed resources (Doyle & Sambanis 2006), organizational problems (Autesserre 2010; Howard 2008), lack of credible commitments (Howard 2008: 21–7), so-called spoilers (Steadman 1997; Nilsson & Soderberg-Kovacs 2011), and lack of sufficient number of soldiers and lack of training (Kreps 2010). Larsdotter (2011) also highlights that much research operates with different measures of success as well as different methodologies, which further complicates comparisons of results.

As in regular interstate land operations, there is fierce debate regarding to what extent numerical preponderance, technology, or maneuver can explain tactical outcomes in externally conducted counter-insurgencies. It could, for example, be claimed that Western technology provides an advantage in terms of surveillance, communications, and firepower, making Western forces superior to its opponents. This technological superiority operates in two ways. While gradually wearing down the insurgents through strikes, it also operated as a tool to decapitate the Taliban leadership. In particular, drone strikes against the leadership were thought to paralyze the Taliban in Afghanistan and increasingly too in Pakistani border areas by disrupting the command and control chain (Price 2012; Johnston 2012). Another way of increasing firepower is of course through more "boots on the ground." Numerical preponderance has also been a central idea in both Iraq and in Afghanistan through the so-called "surges" and through building stronger local armies (Grissom 2013). The effect of the surge in Iraq is, however, questioned by some. Instead of the quick increase in number of US soldiers being the explanation of the decreasing violence in Iraq, it has been pointed out that the surge coincided with changes in the distribution of power in local dynamics of the conflict, in particular between the Sunni and Shia, and that it was these changes that caused the Sunni to align with the US against the Iraqi insurgents. This suggests that the surge was merely a correlate, rather than a cause of stabilization in Iraq (Biddle et al. 2012). On the side of using more force in counter-insurgency, Merom (2003) suggests that the nature of democracy explains why democracies win interstate wars, but loses small wars (cf. Brown, et al. 2011). The idea is that people will agree to be mobilized if the opponent is perceived to threaten the existence of the state. But if the enemy is a national liberation movement on the other side of the globe the same people will not allow excesses of violence from their own units, something that is held to be needed to win in these conflicts. Some also suggest that the degree of organizational learning or ability to adapt during war is key to winning these wars (e.g. Nagl 2002; Ucko 2009; Simpson 2012; Egnell & Ucko 2013). Rather than stressing how the parties fight, Mack (1975) suggests that the key problem in interventions and asymmetric conflicts is that the parties have different aims. The intervening side will not have the same interest in pursuing the war as the local parties. The locals will therefore be able to cope with losses, sustain their effort over a prolonged period, and thereby have a comparative advantage.

Although winning the "hearts and minds" of the local population in, for example, Afghanistan (including maintaining the support of those already committed, convincing the neutrals to increase the support, and changing the minds of those helping the Taliban) may have seemed easy in theory, it was clearly laden with problems, and the theories that underpin the various strategies cannot unambiguously explain the outcome of interventions in civil wars. Legitimacy is also notoriously difficult to measure and predict. Strategies and tactics can therefore easily have effects other than those intended.

Conclusions

Theories of land operations constitute an extensive area of research and study. What has been conveyed in this chapter is more akin to a snapshot of the contemporary theoretical debate on military land operations rather than presenting all the military theories of land warfare. The chapter has attempted to introduce modern theories of land warfare and how the construct of these theories has dealt with the inherent problem of time, space, fire, movement, and protection. The first part of the chapter dealt with theories of land operations that are mainly of interest to an interstate context. The second part of the chapter introduced three schools of thought on guerrilla warfare and counter-insurgency, where the interaction between rebels, government, and (in some cases) intervening powers takes center stage. The chapter has also discussed methodological issues. For example, we pointed out that there is a problem of interpretation in many of the classical theorist's texts. Since it is not always perceived as essential to make the distinction between land warfare as such and warfare in general, it is possible to interpret these theories in different ways.

Theories of land operations, as explanatory military theory, can be said to have made valuable contributions to the study of war and warfare. The two logical constructs, maneuver warfare and attritional warfare, can, combined with a differentiation between the different levels of warfare, improve the ability to understand complex relationships in land war and make them more accessible. However, there is a tendency to equate successful war with maneuver warfare and unsuccessful war with attritional warfare. The examples of maneuver warfare expressed in the literature are almost exclusively those wars which ended with a victory for the side that carried out maneuver warfare, but this is invariably done in retrospect, and not as an explanation for the outcome of the war.

Theories on land operations, as normative theory, give us good insights into the relevant factors for the conduct of land warfare. The five land warfare elements – time, space, fire, movement, and protection – can be said to illustrate the dilemmas that practitioners face when carrying out an operation. To what extent can space be traded for time and fire for movement? Is such reasoning based on a passive opponent? To what extent can one's actions be neutralized by the opponent changing focus from one element to another? The five elements are important for understanding the trade-offs in land warfare and the allocation of scarce resources, but simple and credible answers about how to win wars are difficult to find. For this, land operations are far too complex.

Questions for discussion

1. How do time and space relate to one another in various forms of land operations?
2. Is public support more important in wars of attrition than in guerrilla warfare?
3. What are the differences between terrorism, guerrilla warfare, and civil war?
4. Is mission-type command necessary for maneuver warfare and guerrilla warfare?
5. Are there hidden assumptions about quantity when reasoning about maneuver warfare and attritional warfare that make these theories problematic for small states?
6. What different roles does center of gravity play in maneuver warfare and small wars?

Further reading

Stephen Biddle, *Military Power: Explaining Victory and Defeat in Modern Battle* (Princeton, NJ: Princeton University Press, 2004).

David G. Chandler, *The Art of Warfare on Land* (London: Penguin, 2000).

Robert Egnell & David Ucko, *Counterinsurgency in Crisis: Britain and the Challenges of Modern Warfare* (New York: Columbia University Press, 2013).

Richard D. Hooker (ed.) *Maneuver Warfare: An Anthology* (Novato, CA: Presidio Press, 1993).

Edward N. Luttwak, *Strategy: The Logic of War and Peace* (Cambridge, MA: Belknap Press, 1987).

Stathis Kalyvas, *The Logic of Violence in Civil Wars* (Cambridge: Cambridge University Press, 2006).

Paul Rich & Isabelle Duyvesteyn (eds.), *The Routledge Handbook of Insurgency and Counterinsurgency* (London: Routledge, 2012).

Emile Simpson, *War From the Ground Up: Twenty-First Century Combat as Politics* (Oxford: Oxford University Press, 2012).

Hew Strachan, *The First World War: Volume 1: To Arms* (Oxford: Oxford University, Press 2003).

8   Sea operations

Introduction

Around 600 BC, the Chinese thinker Lao Tze said that "there was nothing in the world more soft and weak than water, yet for attacking things that are firm and strong, nothing surpasses it." Some hundred years later, Greek general Themistocles stated that "he who commands the sea, has command of everything," and in 1597 the English Renaissance philosopher Sir Francis Bacon concluded that "he that commands the sea is at great liberty, and may take as much or as little of the war as he will" (Tangredi 2002: 117; cf. Rodgers 1967; Harding 1999; Sondhaus 2001; cf. Heinl 1966: 288). Modern thinkers on the subject have not significantly revised these positions, but continue to emphasize the importance of sea power. About 70 percent of the earth's surface consists of water and over 90 percent of the world's international trade, in both volume and weight, is transported by sea. Moreover, a majority of the world's cities and population centers are located at or near the coast. The resources and communications that the sea makes possible are simply essential to the prosperity of mankind and life on earth.

But what is seapower and how is it related to other forms of military power? What are the ends and means? How can naval forces be employed and how can wars at sea be won? The purpose of this chapter is to introduce the theories of seapower and to describe how naval forces are used in sea operations in times of war and peace (cf. Till 2013; Lambert 2010; Tangredi 2002; Speller 2008). As with other chapters in this book, the guiding theme is the dualistic character of military theory – its normative and explanatory qualities. What explanatory power has seapower theory and what normative statements are provided for ways to win such wars? The chapter begins with a discussion of how seapower can be defined, what its ends and means are, and briefly how seapower differs from other forms of military power. Since war is commonly understood as a political instrument, the chapter continues with a discussion of the use of naval forces in peacetime and for political purposes, something usually referred to as naval diplomacy. In this section we place the use of seapower into its political context. We then move on to a discussion of the military uses of naval forces in war. This is facilitated through the introduction of a central concept in classical seapower theory, namely "command of the sea," or "sea control" as it is often called in modern parlance. While the concept may be viewed as the primary objective in naval operations, it is also an important means in order to realize the ultimate strategic purpose, that is, to win wars. In the sections that follow we discuss methods for securing, exercising, and disputing command of the sea. Here we present the problems involved concerning decisive battles and blockades as methods to secure command of the sea, maritime power projection and use of sea-lines of communications as methods for exercising command of the sea, and finally, fleet-in-being, war on commerce, and coastal defense as methods for disputing command of the sea.

Seapower

In general terms, seapower can be defined in two ways – a broad definition that encompasses political, economic, commercial, and military aspects, and a narrower one, which primarily focuses on its military use in war. Alfred Thayer Mahan famously argued in his classical treatise of seapower that the concept included not only the naval forces controlling the sea by force of arms, "but also the peaceful commerce and shipping from which alone a military fleet naturally and healthfully springs, and on which it securely rests" (Mahan 1890: 28). Here, the economic and commercial aspects are clearly visible. Sam Tangredi (2002: 114) also employs a broader definition:

> [T]he combination of a nation-state's capacity for international maritime commerce and utilization of oceanic resources, with its ability to project military power into the sea, for the purposes of sea and area control, and from the sea, in order to influence events on land by means of naval forces.

In this latter definition, the concept describes an ability not only to use naval forces in war but also to control international trade, its maritime communications, and the exploitation of naval forces as a political/diplomatic instrument in peacetime. Civilian and commercial aspects of seapower include guarding and policing the coast, law-enforcement, commerce and trade, activities in ports, natural resources under water such as oil and gas, and fishing.

A narrower definition of seapower is provided by British scholar Eric Grove (1990: 3), who describes it as "a military concept, [and] the form of military power that is deployed at or from the sea." Here, seapower is something to be employed and no distinction is made whether such forces are used in peacetime or war. Nor are any of the economic and civil aspects of seapower included. In this chapter, seapower shall be understood as the political and military use of naval forces in war and peace. Seapower thus becomes a resource or capability that is employed in war and peace for political and military ends. Seapower may also represent a state or state-like entity where the sea will significantly affect its existence and political ambition. Naval forces, in turn, means armed platforms and troops operating at and from the sea (naval ships and marine infantry, etc.), below the surface (submarines, etc.), and in the air above the sea and the shoreline (naval aviation).

In order to exercise seapower we first need an idea of what it will be used for and how, i.e. an idea of the ends and means involved. In short, we need an idea concerning strategy. Mahan (1991: 24) argued that naval strategy has "for its end to found, support, and increase, as well in peace as in war, the seapower of a country." For him, naval strategy was a means to support a state's seapower, which in turn worked to ensure national security and prosperity. In his classic book *Some Principles of Maritime Strategy* (originally published in 1911), Julian Corbett distinguished between maritime strategy and naval strategy. For him, maritime strategy was the principles that guided the conduct of a war where the sea played an important part. It also determined the role the navy had to play in the overall strategy and in relation to forces from other armed services. Naval strategy, on the other hand, was only that part of the maritime strategy which determined the employment of the naval forces (Corbett 1988: 15; cf. Widen 2012: 85–7). Maritime strategy, therefore, was according to Corbett, a more general concept relating to the overall use of a state's forces in war, a war in which the sea played a major role. Naval strategy, on the other hand, related to the sole use of naval forces in the context of this overall strategy. As apparent, Corbett was mainly interested in the role of seapower in the war, rather than as a political instrument in peace.

Seapower provides a range of strategic options. It represents the part of military power that takes place at sea, from the sea, or in connection with the sea. The employment of brute force in the naval context consists of using naval forces to destroy or block opposing forces by violent means. Naval coercion involves using threats of violence to force the opponent to do things that favor one's interests, while naval deterrence involves the utilization of naval forces to convince the opponent to refrain from actions that threaten one's interests. The Swedish naval thinker, Captain Daniel Landquist (1891–1962), argued that naval warfare in a strategic sense, unlike war on land, was mainly carried out in an area that lacked ownership, which, according to international law, could not be permanently and completely claimed by any one actor (Landquist 1935: 20). In these waters, also, neutral countries operated commercial ships and naval forces. The principle of an ownerless sea applies in both peace and war and constitutes the foundation for the idea of the "freedom of the seas." Mahan (1991: 27) has described this domain in somewhat more poetical terms:

> [A] wide common, over which men may pass in all directions, but on which some well-worn paths show that controlling reasons have led them to choose certain lines of travel rather than others. These lines of travel are called trade routes; and the reasons which have determined them are to be sought in the history of the world.

Although there is an increasing trend towards "territorialization" of the seas, as evident, for example, by new techniques to exploit natural resources from the seabed, the idea of the freedom of the seas is still dominant.

The theatre of naval operations often has characteristics similar to a flat surface and does not offer opportunities (at least not on the high seas) for defensive positions and obstacles, to the same extent as is common on land. In the littorals, in narrow waters, and archipelagos, there are choke-points, islands, and shoals that affect the possibilities for maneuver and passage. This difference between the naval and land theatres of war has contributed to some thoughts on the pros and cons of offensive versus defensive types of warfare. Furthermore, naval warfare can take place over wide areas rather than along narrow frontlines, as is often the case in ground warfare, although naval bases may be viewed as a natural starting point for operations and an aim for a possible retreat (Landquist 1935: 124; cf. Lindberg & Todd 2002).

Naval diplomacy

Although naval diplomacy – or "gunboat diplomacy" as some prefer to call it – has been used widely by rulers throughout history, it has only rarely been treated by the classical theorists of seapower (Widen 2011: 717–21). Mahan and Corbett, for example, were primarily interested in the use of seapower in war rather than as a diplomatic instrument in peacetime. These "gaps" have been partly remedied by some modern thinkers active in the nuclear era, who saw the value of more limited naval operations. The threat of nuclear retaliation and possible escalation tended to increase the utility for limited operations short of war. Gorshkov (1979: 247–8), for example, claimed that:

> [D]emonstrative actions by the fleet in many cases have made it possible to achieve political ends without resorting to armed struggle, merely by putting on pressure with one's own potential might and threatening to start military operations. Thus, the fleet has always been an instrument of the policy of the states, an important aid to diplomacy in peacetime.

The scope and need for naval diplomacy can be said to have increased even more after the Cold War and thoughts in this regard have been formalized in British and American maritime doctrines. In the US Navy and Marine Corps jointly developed doctrine, *Forward . . . From the Sea*, from the mid-1990s, it was found that:

> [N]aval forces are an indispensable and exceptional instrument of American foreign policy. From conducting routine port visits to nations and regions that are of special interest, to sustaining larger demonstrations of support to long-standing regional security interests . . . U.S. naval forces underscore U.S. diplomatic initiatives overseas.

Changes in the international environment during the last decade and a half have not altered the relevance of this statement. What about the theories of naval diplomacy? Following seminal works on deterrence and coercion (e.g. Schelling 1966; George & Smoke 1974) during the Cold War, research on naval diplomacy blossomed under a new generation of seapower theorists (e.g. Martin 1967; Cable 1971; Luttwak 1975; Booth 1977). Perhaps the most widely read of these is British diplomat James Cable. He (1994: 14) defined "gunboat diplomacy" as

> the use or threat of limited naval force, otherwise than as an act of war, in order to secure advantage, or to avert loss, either in the furtherance of an international dispute or else against foreign nationals within the territory or the jurisdiction of their own state.

According to Cable, the concept thus implies a use of, or threat of using, restricted naval force in situations not involving an act of war, and in order to secure and prevent loss of certain values. These forces are thus means employed in international disputes with foreign powers on their territory. Gunboat diplomacy is therefore an activity occurring in the gray zone between war and peace. It serves political purposes short of war with naval forces as the means. Cable's argument clearly echoes Clausewitz's thoughts about war as a political instrument. Cable distinguishes between four different types of gunboat diplomacy:

- "definitive force," which attempts to create a fait accompli by depriving the opponent of parts of his resources. This corresponds closest to brute force. A well-known example of the definitive type, which Cable highlights, is the North Korean capture of the intelligence vessel, USS Pueblo in 1968. In this case the U.S. government was presented with a fait accompli, forcing them to choose between war (or threat of war), to negotiate with North Korea, or simply to yield (Cable 1994: 15–33).
- "purposeful force," which explicitly attempts to persuade an opponent to change its policy (Cable 1994: 33). The Cuban missile crisis in October 1962 is a clear example of an operation in which one party tried to force a change in behavior through threats and the use of naval forces. This crisis arguably highlights aspects of military power that can be likened to coercion and persuasion.
- "catalytic force," which aims to influence an opponent through naval presence, rather than to induce him to perform a particular action (Cable 1994: 42). Here we can observe a more subtle form of deterrence. The US Navy's presence in the Persian Gulf during the Iran-Iraq war of 1980–88 was not only a means to protect shipping in the area, but also an operation aimed at limiting hostilities and to protect US allies in the region.
- "expressive force," which aims to reinforce the impressions of one's own policy, but without specifically stating what is envisaged by the operation. This type differs from

the "purposeful" by its larger element of ambiguity in terms of objectives and the stated mission (Cable 1994: 15–64). Here, one can neither speak of brute force, coercion, or persuasion, but possibly a subtle form of deterrence. A US aircraft carrier battle group that leaves harbor a day after a military coup has taken place in a South America country, steering south, could well serve as an example of such a subtle signal of American policy and interests in the region.

Cable's categorization has merits but also shortcomings. For one, he clearly distinguishes between the different objectives of naval diplomacy. No doubt a single operation is likely to contain phases where several of these types exist or even co-exist. But Cable's conceptual framework also has problems. First, the model only cites the different objectives that exist in naval diplomacy, and not the means to be employed. For example, to what extent do the ends in such operations determine the means and vice versa? Second, the model is somewhat one-dimensional since it simply describes a subject-object situation which does not take into account the possible counter-moves by the opposite party and the interaction that this entails.

What components is naval diplomacy made up of and how do these differ? According to British scholar Geoffrey Till, naval diplomacy is a phenomenon located somewhere in the spectrum of expeditionary operations, where the aim is often to conquer or occupy a territory, and humanitarian operations, where the goal is to help states and civilians affected by natural disasters, such as famine, drought, and diseases. Naval diplomacy is therefore different, he suggests, from expeditionary operations with their higher degree of threat and deterrence and full-scale military operations with military strategic purposes. It is also different from humanitarian operations which aim to help a state or its people in need, rather than to force them to do something (Till 2013: 225–8).

Naval diplomacy is largely based on the idea of naval presence in those areas where important interests are at stake. The value of naval presence consists of the potential it creates for those in power. Naval forces have a number of competitive advantages, according to Till, which other military instruments of power lack, partially or wholly. Because they can travel in international waters, they are often perceived as less provocation for the local population than ground or air combat units. Furthermore, naval forces have strategic reach, mobility, and flexibility that makes them effective as an instrument of political power. He therefore argues that

> maintaining a maritime presence in an area increases national readiness, contributes to the capacity to signal strategic interest, offers a means by which the strategic environment may be shaped to national advantage and facilitates the activities that may need to follow.
>
> (Till 2013: 229)

According to Till, the presence of naval ships on the seas creates the conditions for three things: coalition building, which includes naval visits and contacts in foreign countries; picture-building (or intelligence gathering) concerning foreign activities both at sea and ashore; and finally coercion, which is a phenomenon already discussed above. Often enough, a naval force can perform many of these types of tasks simultaneously or in sequence (Till 2013: 221–51). Added to these three are also operations that aim to assert the right of free passage through different maritime zones covered by international maritime law.

As described above, naval diplomacy serves as an effective means to influence the behavior of other actors. But there are also practical and theoretical problems connected with employing such means. Till argues, for example, that it is often difficult to prove empirically to what extent naval diplomacy has been "successful" in a particular case, since it represents only one of many diplomatic activities that a state or state-like entity does to influence an opponent. Moreover, naval diplomacy cannot be assessed in isolation, Till claims, but must be viewed in relation to the objective one tries to achieve. Also, operations can be successful at the operational level but a failure at the political level, and vice versa. This requires a certain balance between ends and means. Finally, Till argues, a conflict often arises between the demands set by naval operations in a diplomatic context and the requirements of naval combat between opposing fleets. Since the tasks are inherently different, and this is reflected in the design and organization of the naval platforms, the optimal allocation between "battleships" and "patrol vessels" are often difficult to make. The struggle for scarce resources is timeless and it is therefore important to have a strategy that coordinates political and military objectives with the naval means available (Till 2013: 247–51).

Command of the sea

While command of the sea (or sea control) is often an important means to fulfill the ultimate purposes of seapower in the overall war, it is also considered to be the main goal of naval operations (cf. Landquist 1935: 28). Corbett is clear on this point and concludes that "the object of naval warfare must always be directly or indirectly either to secure the command of the sea or to prevent the enemy from securing it" (Corbett 1988: 91). Thus, while command of the sea is a question of means at the strategic level, it serves as an important objective at the operational and tactical levels (Till 2013: 157). Command of the sea does not constitute a right to possess but rather the possibility of utilizing the sea-lines of communications (Landquist 1935: 23). The value of gaining command of the sea is not a conquest in the physical sense, as is often the case in land warfare, but rather how this control can serve as a means. Corbett (1988: 94) argued that command of the sea "means nothing but the control of maritime communications, whether for commercial or military purposes. The object of naval warfare is the control of communications, and not, as in land warfare, the conquest of territory." Castex (1994: 56) agreed with this understanding of the concept and claimed that command of the sea ("mastery of the sea" in his vocabulary) meant the control of "essential maritime communications."

Most seapower theorists agree that command of the sea is not an absolute, but a relative, concept. Castex (1994: 53) claims for example that "mastery of the sea is not absolute but relative, incomplete, and imperfect." For his part, Corbett (1988: 104–5; cf. Widen 2012: 95–104) stated that command of the sea could be general or local, permanent or temporary, but never absolute. This limited form of command, in time and space, he sometimes described as a "working command." By this, Corbett meant that one's own shipping and naval operations were never completely safe from an attacker, but, if working command was in effect, no effective threat was possible against the implementation of the objectives of war. General control was either permanent or temporary, whereas local control was usually temporary. Castex (1994: 55–6) made it somewhat easier for himself and claimed that mastery of the sea was divided into local and temporary control. Corbett was careful to point out that if a belligerent party lost control of a maritime area, this did not automatically mean that the opponent gained control. As a rule, no one had control and command of the sea was a matter of contention. It was this normal state of dispute that naval strategy was mainly concerned with (Corbett 1988: 91).

The relative degree of command of the sea a state enjoys is not only dependent on the capabilities of its naval forces (in a quantitative and qualitative sense), but also dependent on time and space. Former British Prime Minister Winston Churchill (1874–1965) captured this subtle distinction:

> [W]hen we speak of command of the seas, it does not mean command of every part of the sea at the same moment, or at every moment. It only means that we can make our will prevail ultimately in any part of the seas which may be selected for operations, and thus indirectly make our will prevail in every part of the sea.
>
> (Tangredi 2002: 123)

Seapower thus represents the ability to establish control of important maritime communications and the capacity to prevent the enemy from securing such control. It means that even small maritime powers can establish local or temporary command.

This being said, we now turn to another important naval concept, namely sea denial. This concept can be defined as "the ability to prevent an opponent from using the sea without attempting to establish local sea control" (Tangredi 2002: 123). Till holds that sea denial works in two ways. First, it is an alternative to command of the sea for the actors that do not need such control for their own strategic purposes, but who are primarily interested in preventing an enemy from using important sea-lines of communications. Many smaller states with a mainly defensive posture and a focus on coastal defense can be attracted to this idea. Second, sea denial can work as a complement to command of the sea or even as a contribution to the ambition of general control. Even countries with a large navy may need to make use of sea denial in certain areas or during certain periods, in order to secure sea control in others that are more important. In the latter case it can be seen as an indirect approach aimed at command of the sea. However, to combat the opponent's capacity to prevent one's own use of important maritime communications is not sea denial, according to Till, but rather a struggle for command (see section below on methods for disputing command of the sea) (Till 2013: 152–4).

Methods for securing command of the sea

There are essentially two ways for a naval force to establish command of the sea and these are usually referred to as decisive battle and blockade. Some, e.g. Till (2013), tend to include fleet-in-being in this category, but because of this method's defensive nature, we have chosen to treat this in a later section on how to dispute command.

Decisive battle

Mahan is often mentioned as the most famous proponent of the importance of decisive battle at sea. According to him, this method aimed at the total annihilation of the opponent's fleet in battle, which was also considered the best way of securing command of the sea. In one of his many books, Mahan (1991: 297–8) claimed what he believed was the fundamental principle of all naval warfare, namely that "defense is insured only by offense, and that the one decisive objective of the offensive is the enemy's organized force, his battle-fleet." Mahan, however, was careful to distinguish between sea battles with a decisive effect and battles for their own sake. Winning a battle was only a means to obtaining a decision, i.e. by extension command of the sea, not an end in itself. Mahan's ideal of a decisive naval battle was

Nelson's victories at the Nile in 1798 and at Trafalgar in 1805. These two battles, he claimed, were crucial since they decided (at the operational level) the naval war in Britain's favor, and later, at the strategic level, indirectly decided the war on land against Napoleon.

Till (2013: 158–62) argues that the argument for the former case is much stronger than for the latter. The battle at Trafalgar effectively stopped the plans for a French invasion of Britain, but the fact that Napoleon finally was defeated in 1815 was mainly due to other factors. Naval battles, Till claims, may also be decisive in preventing an opponent from changing the geostrategic situation in his own favor. Examples of such battles are Tsushima (1905), Jutland (1916) and Midway (1942). These battles were important turning points in wars that lasted for many years. It is easy to imagine the great consequence on both operational and strategic levels if the outcome of these battles had been different (Till 2013: 159; cf. Keegan 1989; Hough 1999; Robinson 1942; Fioravanzo 1979; Palmer 2005; Stavridis & Mack 1999).

Corbett, meanwhile, was skeptical of the fixation often found in naval circles regarding the value of decisive battle. He argued that a misguided quest for obtaining a decision with the enemy's main force was unwise for three main reasons. First, there were practical difficulties in bringing about such a battle. Decisive victories were usually dependent on some kind of superiority, such as favorable maritime geography, better ships and weapons, greater operational and tactical skills, and better crews or numerical superiority. These factors in turn were often known by the inferior party, which naturally reduced their willingness to seek battle (Till 2013: 160–1; Corbett 1988: 178). Thus, there was a tendency that the more the stronger party sought such a confrontation, the more the weaker party tried to avoid such a battle. Since it was often easier to avoid battle than to force a decision, many naval wars consisted, for the most part, of a cat-and-mouse game resulting in no major clashes of arms.

Second, Corbett argued, naval battles were seldom decisive since it was almost impossible to concentrate naval forces in time and space to meet the enemy's main force. Often enough, some ships were under construction, being repaired, in transit from one place to another, or performing other assignments in other places. During the Battle of Trafalgar in 1805, often described as the ideal decisive battle, only a small portion of Napoleon's naval forces were destroyed and only one-sixth of the British fleet was engaged in battle. Consequently, even those who lose a great naval battle are provided an opportunity to replace, redistribute, and then concentrate their forces again – this time well aware of the dangers of seeking a decisive battle. As a rule, naval wars tend to be determined by slow attrition, rather than decided in a single battle (Till 2013: 160–2).

Third, Corbett claimed that there were also other important objectives that a naval force must occupy itself with. Often a naval power at war was forced to seek a balance between, on the one hand, the ambition of a decisive battle to secure command of the sea, and, on the other hand, to protect convoys or to support ground operations ashore. These latter activities no doubt served the higher purposes of winning the war as a whole. Corbett thus argued that while decisive battles at sea were preferred in most cases, there were also many risks and difficulties with bringing them about, and that the pursuit of such battles should be done with great care and not at the expense of other important goals (Corbett 1988: 171–6).

Blockade

Blockade is a frequently used method in naval warfare (Till 2013: 178–83; Davis & Engerman 2006). Here it is important to distinguish between commercial blockades, designed to cut off the enemy's supplies and routes of transportation, and naval blockades which have a distinctly military purpose. In practice they tend to be interconnected, but for analytical purposes they are best kept separate. Commercial blockade is primarily a method for exercising command of the sea and will be discussed further in this chapter, while naval blockade is a method used when one tries to secure control of the sea. A naval blockade, Till (2013: 178) argues, usually aims to "prevent the enemy interfering in a substantial way with the blockading navy's capacity to use the sea as it wished." If such a blockade succeeds in neutralizing the enemy's ability to disrupt one's own operations, a command of the sea has been created at the outer limits of the blockade and other ships (which are not assigned to secure the blockade) can then exploit the situation. The general advantages of a blockade are, Till claims, that it increases the chances of knowing more precisely where the enemy is located, while reducing the trapped party's ability to concentrate its naval forces (Till 2013: 183–5; cf. Corbett 1988: 177–9).

It is also common to distinguish between close and distant blockade. The former refers to a blockade in which one's own fleet, more or less permanently, operates close to the enemy's naval bases. The latter refers to a blockade which mainly monitors enemy activities from a distance and only from time to time approaches the enemy bases in order to maintain some control over the area in question. Close blockades were more common before torpedoes, mines, land-based planes, and guided weapons were introduced, since the capability of these weapons increased the risks of such a method. The difference between the two types is mainly a matter of degree, and is, besides the proximity to the enemy bases, dependent on the extent to which contact is possible with the enemy when he is leaving his bases (Vego 2003a: 157–67).

The benefits of a close blockade, in comparison to a distant blockade, are, according to Till, that one is better placed to keep abreast of where the enemy is and what he is doing. Furthermore, a close blockade usually results in decreased performance capability of the affected party, because it cannot conduct training exercises in an optimal way. This restriction in maneuverability also tends to affect morale in an adverse manner. The predicament of the Soviet Baltic Fleet during 1941–44 is an example of this, Till argues. During this period it was largely impossible for the Soviets to conduct naval operations with surface ships in the Baltic Sea from bases in the Gulf of Finland, due to the advancements of the German Army and German fleet operations. Finally, close blockade have the advantage of making it harder for the enemy to enter the open sea, because of the proximity of the blockading party's forces (Till 2013: 179–80).

The benefits of a distant blockade, meanwhile, is that it avoids some of the wear and tear on ships, air craft, and crews that is caused by greater distances to the blockading party's own bases (maintenance, supplies, fuels, etc.). Furthermore, a distant blockade often requires fewer resources to be ear-marked for this specific task, resources that can instead be used elsewhere and for other purposes as well. With a close blockade there is a risk of tying up more resources than the enemy is forced to forsake, which in practice means that the trapped party functions as a fleet-in-being (see below on methods for disputing command of the sea). If the objective of the blockading fleet is primarily to lure the enemy out in the open sea to force a decisive battle, rather than just to bottle him up, a distant blockade is typically the preferred choice. Finally, a distant blockade tends to reduce the risk of surprise attacks, raids, and pinprick operations from the blocked party (Till 2013: 180).

The categorization of blockade as a method for securing command of the sea is somewhat problematic, since it can also be used to exercise such command. In reality, an effective blockade often requires a certain degree of command of the sea and the concept seems then to be both cause and effect, which is logically unsatisfactory. Blockade may even be used to dispute command of the sea although the effects of such an operation are likely to be local and temporary in nature. Germany, for example, tried to impose embargoes against Britain during both world wars mainly by means of submarines. Also, the causal relationship regarding decisive battle as a method to secure command of the sea is problematic since such command is not only a result of a decisive battle, but sometimes also a prerequisite. Here, command of the sea tends to serve as both cause and effect, which is problematic in a logical sense.

Methods for exercising command of the sea

The purpose of securing command of the sea is that such control may serve higher strategic interests, while preventing the opponent from achieving similar benefits. In general, command of the sea can be exercised in two ways: the ability to project military power, which includes the carrying out of amphibious operations, bombardment of enemy coastlines, peacekeeping operations, and various forms of deterrence, and finally the ability to use the sea to transport goods, armed forces, and other strategic resources.

Maritime power projection

Till (2013: 184) defines the concept of maritime power as "the use of seaborne military forces directly to influence events on land." Such operations, he claims, include everything from full-scale invasion to occupying entire territories, to small-scale raids, and coastal bombardment using naval and amphibious forces. The latter of these may conceptually at times be part of naval diplomacy, something that was discussed earlier in this chapter. Maritime power projection may indeed vary as to its objective, type of operation, and intended strategic effect (Vego 2003a: 184–5; Till 2013: 184).

Corbett held the opinion that perhaps the most important reason to have naval forces in the first place, and acquire command of the sea, was precisely the capacity for such power projection. This ability could often be a decisive factor in war as it provided the opportunity to strike at an enemy's weak points. Some have argued against this thesis, stating that amphibious operations were rarely as decisive as portrayed by Corbett and that modern technology made such operations increasingly difficult to conduct (Till 2013: 62–3, 184). Gorshkov went even further than Corbett, arguing that the ability to influence events on land was the ultimate purpose of naval warfare and by far the most effective way to use naval forces. Decisive action on land was much more important than decisive action at sea, Gorshkov (1979: 214) claimed, since the latter only created the conditions for the former. Naval forces used directly for decisive action on land would not need to take an indirect detour via the opponent's fleet.

The value of maritime power projection for winning wars is, however, a difficult question to answer. First, it is dependent on the situation at hand and the context in which it is employed. What kind of war is being waged and in which geographic context? Second, maritime power projection can be successful at the tactical and operational level, but unsuccessful at the strategic level. America's role in the Vietnam War is an example of this. Here, the US Armed Forces had more or less unchallenged naval and air superiority but still failed to have a decisive impact at the strategic level. Third, the more maritime-oriented the opponent is, the more effective is usually the use of maritime power projection (Till 2013: 185). For example, German campaigns against Britain during both world wars might very well have been decided at sea, while campaigns against the Soviet Union could hardly be determined in this manner.

As previously mentioned, maritime power projection can be conducted in many different ways and this is typically dependent on the purpose of the operation. Such operations have of course multiple purposes, simultaneous or sequential ones, which often create problems, both in terms of practical execution and at the conceptual level. The purpose of maritime power projection may, for example, be sought to decide a conflict. Empirical examples of this are the American war in the Pacific against Japan during World War II and Britain's recapture of the Falkland Islands in 1982. The far-reaching and ambitious objective of this type of operation also affects the means employed, which naturally tends to be extensive and numerous. Another purpose might be to open up new operational fronts. The German invasion of Norway and Denmark in April 1940 and the Allied landing in Normandy in June 1944 are examples of such operations. The idea here is to change the strategic situation in a positive way by launching military operations into new areas and to divide and disrupt enemy forces (Till 2013: 186–7; cf. Bartlett 1983; Alexander & Bartlett 1995; Lovering 2007).

A third objective might be to provide direct support to ground forces. Such operations were often conducted by Germany and the Soviet Union on the Eastern Front during World War II. Soviet naval forces, for example, developed a concept using small-scale, often improvised, tactical amphibious assaults, with the aim to evade and encircle German defensive positions from the sea. A fourth objective may be to use amphibious operations to force the enemy into an unfavorable disposition of his forces, which is usually referred to as force displacement. Corbett claimed that such operations could generate disproportionate strategic effects since defense against such operations often required far more troops than were needed to conduct them. At the beginning of the nineteenth century, Napoleon Bonaparte famously lamented the fact that 30,000 troops on the English side of the English Channel required 300,000 French soldiers to defend the French coast. These troops, he argued, were sorely needed elsewhere to keep his other enemies in check. Further objectives of maritime power projection may be to engage in economic warfare by controlling an economically important part of an enemy's territory, to attack especially valuable naval bases and ports, but also to serve as a means of political pressure (Vego 2003a: 267–70; Till 2013: 186–9; Corbett 1988: 60–71).

Sea-lines of communications

As mentioned previously, the ability to use the sea as a means of transport is an important part of exercising command. The ability to exploit these sea-lines of communications and to deny them to the enemy is crucial both for purely military purposes such as maritime power projection and to ensure transportation via the seas. According to Mahan (1991: 27–31), foreign trade and shipping were not only the basis on which a country's strength and prosperity rested, but also the very reason why naval forces were needed at all, i.e. as armed protection for shipping and sea-going trade. Consequently, questions about how to defend and attack maritime communications are of great importance in all theories of maritime strategy (see section below on how to dispute command of the sea). An important problem that naval thinkers have wrestled with over the years is how these sea-lines of communications can be protected and maintained. To what extent should one protect the sea lanes themselves, or rather the ships sailing on these lanes? Mahan argued that in order to protect the sea-lines of communications a necessary condition was to acquire command of the sea by means of decisive battle with the enemy fleet and blockade. Such control of relevant maritime areas would make it impossible for most opponents to operate at all on the seas and give the escorting warships and merchant ships the needed protection against any attacker who still ventured out at sea (Mahan 1991: 185–98; Till 2013: 216–18).

The competing idea held that warships should patrol and protect the most important sea lanes and certain strategic areas rather than focusing on the merchant ships. These patrolling warships would then be supplemented by special hunting groups tasked with seeking out and destroy enemy ships. This tactic was not limited to certain periods or phases but was supposed to continue throughout the war. In this way, permanently protected zones were created and merchant ships could use them for their operations both in war and peace (Till 2013: 217–18). Corbett was a promoter of these ideas, being critical of the convoy system. He argued (1988: 264–70) that technological developments relating to ships and telecommunications (in the early twentieth century) had increased the possibilities for protection against attacks on the high seas. He also claimed that the convoy system had financial and strategic drawbacks. Developments during World War I and World War II proved Mahan correct, rather than Corbett.

During the first half of World War I and in the early stages of World War II, efforts were made to protect shipping routes and to establish hunting groups but with poor results. It was, however, a recurring theme during both wars that casualty figures dropped, sometimes drastically, when merchant ships traveled in convoys and under escort. The German navy countered with "wolf-pack tactics" using submarines, but improved protection from the air, more efficient radars, and improved anti-submarine weapons tended to neutralize the effect of this tactic. Grove (1990: 11–12, 17–19), for example, argues that Allied resistance to the convoy system during both world wars almost led to defeat.

While the experience from the first half of the twentieth century demonstrates the benefits of the convoy system instead of protecting the sea lanes as such, this is dependent on variables that are constantly changing. During the Cold War, and only a few decades after World War II, new voices emerged who argued for more "offensive methods" (read: hunting groups) and protected sea lanes. The main reason for this was considered to be faster and better-armed submarines that with external help could find their targets significantly easier than before. Improved detection-systems would make it easier to track convoys; faster submarines with more effective weapons could keep pace with surface warships and cause greater damage. To put all the eggs in one basket was considered by many to be increasingly difficult and this increased the criticism of the convoy system. As can be seen, this is a timeless problem that depends on ever changing, situation-bound, and uncertain factors (Till 2013: 217–18).

Methods of disputing command of the sea

If decisive battle and various forms of blockade are methods to secure command of the sea, then fleet-in-being, war on commerce, and coastal defenses are ways to challenge and dispute an enemy's command. These methods will now be described and assessed.

Fleet-in-being

Fleet-in-being is a defensive method of naval warfare intended to reduce the strategic value of an enemy's command of the sea. The method was commonly used by the inferior party, but it can also apply to a generally superior naval force, temporarily or locally weakened due to, for example, offensive operations in other places. A naval force applying the principle of fleet-in-being tries to avoid a decisive battle with the superior opponent. However, by its very existence and by skilled maneuvers, it can still threaten the opponent and thereby tie up much of his forces and compel him to suspend or restrain his hostile activities. Such behavior has, for example, often been the natural response to a naval blockade. The method can also serve to deter or delay the implementation of large amphibious operations and force the party seeking to secure command of the sea, to unfavorable dispositions of their naval forces (Vego 2003a: 207–8; Till 2013: 173–4).

The term fleet-in-being derives from an acclaimed event in British naval history later described by Philip H. Colomb (1990). Admiral Lord Torrington, the commanding officer of a joint Anglo-Dutch naval force in June 1690 near the Isle of Wight, facing a superior French fleet and landing force, supposedly recommended his superiors to avoid battle against the superior French force and await reinforcements, rather than going on the offensive. His recommendation was considered to be too passive and was therefore rejected, and in the ensuing battle – the Battle of Beachy Head – his forces were soundly defeated. In the inquiry that followed, Torrington defended his cautious approach and argued that it had served the overall aim of the operation, i.e. to deter the French side from landing on the British Isles – "for I always said, that whilst we had a fleet in being, they would not dare to make an attempt." The court set up by Parliament and Torrington's superiors finally accepted this explanation, at least to some extent, and he was acquitted. However, the fact that Torrington never held command again may be an indication of how his actions were perceived by his contemporaries (Colomb 1990: 140–62; cf. Corbett 1988: 37–8, 212–20; Till 2013: 173–4; Widen 2012: 132–4).

Ever since Colomb's analysis of the fleet-in-being-principle, the question of its military value has been a contentious topic. Colomb (1990: 12, 154) claimed that Torrington had done the right thing and that an amphibious landing was not feasible as long as a fleet-in-being existed. Instead, Mahan argued that Torrington's fleet-in-being strategy had not been crucial in preventing a French invasion of the British Isles. The chief causes were rather the incompetence of the French commander Admiral Tourville and that the French fleet lacked enough troops on board to make a successful landing possible. However, Mahan (1991: 194, 247) saw some value in a fleet-in-being strategy for an inferior naval force, but only if the operation was active in nature and avoided dispersing its forces, while trying to disrupt the enemy (Till 2013: 174–5). Corbett (1988: 212) felt that Torrington had acted correctly and that the event clearly illustrated the advantages with a defensive posture. He warned, however, like Mahan, against passivity and argued that a proper defensive strategy meant "keeping the fleet actively in being – not merely into existence, but in active and vigorous life." Castex argued (1994: 338–45), in accordance with Mahan, that the reason why the British Isles had not been invaded was due to French incompetence rather than Torrington's fleet-in-being strategy. Castex was critical of the idea that the mere existence of a fleet could have any effect on the fleet holding command of the sea, if not actively used against the enemy.

A classic example of a fleet-in-being from World War II is the German Navy's deployment of the battleship *Tirpitz* from early 1942 until it was finally sunk by British bombers in November 1944. From its many bases along the Norwegian coast, *Tirpitz* and her escort became a constant threat to British and Allied convoys en route to Murmansk and Arkhangelsk in the Soviet Union (Lunde 2010; Haarr 2010). Through the ship's very existence and active use against these convoys, the Germans managed to tie down a much larger allied naval force, ships, aircraft, and resources that were greatly needed elsewhere (Friedman 2001: 84–5; Zetterling & Tamelander 2009; O'Hara 2011). In summary, one can thus conclude that the value of a fleet-in-being strategy, according to most naval theorists, mainly depends on how actively it is used. It is a defensive strategy with counter-attacks as the primary means or a temporary strategy until sufficient strength has been accumulated and a decisive battle may be sought with the enemy force. The question whether a fleet's very existence constitutes a workable fleet-in-being is, however, still controversial.

War on commerce (Guerre de course)

Another common method used to challenge and dispute an opponent's command of the sea is war on commerce, or *guerre de course* as it is termed in French. This method was the natural response to a superior force's tendency to blockade the weaker party. To undermine the opponent's trade and economy would reduce the capacity to wage war. Also, to attack a stronger opponent's shipping and maritime communications constituted a sort of asymmetric warfare that appealed to many inferior naval powers. Conducting a war on commerce was also a natural remedy in cases when wars were caused and determined by mainly economic issues.

A first attempt to theorize on these matters was made by the French *Jeune École* ("young school"). These thoughts appeared in the second half of the nineteenth century, and were based on the idea of increased firepower to be spread over many vessels, and the introduction of new technologies (torpedoes, mines, and later submarines). In effect, it was an attempt to find cost-effective means for the inferior naval power to challenge an opponent with command of the sea. The ambition was that these new weapons should be spread out on as many platforms as possible, that these smaller ships – first torpedo boats and later submarines – would be deployed along the coast and then concentrated at sea to create local superiority. These smaller ships could also be employed for bombarding the enemy's coastline and used against his maritime communications (Röksund 2007; Wedin 2007).

According to these thinkers, war on commerce would be a suitable form of warfare, since it struck directly at the economical and commercial structures underpinning the power of maritime states/empires like Britain (and later the US). Progress in weapons technology during the late nineteenth century increased the credibility of these arguments, and most thinkers agreed that threats to larger surface vessels, including battleships, had increased significantly. Followers of the *Jeune École* did not believe that a war against Britain, for example, could be won solely by starving out the population through a war on commerce. On the contrary, it was believed that an attack, mainly by torpedo boats, against the sea-lines of communications in a country dependent on shipping and trade, would create such a panic among the population and strong commercial interest groups that the government would immediately be forced to sue for peace (Till 2013: 68–70). Clearly there are similarities with early air power theorists who claimed that bombing civilian targets, in the initial stages of a war, would immediately force the government subjected to such bombing, to seek peace.

The *Jeune École* had a strong influence on many naval thinkers in Europe during the late nineteenth and early twentieth centuries. It would soon subside, however, although the ideas were still influential in countries such as Germany, the Soviet Union, and Sweden. There were several reasons for this declining interest. Among other things, the technological assumptions on which the theories rested proved slightly dubious. The torpedo boat was not the serious threat to larger surface vessels that enthusiasts had expected, since its seaworthiness was often poor, new radio equipment made fleets less vulnerable, new ships were developed to counter the torpedo boat threat, and ship design improved to the detriment of the torpedo attack (Till 2013: 66–70).

War on commerce, however, continued to be an attractive idea for many weaker maritime powers. This form of warfare was based primarily on the idea that the offensive, and not the defensive, was the stronger form of warfare at sea. This meant that the party who practiced a war on commerce would generate a disproportionately large effect on the defending party's finances. A war against shipping also appeared to be an effective method of dividing the naval forces of the stronger power, as the latter would have to defend its shipping and maritime communications rather than concentrate its forces for a decisive battle (Till 2013: 214). As for the argument of cost-efficiency, Gorshkov (1979: 118–20; cf. Vego 1992) argued that the experience of World War II had showed that German submarine warfare had generated a disproportionately large effect, given the resources and effort spent on the German side. Replacing the sunken merchant ships and hunting submarines across the Atlantic and elsewhere was thus, according to him, much more expensive and more demanding than to wage the submarine war itself.

The effectiveness and value of a war on commerce have been hotly contested. First, it is difficult in purely analytical terms to distinguish the effects of such a war from other matters in war, because it has usually been part of a wider war effort that was played out in many areas. Second, a war on commerce can be relatively effective on the tactical and operational level but end up rather unsuccessful at the strategic level. The German submarine war in both world wars is a case in point. In the end, the Allies built merchant ships faster than the Germans could sink them. One might also imagine a war in which a war on commerce is relatively ineffective at the tactical and operational levels but still decisive at the strategic level. All these problems lead to difficulties in assessing the phenomenon. Hence, the general value of a war on commerce is not only difficult to determine, but also reliant on factors such as current levels of military technology. Technical breakthroughs in weaponry, sonars, and radar equipment can have major consequences for conditions in such a war at sea.

Of the classical naval thinkers, most of them were skeptical of the possibility of winning a war using such methods. The main argument was that great maritime powers often had such vast resource that losses could be handled. In any case, a truly effective warfare against shipping had to be performed in the most barbaric and immoral manner, something that would certainly backfire on the party using such methods. Germany's decision to begin unrestricted submarine warfare in 1917 and America's subsequent entry into the war is an example of this. However, the most important argument, one that both Mahan and Corbett agreed on, was that maritime powers holding command of the sea would always be superior and therefore ultimately prevail (Till 2013: 214–15).

Another objection raised by the French theorist Castex (1994: 357–84), in many ways a critic of the *Jeune École*, held that a war on commerce needed support from warfare on the ground and in the air to have decisive effect in the war as a whole. Performed in isolation and geared solely towards the maritime communications and trade, such a method would fail, he argued. Gorshkov (1979: 120–1) also agreed on this point, stating that this was the reason why Hitler's submarine warfare during World War II had proved unsuccessful. Finally, many considered a war on commerce to be much more effective when performed by maritime powers holding command of the sea, the successful US submarine warfare against Imperial Japan during World War II being a case in point. This also reduced the attraction of this method for smaller and weaker fleets as it was better as a method of exploiting command of the sea rather than disputing such command (Till 2013: 69–70).

A variation of the method described as war on commerce is *Kleinkrieg*, something brought forth by German naval thinker Otto Groos (1929). The German approach during World War I (and in fact also World War II) provides the model, although ultimately an unsuccessful one. Using submarines and mines, the German Navy tried to equalize the balance of forces at sea, while the main battle force was being held back pending a chance at a decisive blow once the balance of power was favorable. This approach also characterized Russian naval warfare in the Baltic during World War I. Based on his earlier works, Mahan would certainly have been of the opinion that such a method was doomed to failure because only deployment of large and concentrated forces could achieve decisive results at sea.

Landquist (1935: 51–53) argued that this form of warfare contained logical problems. How was it possible to reduce an enemy's superiority by only inserting a portion of one's already inferior forces? According to Landquist, this method built on the assumption that submarines and mines were more or less invulnerable and very hard to combat even for a great seapower with a large fleet. However, the development of technology and doctrine in naval warfare, in for example the Atlantic and the North Sea during World War I (and later World War II), showed the possibilities of finding effective countermeasures against these weapons, and thereby neutralizing them (cf. Friedman 2009).

Coastal defense theory

Coastal defense theory (or "fortress fleet") constitutes a radically different view of maritime operations and serves as a purely defensive strategy. Such a method of disputing command of the sea has also proved attractive to states with smaller navies. US maritime strategy in the nineteenth century was party based on such ideas, something that was reflected in the extensive fortifications along the east coast, with a focus on mines and the construction of small vessels optimized for coastal operations. Moreover, strategists in the German general staff, from 1870 onwards, developed ideas of a fleet entirely under army command and on similar principles, primarily intended for coastal defense. Observers on the coast would alert when the enemy was approaching, and naval warships would rush out from their fortified bases, while ground troops was concentrated to the threatened area by railways (Till 2013: 71–2).

A more complete doctrine concerning coastal defense theory would have to wait until the end of the 1920s and early 1930s, when representatives of the "new school" in the Soviet Union formulated their thoughts on the subject. They emphasized the value of joint operations and command, as well as using modern means of communications. The coastline would be protected against naval and amphibious attacks from the sea through an integrated system of mines, coastal artillery, aircraft, submarines, and torpedo boats. According to Till (2013: 71–3), this doctrine was based on the assumption that new technology in the form of airplanes and submarines had undermined traditional naval warfare in a fundamental way and made battleships and aircraft carriers vulnerable. Some even claimed that the idea of command of the sea itself had become obsolete due to these developments. As we can see these ideas are similar to the ones presented by the *Jeune École*, with the addition of new elements of joint command and operations.

This increased emphasis on joint thinking is very much present in the contemporary discussion of coastal defense. A contemporary Norwegian scholar, Jacob Børresen (2004: 252–55; cf. Hughes 2000), for example, argues that the small coastal state perspective on naval power is usually characterized by a tendency to maximize the use of joint operations and coastal topography. The coastal fleet in such small states aims to deter large-scale naval operations from a hostile great power by causing him serious losses rather than trying to defeat him. A coastal fleet should therefore be as balanced as resources allow and tailored for the local environment. Many methods to dispute command of the sea, could also serve as methods to secure such command. Fleet-in-being, for example, is an often used method to retain a local and temporary command at sea while waiting for an opportunity to seek a decisive battle, as was the case with Torrington's strategy before the Battle of Beachy Head. The same applies to war on commerce that is also widely used as an attempt to secure a command of the sea in the long term. Here, the method of coastal defense stands out because it often questions the relevance of controlling the sea except for maritime areas near the coast.

Conclusions

As is evident from the discussion in this chapter, seapower is far from being a simple and unambiguous concept. The ends and means depend on a number of factors that are located outside the domain where seapower is played out. Seapower is thus part of a greater whole and serves as an important element in the use of military power. Today's technological development, with guided weapons, satellite surveillance, and communications in near real time, has affected the very foundations on which seapower is resting although not enough to substantially revise them. The sea is still indispensable for the transport of vital raw materials and processed goods, and thus fundamental to global economic prosperity. The maritime communications on which these goods are carried still needs to be protected and naval forces are an important means of achieving this. The sea also offers opportunities for projecting military power, and naval forces therefore serve as an important political instrument.

As an explanatory theory, seapower has some problems with its logical consistency. The crucial causal relationship centers on command of the sea, which is portrayed as an independent variable in explaining the outcome of war. Problems do exist, however, since the factors and the methods that are said to produce command of the sea, in turn, depend not infrequently on having such command. Thus, sea control serves as both cause and effect, which is logically unsatisfactory. Furthermore, the theoretical focus on methods for securing, exercising, and disputing command of the sea is also problematic. Many of the methods may in fact serve all three properties and this makes the categorization difficult to employ analytically.

Seapower as a normative theory can provide a wide range of ideas about ways to act both to win a war at sea and to win the general war by means of naval power. Many of the classical theories of seapower, such as how best to protect maritime communications and conduct war on commerce, have been challenged based on the experiences of the wars of the twentieth century, especially World War I and World War II. Even though they have not been falsified, there is certainly a need to review them and place them in a modern context, and technological development has been a crucial variable in this regard.

Questions for discussion

1. To what extent are the ends and means of seapower changing over time?
2. Is command of the sea enough to win a war?
3. To what extent can naval power compensate for supremacy on the ground and in the air?
4. What are the greatest challenges when carrying out, and defending against, amphibious operations?
5. What are the pros and cons of using naval forces as a diplomatic instrument?
6. How relevant is the concept of command of the sea for small states?

Further reading

Ken Booth, *Navies and Foreign Policy* (New York: Holmes & Meier Publishers, 1979).

Julian S. Corbett, *Some Principles of Maritime Strategy* (Annapolis, MD: Naval Institute Press, 1988).

Colin S. Gray, *The Leverage of Seapower: The Strategic Advantage of Navies in War* (New York: The Free Press, 1992).

Alfred T. Mahan, *Mahan on Naval Strategy: Selections from the Writings of Rear Admiral Alfred Thayer Mahan* (Annapolis, MD: Naval Institute Press, 1991).

Arne Röksund, *The Jeune École: The Strategy of the Weak* (Leiden and Boston, MA: Brill, 2007).

Ian Speller, *Understanding Naval Warfare* (London: Routledge, 2014).

Geoffrey Till, *Seapower: A Guide for the Twenty-First Century*, 3rd edn. (London: Routledge, 2013).

J. J. Widen, *Theorist of Maritime Strategy: Sir Julian Corbett and his Contribution to Military and Naval Thought* (Farnham: Ashgate, 2012).

9   Air operations

Introduction

Airpower has been an indispensable part of Western use of force after the Cold War. This has given rise to a sometimes-heated debate on airpower and its limitations. It has been suggested that the quick collapse of Iraqi troops during the 1991 Gulf War once the coalition ground offensive began can be explained by the month-long air bombing that preceded the ground war. The air campaign, the argument goes, neutralized the Iraqis' ability and undermined their will to continue the fight. In this way, operations seemed to confirm the notion that airpower and air superiority were crucial to the outcome of modern war. Air force operations in Bosnia in 1994–5, but above all in Kosovo in 1999, Afghanistan in 2001, Iraq in 2003, and Libya in 2012 further strengthened the impression that airpower was a relatively cheap, effective, and politically viable way to wage war. The Kosovo War, in particular, has even been regarded as a watershed in the history of warfare, because Serbia was defeated by action from the air alone (e.g. Olsen 2003; Lambeth 2001).

But how credible is the claim that airpower alone can win wars or that air superiority is tantamount to winning wars? Studies of the wars in Chechnya, where Russia unquestionably enjoyed air superiority, show that the relationship between airpower and victory is not entirely unambiguous (de Haas 2004). Later research on the 1991 Gulf War, moreover, has shown that it is debatable to what extent the Iraqis' will and capacity for continued resistance was affected by the initial bombing (Press 2001). The real value of the so-called "Afghan Way of War" has also been questioned (Biddle 2007). Similarly, it has been questioned as to what extent the Serbian leader Slobodan Milosevic's decision to withdraw from Kosovo and meet the conditions of the Rambouillet Agreement was caused by NATO bombing, lack of Russian support, the threat of a ground invasion, the Kosovo Albanian guerrilla resistance, or the threat to indict the Serbian leader at the International Crimes Tribunal in the Hague (Lambeth 2001; Hosmer 2001; Gow 2003; Byman & Waxman 2000).

The independent causal power of airpower on the outcome of war and militarized crises is one of several cross-cutting themes in the theoretical discourse of airpower. This means that the relative utility of airpower is surrounded by similar questions as the use of force in other domains. It also means that there is an implied causal link between the use of airpower and victory in war. How have ideas about this relationship developed? How are the normative and explanatory aims of military theory understood in the airpower debate?

The aim of this chapter is to introduce modern airpower theory and its core assumptions. The central theme running through modern airpower debate is how effective airpower is for achieving tactical, operational, and strategic effects. The great divide in this debate is between those who believe that airpower alone can induce the opponent in a conflict to behave in a desirable way and those who believe that airpower – as other means at the state's disposal – must be understood in a broader strategic context. In this way, the central debate is between those who believe that airpower should be seen as an independent strategic resource and those who believe that it primarily should be used for operational-tactical purposes to support ground and naval forces. Since the latter idea has already been discussed in Chapter 6 on joint operations, the focus of this chapter is on how airpower as a stand-alone resource and how it is considered to contribute to military power. Obviously, airpower can be used for both purposes, but because strategy is constrained by scarce resources, one must prioritize.

The American Colonel Peter Faber (1997a; cf. Garden 2002) suggests that air warfare contains offensive operations, control of airspace, supporting air operations, and logistics. Of these components, the main focus of airpower theory has been kinetic air force operations. Logistics, reconnaissance operations, and control of airspace from the ground (through radar) have received far less attention in airpower theory. Similarly, space – sometimes included in the concept of airpower – has not received extensive theorizing (Gray 1996a; DeBlois 2004). It is also worth pointing out that airpower theories have been developed by, or for, the great powers. On the one hand, it may be argued that this does not matter. The logic of targeting and strategic effect, in short, should hold regardless of whether it is a Danish F-16 or a US F-16 that drops a bomb on a power plant. On the other hand, airpower is associated with access to capital-intensive high-technology, commonly associated with great powers and their comparatively larger defense budgets. There are thus confounding variables involved in airpower theory. In the above example of F-16:s, it is not entirely obvious that the strategic outcome of bombings will be similar since the targeted state in all likelihood are aware of the fact the US have much more latent military resources than Denmark. The fact that the Great Powers possess so-called escalatory dominance (cf. Chapter 3) thus makes airpower theorizing suffer from potential biases.

Airpower: concepts and strategic context

We begin the chapter with a discussion of key concepts, before moving on to the causal logic implied in airpower theory. As in the other chapters on military operations, this conceptual discussion has clear connections to Chapter 2 on war and Chapter 3 on strategy. A conceptual discussion of airpower should relate to its nature, air superiority, and the strategic context in which airpower is relevant.

Air power and its characteristics

What does the term "airpower" mean? Philip Meilinger (2003: 1) defines airpower as "the ability to exercise power from air or space to achieve strategic, operational or tactical objectives." At least two aspects of this understanding of the concept deserve more attention. First, it includes space, which sets it apart from previous definitions, and it makes contemporary satellite systems into an integral and essential resource in the use of airpower (cf. Klein 2004). Not only are monitoring and intelligence gathering facilitated by satellites, but also command and control. For example, the US Air Force is already using its satellite system to obtain information on weather, targets, and to evaluate effectiveness, and it can designate targets from the ground directly to manned or unmanned aircraft. Second, airpower includes "the exercise of power." What is somewhat surprising, however, is that there is a lack of analysis of the concept of "power" among airpower theorists. It is surprising since neighboring disciplines such as political science and sociology usually consider "power" as an "inherently contested concept." The political science literature on the concepts of power or freedom often distinguishes between "power to act" and "the power to protect from." Similarly, it is common to separate "freedom to" and "freedom from."

These two dimensions of the concept of power are also relevant in airpower theory, as will become evident in the discussion of the concept of "air superiority." What Meilinger seems to have in mind with his understanding of airpower is similar to Dahl's concept of power, since Meilinger's concept is intimately associated with incompatible interests involved in war. In his classic formulation, Dahl (1957; 1991) suggested that "A has power over B to the extent that A can get B to do something B would not otherwise have done." Similarly, Meilinger understands airpower is a relational concept insofar as the use of "power" includes at least two actors. Dahl's understanding of power is also intentional and causal, i.e. the use of force is deliberate and such conscious acts causes an effect. Power, in short, is used to accomplish goals. For example, in 1990, Iraq could wield its airpower against Kuwait, but not against the US at the same time. Hence, airpower is not an objective resource, but must be seen in relation to other actors.

Another recurring theme in the development of airpower theory is the extent to which it can be understood as inherently offensive. Almost all of the early airpower theorists in the 1920s held that airpower was offensive by nature. Air forces would not get stuck in trench warfare similar to the Western Front, it was argued. This position was further reinforced by the absence of a functioning air defense system with radar and long-range air defense systems. These theorists envisioned air forces as cavalry in the air that, unhindered by trenches or minefields, could envelop opposition units easily and cordon off the battle space. One of the early "pioneers" of airpower theory, the Italian General Guilio Douhet (1869–1930), assumed that it was impossible to defend against airpower. The US General William Mitchell and other early American airpower theorists held similar positions. A text from the US Air Corps Tactical School (ACTS) in 1926 even suggested that "it was futile to try to prevent hostile air operations . . . As soon as the bombers were in the air, they were practically impossible to prevent." (West 1999: 7) In Britain, Hugh Trenchard emphasized that air forces were inherently aggressive and claimed that "nothing is more annoying than being attacked by something you cannot defend yourself against" (Meilinger 2003: 46). According to Faber (2002), this has subsequently led airpower theorists to mostly ignore theorizing about defensive air power.

The notion that you cannot defend against airpower also meant that early theorists such as Douhet (1999) argued that air forces should be used for pre-emptive strikes. If you are unable to defend against assault from the air and the effort of air forces determine the outcomes of war, it becomes rational to pre-empt the opponent's attack by launching an attack in advance. The emergence of airpower, in short, implied that victory in war was determined by whoever attacked first. This line of thought was later elaborated in more detail by Bernard Brodie in the 1950s. Brodie (1959: 402) suggested that nuclear weapons made Douhet's ideas about the anticipatory attack relevant. It is worth noting that Brodie wrote his text before the Cold War superpowers had developed robust second-strike capabilities, which made the logic behind pre-emptive strikes less relevant. Meilinger (2001: 105) notes that "if the only thing that makes Douhet relevant is nuclear weapons, then he is completely irrelevant" because none of the superpowers from the 1960s onwards could defeat the other instantly, always risking a devastating second strike. It is, moreover, not only the early airpower theorists that assumed that air forces are inherently offensive. US colonel and influential modern airpower theorist John Warden (2000: 21–3) emphasizes that the offensive has advantages over the defensive in air warfare. Warden even claims that a defensive strategy can never lead to victory – only "drawn" results in war. Hence, to some extent airpower theory is still characterized by the "cult of the offensive" (cf. J. Snyder 1984).

A further recurring theme in the history of airpower theory is the notion of decisive battle. This, of course, demonstrates the close relationship between Western strategic thought in general and airpower theory. Being able to defeat the opponent in a great battle and thus determine the outcome of the entire war has consistently been held as an ideal in Western military theory – at least since Clausewitz. Mahan's discussion of the decisive naval battle (see Chapter 8) is another manifestation of this idea. It is also a recurring theme in airpower theory. We can consider Douhet's suggestion of bombing of civilians, ACTS thinkers' ideas about bombing nodes in the society to achieve system collapse, Wardens ideas about decapitating enemy leadership, and the late 1990s thoughts on "shock and awe," as expressions of accomplishing the ideal of determining the outcome of war by one, decisive blow.

Airpower advocates also highlight a number of other characteristics of airpower that distinguishe air forces from other services. Both British Air Marshal Timothy Garden (2002: 137–57) and Meilinger (2003: 1–2) argue that airpower has innate strengths and weaknesses. Airpower is flexible, they suggest, because it can be used for a wide variety of tasks. It is also attractive to decision-makers – both civilian and military – since air power offers a way to quickly exert military power over long ranges, with relatively low risks of suffering losses. Air forces are also quick to withdraw from the conflict if necessary. The new development of precision-guided munitions, moreover, has led to the political level being able to control the military operations more carefully and even participate in the targeting process to a greater extent than before. Since the sky is omnipresent, it is also suggested that air power by definition increases the possibility of surprise, since it can attack from all directions. Garden and Meilinger also point out, however, that airpower is capital-intensive and air forces are dependent on often vulnerable base and logistics infrastructure. Another inherent limitation of airpower is its transient nature, i.e. air forces cannot permanently occupy their domain, but are dependent on land or sea operations for such tasks. Another inhibiting and related factor for airpower is that it cannot control territory, although it can greatly limit the opponent's ability to maneuver and master the same territory.

Air superiority and its significance

Perhaps the clearest sign that airpower is exercised is that one party holds air superiority in a war. How has the latter term been understood? Douhet (1999: 297) suggested "to have command of the air means to be in a position to prevent the enemy from flying while retaining the ability to fly oneself." Douhet's concept set forth two fairly tough demands: you should be able to operate freely in the air, while the opponent should not be able to fly at all. Douhet thus understood airpower in terms of freedom of maneuver, to operate freely from the opponent's operations. It is also clear that he understood the concept as binary; either you have air superiority, or you do not. Those suggesting that air superiority was a relative concept and could be differentiated in time and space were dismissed for mistaking command of the air for local, short-term superiority. Douhet (1999: 297) went as far as to claim that (emphasis in original):

> [T]o have command of the air means to be in a position to wield offensive power so great it defies human imagination. It means to be able to cut an enemy's army and navy off from their bases of operation and nullify their chances of winning the war. It means complete protection of one's own country, the efficient operation of one's army and navy, and peace of mind to live and work in safety. In short, it means to be in a position

to win. To be defeated in the air, on the other hand, is finally to be defeated and to be at the mercy of the enemy, with no chance at all of defending oneself, compelled to accept whatever terms he sees fit to dictate.

In contrast, John Slessor argues that air superiority is not a permanent state of affairs, but only a phase that is possible in a smaller theater of operations for a limited time. Slessor maintained that this is sufficient since the decisive moments in war by definition only take place at a specific time and place (Meilinger 2003: 69). Warden, meanwhile, differentiated the concept even more. Air superiority, according to him (2000: 10), ought to be understood as "sufficient control of the air to make air attacks – manned or unmanned – on the enemy without serious opposition and, on the other hand, to be free from the danger of serious enemy air incursions." His understanding seemingly follows Douhet's, but with some qualifications. Warden also distinguishes sub-categories such as "air supremacy" (identical to Douhet's "command of the air"), and – like Slessor – insists that air superiority can be "local," i.e. limited to a given battle space; "operational," i.e. limited to an entire "combat theatre," or even "neutral," i.e. "neither side has won sufficient control of the air to operate without great danger" (Warden 2000: 10–11). For Warden, and unlike Douhet, therefore, air superiority is a relative term.

The most central of the causal claims involving air superiority within airpower theory is that holding such superiority leads to victory in war. This claim is firmly entrenched in airpower thought from Douhet to current air force doctrines, such as British Royal Air Force doctrine *AP 3000* (2009). Douhet (1999: 298; cf. MacIsaac 1986: 627; Buckley 1999: 22–42) claimed that "to have command of the air is to have *victory*. Without this command, one's portion is defeat and the acceptance of whatever terms the victor is pleased to impose" (emphasis in original). Even current airpower theorists strongly argue in favor of this causal relationship. The causal story, in short, is that the holder of air superiority has an advantage compared to its counterpart, because the holder can implement their offensive operations undisturbed. This allows the holder to influence the opponent at will, while the opponent cannot respond. This means that air superiority is an end in itself for the air force, even if it serves as a means to influence the outcome of the war as a whole. It is only when air superiority is achieved, Warden (2000: 13–20) maintains, that air forces' full potential can be realized.

There are, however, some problems with the causality in the claim that air superiority will lead to victory in war. First, Faber (2002) points out that the causal stories and mechanisms of the theories rely far too heavily on metaphors. Even if this is seemingly convincing, metaphors rarely capture the full complexity of the phenomenon to be explained. For example, following ACTS propositions about targeting key nodes in the opponent's social and economic system, US Air Force General Frank Andrews (1884–1943) suggested that modern society was "as sensitive as a precision instrument." This suggested that if you destroyed or disrupted a vital part of a watch, it would not work (Faber 2002: 56–7). The problem – of course – is that modern societies or states are not identical to a wrist watch. Similarly, it is certainly true, as Warden argues, that a human body ceases to function if you cut off its head. However, this does not necessarily mean that the same applies to a state that loses its leadership. States can naturally replace their leadership more easily than a human body can grow another head. Ultimately, relying upon metaphors in the planning and targeting decisions can be misguided and lead to unnecessary death and destruction as well as poorly utilized resources.

Second, it is almost impossible to separate the independent causal powers of one tool in war from others. For example, if we claim – as some airpower theorists do – that air superiority leads to victory in war, it is extremely difficult to prove it, since there are a number of confounding variables. Often the party with air superiority also has dominance on land. This is of course related to the fact that air forces are capital-intensive and the side with the largest defense spending and largest disposable forces is therefore also the most likely to achieve a dominant situation both on land and in air. Operations in air, moreover, influence the conduct of ground operations. It is easy to conceive of situations where ground offensives are made possible by air superiority and equally easy to conceive of situations where ground offensives hamper the opponent's air operations. Moreover, since war by definition involves at least two sides there are also problems related to the interchange of strategic and tactical behavior. If, for example, the opponent uses a strategy of dispersion and concealment to protect its air forces during an initial campaign to suppress opponent air forces, it may still be the case that one's own bombing fleet is not protected when the initial campaign is over. And if we cannot isolate the effect of airpower but instead are caught in a series of interaction effects, it is difficult to prove the independent causal powers of air superiority.

Strategic context and airpower strategy

Theories of the utility of airpower are also based on implicit assumptions about the strategic context and a particular understanding of the opponent. In particular, the absence of clear and explicit assumptions about the opponent has generated criticism that airpower theory tends to be static and one-dimensional. This is a problem in the sense that war is a struggle between at least two actors, who only partially set the agenda on their own. For example, an opponent whose industrial resources are subjected to heavy bombing can reallocate resources, find alternatives, and thus avoid system collapse. Moreover, most airpower theory focuses on one actor's perspective, instead of understanding airpower as a phenomenon in the relationship between two parties. This is likely to provide a distorted picture of air warfare since it has led airpower theory mainly to be deduced from technological potential, rather than as a theory of war encompassing interaction between actors. A military theory that ignores the other party's behavior could also provide misleading normative proposals (Byman & Waxman 2002: 18–21). One manifestation of this is the US plan to bomb Nazi Germany into submission in merely six months. Targeting, bombings, and reconnaissance were planned in detail, but the plan nevertheless failed as it underestimated German ability to retaliate, persist, and resist.

The lack of strategic context in much airpower thought can also be a result of, in particular, the airpower pioneers' – e.g. Douhet, Mitchell, and Trenchard – shared vision of an independent air force. Hence, rather than the result of cool, calculated objective analysis of the optimal combination of use of force, airpower theory is intended to form the intellectual justification for the air force as an independent armed service. Johansson (1988: 286) makes a similar observation, arguing that the early airpower theorists are equally interested in trying to show what the air force *can* do in the future as opposed to what it *should* do in order to reach strategic aims. In this way, they were trying to justify why the air force should be an independent armed service.

Most airpower theorists also presuppose that the opponent is a state. John Warden (1995) is a rare exception that specifically includes non-state actors in his theory of the utility of airpower. But to what extent can airpower reach strategic or tactical aims in small wars? To begin with, we can note that theory in this area is still somewhat rudimentary (cf. Corum & Johnson 2003). What we can conclude, however, is that airpower faces at least two unique challenges in small wars as compared with regular, interstate wars. Both of these challenges can be derived from the fact that the opponent in asymmetric small wars is a non-state group. Unlike conventional opponents, guerrillas or insurgents tend not to mass their forces and thus rarely offer opportunities for large-scale bombing campaigns. The guerrilla small-unit tactics also means that they are not dependent upon sustained large-scale logistical networks. Hence, airpower will struggle with the targeting in small wars. In Afghanistan in 2001, the greatest impact of airpower was against Taliban fixed positions or in tandem with Northern Alliance forces (Biddle 2007). Instead of targeting insurgents, some suggest that airpower should be used to gather intelligence, psychological operations, reconnaissance, surveillance, and transportation (Corum & Johnson 2003: 8).

The few airpower theorists that explicitly address strategic context largely follow mainstream conceptual frameworks. Coercion and deterrence are closely related, according to Robert Pape (1996), who argues that deterrence is about persuading the other party not to change their behavior, while coercion is about persuading the other party to change their behavior. Both of these ways of war are fundamentally about power. This is also evident in Waxman's and Byman's (2000: 9) understanding of coercion, which is strikingly similar to Dahl's concept of power; "threat of use of military force, or the use of limited force, to compel another party to act in a way that he would not otherwise do." Airpower can be used in all four forms of military power outlined in Chapter 1. In order to persuade, for example, airpower can assist information operations by spreading flyers or jamming opposition broadcasts or relay own transmissions providing alternative information to the opponent. For example, air force units released nearly thirty two million leaflets over Iraq during the Iraq war in 2003. Airpower can of course also be used to discourage opponents from choosing certain policy options deemed less favorable. As shown below, this was one of the basic ideas of nuclear strategy during the Cold War. Conventional airpower can also be used for deterrence, coercion, and brute force. Indeed, airpower theory has mostly focused on these three ways to wield military power.

To provide airpower theory an even clearer strategic framework, Pape (1996: 56) identifies four categories of airpower strategies, i.e. the links or the "mechanisms by which the destruction of a target set is supposed to translate into changed enemy behavior." The concept thus catches the logic of operational art of airpower, i.e. how tactical successes are translated into strategic results. Pape (1996: 55–6) suggests that we can distinguish four different forms of operational art in the context of independent airpower; punishment, risk, denial, and decapitation.

1. The first category is *punishment* campaigns. The inherent logic suggests that by punishing undesirable behavior of the opponent, you raise the costs for the opponent to choose some courses of action. Therefore, gradually, the opponent will learn what behavior to choose in order to avoid punishment. Examples of this logic have been plentiful in the history of air bombing and it has often been understood (and conducted) as punishing the civilian population, in the hope that the civilians would put pressure on its government to behave in a certain way. The airpower theories of Douhet as well as much of the logic underpinning Allied bombing campaigns during World War II share striking similarities to this kind of punishment strategy.

2. The second category is *risk* campaigns. These are essentially similar to punishment when it comes to targeting and the underlying logic of increasing the cost of certain behavior for the opponent. However, rather than maximizing the punishment, the typical risk campaign tries to signal desired behavior through using variation in intensity of bombing. This gives the opponent time to think and change its behavior at an earlier (and therefore less costly) stage than in a punitive operation. The idea is thus closely associated with Schelling's (1960) concept of "gradual escalation." The US operation Rolling

Thunder against North Vietnam 1965–68, in which they made continuous operational pauses to try to communicate with North Vietnam is an oft-cited example of this kind airpower strategy.

3. The third category is *denial* campaigns. The logic here is that through bombing you deny the opponent the opportunity to choose certain strategies. Hence, rather than raising the cost of certain behavior, you make those options unavailable for the opponent. Central in this regard is the defeat of opposition military capabilities to prevent the opponent from implementing its strategy. Perhaps the most important target for the bombing is the opponent's armed forces. In particular, the idea is to cut off the enemy front positions from the rear through battlefield (or theater-wide) interdiction. Effectively, this leads to cutting the logistics chain as well as denying the opponent the ability to mass reinforcements using reserves. Once the opponent's military options are gone, it can only choose the option that is desired. An empirical example of this operation art is America's operation Linebacker against North Vietnam in 1972.

4. The fourth category is *decapitation*. The idea here is to achieve your strategic goals through either eliminating or severing the leadership of the military units from the rank-and-file. Accordingly, you effectively generate system collapse or nullify the military front units since they are incapable of massing and conducting a concerted campaign. Hence, strategic goals are reached either through replacing the elites to those favorable to you or through forcing the opponent to cease resistance. One empirical example is the US-led coalition's air operations during the initial phase of the Iraq War in 2003. During this campaign, there were several attempts to eliminate the ruling Iraqi elite as well as attacking its command and control structure. Moreover, the currently ongoing US drone campaign in the wider Middle East can be understood as a decapitation campaign in the war on terrorism. Arguably, the major proponent of this category of airpower theory is John Warden (1998) and his theory of the "enemy as a system."

None of these four categories of airpower mechanisms make explicit assumptions about the balance of power between the parties. However, there are some implicit assumptions made regarding capabilities. For example, both decapitation campaigns and denial campaigns require precision-guided munitions to be effective (Warden 1998: 188–9; Pape 2004: 109–12). Decapitation campaigns that cannot destroy individual command and control centers, for example, will hardly be effective. Moreover, if battlefield interdiction is to be effective, it may involve destroying individual roads or tracks that are used to support front units or for reinforcements. Meanwhile, risk and punishment campaigns do not rely equally heavy on precision-guided bombs or drones. Here, the targets are of a different nature.

The utility of airpower

The major distinction in theories of airpower and air warfare is between those who believe that airpower has the greatest impact as a strategic stand-alone resource and those who believe that airpower instead should be used at the operational-tactical level to support ground or sea combat units, i.e. as a "flying artillery." Most of the answers to how airpower can help win wars fits into these two traditions. The latter school of thought relates to how airpower is used most effectively combined with land and naval forces. These theories have largely been dealt with in Chapter 6 on joint operations. Our focus in this chapter is rather on variation in the first school of thought. Although there are similarities between the supporters of independent air forces (all advocating strategic bombing to win the war), there are also major differences, not the least regarding targeting, causal logic, and sequencing of targets. What is the logic behind these target selections and sequencing? What causal mechanisms do they rely upon, explicitly and implicitly?

Figure 9.1 shows the hypothesized relationship between a series of target selections and the utility of airpower. The early use of airpower – from air balloons, airships, and early aircraft – focused primarily on the direct destruction of opponent armed forces. During the interwar period ideas about an indirect approach began to emerge. Rather than focusing directly on the destruction of military capabilities, it was more about attacking the opponent's *will* to continue to resist. Strategic bombing theory has largely followed these two tracks. You either conceptualize bombing as directly decimating military capabilities or frame it as bombing indirectly decimating military capability through decimating public will, elite will, or the military will to continue to resist. Willingness and capabilities are, of course, intimately connected because will can be affected by skills and capabilities, while capabilities can be affected by will. By separating them analytically, we can better examine the logic of the theories. Admittedly, hardly any of the airpower theorists have a one-sided, simplified view on this either.

The pioneers

The Italian General Guilio Douhet is often considered as the pioneer among airpower theorists and his theorizing belongs to the most scrutinized and well-analyzed in the field (e.g. Meilinger 1997: 1–40). In his most famous book, *Il Dominio dell' Aria* (1921), he argued that massive bombings of cities, including blasting them with fire- and gas munitions in "correct proportions", would quickly result in victory. By bombing the population, Douhet suggested, it would threaten the incumbent government with revolution to change its policy

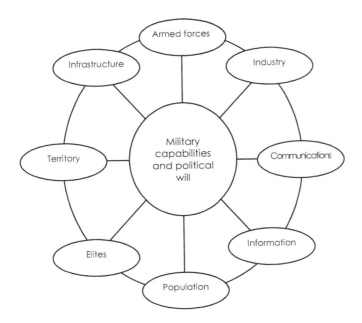

Figure 9.1 Airpower targeting (adapted from Meilinger 2003: 174).

and thus stop the war. Douhet's ideas, however, are based on assumptions that rest on a shaky foundation.

First, he assumed that airpower and the air force was a fundamentally offensive weapon. Unlike ground forces, air force had intrinsic characteristics – speed, altitude, and range – that could be exploited to avoid getting caught in a stalemate. Douhet did not suggest that airpower alone could win wars. Instead, he (1999: 289–93) emphasized, which is often forgotten, that strategic bombers in combination with defensive land operations was the key to success in war. This combination, in turn, was based on the premise that air operations were inherently offensive, while land operations were static and defensive. For those experiencing German *Blitzkrieg* two decades later, this assumption appeared odd, but among Douhet's contemporaries who had experienced the stalemate of trench warfare on the Western Front during World War I, the assumption was not only defensible, but also had numerous supporters.

Second, Douhet (1999: 339–56) also assumed that no one would be able to defend against bombers. This made him even more focused on arguing that it was only by concentrating on building large bomber fleets that breakthroughs could be realized. Douhet was not alone in holding this position. Other contemporary early airpower theorists also suggested that defensive air operations were difficult or impossible. This hints at a possible contradiction within airpower theory. While often stressing technological developments and relying upon deducing propositions from the technology, it seems oddly inept to ignore that other technologies may make earlier ideas redundant. For example, the invention of radar clearly created sufficient conditions to wage air war defensively.

Third, central to Douhet's claim was the assertion that popular will would be broken by mass bombings. That the will to continue to fight could be strengthened by the aerial bombings against civilian targets – as occurred during the London Blitz during World War II – was not predicted by Douhet. Instead, he imagined that society would collapse quickly as the bombs started to fall. He (1999: 331–3, 336, 386–7) even asserted that bombing campaigns against civilian population centers was more humane than to bomb military forces, since the war would be shorter – and therefore fewer lives would be sacrificed – than through protracted aerial bombings against the more durable and better protected military units. This does not mean that Douhet ignored the effects that civilian targeting would have on front line military units. Instead, he also stressed that "the armed forces will, in fact, suffer terrible moral pressures" if their homes and cities are bombed while they are away (Johansson 1988: 279).

There is a further contradiction in Douhet's theory when it comes to the importance of air superiority. He claimed, on the one hand, that it was crucial to establish air superiority, but on the other hand, that it was impossible to defend against bomber fleets (Douhet 1999: 283, 293, 307). These two claims cannot be combined, since air superiority cannot be important if bomber fleets can break through anyway. Air superiority would then be irrelevant. This suggests that there are other implicit assumptions in Douhet's theorizing. Perhaps most importantly in this context, he must have thought that bombing civilians in cities is only of secondary importance. The first target must have been the opponent's air force. If the opponent's air force were to be defeated, it could not threaten you. Traces of this assumption can also be observed in Douhet's idea of pre-emptive attack. In this regard, he (1999: 303, 334) claimed that by building bomber fleets the offensive would be much stronger than the defensive, resulting in whomever attacked first also winning the war.

Douhet's theory was not undisputed and he had critics even in his native Italy. For example, contemporary theorists Gianni Caproni and Nino Salvaneschi based their theories on a very different logic than Douhet. Instead of mass bombings on population centers, they argued that the strategic bombing campaign should be concentrated against enemy factories which produced munitions and other military equipment. This would force a favorable asymmetric relation between the ground troops, which, in turn, would lead to victory. Unlike Douhet's focus on the will of the population, they argued, that it was by defeating the opponent's military units that victory could be achieved (Faber 2002: 56). Douhet's ideas about unstoppable bomber fleets were also criticized by Mecozzi, who emphasized fighters and interdiction (see Chapter 6).

Meanwhile, airpower theorizing also continued to develop in both the US and Britain (Davies Biddle 2002; Meilinger 1997). In the US, General William Mitchell (1879–1936) emerged as the leading figure both in terms of airpower theory and the institutionalization of the air force as a separate branch of the armed forces. Like Douhet, Mitchell had served in World War I, mostly in various staff positions. Although sometimes held to be less of an original thinker than Douhet, Mitchell was far more successful in serving as an inspiration to others as well as leading the development of airpower theory (MacIsaac 1986: 631). Similar to Douhet (although it is unclear if he developed his ideas independently of Douhet or if he was influenced by Douhet, see Clodfelter 1997: 98; Meilinger 2001: 11–12), Mitchell stressed the importance of strategic bombing. Unlike Douhet, however, Mitchell suggested a different target strategy and different mechanisms through which airpower would lead to victory. Consequently, Mitchell also attributed different weight to air superiority. The war of attrition on the Western Front during World War I also influenced Mitchell, insofar as he immediately after the war suggested the majority of air force bombings should be carried out in support of the ground troops to enable breakthroughs. Gradually, however, Mitchell's ideas grew more radical and in *Winged Defense: The Development and Possibilities of Modern Air Power: Economic and Military'* (1925), he advocated a more independent and central role for the bombers.

In short, Mitchell claimed that strategic bombing would lead to victory in war if the opponent's industrial and economic centers were targeted. Like Douhet, he hypothesized that the population eventually would rebel against the government or force a change in policy. The causal mechanism was not, as in Douhet's theory, that the population suffered deaths directly, but rather indirectly through the destruction of the economic centers. Unlike Douhet, Mitchell stressed that targeting economic centers would deprive military front line units of logistical support, means of transportation, and in the long run also military equipment. The military would therefore be denied the means to continue the war. In this sense, Mitchell thought he had come up with a way of winning war that both decimated the will to continue the war and the means with which to do so (Clodfelter 1997: 96–7). Like Douhet, Mitchell also believed that pre-emptive strikes were the logical way to win wars. The country with the fastest and most efficient air force, Mitchell (1999: 436) claimed, "will bring a lasting and quick victory." Since Mitchel's reasoning was largely similar to Douhet's, his theory is based on similar assumptions.

The so-called "Bomber mafia" at ACTS – founded in 1920 in the US – continued development of airpower theory after Mitchell was dismissed from the air force, due to slandering his superiors after an accident. Theorists at ACTS soon launched the so-called "industrial web theory," in which the opponent was assumed to operate as a system. Here, the idea was that strategic bombing would be directed against economic "nodes" in the system. Destroying these nodes, it was hypothesized, would generate social and economic collapse. The opponent's will to continue the war would thus be broken and defeat would be certain. Unlike Douhet and Mitchell, the ACTS theory made explicit assumptions about the nature of the opponent, instead of just prophesizing how the opponent would be defeated. By being explicit, the ACTS theorists essentially refined Mitchell's thoughts to make them more empirically testable. It also paved the way for thinking about targeting in different ways. By understanding the state as a complex system of economic and social dependencies, it was possible to conjure new ways of inducing collapse of this system. By destroying key nodes, the system as a whole would suffer problems of communication between different functions and chain reactions would be created throughout the system. Bombing cities would not accomplish this. Instead, industrial targets, factories, communications, railroads, electricity plants, and distribution would cause the system to collapse and the will of the people to be broken. Several of those who were active in the ACTS later appeared in the bomber command that planned and implemented the US bombing operations of Nazi Germany and Japan (Faber 1997b).

Meanwhile, in interwar Britain, the development of airpower thought followed a slightly different path. Like Douhet and Mitchell, the British airpower pioneers – the Air Marshals Sir Hugh Trenchard (1873–1956), Sir John Slessor (1897–1979), and Sir Arthur "Bomber" Harris (1892–1984) – advocated strategic bombing. In a similar way as in the US and Italy, the British theorists were prominent officers who also advocated an independent organization for the air force. The tactical use of aircraft in World War I convinced the British to establish a separate branch – the RAF – as early as 1918. The three air marshals represented similar ideas that emerged in continental Europe and the US. Slessor advocated a bombing strategy similar to ACTS and Mitchell, insofar as he wanted to target factories and the production lines of military equipment and thereby weaken the will and capability of continued war. "Bomber" Harris, in turn, advocated a similar idea to Douhet insofar as targeting the population with area bombings was concerned. Harris' ideas partly informed the British aerial campaign against Nazi Germany during World War II, including the fire bombings of population centers such as Hamburg and Dresden. Unlike the Americans, however, Trenchard suggested that strategic bombing led to victory by decimating the opponent's armed forces. By bombing the enemy front units as well as roads and transportation, it was thought that the front line units would be starved of equipment and ammunition as well as reserves. Gradually, therefore, the opponent's capability to continue to fight would be decimated, resulting in operational paralysis (Meilinger 2003: 36–74).

Nuclear strategy and airpower

During the Cold War, the development of airpower theory was intimately connected to the development of nuclear deterrence between the superpowers (e.g. Freedman 2003, 2004). Unlike much other military theorizing, this was almost exclusively a domain for civilian theorists. Nuclear strategists such as Bernard Brodie, Herman Kahn, Albert Wohlstetter, Thomas Schelling, and others contributed as much to the development of strategic theory in general as to the development of airpower theory. Although nuclear weapons in many circles initially were understood as a weapon among others, there were also those that early on argued that the unprecedented destructive powers of the atom bombs radically changed the rules of the game. As early as 1946 in *The Absolute Weapon: Atomic Power and World Order*, Brodie observed that the tremendous effect of the new weapon made war irrelevant as a solution to conflicts. Nuclear weapons' only rational use, he argued, was deterrence. He thus set the conditions for the strategic debate for two generations of strategic thinkers during the Cold War.

Nuclear weapons challenged the classical approach to strategy in two ways. First, they made the prevailing concept of victory problematic if a war could escalate into a large-scale nuclear war. In particular during the 1940s and 1950s, this was not as obvious as later on, since the superpowers' nuclear arsenals were quite limited both in terms of warheads and the destructive powers of each of the bombs. Nuclear weapons, moreover, seemingly offered what initially was understood to be a more cost-effective alternative to the maintenance of large-scale conventional forces. As nuclear arsenals grew, delivery vehicles and warheads were refined, and home bases were made less vulnerable, however, it was realized that victory was an illusion. Liddell Hart argued in 1960 that "trying to win a nuclear war was nothing but pure madness" (Baylis & Garnett 1991: 1). The traditional understanding of strategy and victory was rendered almost meaningless when the two sides in the Cold War acquired so-called "second strike capability" (Wohlstetter 1956; Rosecrance 1991). The ability to destroy the opponent even after the opponent had carried out an initial surprise attack made arguments about the utility of pre-emptive strikes that had thus far dominated the debate meaningless. There was no longer any rationality in the use of nuclear weapons except as a deterrent and as a last resort.

Second, the advent of nuclear weapons also changed the logic of deterrence. Since each of the Cold War opponents realized that the use of nuclear weapons was potentially self-destructive, signaling a *credible* deterrent became highly problematic. On the one hand, not using nuclear weapons as part of the deterrence would have signaled indecisiveness of their use and thus weakened the deterrent. On the other hand, the mutually shared knowledge that the use of nuclear weapons would devastate both the superpowers made nuclear deterrence less credible.

During the Cold War, much thought on both sides of the Iron Curtain was devoted to managing these two issues, as is evident in the development of nuclear doctrines. The US strategy of "massive retaliation" in the 1950s came under severe criticism due to lack of credibility. Critics argued that it simply was not credible that the US would deploy nuclear weapons to counter a limited conventional provocation from the Soviet Union. If the strategy was not credible, it rather invited the Soviets to act aggressively. In addition, the fact that both of the super powers gradually acquired intercontinental missiles, as well as submarine-based missiles, made the strategy appear redundant and lacking in credibility. The strategy, in short, would not deliver any deterrence if the situation of mutual assured destruction made nuclear weapons surplus to requirements. Eventually this was untenable and the US modified its strategy in the 1960s into so-called "flexible response." Rather than an all-out nuclear assault for any form of Soviet provocation, flexible response meant that the US would meet Soviet aggression with graduated and proportional responses. Hence, a conventional attack would be met with conventional weapons, while a nuclear attack would render a nuclear response. This resulted in a greater credibility for nuclear deterrence because it acknowledged that the US could respond to any provocations without necessarily resorting to nuclear weapons. A graduated response implied that political intentions could be signaled by controlled patterns of escalation and de-escalation. This gave nuclear weapons perhaps their most relevant role in the military use of force; they were weapons that had their greatest impact by their very existence (Freedman 1986: 740–5, 757–9).

According to strategist and later Nobel Prize laureate, Schelling (1966), nuclear weapons and airpower shared the peculiar characteristic that their main advantage and strength in the use of force was their latent capability. They were effective in realizing political goals since their effects were predictable. By increasing or decreasing the intensity of the threat or the intensity of conventional bombing directed against the population – the so-called theory of gradual escalation – actors could, according to Schelling, clearly signal their resolve and their preferences. The logic implied that the state that was put under the sword would understand and interpret correctly shifts in the intensity and specific targets that were bombed and could adapt its behavior accordingly. To put it in more formal theoretical terms, by varying the bombing, one changes the opponent's expectation about the future cost-benefit calculus of certain policies. Once it became clear to the opponent which policy it should pursue to avoid further bombing, gradual escalation had the intended effect. A key element in the use of airpower in support of a strategy of gradual escalation was to continually provide the opponent with the opportunity to respond or to obey. Similarly, not bombing certain targets was understood to send important signals. Schelling hoped that since airpower could be used to signal intent and resolve, it implied that even a major war would not degenerate into a nuclear war, because both parties would be able to use airpower to signal that they wanted to avoid nuclear escalation.

Schelling's logic is heavily influenced by rationalist theory. The assumption of actors in war as rational and unitary has already been briefly discussed, but there is reason to return to some elements. Schelling's ideas presuppose that parties understand each other's intentions by observing (or suffering the consequences of) behavior. However, behavior is not like a shared language. It is far from certain that such blunt variation in "language" as intensity and targeting sequences will send an unequivocal message. There is even a risk that gradual escalation can be understood as being indecisive. Moreover, Schelling assumes that the parties will react in a similar way to variation in threat level. This presupposes that the parties essentially share the same structure of preferences or at least that it is possible to ascertain the opponent's structure of preferences. In many cases of bargaining, however, actors – according to the same unyielding rationalist logic – have incentives to manipulate information about (or keep secret) their preferred policy options and goals. Political psychologists (e.g. Vertzberger 1990; Jervis 1976) have pointed out that in such contexts, mirror imaging and cognitive distortion easily take hold and supersede the decision-making. Furthermore, it may also be the case that one exaggerates the extent to which the opponent acts as a unified actor. There are, most likely, more or less pronounced power struggles and debates of policy options in all states, especially if they are being exposed to strategic bombing. By mistakenly believing that the opponent is unitary, gradual escalation may send the wrong signals.

The development of nuclear strategy was much influenced by interwar airpower theory. The close link between nuclear strategy and airpower theory originated from the fact that airplanes initially were the only available carrier for strategic nuclear weapons. It was not until the early 1960s that the superpowers had developed credible alternative options such as intercontinental or submarine-launched ballistic missiles. Even later, the strategic bombers were still significant for the superpowers to maintain sufficient flexibility for a credible second-strike capability. Accordingly, circles within the Strategic Air Command (SAC) dominated theorizing on nuclear strategy among the military in the US (e.g. Roman 1995). Both Freedman (1986: 761) and Mueller (1997: 290–3) point out that this meant that theorizing on nuclear weapons wwas heavily influenced by airpower theory.

The close relationship between early airpower theory and nuclear strategy is evident when comparing the causal mechanism of how it was hypothesized that nuclear strikes were to lead to victory in war. First, as in early airpower theory, nuclear weapons were considered as inherently offensive and favoring pre-emptive strikes. Second, the logic of targeting in early airpower theory was essentially reproduced in theorizing on the use of nuclear weapons. There were, on the one hand, those that advocated the bombing of population centers – the so-called counter-city strategy – and on the other hand those that favored striking the opponent's armed forces – the so-called counter-force strategy. The first school of thought claimed that nuclear strikes on cities would cause such a devastating blow to the opponent that he would not dare to either provoke or continue to fight. The social fabric and economic system of the state would simply cease to exist if its cities were destroyed. Meanwhile, the second school of thought argued that nuclear strikes were to be directed at the opponent's strategic nuclear forces. Here, the logic implied that if you were able to destroy the opponent's nuclear arsenal while grounded, he would have little option but to follow your preferred policies. This idea is a clear heir of Douhet's and Mitchell's assumptions of airpower as unstoppable once the planes have taken off from the runways. Even the ideas of limited, tactical nuclear war had their intellectual inspiration from airpower theory. Here, theorizing on nuclear strikes followed Russian and German interwar airpower theory stressing the potential of nuclear strikes as operational interdiction. Once nuclear strikes were launched, the blast areas could be used to achieve breakthroughs in enemy lines to facilitate deep attacks by armored units. Both these ideas were directed at the opponent's military capability (Freedman 1986: 746–51).

Nuclear strategy can also be seen as a precursor to innovation in conventional airpower theory in the 1980s and 1990s. Fortunately for mankind, much theorizing on nuclear arms has not been possible to test empirically. The absence of systematical empirical testing of theories and hypotheses is yet another similarity to early airpower theorists. As such, nuclear strategy is also heavily influenced by assumptions of rational actors and deductions from technological capabilities. The advantage of this for intellectual purposes was that a lot of effort was put in to outline the logic of nuclear strategy. Perhaps this is also the main contribution of nuclear strategy, and it made not only airpower theory, but military theory in general, more logically coherent. It also set the foundation for the airpower theorists of the 1990s. They had a more coherent, sound theoretical platform to depart from in their analyses of the air campaigns in the Persian Gulf War as well as the wars in the Balkans. Peter Faber (2002: 87) claims that the link to nuclear strategy was crucial in re-invigorating modern *conventional* airpower theory. The connection to nuclear strategy symbolized "an evolving recognition that airpower was much more than a blunt tool, destruction-centered instrument of total war. Instead, it had the potential to function as a tool that deterred, compelled, and coerced others." Although the Cold War is over, we should not forget, moreover, that the logic of nuclear strategy is still valid and highly relevant. Indeed, as more states acquire nuclear arsenals, it may even have more relevance today than before, although the number of warheads in the arsenals of the superpowers has been reduced.

The independent role of the air force in conventional warfare is rediscovered

During the 1980s, the development of airpower theory in the US stagnated, and positions gradually became entrenched between SAC and its advocacy of strategic bombing and those in favor of the then newly published AirLand Battle doctrine that prescribed joint operations and close collaboration with the army. At that point, John Warden published his book *The Air Campaign: Planning for Combat* in 1986. Warden's book had a tremendous effect, reviving conventional airpower theory in the US and breaking the deadlock in the debate (Olsen 2007; van Creveld 2011: 241–2; Fadok 1997). Warden suggested that the prevailing airpower theory was at an intellectual dead end and inhibited the potential effects of air forces in modern war. He argued that independent conventional strategic strikes against enemy centers of gravity could be decisive in warfare. In short, Warden suggested that striking at the opponent leadership (or at least communications) would paralyze its armed forces and force opposing troops to collapse. This clearly falls into the category of a strategy of decapitation. He (2000: *x*, 1995: 13–14) was particularly critical of strategic bombing of military units. There were a number of similarities between Warden's theory and "industrial web theory" as it was developed by ACTS in the 1930s. In both cases, for example, it was assumed that the enemy operated as a system. Both emphasized the alleged offensive nature of airpower and understood the destruction of opponent infrastructure as critical to success. However, there were also differences.

Warden's theory was based on two main assumptions. First, he presupposed that John Boyd's theory of decision-making cycles was correct. Without this assumption, there is no reason to conclude that attacking the opponent's systems of command and control would lead to system collapse. Boyd's theory of decision-making cycles (as discussed in Chapter 7), in short, set forth the idea that, by being better to respond to new decision-making situations, an actor would gain a relative advantage by increasing the rate of such new cycles of decision-making. Ultimately, the actor that is slow to respond will be thrown off-guard, fail to make necessary decisions, and collapse. By targeting the opponent's systems for communication as well as for command and control, Warden suggested that the opponent would be impaired and eventually unable to respond. There were some differences between Boyd and Warden, however, when it comes to the level of abstraction. While Boyd assumed that the actor is an individual – and thus that the theory can be derived from cognitive psychology – Warden assumed that the logic applied to collective actors.

Second, Warden assumed that it is possible to characterize the opponent as a system and that it is possible to induce system paralysis by decapitation of the system's core. In 1995, Warden further developed his arguments and elaborated on the theory of the "enemy as a system." Here, Warden was explicit insofar as suggesting that all organic systems consisted of the same five basic elements: (1) a leadership to direct the system, (2) system essentials to transform energy from one part of the system to another, (3) infrastructure to maintain the system, (4) a population inhabiting the system, and (5) armed forces that protect the system from external threats. Warden suggested that these basic elements were organized as five rings with the leadership at the core of the model and the protective forces at the periphery. His main theoretical claim was that if the leadership – or at least communications and the command and control that underpinned the leadership – is targeted, the system will

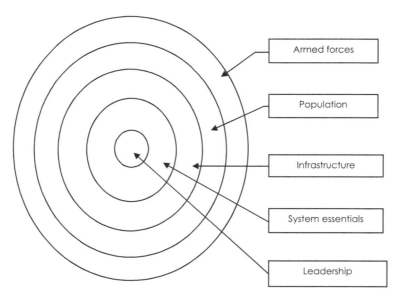

Figure 9.2 Warden's (1995) model of the enemy as a system.

either collapse or the leadership will be isolated, and the outer rings can be easily defeated (Warden 1995).

By now, Warden's theory was heavily criticized. It was pointed out that the logic of the model relied on metaphors that were highly debateable. For example, the construction of the enemy as a system is based on the assumption that a collective actor – the state – is akin to a human being. This is far from self-evident. While humans cannot grow new brains, a state is an open system that allow for reproduction or replacement of its leadership (Faber 2002: 56–7). It is equally important to emphasize that Warden's theory is not empirically substantiated in any systematic large-N study. As with the vast majority of airpower theorists, Warden's theory is based instead on technological deductions or cherry-picking from a few cases that seem to be selected to fit his theory, rather than being representative of the whole population of air campaigns. This criticism does not invalidate the theory as such, but it means that we should regard it as a hypothesis rather than an empirically proven theory.

In *Bombing to Win: Air Power and Coercion in War* (1996), one of Warden's critics, Robert Pape, argued that decapitation strategies had both logical and practical problems. Pape advanced the argument that it is extremely difficult to locate, and then successfully target, the opponent's leadership – even with today's advanced precision-guided munitions. Moreover, he also suggested that to decapitate the opponent is counterproductive. If war is an instrument of policy, which both Warden and Pape assume, then war is also a tool for sending messages to the other party. If you continuously eliminate the leadership of the opponent, there is no one to receive the signals and thus war drags on longer than if there was an opponent that could realize that it has been defeated. Certainly, forcing a new leadership onto your opponent in the midst of war can be successful, but the empirical record also shows that it can backfire. It is, in theoretical terms, difficult to assess the new leadership's preferences (Pape 1996: 79–86; Pape 2004: 116–30). For example, fearing a large-scale uprising in Cyprus, the British Field Marshal Sir John Harding imprisoned what he saw as the leader of the Cypriote EOKA movement aiming for *Enosis* – unification with Greece in 1955. However, as it turned out the imprisoned Archbishop Makarios had belonged to the moderate wing of the EOKA, thus far preventing violence and Harding's attempted decapitation of the movement effectively conferred the reins of EOKA to hardliner Georgios Grivas, prompting immediate violence (e.g. Corum 2008).

Instead of decapitation, Pape suggests that it is more effective to target the opponent's armed forces. The claim caused furor among air force circles (e.g. Frankel 2001; Bratton 2003). In classical, Clausewitzian manner, Pape argues that as long as you deprive the opponent of the means to continue the fight, you are in a position of strength and can dictate the terms of the new peace. Denying the opponent the opportunity to pursue some policy options by depleting the armed forces thus ultimately ensures that the opponent will choose the preferred option. According to Pape (1996: 69–79), this can be done in three principal ways. First, airpower can be used to support advancing ground troops. This is the same idea as we elaborated upon in Chapter 6 on joint operations. Airpower can facilitate breakthroughs. Second, airpower can be used for strategic interdiction. Here, the idea is to strike at the opponent's production lines for military equipment, thus creating a more favorable future balance of power on the battlefield. Third, airpower can be used for operational interdiction. In operational level interdiction, the idea is to decimate the capabilities of front line units through denying them reinforcements as well as logistical support. This in turn creates a favorable balance of power in a quicker way, than the more long-term strategic interdiction.

Pape's theory shares some of the features of "industrial web theory" and John Slessor's ideas about interdiction as a method to weaken the opponent's military units. Unlike much airpower theory, it should be emphasized that Pape's conclusions are empirically substantiated (Horowitz & Reiter 2001). This provides Pape's claims with a completely different weight than the more futuristic technological deductions of much airpower theory. However, there are still problems with Pape's arguments. Like Schelling, Pape relies upon the assumption of rational actors. Moreover, Pape's interpretations of his case studies have been criticized, not least the extent to which Japan and Germany were influenced in their decision-making by allied bombing campaigns during World War II (e.g. Mueller 1998). Pape's theory is also very much geared towards explaining the role of airpower in large-scale conventional warfare, but airpower can be used in other contexts and it is far from certain that interdiction is an efficient method for coercion short of open war.

In the late 1990s, airpower theory continued to develop. The technological developments with improved precision-guided munitions and communications paved the way for new ideas of how airpower could lead to victory in war. Not implemented until the Iraq War in 2003, operational concepts such as "effects-based operations" (EBO), parallel warfare, rapid dominance, and "shock and awe" had a major impact on the airpower debate (e.g. Deptula 2001; Davis 2001; Ullman & Wade 1996; Chisholm 2003). Most of these new ideas were developments of Warden's theory of the enemy as a system, but much refined as the development of technology progressed. Central to these sets of hypotheses was the assertion that stealth technology, precision-guided weapons, and better situational awareness enabled parallel – instead of serial – warfare. Rather than using air forces to attack targets one at a time, and nitpicking over the proper sequencing, the new airpower theorists advocated parallel attacks. Simultaneity was made possible through surgical strikes. Thus, the destruction of targets did not require scores of bombing sorties. By striking simultaneously and with strategic depth, it was hypothesized that the opponent would not have the time to recuperate losses or repair critical infrastructure. This, in turn, would create a shock wave through the system. Although impressive in detail in terms of targeting principles, modern airpower theory can be criticized for being overly reliant upon the US as the presumed actor. In terms of explanatory power, this creates a confounding variable. It may not be the hypothesis on air targeting that explains victory, but rather the fact that it is the US with its incomparable overall military supremacy. It also limits the practical utility of these concepts. To use them effectively depends on possessing certain capital-intensive infrastructure, satellites, etc. that only the US has access to.

The solution to the problem of sequencing and pooling operations, according to David Deptula (1991: 3–13), is so-called "effects-based theorizing." Thinking in terms of effects, rather than in terms of sets of targets, implies that the focus changes from destruction to aims in war. Hence, instead of thinking of how to find and bomb individual enemy fighter jets, you can focus on ways of making the air defense system unusable. Instead of flying hundreds of surveillance sorties to establish a targeting sequence, you can target the power plant and the transformer station that supplies electricity to the opponent's air defenses. Deptula argued that thinking in effects, rather than targets, freed resources that can be better spent elsewhere. This theory, too, is dependent upon stealth technology and precision-guided strikes. If hitting the transformer station required vast number of sorties and bombs, parallel warfare would still be an illusion. The effects of precision-guided munitions should not be taken lightly. For example, one plane with precision-guided bombs during the Gulf War in 1991 accomplished the same result, presumably, as 1,000 planes with over 9,000 bombs during World War II.

The essence of effects-based theorizing and EBO in a military context is to conquer not by destruction, but by making the opponent's weapons systems inoperative. On the one hand, this line of thought is in line with much Clausewitzian thought, since it generates a focused effort in line with the war aims. On the other hand, it is also distinctively non-Clausewitzian, since Clausewitz stressed the need to destroy opponent's military capabilities and then be in a position to dictate the peace. EBO also requires excellent intelligence about the opponent's infrastructure, transportations, command, and control system. It is far from certain that it is possible to possess such intelligence. Furthermore, although the EBO-logic promises quick and cheap returns for bombing campaigns, the idea that surgical pinprick strikes can generate system collapse is empirically doubtful (Echevarria 2001). For example, US bombers destroyed 90 percent of the power plants in North Korea in 1953 and North Vietnam in 1968. Still, the population did not rebel or surrender. Neither did the armed forces surrender. In Germany and Japan towards the end of World War II as much as 20 percent of the population was homeless as a result of the allied bombing, but the societal fabric did not collapse (Pape 1996: 320). Finally, if we think in terms of rationalist theory of war and costly signals, it may be the case that a surgical strike with a drone or Tomahawk-missile may be too subtle a signal. The opponent may, in fact, interpret this limited strike as "cheap talk" and conclude that you are not determined to win the dispute. Hence, although the EBO-logic seemingly is an effective method for coercion, it may also be counterproductive at times. The surgical strikes, moreover, reduces the fear of the unexpected in war. Increased efficiency in the military means can, paradoxically, lead to decreased ability to exercise military power.

Conclusions

Like other kinds of military theory, airpower theory has proved to have a dual nature: one normative and one explanatory. In this chapter, we have introduced airpower theory and demonstrated how various theorists have hypothesized the causality between airpower and victory in war. To put airpower theory in a strategic context, much theorizing has been devoted to how war aims should be translated into targeting and sequencing charts for the bomber commands. It is important to stress that the theories presented here are not the only ones, or even necessarily the most dominant ones, or those that inform practical air campaigns the most. It may very well be, from time to time, that those advocating air forces as mainly supportive of armies are most successful in terms of institutionalizing their arguments in doctrines.

As explanatory theory, we have demonstrated that airpower theory has both strengths and weaknesses. In particular, after the advent of nuclear power, airpower theory has largely been deductively sound and coherent. Hence, empirical testing to a larger extent than what has been carried out so far should prove valuable and realizable. In particular, airpower theory is commendable in outlining the hypothesized causal chains. As normative theory, airpower theory also has a set of weaknesses and strengths. We have, for example, stressed how the absence of closer analysis of the opponent and the strategic context is especially problematic for some of the theories. There has generally been much focus on targeting and how to find, identify, and destroy targets, but less focus on why specific targets are destroyed.

Table 9.1 summarizes much of airpower theorizing and highlights the causal chain as it has been suggested. As pointed out above, many of these theories are not empirically substantiated in systematical empirical studies and should rather be understood as a collection of hypotheses. This has sometimes rendered critique that airpower theorists are mainly visionaries and prophets, rather than social scientists (Holley Jr. 1997: 579–99). The lack of empirical studies to substantiate the causal claims must, however, be put into context. Nuclear strategists especially, but also airpower pioneers, simply did not have any empirical data to access. Although the Italians carried out trial bombings of Turkish units already in

Table 9.1 Overview of suggested causal relations in airpower theory (adapted from Faber 2002)

Theorist	Targeting	Mechanism	Effect
Douhet	Population	Public uprising	Overthrow government or change policies
Mitchell	Economic centers	Public uprising	Overthrow government or change policies
ACTS	Nodes in the industry	Socio-economic collapse	Overthrow government or change policies
Trenchard	Military equipment, transportations, and logistics	Operational paralysis	Overthrow government or change policies
Slessor	Troops, supplies, and production	Decimate capability	Military defeat
Schelling	Population	Gradual escalation	Changed policies
Warden	Leadership	Decapitation	Military defeat through leadership paralysis
Pape	Troops	Decimate front line military capability	Military defeat
Deptula	Nodes for system effects	Units and functions unusable	Systemic collapse

1911 and Germany bombed London in the summer of 1917, no large-scale use of strategic bombing occurred until the Spanish Civil War and, above all, World War II.

The early lack of empirical evidence has also led to the notion (and defense of its propositions by advocates) that airpower theory does work, but only when technology catches up. Hence, there have been suggestions that the interwar theories of Douhet and Mitchell were being validated only in the 1990s, with the introduction of precision-guided munitions (Meilinger 2003: 8). The lack of empirical data is also a problem for practitioners. The planning procedures required to estimate sometimes causal chains consisting of multiple links (as many EBO-hopefuls seem to advocate), in particular, is very time-consuming. Airpower theory also seems to exaggerate the potential effects. Those proposing strategic area bombings overestimate the psychological effects of bombing, while those favoring system collapse through surgical strikes, underestimate the resilience of the modern state.

Questions for discussion

1. Is airpower inherently offensive?
2. To what extent is air superiority a precondition for victory in modern war?
3. How are theories of airpower relevant for small, medium, or great powers?
4. How can airpower contribute to the pursuit of victory against terrorists or non-state actors?
5. How can we design empirical studies that test the main tenants of airpower theory?
6. At what level of warfare is airpower most important?

Further reading

Bernard Brodie, *Strategy in the Missile Age* (Princeton, NJ: Princeton University Press, 1959).

Martin van Creveld, *The Age of Airpower* (New York: Public Affairs, 2011).

James S. Corum & Wray R. Johnson, *Airpower in Small Wars: Fighting Insurgents and Terrorists* (Lawrence, Kansas: University Press of Kansas, 2003).

Lawrence Freedman, *The Evolution of Nuclear Strategy*, 3rd edn (London: Palgrave Macmillan, 2003).

Philip S. Meilinger (ed.), *The Paths of Heaven: The Evolution of Air Power Theory* (Maxwell, AL: Air University Press, 1997).

John Andreas Olsen (ed.), *A History of Air Warfare* (Washington DC: Potomac Books, 2009).

Robert A. Pape, *Bombing to Win: Air Power and Coercion in War* (Ithaca, NY: Cornell University Press, 1996).

John A. Warden III, *The Air Campaign: Planning for Combat*, 2nd edn (New York: ExCel, 2000).

10 The dynamics of war
Some conclusions

Introduction

This book has dealt with theories of war and warfare. It has introduced classical and modern military theory by focusing on the theories, the concepts they are made of, and the relationship between them. In particular, the two key issues in the study of the dynamics of war – the nature of war and how to win wars – have been the center of attention. It has also outlined the most important debates in the theory of war and warfare. In doing so, we have aimed to continuously criticize and analyze the theories and their claims. How to understand war and its dynamics has thus permeated this book. In this concluding chapter, we will summarize some of the central debates in terms of the general themes of military theory. Hence, we will elaborate on the extent to which the levels of warfare can help us understand the conduct of war, the extent to which the concept of power is fruitful when we analyze war and warfare, the extent to which social science methodology can contribute to a better understanding of war and warfare, and the extent to which theory and practice in war are interchangeable. We will conclude the chapter by outlining a framework on how to analyze the dynamics of war.

Military theory and the levels of war

The first general theme that permeates the book is the idea of levels of war. Dividing war into strategic, operative, and tactical levels is commonly understood to be an analytical tool used to better understand the conduct of war. The levels of war, however, do not only serve analytical purposes in order to understand a complex reality, but also have more direct and practical purposes. The levels of war usually coincide with levels of command and are therefore a critical part of how armies organize and prepare for war. In this way, levels of warfare are not just a way to analyze and understand war, but also a tool to plan and wage war.

When trying to understand war and warfare, using a three (or four)-tiered analytical instrument is fruitful insofar as it divides a complex matter into smaller and more manageable parts. By understanding the parts and the relationship between the parts, one can better grasp the whole. Furthermore, a tiered analytical tool increases theoretical rigor and facilitates scholarly debate. For example, victory manifests itself differently on the tactical level in comparison with the strategic level. By using the levels of war we can make this distinction and thus be more precise in how we conceptualize victory.

The levels of war change over time. The change concerns both how we name the levels, the contents of the levels, and the number of levels. Whereas pre-modern military thought in Western Europe was mostly concerned with tactics, the strategic level was gradually introduced during the eighteenth century. For Jomini and Clausewitz, the duality of strategy and tactics was central to their reasoning. While Jomini (1987: 460) understood the distinction as the art of war on maps (strategy) and the art of war on the battlefield (tactics), Clausewitz (1993: 146) suggested that strategy was the art of using battle for the purposes of the war and that tactics was the art of using armed forces in combat. Dividing warfare into levels thus increased the precision in the military theoretical debate at the time. Gradually, technological, industrial, and economical developments made it common in the theoretical debate to include three or four levels of war. For example, in Chapter 4 we described how the US in the aftermath of the failed war in Vietnam rediscovered the need for an operational level, between the strategic and tactical level, to optimize coordination of forces, strategic ends, and tactical means.

Explanations of how levels of war wax and wane are not plentiful. In one of the exceptions, Christopher Bassford (1997: 21) suggests that the number of intermediate levels of war is best understood as "administrative matter and only an organizational response to the specific distance that exists between the tactical operations and the political impact of a given conflict." In short, the greater the war and the larger the forces involved, the more levels of war will be introduced by leaders and commanders. In a conflict similar to World War II, it took many tactical battles to achieve political effects. Hence, more levels of war are necessary. At other times, in more limited small-scale conflicts, political and strategic effects can be achieved by smaller units or even by individuals. Hence, fewer levels of war are necessary. In the attacks on the World Trade Center and the Pentagon in September 2001, only a few individuals were involved, yet, they managed to set the strategic and political agenda for the better part of the decade. The assassination of the Austrian Crown Prince Franz Ferdinand and his wife in Sarajevo in July 1914 is another example where a single event conducted by one or a few people seems to have had great political impact.

Changes in, and the relative utility of, the levels of war is therefore contextual and intimately linked to the development of war and warfare in general. While we could observe an increase in the number of levels of war when army sizes grew during the nineteenth century, technological changes in missiles, aircraft, and means of communications in the late twentieth century have rather compressed the levels of war. Today, political elites have far greater opportunities to directly intervene in what 50 years ago would have been decisions better suited to company or even platoon commanders. On the one hand, this development should perhaps be applauded since it increases the accountability of the political leadership. On the other hand, it may also tempt decision-makers to increase their use of force (Betts 2012). Interaction between belligerents and the inner dynamics of war, where actors strive to defeat each other, will probably continue to make war change. New methods of warfare and the acceleration of technological development will continue to challenge how we manage organized violence. As the nature of force changes, so will the organization of the armed forces and the levels of war.

Military theory and military power

The second major theme of military theory is that war and its conduct can be understood as the use of military power. Waging war is therefore a way to exercise power. From this perspective, the conduct of war has more similarities than differences to other social and political phenomena. Military theory can thus earn insights from the study of power in related fields such as political science and sociology. The concept of power is hotly debated within the latter disciplines and there is a wealth of concepts and theoretical approaches that would enrich the study of military affairs. In Chapter 1, we showed how Robert Dahl's and Thomas

Schelling's understanding of power could be linked to the notions of coercion, deterrence, and brute force. This is but one example of how military theory would benefit from borrowing from more developed disciplines. We can, for example, follow Steven Lukes' (1974) differentiation of three dimensions of power and portray military power in similar fashion.

The first dimension consists of influencing someone to do what you want. This is what we often equate with the term "power" and also what most often is studied. As such, the first dimension of power is the one most clearly expressed in existing military theory. In regular party politics, the first dimension of power includes, for example, majorities having their way over minorities through voting. In military power it entails the attempt to destroy the opponent's armed forces, force the opponent into submission, and therefore be able to dictate the terms of the coming peace. Notions of decisive battles on land and at sea are clear expressions of this form of power. The first dimension of military power does not only include active use of force, but also threats to use force. Hence, more or less the entire literature on coercion and brute force (e.g. Schelling 1966; Freedman 1998) demonstrates further examples of theorizing on the first dimension of power.

The second dimension of military power includes the power to influence the agenda and thus the power to make non-decisions. Here, we can rather think of a form of power where one avoids direct influence by controlling the issues to be decided upon. Again, drawing upon the example of party politics, the second dimension of power would include, for instance, elites not adding controversial issues on the agenda before party conferences to avoid suffering defeats that will push them into pursuing specific policies. By denying others the chance to express their power, the elites in this case used the second dimension of power. In military terms, this form of power is also prevalent. Perhaps the most obvious example is various forms of deterrence. By preventing the opponent from choosing its optimal strategy, you effectively remove options for the opponent. A fleet-in-being or a blockade in naval warfare are also cases in point. By maintaining the coherence and strength of a military force, you constantly pose a threat to the opponent that denies the freedom to choose.

The third dimension of power refers to power over the way we think. Essentially, this boils down to influencing someone without the other party noticing that the use of power occurs. By shaping the opponents' mental schemes or frameworks of mind, one conditions how and what the opponent thinks. For example, by creating routines, one can influence decision-making and even create or foster certain values and identities that you want to create for the opponent. In this way, the counterpart may even think that it is acting upon free will, while it is actually influenced. The third dimension of power occurs in military thought as well as in military practices. The logic of a strategic narrative, information-warfare, as well as creating strong cohesion among your troops by inferring discipline, all belong to this dimension of power. Through manipulating information, it is possible to condition how your opponent thinks. This can occur in terms of constructing how the opponent conceives of causal relations upon the battlefield, by influencing the opponent's understandings of the available choices, or ultimately by shaping how the opponent understands its political ends. Yet another example of literature that attempts to study the impact of the third facet of power is the literature on strategic culture (Chapter 3) and the logic of emulation as the key dynamics of war (see p. 176).

Military theory and methodology

The third central theme of military theory is scientific methodology. What should be considered evidence in military theory? How do assumptions on methodology shape the substance of what we are trying to study? How do we know what we think we know? One example is to what extent we can draw inferences from targeting patterns. The obvious problem is that bombing something can be done with multiple purposes in mind, making it difficult to test causal relations with targeting patterns.

Methodology is important in military theory not only because it is a tool with which to improve the accuracy of our theorizing, but also because it contributes to the development of the field in general. So far, we have mainly stressed that the development of theorizing can be attributed to changes in the conduct of war. In short, the great variation of the history of war can explain how theories develop. However, there are also, for the scientific community, "internal" causes of the development of knowledge (Kuhn 1996; Shapin 1995). Rather than explaining theoretical variation through empirical developments in the technology or techniques of war, this suggests that development of knowledge in neighboring fields also have an impact on how we theorize in the study of war. For example, the development of game theory in economics and mathematics in the 1940s and 1950s led Thomas Schelling to his path breaking theories on military coercion and deterrence. Similarly, as Gat (2001) has demonstrated, the ideals of the Enlightenment in the late eighteenth century shaped much of the debate between Jomini and Clausewitz. How we understand and approach methodological issues also influences what we think we can acquire knowledge about. Kalyvas (2003), for example, shows that how we approach the phenomenon of civil war has a direct influence upon whether we think that the conflict is driven by local or nationwide grievances, i.e. if individuals rebel because of local concerns and social ties or if nationwide political programs can mobilize rebels.

Borrowing ideas from other fields is not as straightforward as it may appear, though. Most importantly, it challenges prevailing knowledge and it therefore begs the question of what counts as legitimate knowledge in military theory. This question has often boiled down to whether or not battle experience is a necessary requirement, or if one can "just" study war to make valid knowledge claims about war. The importance of this issue should not be underestimated. In his much-appraised study of combat, well-renowned military historian John Keegan (1991: 15–78) goes to great lengths to stress why he has something important to say about battle even if he has no first-hand experience. Even Lawrence Freedman (1985: 29) has noted that, until recently, civilian analysts of warfare were met with great suspicion in military quarters. On the one hand, it can be claimed that the experience of combat is necessary to earn a deeper understanding of war. On the other hand, it can be claimed that individual experience is too narrow and, due to the intense nature of combat, threatens to condition and bias our future observations of war. Liddell Hart (1991), with experience of the trench warfare on the Western Front during World War I, dismissed the notion that battle experience was necessary:

> [D]irect experience is inherently too limited to form an adequate foundation either for theory or for application. At the best it produces an atmosphere that is of value in drying and hardening the structure of thought. The greater value of indirect experience lies in its greater variety and extent. 'History is universal experience' – the experience not of another, but of many others under manifold conditions.
>
> (Liddell Hart 1991: 3–4)

Due to the complexities of war and the sometimes-heated argument that we should understand warfare as an art, it has also been questioned as to what extent social science methodology can help us understand war and warfare. The continued importance of this issue is indicated by the fact that military theorists from Clausewitz (1993: 172–4) to Fuller have been forced to position themselves in the debate. Fuller (1926: 36, emphasis in original) maintained that

> it is beyond question that war, like all other human activities, may be examined scien-
> tifically, and it is in its examination, and not in what it may be in itself, that practical
> knowledge is to be sought, for it is a recognized fact that any branch of study 'should be
> classed as a science, not in virtue of the nature of the things with which it is concerned,
> but rather in virtue of the *method* by which it pursues knowledge.'

Fuller voices a modern argument suggesting that it is not the nature of the object of study that determines whether or not we can study it scientifically, but it is rather the process of accumulating data in a neutral way and systematically analyzing this data that determines whether or not arguments are valid or biased.

Methodology is thus important since it influences the quality of our knowledge and theo-ries. To illustrate the importance of this claim, we will briefly mention a few common meth-odological problems in the study of war. First, cherry-picking empirical cases to seemingly prove a point, rather than systematically testing theoretical claims, is commonplace. Selec-tion is thus critical. In his oft-cited analysis of the American way of war, Russell Weigley (1973) bases his analysis on a sample of US wars including the Civil War, World War I, World War II, and the Korean War. He concludes that the US wages its wars by relying upon technology, mass, overwhelming firepower, and with the aim of totally defeating the oppo-nent. The problem, however, is that Weigley's sample is not representative of US wars. By instead selecting cases of US warfare in small wars, Max Boot (2002) emphasizes that most of the wars that the US has been involved in have had limited ambitions and that US troops often act more like "social workers" rather than soldiers. Second, theorizing needs to strike a balance between its ambitions to generalize and historical reductionism. This suggests that although the ambition of theory is to generalize, this needs to be done with caution. A com-mon problem is that we tend to project our modern categories backwards when we analyze historical cases. During the height of the Cold War, it was, for example, common to liken the Peloponnesian Wars between Athens and Sparta to the relations between the two Cold War superpowers the US and the Soviet Union (cf. Lebow & Strauss 1991). Third, there is an inherent problem in the interpretation of historical texts. Can we interpret historical texts free of the concerns of our modern time or are we bound by the context? Can we, for example, understand the classic military theories of Sun Tzu or Vegetius without know-ing the world in which they lived? And how do we translate these thoughts and words into modern language?

Military theory as theory and practice

The final, central theme of military theory relates to its dual purposes of making explanatory claims on the one hand, and providing guidance for practitioners on the other. Throughout the discussion of various theories, we have separated these aims from analytical purposes. The basis for much of our criticism of the theories as practical guidance is found in Chapters 3 and 5, where we point out that war is an inherently interactive and dynamic phenomenon, in which none of the belligerents control events single-handedly. The logical consequence of this is that if you follow any particular theory slavishly, you will be predictable and therefore easier to defeat. Military theories have also been consistently criticized for lack of logical consistency and empirical testability. A final question that needs to be discussed, however, is to what extent it is fruitful and possible to distinguish between theory and practice. Are the explanatory and normative aims just different sides of the same coin?

Although it is possible to analytically distinguish theory from practice, it is impossible in an ontological sense. From this perspective, it is not feasible to discriminate between the search for academic excellence and theoretical precision on the one hand, and practical utility on the other. If causal relationships can be determined, it would be useful knowledge also for practitioners. Moreover, the distinction between theory and practice is an idea itself, rather than an empirical fact (e.g. Smith et al. 1996: 1; Smith 2004). How a military unit solves a tactical challenge, therefore, is just a reflection of how its commander thinks about possible solutions. The theories constructed are, from this perspective, both catalysts, as they enable action by allowing us to "see" solutions and intellectual prisons insofar as they prevent us from seeing other solutions. Theories condition how we categorize and perceive observations and practical solutions are therefore always "theory-laden" (Quine 1953; Carr 1964: 11; Waltz 1979: 1–17; Popper 1970: 52). At the same time, the practice of waging war is the most important source for theory development. This means that theory is "practice-laden" as well.

Theory and practice, explanatory and normative, can thus be understood as two sides of the same coin. Rather than a choice between practical utility and explanatory value, military theory is a means of achieving both objectives. In a similar manner, Robert Keohane claims that it is not possible to distinguish between theory and practice. Theories, Keohane (1986: 5) suggests, is to some extent inevitable, because "no one can cope with the complexities of world politics without the aid either of a theory or of implicit assumptions and propositions that substitute, however poorly, for theory." Arnold Wolfers (1962: *xiii–xiv*, emphasis in original), too, argued:

> [T]hough it would be foolish to underestimate the role of the intuitive touch – what the Germans call *Fingerspitzengefühl* – it is self-delusion on the part of the decision-maker to believe that he can get along without theoretical propositions. If one looks more closely, one discovers that rather than emerging out of an intellectual vacuum, his hunches rest, in fact, on generalizations of some sort. . . . The choice, then, is not between theory and no theory, but between relatively informed, sophisticated, and objective theoretical propositions carefully formulated in the course of disciplined and dispassionate analysis, and crude hit-and-miss 'theories' against which the statesman, even if aware of the pitfalls, may not be able to immunize himself.

Just like politics, war and warfare, without theory, are also in danger of being controlled by prejudice, gut feelings, and untested and potentially invalid causal propositions. Although military theory – as other social science theory – does not have a spotless track record of predicting the future development of war correctly, we can at least put our faith in the inherent critical dimension of science. The scientific process, in short, discourages overly broad conclusions from being drawn in the study of war.

Assuming that military theory is both explanatory and normative, we are able to more precisely identify the practical utility of military theory. First, military theory is of indirect utility insofar as it contributes to the education of the commander and thus partly conditions the decisions of the commander. An example of such reasoning can be found in Clausewitz's theorizing. He (1993: 163) suggested that:

[T]heory exists so that one need not start afresh each time sorting out the material and plowing through it, but will find it ready to hand and in good order. It is meant to educate the mind of the future commander, or, more accurately, to guide him in his self-education, not to accompany him to the battlefield.

Similar arguments are brought forward by Corbett (1988: 3–4, 6) and many others. The French Field Marshal Ferdinand Foch, for example, claimed that: "Historical Studies create the possibilities for preparing for the concrete experience of war, learning the art of command and finally, implanting the habit to act properly without long deliberations" (Johansson 1988: 14). The nineteenth century German Chancellor Otto von Bismarck had a similar view of the importance of experience and allegedly claimed that: "fools learn from experience. I prefer to learn from the experience of others."

Second, military theory – as science in general – may also be of direct practical utility. Jomini, for example, heavily criticized Clausewitz for his reluctance to attribute more importance to science in the conduct of war (Johansson 1988: 51–2). Science, Jomini suggested, would not only help us better understand war, but also contribute to a more efficient conduct of war. In holding such views, he was not alone. As we have seen in both nuclear strategy and airpower theory, science and technology play an important role in underpinning various targeting strategies. Both Clausewitz's and Jomini's positions take for granted that it is possible to use theoretical knowledge for practical utility. This assumes that there are features of reality that are generalizable and it presupposes that we can test theories against empirical conditions. However, it is far from certain that the course of history can be regarded as a laboratory for testing hypotheses. On the one hand, there are modern social scientists that suggest that history can be used to test our hypotheses and to generate theories (e.g. Rosecrance 1973: 25). In his monumental, *A Study of War*, Quincy Wright (1941: 438–49) suggested that generalizations are possible if one can identify the right perspective; a leaf that turns yellow and falls from the tree is unique for the leaf, but not for the tree. On the other hand, there are those (e.g. Gaddis 1997) who maintain that history does not allow us to replicate experiments in social science, since exactly the same conditions and actors cannot be recreated in a controlled manner.

Two perspectives on the dynamics of war

After summarizing and elaborating on the key themes of military theory, we can, by way of conclusion, outline two rivaling perspectives on the dynamics of war. Both of these two theoretical frameworks, it should be stressed, share the assumption that the development of a particular war is largely dependent upon the interaction in war, as described and theorized by, for example, Clausewitz. Although military adaptation can be explained by factors such as the internal characteristics of military organizations and the composition of and decision-making procedures of strategic elites (e.g. Murray 2011; Horowitz 2010; Grissom 2006; Farrell et al. 2013), both these frameworks stress the importance of interaction.

Escalation and adaptation in war

Traditionally, strategy and the dynamics of war have centered on cycles of escalation and de-escalation. According to this framework, adversaries adapt to each others' behavior and try to overcome their opponents. For a long time, Western powers have focused on gaining the upper hand through escalating quicker and more decisive than their opponents. The central strategic problem of how to translate political aims into military targets has been solved by trying to defeat the adversary's armed forces. Defeat of the opponent's armed forces would imply that one could dictate the conditions of the future peace on one's own terms. The problem, of course, is that it is impossible to know in advance how much force and what kind of force that should be applied. Moreover, if you face a much weaker, yet politically determined, opponent, the latter may choose to escalate in other dimensions than military numerical preponderance. Hence, even if escalation can have different expressions, the traditional understanding is that actors adapt new ways of fighting depending upon the behavior of the opponents (e.g. Schelling 1966; Smoke 1990; Posen 1984; Resende-Santos 2007; Buzan & Herring 1998).

Adopting new ways to wage wars as a result of escalation or expectations of escalation is an inherently rationalistic idea. Here, actors adopt their strategies depending upon the adversary's behavior. Much of the theorizing displayed in this book follows these assumptions. For example, it is precisely the conventional superiority of Western forces that has made non-state actors turn to guerrilla warfare to negate the comparative advantages of Western military power. The literature on military adaptation has often dealt with how military organizations try to plan and adapt in peace time. Treating adaptation in this way has made learning and innovation, not the least technological innovation, key parts of this literature. Lately, however, some have studied the problem of adaptation within war. The particular challenges of adaptation in war are manifold and relate partly to the internal organization and culture of the armed forces as well as dyadic nature of war. Traditionally, many armies have deemed it to be critical for battle success that soldiers strictly adhere to orders from superior officers. A culture of following orders without questioning them, however, is not conducive to adaptation, which by definition means changing behavior (cf. Murray & Millett 1996). Murray (2011: 1–2) continues:

> [I]n Clausewitzian terms, war is a contest, a complex, interactive duel between two opponents. It is a phenomenon of indeterminate length, which presents the opportunity to the contestants to adapt to their enemy's strategy, operations, and tactical approach. But because it is interactive, both sides have the potential to the conflict at every level, from the tactical to the strategic. Thus, the problems posed by the battle space do not remain constant; in fact, more often than not, they change with startling rapidity.

The standard explanation of the emergence of adaptation in warfare adheres strictly to this logic. It is the interactive nature of war and Western supremacy in large-scale conventional warfare that has made some actors find alternatives that can negate the advantages of the West. The development of the strategies of the weak, however, does not necessarily make sense unless one takes resources and military capabilities into account. Classical insurgency and counter-insurgency theory often relied on the assumption that insurgency was a response to relative weakness against a much stronger colonial power. Initial weakness and a gradual military build-up were an essential idea in both Mao's and later Giap's ideas on national liberation.

Even so, the logic is not restricted to situations of asymmetries in power. Also, nominally equally strong actors interact in war, seeking to exploit weaknesses and in doing so try to outmaneuver one another to defeat the opponent. We can easily detect the same logic in arms races and in the logic of deterrence as understood by generations of strategists during the

Cold War. Once the Soviet Union changed its nuclear arsenal by adding new missiles, the US and its NATO allies tried to adapt and respond proportionately. And then the cycle of adaptation started again.

Emulation and adaptation in war

An alternative frame of reference to escalation as the key dynamic involved in war and the variation of strategies employed is emulation. Rather than trying to gain the upper hand by increasing the level of violence or size of armed forces, emulation suggests that parties learn from and copy each other in war. In other words, what goes on in war is not necessarily the use of overwhelming force as a means to reach political goals, but a particular form of communication in which the parties gradually develop a new, common language and learn to speak it, thus opening the path to reaching a political settlement (cf. Honig, forthcoming).

Several things need highlighting regarding this framework. First, it would be misleading to think that only the weak party learns to adapt its strategy in relation to the strong. It is a new language that both parties ascertain from one another and create (or construct) in their interaction. In this way, the strong will learn as much from the weak as the other way around. Moreover, if we consider the use of force as a language, a shared language is necessary to reach a politically stable post-war peace. Gradually, therefore, it will not only be – as Branislav Slantchev (2011) and bargaining theory in general (e.g. Reiter 2009; Blainey 1988) hold – that the parties learn about each others' preferences and thus are able to credibly commit to courses of action, but emulation will also be key to identifying a shared meaning of a particular strategic behavior. Through progressively learning and by emulating their respective strategies, the adversaries learn each others' norms and discover how the opponent understands the manner in which force leads to political results. And when the adversaries agree upon a certain set of norms, they will be in a position where force influences the outcome of the war. Through emulation, therefore adversaries can reach a more durable peace.

Second, as opposed to the logic of escalation described above, the logic of emulation is inherently constructivist. Actors emulate one another in war in order to confirm their identity, and through this act, and through the interaction that occurs, adversaries recognize each other and reach common understandings and common languages of how force operate and how the conflict can be solved peacefully. Within the literature, only a few have used constructivist arguments and focused on the larger issue of military reform or acquisition of military capabilities at large. For example, it has been pointed out that the spread of advanced weapons systems (for example, modern high-tech fighter jets) in the developing world can be understood rather as acts to claim a particular form of identity as modern states, than calculated rational strategic choices responding to external threats (Eyre & Suchman 1996; Ralston 1990; Angstrom & Honig 2012).

Third, emulation may be observed as copying each others' tactics, weaponry, organization, and strategy, but these are just expressions of a particular set of strategic norms. The underlying assumption of emulation as the key dynamic in war is that the way actors wage wars reflects how they think of strategy. It also reflects how they think about using violence legitimately and how they consider themselves. Following Peter Katzenstein (1996: 1–32), norms are not only regulative, but also constitutive. Ideas and norms determine – according to this framework – more than just the conduct of war. Instead, they influence what kind of behavior that can be considered as acts of war to begin with. War, in Martin van Creveld's (2008: 147) words, "cannot take place without rules to define what it is, and is not, about."

The influence of norms does not only provide certain violent behavior meaning as war and other violence as crime, but also gives direction to how military force is translated into political aims and how military force is created. In order to have an impact, norms need a carrier and when it comes to strategic norms the military organizations are the usual culprit. Theo Farrell (2005; cf. Farrell & Teriff 2002; Farrell et al. 2013), for example, has argued that norms become embedded in organizations which are created to solve security problems. Similarly, Elisabeth Kier (1997) has demonstrated that the different conclusions about future war reached by the strategic elites in interwar Europe were reflected in the different norms upheld in the armed forces at the time.

Understanding military theory

Following from the discussion of these two frameworks, we can develop further positions on how military theory should be understood. First, we can understand military theory as inherently practical – a craft. Just as doctrine, military theory is prescriptive (even normative) and the difference between doctrine and theory is merely the fact the former has been formally sanctioned as important by the armed forces. Military theory should focus on the internal dimension, where staff procedures and command processes are central. Instead of demanding that military theory should accommodate the requirements of modern social science methodology, the relevant test of military theory is whether or not you succeed in war by following a particular theory. Hence, it is not explanatory power that matters, but success.

Second, we can understand military theory as the history of ideas. It is not reasonable to insist that classical military theory should follow modern scientific ideals. We do not generally discard the political thought of Thomas Hobbes or Jean-Jacques Rousseau just because they could not empirically prove that such a thing as a state of nature had existed. Why should we have higher demands of Jomini or Clausewitz? Instead, we should understand military theorizing within a given context and the interesting phenomenon to be studied is how this context interacts with our theorizing. The appropriate test of relevance for military theory is thus what we can infer about the past and present by following the development of ideas. Moreover, theorizing is of practical utility only due to the fact that it contributes to the education of future generations of commanders.

Third, we can understand military theory as social science theory. Accordingly, it should be measured against the same yard stick as other social sciences such as economics, political science, or sociology. Theories must be able to explain and predict events, and if they cannot do so then the pursuit of better theories should continue. It is through explanatory power that military theory can underpin and provide an evidence-based practice.

Throughout the book, we have illustrated how the two dynamics of war pan out in different domains, at different levels of war, and in different kinds of war. We have even seen how differences in the understanding of the concept of "theory" lead to different conclusions regarding the practical utility of military theory. The tension between understanding war and its conduct as a rational and calculated phenomenon, or understanding it as a rule-circumscribed and identity-based phenomenon, runs through much of contemporary military theory. Both of the frameworks imply that wars can appear in many shapes and forms as well as include vastly different strategies and tactics. It is the tension between these frameworks, and the tension between the dual nature of military theory as both normative and explanatory, that promises that military theory will continue to be a vibrant field of study. By continuously debating the borders of legitimate knowledge in the field, military theorizing will continue to be exciting, relevant, and rich.

Questions for discussion

1. What are the prospects for future military theory?
2. How and to what extent does doctrines influence military theory and vice versa?
3. Why is it important to study military theory for civilians and military alike?
4. Is military theory best understood as history of ideas, social science theory, or practitioners' craft?
5. To what extent is theorizing dependent upon practice and vice versa?
6. How should we best understand the dynamics of war: as escalation or emulation?

Further reading

Martin van Creveld, *The Culture of War* (New York: Random House, 2008).

Theo Farrell, Sten Rynning, & Terry Teriff, *Transforming Military Power since the Cold War: Britain, France, and the United States, 1991–2012* (Cambridge: Cambridge University Press, 2013).

Azar Gat, *War in Human Civilization* (Oxford: Oxford University Press, 2006).

Beatrice Heuser, *The Evolution of Strategy* (Cambridge: Cambridge University Press, 2010).

Jan Willem Honig, *Winning Wars* (Cambridge: Cambridge University Press, forthcoming).

Anthony King, *The Transformation of Europe's Armed Forces: From the Rhine to Afghanistan* (Cambridge: Cambridge University Press, 2011).

John A. Lynn, *Battle: A History of Combat and Culture* (New York: Basic Books, 2008).

Steven Pinker, *The Better Angels of our Nature* (Cambridge, MA: Harvard University Press, 2011).

Hew Strachan & Sibylle Scheippers (eds.) *The Changing Character of War* (Oxford: Oxford University Press, 2012).

References

Abrahamsson, Bengt (1972) *Military Professionalization* (London: SAGE).

Adamsky, Dima (2010) *The Culture of Military Innovation: The Impact of Cultural Factors in the Revolution of Military Affairs in Russia, the US and Israel* (Stanford, CA: Stanford University Press).

Afflerbach, Holger & Hew Strachan (eds.) (2012) *How Fighting Ends: A History of Surrender* (Oxford: Oxford University Press).

Agrell, Wilhelm (2002) *Svenska förintelsevapen: Utveckling av kemiska och nukleära stridsmedel 1928–1970* (Lund: Historiska Media).

Alexander, Joseph H. & Bartlett, Merrill L. (1995) *Sea Soldiers in the Cold War: Amphibious Warfare, 1945–1991* (Annapolis, MD: Naval Institute Press).

Alger, John I. (1982) *The Quest for Victory: The History of the Principles of War* (Westport, CT: Greenwood Press).

Allison, Graham T. (1971) *Essence of Decision: Explaining the Cuban Missile Crisis* (New York: Harper Collins).

Anderson, Benedict (1991) *Imagined Communities* (London: Verso).

Angstrom, Jan (2013) "The Changing Norms of Civil and Military and Civil-Military Relations Theory," *Small Wars & Insurgencies*, 24(2): 224–36.

Angstrom, Jan (2011) "Mapping the Competing Historical Analogies of the War on Terrorism: The Bush Presidency," *International Relations*, 25(2): 224–42.

Angstrom, Jan (2005) "Introduction: Debating the Nature of Modern War," in Jan Angstrom & Isabelle Duyvesteyn (eds.) *Rethinking the Nature of War* (London: Frank Cass).

Angstrom, Jan (2001) "Towards a Typology of Internal Armed Conflict: Synthesising a Decade of Conceptual Turmoil," *Civil Wars*, 4(3): 93–116.

Angstrom, Jan & Jan Willem Honig (2012) "Regaining Strategy: Small Powers, Strategic Culture, and Escalation in Afghanistan," *Journal of Strategic Studies*, 35(5): 663–87.

Angstrom, Jan & Isabelle Duyvesteyn (eds.) (2010) *Modern War and the Utility of Force: Challenges, Methods and Strategy* (London: Routledge).

Angstrom, Jan & Isabelle Duyvesteyn (eds.) (2007) *Understanding Victory and Defeat in Contemporary War* (London: Routledge).

Ardant du Picq, Charles (1987) "Battle Studies," in *Roots of Strategy*, vol. 2 (Mechanicsburg, PA: Stackpole Books).

Army Staff Field Manual (1962) *Heeresdienstvorschrift HDV 100/1 Truppenführung* (Bonn: The Federal Ministry of Defense).

Arntzen, Arent and Tor Olav Grotan (2011) "A New Chance for Network Centric Warfare in the Context of Modernity," in Karl Erik Haug & Ole Jorgen Maao (eds.) *Conceptualising Modern War* (New York: Columbia University Press).

Aron, Raymond (1985) *Clausewitz: Philosopher of War* (Englewood Cliffs, NJ: Prentice-Hall).

Arquilla, John & David Ronfeldt (2001) *Networks and Netwars: The Future of Terror, Crime and Militancy* (Santa Monica, CA: RAND).

Arreguin-Toft, Ivan (2007) "How to Lose a War on Terror: A Comparative Analysis of Counterinsurgency Success and Failure," in Jan Angstrom & Isabelle Duyvesteyn (eds.) *Understanding Victory and Defeat in Contemporary War* (London: Routledge).

Asprey, Robert (1975) *War in the Shadows: The Guerrilla in History*, vols. 1 and 2 (New York: Doubleday).

Autesserre, Séverine (2010) *The Trouble with the Congo: Local Violence and the Failure of International Peacebuilding* (Cambridge: Cambridge University Press).

Avant, Deborah (2005) *The Market for Force: The Consequences for Privatizing Security* (Cambridge: Cambridge University Press).

Axelrod, Robert (1984) *The Evolution of Cooperation* (New York: Basic Books).

Baldwin, David A. (2002) "Power and International Relations," in Walter Carlsnaes, Thomas Risse, & Beth A. Simmons (eds.) *Handbook of International Relations* (London: Sage).

Ballentine, Karen & Jake Sherman (eds.) (2003) *The Political Economy of Armed Conflict* (Boulder, CO: Lynne Rienner).

Barany, Zoltan (2012) *The Soldier and the Changing State: Building Democratic Armies in Africa, Asia, Europe, and the Americas* (Princeton, NJ: Princeton University Press).

Barkawi, Tarak & Shane Brighton (2011) "Powers of War: Fighting, Knowledge, and Critique," *International Political Sociology*, 5(2): 126–43.

Bartlett, Merrill L. (ed.) (1983) *Assault from the Sea: Essays on the History of Amphibious Warfare* (Annapolis, MD: Naval Institute Press).

Bassford, Christopher (1997) "Policy, Politics, War and Military Strategy" (National War College), unpublished manuscript available online at www.clausewitz.com/strategybook/wholething.html (accessed April 7, 2014).

Baylis, John & John Garnett (eds.) (1991) *Makers of Nuclear Strategy* (London: Pinter).

Baylis, John, Wirtz, James, & Gray, Colin S. (eds.) (2010) *Strategy in the Contemporary World: An Introduction to Strategic Studies*, 3rd edn. (Oxford: Oxford University Press).

Beaufre, André (1963) *Modern strategi för fred och krig* (Stockholm: Prisma).

Beaumont, Roger A. (1993) *Joint Military Operations: A Short History* (Westport, CT: Greenwood Press, 1993).

Beckett, Ian F.W. (2001) *Modern Insurgencies and Counter-Insurgencies: Guerrillas and their Opponents since 1750* (London: Routledge).

Beevor, Anthony (2007) *Berlin: The Downfall 1945* (London: Penguin).

Beevor, Anthony (2009) *D-Day: The Battle for Normandy* (London: Penguin).

Bellamy, Christopher (1990) *The Evolution of Modern Land Warfare: Theory and Practice* (London: Routledge).

Bellamy, Christopher (1997) *Knights in White Armour: The New Art of War and Peace* (London: Pimlico).

Bennett, Huw (2013) *Fighting the Mau-Mau: The British Army and Counter-Insurgency in the Kenya Emergency* (Cambridge: Cambridge University Press).

Berkowitz, Bruce (2003) *The New Face of War: How War Will be Fought in the 21st Century* (New York: The Free Press).

Betts, Richard K. (2012) *American Force: Dangers, Delusions, and Dilemmas in National Security* (New York: Columbia University Press).

Betts, Richard (1997) "Should Strategic Studies Survive?" *World Politics*, 50(1): 7–33.

Betz, David (2012) "Cyberpower in Strategic Affairs: Neither Unthinkable nor Blessed," *Journal of Strategic Studies*, 35(5): 689–711.

Betz, David (2011) 'The Mystique of "Cyberwar" and the Strategic Latency of Networked Social Movements', *Strategic Insights*, 10(3): 85–105.

Biddle, Stephen (2007) "Toppling the Taliban in Afghanistan," in Jan Angstrom & Isabelle Duyvesteyn (eds.) *Understanding Victory and Defeat in Contemporary War* (London: Routledge).

Biddle, Stephen (2006) "Seeing Bagdad, Thinking Saigon," *Foreign Affairs*, 84(5): 87–104.

Biddle, Stephen (2004) *Military Power: Explaining Victory and Defeat in Modern Battle* (Princeton, NJ: Princeton University Press).

Biddle, Stephen (1998) "The Past as Prologue: Assessing Theories of Future Warfare," *Security Studies*, 8(1): 1–74.

Biddle, Stephen, Jeffrey Friedman, & Jacob Shapiro (2012) "Testing the Surge: Why did Violence Decline in Iraq in 2007?" *International Security*, 37(1): 7–40.

Blainey, Geoffrey (1988) *The Causes of War*, 3rd edn. (New York: Free Press).

Bobbitt, Philip (2008) *Terror and Consent: The Wars for the Twenty-First Century* (London: Penguin).

Boin, Arjen, Paul't Hart, Eric Stern, & Bengt Sundelius (2006) *The Politics of Crisis Management: Public Leadership under Pressure* (Cambridge: Cambridge University Press).

Bonaparte, Napolean (1985) "The Military Maxims of Napoleon,", in *Roots of Strategy*, vol. 1 (Mechanicsburg, PA: Stackpole Books).

Bond, Brian (1998) *The Pursuit of Victory: From Napoleon to Saddam Hussein* (Oxford: Oxford University Press).

Bond, Brian (1977) *Liddell Hart: A Study of his Military Thought* (London: Cassell).

Bond, Brian & Martin Alexander (1986) "Liddell Hart and De Gaulle: The Doctrines of Limited Liability and Mobile Defence," in Peter Paret (ed.), *Makers of Modern Strategy* (Princeton, NJ: Princeton University Press).

Boot, Max (2002) *The Savage Wars of Peace: Small Wars and the Rise of American Power* (New York: Basic Books, 2002).

Booth, Ken (1977) *Navies and Foreign Policy* (London: Croom Helm).

Børresen, Jacob (2004) "Coastal Power: The Seapower of the Coastal State and the Management of Maritime Resources,", in Rolf Hobson & Tom Kristiansen (eds.) *Navies in Northern Waters, 1721–2000* (London: Frank Cass).

Bousquet, Antoine (2008) *The Scientific Way of Warfare: Order and Chaos on the Battlefields of Modernity* (London: Hurst).

Bratton, Patrick C. (2003) "A Coherent Strategy of Coercion? The Writings of Robert Pape," *Comparative Strategy*, 22(4): 355–72.

Brehmer, Berndt (2002) "Nätverkskrig för Sverige?" in Berndt Brehmer (ed.) *Krigsvetenskaplig årsbok 2002* (Stockholm: Swedish National Defence College).

Brigham, Robert K. (2006) *Is Iraq Another Vietnam?* (New York: Public Affairs).

Brodie, Bernard (1959) *Strategy in the Missile Age* (Princeton, NJ: Princeton University Press).

Brodie, Bernard (1949) "Strategy as a Science," *World Politics*, 1(4): 467–88.

Brodie, Bernard (1946) *The Absolute Weapon: Atomic Power and World Order* (San Diego: Harcourt).

Brodie, Bernard (1943) *A Layman's Guide to Naval Strategy*, 2nd edn. (Princeton, NJ: Princeton University Press).

Brooks, Risa A. (2008) *Shaping Strategy: The Civil-Military Politics of Strategic Assessment* (Princeton, NJ: Princeton University Press).

Brosché, Johan & Daniel Rothbart (2012) *Violent Conflict and Peacebuilding: The Contining Crisis in Darfur* (London: Routledge).

Brown, Michael E. (1996) "Introduction," in Michael E. Brown (ed.) *The International Dimensions of Internal Conflict* (Cambridge, MA: MIT Press).

Brown, Michael E., Owen R. Coté Jr., Sean M. Lynn-Jones, & Steven A. Miller (eds.) (2011) *Do Democracies Win Their Wars* (Cambridge, MA: MIT Press).

Brown, Michael E., Owen R Coté Jr., Sean M. Lynn-Jones, & Steven A. Miller. (eds.) (2004) *Offense, Defense, and War* (Cambridge, MA: MIT Press).

Browning, Peter (2002) *The Changing Nature of Warfare: The Development of Land Warfare from 1792 to 1945* (Cambridge: Cambridge University Press).

Brownlee, Richard S. (1986) *Gray Ghosts of the Confederacy: Guerrilla Warfare in the West, 1861–1865* (Baton Rogue: Louisiana State University Press).

Buckley, John (1999) *Air Power in the Age of Total War* (London: UCL Press).

Buzan, Barry (1987) *An Introduction to Strategic Studies: Military Technology and International Relations* (London: Macmillan).

Buzan, Barry & Lene Hansen (2009) *The Evolution of International Security Studies* (Cambridge: Cambridge University Press).

Buzan, Barry & Eric Herring (1998) *The Arms Dynamic in World Politics* (Boulder, CO: Lynne Rienner).

Byman, Daniel (2005) *Deadly Connections: States that Sponsor Terrorism* (Cambridge: Cambridge University Press).

Byman, Daniel L. & Matthew C. Waxman (2002) *The Dynamics of Coercion: American Foreign Policy and the Limits of Military Might* (Cambridge: Cambridge University Press).

Byman, Daniel L. & Matthew C. Waxman (2000) "Kosovo and the Great Air Power Debate," *International Security*, 24(4): 5–38.

Cable, James (1994) *Gunboat Diplomacy 1919–1991 – Political Applications of Limited Naval Force*, 3rd edn. (New York: St. Martin's Press).

Callwell, Charles E. (1905/1996) *Military Operations and Maritime Preponderance: Their Relations and Interdependence* (Annapolis, MD: Naval Institute Press).

Callwell, Charles E. (1896/1996) *Small Wars: Their Principles and Practice*, 3rd edn. (London: Bison Books).

Carlyon, L. A. (2003) *Gallipoli* (London: Bantam Books).

Carr, E. H. (1964) *What is History?* (London: Penguin).

Castex, Raoul (1994) *Strategic Theories* (Annapolis. MD: Naval Institute Press).

Cebrowski, Arthur K., & John H. Garstka (1998) "Network-Centric Warfare: Its Origin and Future," *U.S. Naval Institute Proceedings*, 124(1): 28–35.

Cedergren, Anders (2005) "Doctrine, Expertise and Arms in Combination: A Reflection on the Iraq War," in Jan Hallenberg & Håkan Karlsson (eds.) *The Iraq War: European Perspectives on Politics, Strategy and Operations* (London: Routledge).

Chandler, David G. (2000) *The Art of Warfare on Land* (London: Penguin, 2000).

Chenoweth, Erica & Maria J. Stephan (2012) *Why Civil Resistance Works: The Strategic Logic of Non-Violent Conflict* (New York: Columbia University Press).

Childs, David J. (1999) *Peripheral Weapon? The Production and Employment of British Tanks in the First World War* (Westport, CT: Greenwood Press).

Chisholm, Donald (2003) "The Risk of Optimism in the Conduct of War," *Parameters*, 33(4): 114–31.

Chwe, Michael Suk-Young (2013) *Jane Austen: Game Theorist* (Princeton, NJ: Princeton University Press).

Cimbala, Stephen J. (2001) *Clausewitz and Chaos: Friction in War and Military Policy* (Westport, CT: Praeger).

Citino, Robert M. (1999) *The Path to Blitzkrieg: Doctrine and Training in the German Army, 1920–1939* (Mechanicsburg, PA: Stackpole Books).

Citino, Robert M. (2004) *Blitzkrieg to Desert Storm: The Evolution of Operational Warfare* (Lawrence, KS: University Press of Kansas).

Clark, Ian (2005) *Legitimacy in International Society* (Oxford: Oxford University Press).

Clark, Robert M. (2004) *Intelligence Analysis: A Target-Centric Approach* (Washington DC: CQ Press).

von Clausewitz, Carl (1832/1993) *On War*, translation Michael Howard & Peter Paret (London: Everyman's Library).

von Clausewitz, Carl (1987) "Principles of War," in *Roots of Strategy*, vol. 2 (Mechanicsburg, PA: Stackpole Books).

Clodfelter, Mark (1997) "Molding Airpower Convictions: Development and Legacy of William Mitchell's Strategic Thought," in Phillip S. Meilinger (ed.) *The Paths of Heaven* (Maxwell, AL: Air University Press).

Cohen, Eliot A. (2002) *Supreme Command: Soldiers, Statesmen and Leadership in Wartime* (New York: The Free Press).

Coker, Christopher (2010) *Barbarous Philosophers: Reflections on the Nature of War from Heraclitus to Heisenberg* (New York: Columbia University Press).

Coker, Christopher (2002) "Asymmetrical Warfare: Ends or Means?" in John Andreas Olsen (ed.) *Asymmetrical Warfare* (Trondheim: Luftkrigskolen).

Coker, Christopher (2001) *Humane Warfare: The New Ethics of Postmodern War* (London: Routledge).

Coker, Christopher (1997) "How Wars End," *Millennium*, 26(3): 615–29.

Coleman, Katharina P. (2007) *International Organizations and Peace Enforcement: The Politics of International Legitimacy* (Cambridge: Cambridge University Press).

Collier, Paul Anke Hoeffler, & Dominic Rohner (2009) "Beyond Greed and Grievance: Feasibility and Civil War," *Oxford Economic Papers*, 61(1): 1–27.

Collins, John M. (2002) *Military Strategy: Principles, Practices, and Historical Perspectives* (Washington DC: Brassey's).

Colomb, Philip H. (1990) *Naval Warfare: Its Ruling Principles and Practice Historically Treated* (Annapolis, MD: Naval Institute Press).

Condell, Bruce & David Zabecki (eds.) (2001) *On the German Art of War: Truppenführung* (Boulder, CO: Lynne Rienner Publishers).

Coram, Robert (2002) *Boyd: The Fighter Pilot Who Changed the Art of War* (Boston: Little, Brown).

Corbett, Julian S. (1911/1988) *Some Principles of Maritime Strategy* (Annapolis, MD: Naval Institute Press).

Corum, James S. (2008) *Bad Strategies: How Major Powers Fail in Counterinsurgency* (Minneapolis: Zenith Press).

Corum, James S. (1997) "Airpower Thought in Continental Europe between the Wars," in Philip S. Meilinger (ed.) *The Paths of Heaven: The Evolution of Air Power Theory* (Maxwell, AL: Air University Press).

Corum, James S. (1992) *The Roots of Blitzkrieg: Hans von Seeckt and German Military Reform* (Lawrence, KS: University Press of Kansas).

Corum, James & Wray R. Johnson (2003) *Airpower in Small Wars: Fighting Insurgents and Terrorists* (Lawrence, KS: University Press of Kansas).

Corvisier, André (ed.) (1994) *A Dictionary of Military History*, translation Chris Turner (Oxford: Blackwell).

Coser, Lewis (1956) *The Functions of Social Conflict* (New York: The Free Press).

Craig, Gordon A. (1986) "Delbrück: The Military Historian," in Peter Paret (ed.), *Makers of Modern Strategy* (Princeton, NJ: Princeton University Press).

Cramer, Christopher (2006) *Civil War is not a Stupid Thing: Accounting for Violence in Developing Countries* (London: Hurst).

Crenshaw, Martha (1990) "The Logic of Terrorism: Terrorism as the Product of Strategic Choice," in Walter Reich (ed.) *Origins of Terrorism: Psychologies, Ideologies, Theologies, States of Mind* (Cambridge: Cambridge University Press).

van Creveld, Martin (2011) *The Age of Airpower* (New York: Public Affairs).

van Creveld, Martin (2008) *The Culture of War* (New York: Random House).

van Creveld, Martin (2002) *Men, Women and War: Do Women Belong in the Front Line?* (London: Cassell).

van Creveld, Martin (2001) *The Rise and Decline of the State* (Cambridge: Cambridge University Press).

van Creveld, Martin (2000) *The Art of War: War and Military Thought* (London: Cassell).

van Creveld, Martin (1997) "What is Wrong with Clausewitz?" in Gert de Nooy (ed.) *The Clausewitzian Dictum and the Future of Western Military Strategy* (Haag: Kluwer Law International).

van Creveld, Martin (1994) *Air Power and Maneuver Warfare* (Maxwell, AL: Air University Press).

van Creveld, Martin (1991) *The Transformation of War* (New York: The Free Press).

van Creveld, Martin (1989) *Technology and War: From 2000 B.C. to the Present* (New York: The Free Press).

van Creveld, Martin (1985) *Command in War* (Cambridge, MA: Harvard University Press).

van Creveld, Martin (1977) *Supplying War: Logistics from Wallenstein to Patton* (Cambridge: Cambridge University Press).

Crocker, Chester A., Fen Osler Hampson, & Pamela Aall (eds.) (1996) *Managing Global Chaos: Sources of and Responses to International Conflict* (Washington DC: United States Institute of Peace Press).

Dahl, Robert A. (1991) *Modern Political Analysis*, 5th edn. (Englewood Cliffs, NJ: Prentice-Hall).

Dahl, Robert A. (1957) "The Concept of Power," *Behavioral Science*, 2(3): 201–15.

Dalby, Simon, Paul Routledge, & Gerard Toal (eds.) (2006) *The Geopolitics Reader* (London: Routledge).

Danchev, Alex (1998) *Alchemist of War: The Life of Basil Liddell Hart* (London: Phoenix Giant).

Daniel, Donald C. F., Patricia Taft, & Sharon Wiharta (eds.) (2008) *Peace Operations: Trends, Progress, and Prospects* (Washington DC: Georgetown University Press).

Davies Biddle, Tami (2002) *Rhetoric and Reality in Air Warfare: The Evolution of British and American Ideas about Strategic Bombing, 1914–1945* (Princeton, NJ: Princeton University Press).

Davis, Diane E. & Anthony W. Pereira (eds.) (2003) *Irregular Armed Forces and their Role in Politics and State Formation* (Cambridge: Cambridge University Press).

Davis, Lance E. & Stanley L. Engerman (2006) *Naval Blockades in Peace and War: An Economic History since 1750* (Cambridge: Cambridge University Press).

Davis, Paul K. (2001) *Effects-Based Operations: A Grand Challenge for the Analytical Community* (Santa Monica, CA: RAND).

DeBlois, Bruce (2004) "Space Weapons: Crossing the US Rubicon," *International Security*, 29(2): 50–84.

Department of the Navy (1994) *Forward...From the Sea* (Washington DC: Department of the Navy).

Deptula, David A. (2001) *Effects-Based Operations: Change in the Nature of Warfare* (Arlington, VA: Aerospace Education Foundation).

Der Derian, James (2001) *Virtuous War: Mapping the Military-Industrial-Media-Entertainment Network* (Boulder, CO: Westview Press).

Diehl, Paul F. & Daniel Druckman (2010) *Evaluating Peace Operations* (Boulder, CO: Lynne Rienner).

Dixit, Avinash K. & Barry J. Nalebuff (2008) *The Art of Strategy: A Game Theorist's Guide to Success in Business and Life* (New York: W. W Norton).

Dixon, Howard Lee (1989) "Low Intensity Conflict: Overview, Definitions, and Policy Concerns," *CLIC Papers* (Langley, VA: A-AF Center for Low Intensity Conflict).

Doughty, Robert A. (1994) "The Illusion of Security: France, 1919–1940," in Williamson Murray, MacGregor Knox, & Alvin Bernstein (eds.) *The Making of Strategy: Rulers, States, and War* (Cambridge: Cambridge University Press).

Douhet, Guilio (1999) "The Command of the Air," translation Dino Ferrari, in David Jablonsky (ed.) *Roots of Strategy*, vol. 4 (Mechanicsburg, PA: Stackpoole Books).

Downes, Alexander (2008) *Targeting Civilians in War* (Ithaca, NY: Cornell University Press).

Doyle, Michael W. (1997) *Ways of War and Peace: Realism, Liberalism, and Socialism* (New York: W.W. Norton).

Doyle, Michael W. & Nicholas Sambanis (2006) *Making War and Building Peace: UN Peace Operations* (Princeton, NJ: Princeton University Press).

Duffield, Mark (2007) *Development, Security and Unending War: Governing the World of Peoples* (Cambridge: Polity).

Duyvesteyn, Isabelle (2005) "The Concept of Conventional War and Armed Conflict in Collapsed States," in Jan Angstrom & Isabelle Duyvesteyn (eds.) *Rethinking the Nature of War* (London: Frank Cass).

Duyvesteyn, Isabelle (2004) *Clausewitz and African War: Politics and Strategy in Liberia and Somalia* (London: Frank Cass).

Eccles, Henry E. (1965) *Military Concepts and Philosophy* (New York: Rutgers University Press).

Echevarria, Antulio J. (2011a) "Beyond Generations: Breaking the Cycle," in Karl Erik Haug & Ole Jorgen Maao (eds.) *Conceptualizing Modern War* (New York: Columbia University Press).

Echevarria, Antulio J. (2011b) "American Operational Art, 1917–2008," in John Andreas Olsen & Martin van Creveld (eds.) *The Evolution of Operational Art: From Napoleon to the Present* (Oxford: Oxford University Press).

Echevarria, Antulio J. (2007) *Clausewitz and Contemporary War* (Oxford: Oxford University Press).

Echevarria, Antulio J. (2003a) "'Reining in' the Center of Gravity Concept," *Air & Space Power Journal*, 17(2): 87–96.

Echevarria, Antulio J. (2003b) "Clausewitz's Center of Gravity: It's Not What we Thought," *Naval War College Review*, 56(1): 108–23.

Echevarria, Antulio J. (2001) *Rapid Decisive Operations: An Assumptions-Based Critique* (Carlisle, PA: Strategic Studies Institute).

Eck, Kristine (2012) "In Data We Trust? A Comparison of UCDP GED and ACLED Conflict Events Datasets," *Cooperation and Conflict*, 47(1): 124–41.

Edstrom, Hakan, Janne Haaland Matlary, & Magnus Petersson (eds.) (2011) *NATO: The Power of Partnerships* (London: Palgrave Macmillan).

Egnell, Robert (2009) *Complex Peace Operations and Civil-Military Relations: Winning the Peace* (London: Routledge).

Egnell, Robert & David Ucko (2013) *Counterinsurgency in Crisis: Britain and the Challenges of Modern Warfare* (New York: Columbia University Press).

Eikmeier, Dale C. (2007) "A Logical Method for Center-of-Gravity Analysis," *Military Review*, 87(5): 62–6.

Ellis, Stephen (1999) *The Mask of Anarchy: The Destruction of Liberia and the Religious Dimension of an African Civil War* (London: Hurst).

Elman, Colin & Miliam Fendius Elman (eds.) (2001) *Bridges and Boundaries: Historians, Political Scientists, and the Study of International Relations* (Cambridge, MA: MIT Press).

Elshtain, Joan Bethke (1995) *Women and War* (Chicago, IL: University of Chicago Press).

Engelbrekt, Kjell, Marcus Mohlin & Charlotte Wagnsson (eds.) (2013) *The NATO Intervention: Lessons Learned from the Campaign* (London: Routledge).

English, John (1996) "The Operational Art: Developments in the Theories of War," in B. J. C. McKercher & Michael A. Hennessy (eds.) *The Operational Art – Developments in the Theories of War* (Westport, CT: Praeger).

Evans, Michael (2004) *The Continental School of Strategy: The Past, Present and Future of Land Power* (Duntroon, Australia: Land Warfare Studies Centre).

Evans, Michael H. H. (1990) *Amphibious Operations: The Projection of Sea Power Ashore* (London: Brassey's).

Eyre, Dana P. & Mark C. Suchman (1996) "Status, Norms, and the Proliferation of Conventional Weapons: An Institutional Theory Approach," in Peter J. Katzenstein (ed.), *The Culture of National Security: Norms and Identity in World Politics* (New York: Columbia University Press).

Faber, Peter R. (1997a) *Competing Visions of Aerospace Power: A Language for the 21st Century* (Newport, RI: Naval War College).

Faber, Peter R. (1997b) "Interwar US Army Aviation and the Air Corps Tactical School: Incubators of American Airpower," in Phillip S. Meilinger (ed.) *The Paths of Heaven* (Maxwell, AL: Air University Press).

Faber, Peter (2002) "The Evolution of Airpower in the United States: From WW1 to Warden's *The Air Campaign*," in John Andreas Olsen (ed.) *Asymmetric Warfare* (Trondheim: The Royal Norwegian Air Force Academy).

Fadok, David S. (1997) "John Boyd and John Warden: Airpower's Quest for Strategic Paralysis," in Phillip S. Meilinger (ed.) *The Paths of Heaven* (Maxwell, AL: Air University Press).

Fall, Bernard (1998/1965) "The Theory and Practice of Insurgency and Counterinsurgency," *Naval War College Review*, 51(1): 46–57.

Fallwell, Marshall L. (1955) "The Principles of War and the Solution of Military Problems," *Military Review*, 35(5): 48–62.

Farrell, Theo (2005) *Norms of War: Cultural Beliefs and Modern Conflict* (Boulder, CO: Lynne Rienner).

Farrell, Theo & Terry Teriff (2002) *The Sources of Military Change: Culture, Politics, and Technology* (Boulder, CO: Lynne Rienner).

Farrell, Theo, Frans Osinga, & James Russell (eds) (2013) *Military Adaptation in Afghanistan* (Stanford, CA: Stanford University Press).

Farrell, Theo, Sten Rynning, & Terry Teriff (2013) *Transforming Military Power since the Cold War: Britain, France, and the United States, 1991–2012* (Cambridge: Cambridge University Press).

Fast Scott, Harriet & William F. Scott (1982) "Introduction," in Harriet Fast Scott & William F. Scott (eds.) *The Soviet Art of War: Doctrine, Strategy, and Tactics* (Boulder, CO: Westview Press).

Fearon, James D. (1995) "A Rationalist Explanation of War," *International Organization*, 49(3): 379–414.

Fearon, James D. & David D. Laitin (2004) "Neotrusteeship and the Problem of Weak States," *International Security*, 28(4): 5–43.

Feaver, Peter (2003) *Armed Servants: Agency, Oversight, and Civil-Military Relations* (Cambridge, MA: Harvard University Press).

Ferrill, Arther (1985) *The Origins of War* (London: Thames and Hudson).

Fioravanzo, Guiseppe (1979) *A History of Naval Tactical Thought*, translation Arthur W. Holst (Annapolis, MD: Naval Institute Press).

Fishel, John T. (1995) "Little Wars, Small Wars, LIC, OOTW, the GAP, and Things that Go Bump in the Night," *Low Intensity Conflict & Law Enforcement*, 4(3): 372–98.

FM 100-5 *Operations* (1986) (Headquarters, Department of the Army: Washington DC).

Fortna, Virginia Page (2008) *Does Peacekeeping Work? Shaping Belligerents' Choices after Civil War* (Princeton, NJ: Princeton University Press).

Foxton, P. D. (1994) *Powering War: Modern Land Force Logistics* (London: Brassey's).

Frankel, Benjamin (ed.) (2001) *Precision and Purpose: Debating Robert A. Pape's Bombing to Win* (London: Frank Cass).

Freedman, Lawrence (2013) *Strategy: A History* (Oxford: Oxford University Press).

Freedman, Lawrence (2004) *Deterrence* (Cambridge: Polity Press).

Freedman, Lawrence (2003) *The Evolution of Nuclear Strategy*, 3rd edn. (London: Palgrave Macmillan).

Freedman, Lawrence (2002) "The Third World War?" *Survival*, 43(4): 61–88.

Freedman, Lawrence (1998) (ed.) *Strategic Coercion: Concepts and Cases* (Oxford: Oxford University Press).

Freedman, Lawrence (1986) "The First Two Generations of Nuclear Strategists," in Peter Paret (ed.) *Makers of Modern Strategy* (Princeton, NJ: Princeton University Press).

Freedman, Lawrence (1985) "Strategic Studies," in Steve Smith (ed.) *International Relations: British and American Perspectives* (Oxford: Blackwells), pp. 29–44.

Friedman, Norman (2009) *Network-Centric Warfare: How Navies Learned to Fight Smarter Through Three World Wars* (Annapolis, MD: Naval Institute Press).

Friedman, Norman (2001) *Seapower as Strategy: Navies and National Interest* (Annapolis, MD: Naval Institute Press).

Fuller, J. F. C. (1931) *Lectures on F.S.R. II* (London: Sifton Praed & Co.).

Fuller, J. F. C. (1926) *The Foundations of the Science of War* (London: Hutchinson).

Gaddis, John Lewis (2005) *Strategies of Containment: A Critical Appraisal of American National Security Policy during the Cold War*, rev. edn. (Oxford: Oxford University Press).

Gaddis, John Lewis (2002) *The Landscape of History: How Historians Map the Past* (Oxford: Oxford University Press).

Gaddis, John Lewis (1998) *We Now Know: Rethinking Cold War History* (Oxford: Oxford University Press).

Gaddis, John Lewis (1997) "History, Theory, and Common Ground," *International Security*, 22(1): 75–85.

Galtung, Johan (1985) *Det finns alternativ: Fyra vägar till fred och säkerhet* (Stockholm: Gidlund).

Galula, David (1965/2006) *Counter-Insurgency Warfare: Theory and Practice* (Westport, CT: Praeger).

Garden, Timothy (2002) "Air Power: Theory and Practice," in John Baylis, James J. Wirtz, & Colin S. Gray (eds.) *Strategy in a Contemporary World*, 3rd edn. (Oxford: Oxford University Press).

Gardner, Lloyd C. & Marilyn B. Young (eds.) (2007) *Iraq and the Lessons of Vietnam* (New York: New Press).

Gartner, Scott Sigmund (1997) *Strategic Assessment in War* (New Haven, CT: Yale University Press).

Gat, Azar (2013) "Is War Declining – and Why?" *Journal of Peace Research*, vol. 50(2): 149–57.

Gat, Azar (2006) *War in Human Civilization* (Oxford: Oxford University Press).

Gat, Azar (2001) *A History of Military Thought: From the Enlightenment to the Cold War* (Oxford: Oxford University Press).

George, Alexander L. & Richard Smoke (1974) *Deterrence in American Foreign Policy: Theory and Practice* (New York: Columbia University Press).

General Staff War Office (1920) *Field Service Regulations* (London: H.M. Stationery Office).

Giddens, Anthony (1985) *The Nation-State and Violence* (Cambridge: Polity Press).

Glantz, David M. (1996) "The Intellectual Dimension of Soviet (Russian) Operational Art," in B. J. C. McKercher & Michael A. Hennessy (eds.) *The Operational Art – Developments in the Theories of War* (Westport, CT: Praeger).

Glantz, David M. (1991a) *The Soviet Conduct of Tactical Maneuver: Spearhead of the Offensive* (London: Frank Cass).

Glantz, David M. (1991b) *Soviet Military Operational Art: In Pursuit of Deep Battle* (London: Frank Cass).

Glenn, Russell W. (1998) "No More Principles of War?" *Parameters*, 28(1): 48–66.

Glete, Jan (2000) *Warfare at Sea, 1500–1650: Maritime Conflicts and the Transformation of Europe* (London: Routledge).

Goldstein, Joshua (2011) *Winning the War on War: The Decline of Armed Conflict Worldwide* (New York: Penguin).

Goldstein, Joshua S. (2001) *War and Gender: How Gender Shapes the War System and Vice Versa* (Cambridge: Cambridge University Press).

Goldstein, Judith & Robert O. Keohane (eds.) (1993) *Ideas and Foreign Policy: Beliefs, Institutions, and Political Change* (Ithaca, NY: Cornell University Press).

Goodin, Robert E. & Hans-Dieter Klingemann (eds.) (1996) *A New Handbook of Political Science* (Oxford: Oxford University Press).

Gorshkov, S. G. (1979) *The Sea Power of the State* (Oxford: Pergamon Press).

Gow, James (2003) *The Serbian Project and Its Adversaries: A Strategy of War Crimes* (London: Hurst).

Gow, James (1997) *Triumph of the Lack of Will: International Diplomacy and the Yugoslav War* (London: Hurst).

de Graaff, Bob (2005) "The Wars in Former Yugoslavia in the 1990s: Bringing the State Back In," in Jan Angstrom & Isabelle Duyvesteyn (eds.) *Rethinking the Nature of War* (London: Frank Cass).

Gray, Colin S. (2011) *The Strategy Bridge: Theory for Practice* (Oxford: Oxford University Press).

Gray, Colin S. (2007) *War, Peace and International Relations* (London: Routledge).

Gray, Colin S. (2002) *Strategy for Chaos: Revolutions in Military Affairs and the Evidence of History* (London: Frank Cass).

Gray, Colin S. (1999) *Modern Strategy* (Oxford: Oxford University Press).

Gray, Colin S. (1996a) "The Influence of Space Power upon History," *Comparative Strategy*, 15(4): 293–308.

Gray, Colin S. (1996b) "Introduction," in Charles Callwell (1996) *Military Operations and Maritime Preponderance* (Annapolis, MD: Naval Institute Press).

Gray, Colin S. (1992) *The Leverage of Seapower: The Strategic Advantage of Navies in War* (New York: The Free Press).

Gray, Colin S. & Jeannie L. Johnson (2009) "The Practice of Strategy," in John Baylis, James Wirtz, & Colin Gray (eds.) *Strategy in the Contemporary World*, 3rd edn. (Oxford: Oxford University Press).

Grechko, A.A. (1975) *The Armed Forces of the Soviet State: A Soviet View* (Washington DC: U.S. Government Printing Office).

Grissom, Adam (2013) "In Our Image: Statebuilding Orthodoxy and the Afghan National Army," in Robert Egnell & Peter Haldén (eds.) *New Agendas in Statebuilding: Hybridity, Contingency, and History* (London: Routledge).

Grissom, Adam (2006) "The Future of Military Innovation Studies," *Journal of Strategic Studies*, 29(5): 905–34.

Groos, Otto (1929) *Seekriegslehren im Lichte des Weltkriges* (Berlin: E. S. Mittler & Sohn).

Grove, Eric (1990) *The Future of Sea Power* (London: Routledge).

Gudmundsson, Bruce I. (1995) *Stormtroop Tactics: Innovation in the German Army 1914–1918* (Westport, CT: Praeger).

Guevara, Ernesto Che (1969) *Guerrilla Warfare* (London: Penguin, 1969

Guistozzi, Antonio (2009) *Empires of Mud: Wars and Warlords in Afghanistan* (New York: Columbia University Press).

Haarr, Geirr H. (2010) *The Battle for Norway 1940* (Annapolis, MD: Naval Institute Press).

de Haas, Marcel (2004) *Russian Security and Air Power, 1992–2002* (London: Frank Cass).

Hables Gray, Chris (1997) *Postmodern War: The New Politics of Conflict* (London: Routledge).

Hahlweg, Werner (1986) "Clausewitz and Guerrilla Warfare," in Michael I. Handel (ed.) *Clausewitz and Modern Strategy* (London: Frank Cass).

Hahlweg, Werner (1968) *Guerilla: Krieg ohne Fronten [Guerrilla – War without Fronts]* (Stuttgart: W. Kohlhammer GmbH).

Hall, John A. & G. John Ikenberry (1989) *The State* (Milton Keynes: Open University Press, 1989).

Hallett, Brien (1998) *The Lost Art of Declaring War* (Chicago, IL: University of Illinois Press).

Hammes, Thomas X. (2006) *The Sling and the Stone: On War in the Twenty-First Century* (St. Paul, MN. Zenith Press).

Hammond, Grant T. (2001) *The Mind of War: John Boyd and American Security* (Washington DC: Smithsonian Institute Press).

Handel, Michael I. (2001) *Masters of War: Classical Strategic Thought*, 3rd edn. (London: Frank Cass).

Handel, Michael I. (ed.) (1990) *Intelligence and Military Operations* (London: Routledge).

Harding, Richard (1999) *Seapower and Naval Warfare 1650–1830* (London: UCL Press).

Harkavy, Robert E. & Stephanie G. Neuman (2001) *Warfare and the Third World* (New York: Palgrave Macmillan).

Harrison, Richard W. (2001) *The Russian Way of War: Operational Art, 1904–1940* (Lawrence, KS: University Press of Kansas).

Heinl, Robert Debs (ed.) (1966) *Dictionary of Military and Naval Quotations* (Annapolis, MD: U.S. Naval Institute Press).

Hemleben, Sylvester John (1943) *Plans for World Peace through Six Centuries* (Chicago, IL: University of Illinois Press).

Herberg-Rothe, Andreas (2007) *Clausewitz's Puzzle: The Political Theory of War* (Oxford: Oxford University Press).

Herberg-Rothe, Andreas, Dan Moran, Jan Willem Honig (2011) (eds.) *Clausewitz: The State and War* (Hamburg: Franz Steiner).

Herman, Michael (1996) *Intelligence Power in Peace and War* (Cambridge: Cambridge University Press).

Heuser, Beatrice (2010) *The Evolution of Strategy* (Cambridge: Cambridge University Press).

Heuser, Beatrice (2002) *Reading Clausewitz* (London: Vintage).

Hezlet, Arthur (1970) *Aircraft and Sea Power* (London: Peter Davies).

Hicks, George (1997) *The Comfort Women: Japan's Brutal Regime of Enforced Prostitution in the Second World War* (New York: WW Norton).

Higate, Paul (ed.) (2003) *Militarized Masculinities* (London: Praeger).

Hobbs, Richard (1979) *The Myth of Victory: What is Victory in War?* (Boulder, CO: Westview Press).

Hobson, John M. (2000) *The State and International Relations* (Cambridge: Cambridge University Press).

Hoglund, Kristine & Magnus Oberg (2010) *Understanding Peace Research: Methods and Challenges* (London: Routledge).

Hoglund, Kristine and Mimmi Soderberg-Kovacs (2010) "Beyond the Absence of War: The Diversity of Peace in Post-Settlement Societies," *Review of International Studies*, 36(2): 367–90.

Hoiback, Harald (2013) *Understanding Military Doctrine: A Multidisciplinary Approach* (London: Routledge).

Holley, I. B., Jr. (1997) "Reflections on the Search for Airpower Theory," in Phillip S. Meilinger (ed.) *The Paths of Heaven* (Maxwell, AL: Air University Press).

Hollis, Martin & Steve Smith (1991) *Explaining and Understanding International Relations* (Oxford: Clarendon).

Holmes, Richard (ed.) (2001) *The Oxford Companion to Military History* (Oxford: Oxford University Press).

Holmqvist, Caroline (2014) *Policing Wars: On Military Intervention in the Twenty-First Century* (London: Palgrave Macmillan).

Holsti, Kalevi J. (2004) *Taming the Sovereigns: Institutional Change in International Politics* (Cambridge: Cambridge University Press), pp. 275–99.

Holsti, Kalevi (1996) *The State, War, and the State of War* (Cambridge: Cambridge University Press).

Honig, Jan Willem (forthcoming) *Winning Wars* (Cambridge: Cambridge University Press).

Honig, Jan Willem (1997) "Strategy in a Post-Clausewitzian Setting," in Gert de Nooy (ed.), *The Clausewitzian Dictum and the Future of Western Military Strategy* (Haag: Kluwer Law International).

Hooker, Richard, Jr. (1993) *Maneuver Warfare: An Anthology* (Novato, CA: Presidio Press).

Horne Alistair (1977) *A Savage War of Peace: Algeria, 1954–62* (London: Macmillan).

Horowitz, Michael (2010) *The Diffusion of Military Power* (Princeton, NJ: Princeton University Press).

Horowitz, Michael & Dan Reiter (2001) "When Does Aerial Bombing Work? Quantitative Empirical Tests, 1917–1999," *Journal of Conflict Resolution*, 45(2): 147–73.

Hosmer, Stephen T. (2001) *The Conflict over Kosovo: Why Milosevic Decided to Settle when he Did* (St. Monica, CA: Rand).

Hough, Richard (1999) *Naval Battles of the Twentieth Century* (London: Constable).

House, Jonathan M. (2001) *Combined Arms Warfare in the Twentieth Century* (Lawrence, Kansas: University Press of Kansas).

House, Jonathan M. (1984) *Toward Combined Arms Warfare: A Survey of 20th-Century Tactics, Doctrine and Organization*, Research Survey No. 2 (Fort Leavenworth, Kansas: Combat Studies Institute).

Howard, Lise Morjé (2008) *UN Peacekeeping in Civil Wars* (Cambridge: Cambridge University Press).

Howard, Michael (2008) *War and the Liberal Conscience* (London: Hurst).

Howard, Michael (1983a) *Clausewitz* (Oxford: Oxford University Press).

Howard, Michael (1983b) *The Causes of Wars* (London: Unwin).

Hudson, Valerie (2012) *Sex and World Peace* (New York: Columbia University Press).

Hughes, Wayne P., Jr. (2000) *Fleet Tactics and Coastal Combat*, 2nd edn. (Annapolis, MD: Naval Institute Press).

Huntington, Samuel (1957) *The Soldier and the State: The Theory and Politics of Civil-Military Relations* (Cambridge, MA: Belknap Press).

Hurd, Ian (2007) *After Anarchy: Legitimacy and Power in the United Nations Security Council* (Princeton, NJ: Princeton University Press).

Ignatieff, Michael (2000) *Virtual War: Kosovo and Beyond* (Toronto: Viking Books).

Imlay, Talbot C. & Monica Duffy Toft (eds.) (2006) *The Fog of Peace and War Planning: Military and Strategic Planning under Uncertainty* (London: Routledge).

Janowitz, Morris (1960) *The Professional Soldier* (New York: The Free Press).

Jervis, Robert (1978) "Cooperation Under the Security Dilemma," *World Politics*, 30(2): 167–214.

Jervis, Robert (1976) *Perception and Misperception in International Politics* (Princeton, NJ: Princeton University Press).

Jervis, Robert, Richard Ned Lebow, & Janice Gross Stein (eds.) (1985) *Psychology and Deterrence* (Baltimore, MD: The Johns Hopkins University Press).

Johansson, Alf (1988) *Europas krig: Militärt tänkande, strategi och politik från Napoleon tiden till andra världskrigets slut* (Stockholm: Tiden).

Johnsen, William (2004) *Redefining Land Power for the 21st Century* (Carlisle, PA: Strategic Studies Institute).

Johnson, Dominic & Dominic Tierney (2007) "In the Eye of the Beholder: Victory and Defeat in US Military Operations," in Jan Angstrom & Isabelle Duyvesteyn (eds.) *Understanding Victory and Defeat in Contemporary War* (London: Routledge).

Johnson, Dominic & Dominic Tierney (2006) *Failing to Win: Perceptions of Victory and Defeat in International Politics* (Cambridge, MA: Harvard University Press).

Johnson, Loch K. & James J. Wirtz (2010) *Intelligence: The Secret World of Spies*, 3rd edn. (Oxford: Oxford University Press).

Johnson, Robert (2012) *The Afghan Way of War: How and why they Fight* (Oxford: Oxford University Press).

Johnston, Alastair Iain (1995) "Thinking about Strategic Culture," *International Security*, 19(4): 32–64.

Johnston, Patrick B. (2012) "Does Decapitation Work? Assessing the Effectiveness of Leadership Targeting in Counterinsurgency Campaigns," *International Security*, 36(4): 47–79.

Joint Chiefs of Staff (2000) *Joint Vision 2020* (Washington DC: US Department of Defense).

Joint Chiefs of Staff (1996) *Joint Vision 2010* (Washington DC: US Department of Defense).

Jomini, Antoine Henri (1987) "Summary of the Art of War," in *Roots of Strategy*, vol. 2 (Mechanicsburg, PA: Stackpole Books).

Jones, Archer (1987) *The Art of War in the Western World* (Chicago: University of Illinois Press).

Jordan, David, James D. Kiras, David J. Lonsdale, Ian Speller, Christopher Tuck, & Dale C Walton (2008) *Understanding Modern Warfare* (Cambridge: Cambridge University Press).

Kagan, Donald (1997) *On the Origins of War* (London: Pimlico).

Kaldor, Mary (2006) *New and Old Wars: Organized Violence in a Global Area*, 2nd edn. (Cambridge: Polity Press).

Kalyvas, Stathis N. (2012) "The Changing Character of Civil Wars, 1800–2009," in Hew Strachan & Sibylle Scheipers (eds.) *The Changing Character of War* (Oxford: Oxford University Press).

Kalyvas, Stathis N. (2006) *The Logic of Violence in Civil Wars* (Cambridge: Cambridge University Press).

Kalyvas, Stathis N. (2005) "Warfare in Civil Wars," in Jan Angstrom & Isabelle Duyvesteyn (eds.) *Rethinking the Nature of War* (London: Frank Cass).

Kalyvas, Stathis N. (2003) "The Ontology of Political Violence: Action and Identity in Civil Wars," *Perspectives on Politics*, 1(3): 475–94.

Kalyvas, Stathis N. (2001) "New and Old Wars: A Valid Distinction?" *World Politics*, 54(1): 99–118.

Kane, Thomas M. (2001) *Military Logistics and Strategic Performance* (London: Routledge).

Kaplan, Robert D. (2000) *The Coming Anarchy: Shattering the Dreams of the Post Cold War* (New York: Random House).

Karlsson, Hakan (2002) *Bureaucratic Politics and Weapons Acquisition: The Case of the MX ICBM Program*, PhD Diss. (Stockholm: University of Stockholm).

Kassimeris, George & John Buckley (eds.) (2010) *The Ashgate Research Companion to Modern Warfare* (Farnham: Ashgate).

Katz, Paul (1987) "The Additional Principle of War," *Military Review*, 67(6): 36–45.

Katzenstein, Peter (1996) "Introduction: Alternative Perspectives on National Security," in Peter Katzenstein (ed.) *The Culture of National Security: Norms and Identity in World Politics* (New York: Columbia University Press).

Kaufmann, Chaim D. (1996a) "Interventions in Ethnic and Ideological Civil Wars: Why One Can Be Done but the Other Can't," *Security Studies*, 6(1): 62–103.

Kaufmann, Chaim D. (1996b) "Possible and Impossible Solutions to Ethnic Civil Wars," *International Security*, 20(4): 136–75.

Kaufman, Robert G. (2001) "On the Uses and Abuses of History in IR Theory," *Security Studies*, 10(4): 179–211.

Keegan, John (2003) *Intelligence in War: Knowledge of the Enemy from Napoleon to Al-Qaeda* (New York: Alfred A. Knopf).

Keegan, John (1994) *A History of Warfare* (London: Pimlico).

Keegan, John (1991) *The Face of Battle* (London: Pimlico).

Keegan, John (1989) *The Price of Admiralty: The Evolution of Naval Warfare* (London: Penguin).

Keegan, John (1961) "On the Principles of War," *Military Review*, 41(12): 61–72.

Keen, David (2000) "Incentives and Disincentives for Violence," in Mats Berdal & David Malone (eds.) *Greed and Grievance: Economic Agendas in Civil Wars* (Boulder, CO: Lynne Rienner).

Kelly, Justin & Mike Brennan (2009) *Alien: How Operational Art Devoured Strategy* (Carlisle, PA: Strategic Studies Institute).

Kennan, George (1947) "The Sources of Soviet Conduct," *Foreign Affairs*, 25(4): 566–82.

Keohane, Robert O. (1986) "Realism, Neorealism, and the Study of World Politics," in Robert O. Keohane (ed.) *Neorealism and Its Critics* (New York: Columbia University Press).

Kesseli, Pasi (2001) *In Pursuit of Mobility: The Birth and Development of Israeli Operational Art, from Theory to Practice* (Helsinki: National Defence College of Finland).

Khong, Yuen Foong (1992) *Analogies at War: Korea, Munich, Dien Bien Phu, and the Vietnam Decisions of 1965* (Princeton, NJ: Princeton University Press).

Kier, Elisabeth (1997) *Imagining War: French and British Military Doctrine between the Wars* (Princeton, NJ: Princeton University Press).

Kilcullen, David (2009) *The Accidental Guerrilla: Fighting Small Wars in the Midst of a Big One* (Oxford: Oxford University Press).

King, Anthony (2011) *The Transformation of Europe's Armed Forces: From the Rhine to Afghanistan* (Cambridge: Cambridge University Press).

Kipp, Jacob W. (2011) "The Tsarist and Soviet Operational Art, 1853–1991," in John Andreas Olsen and & van Creveld (eds.) *The Evolution of Operational Art: From Napoleon to the Present* (Oxford: Oxford University Press).

Kipp, Jacob W. (1992) "Preface" in A. A. Svechin *Strategy*, translated Kent D. Lee (Minneapolis, MN: East View Information Service).

Kiras, James D. (2002) "Terrorism and Irregular Warfare," in John Baylis, James J. Wirtz, & Colin S. Gray (eds.) *Strategy in the Contemporary World: An Introduction to Strategic Studies* (Oxford: Oxford University Press).

Kitson, Frank (1971) *Low Intensity Operations: Subversion, Insurgency, and Peacekeeping* (London: Faber).

Klein, John J. (2004) "Corbett in Orbit," *Naval War College Review*, 57(1): 59–74.

Kokoshin, Andrei A. (1998) *Soviet Strategic Thought, 1917–91* (Cambridge, MA: MIT Press).

Kollock, Peter (1998) "Social Dilemmas: The Anatomy of Cooperation," *Annual Review of Sociology*, 24: 183–214.

Kozlov, S. N. (ed.) (1977), *The Officer's Handbook: A Soviet View* (Washington DC: U.S. Government Printing Office).

Kreps, Sarah (2011) *Coalitions of Convenience: United States Military Interventions after the Cold War* (Oxford: Oxford University Press).

Kreps, Sarah (2010) "Why Does Peacekeeping Succeed or Fail? Peacekeeping in the Democratic Republic of Congo and Sierra Leone," in Jan Angstrom & Isabelle Duyvesteyn (eds.) *Modern War and the Utility of Force* (London: Routledge).

Kress, Moshe (2002) *Operational Logistics: The Art and Science of Sustaining Military Operations* (Boston: Kluwer Academic Publishers).

Kuhn, Thomas (1996) *The Structure of Scientific Revolutions*, 3rd edn. (Chicago: University of Chicago Press).

Lakatos, Imre & Alan Musgrave (eds.) (1970) *Criticism and the Growth of Knowledge* (Cambridge: Cambridge University Press).

Lake, David (2009) *Hierarchy in International Relations* (Ithaca, NY: Cornell University Press).

Lambeth, Benjamin (2001) *Nato's Air War for Kosovo: A Strategic and Operational Assessment* (St Monica, CA: Rand).

Lambert, Andrew (2010) "Seapower" in George Kassimeris & John Buckley (eds.) *The Ashgate Research Companion to Modern Warfare* (Farnham: Ashgate).

Landquist, Daniel (1935) *Några av sjöstrategiens grunder* (Stockholm: Marinlitteraturföreningens förlag).

Laqueur, Walter (1985) *A World of Secrets: The Uses and Limits of Intelligence* (New York: Basic Books).

Larsdotter, Kersti (2011) *Military Interventions in Internal Wars: The Study of Peace or the Study of War?* PhD dissertation (Gothenburg University).

Laver, Harry S. & Jeffrey J. Matthews (2008) *The Art of Command: Military Leadership from George Washington to Colin Powell* (Lexington: University Press of Kentucky).

Lawrence, T. E. (1997/1922) *Seven Pillars of Wisdom* (Ware, Herts.: Wordsworth).

Lebow, Richard Ned (2010) *Why Nations Fight: The Past and Future of War* (Cambridge: Cambridge University Press).

Lebow, Richard Ned (2008) *A Cultural Theory of International Relations* (Cambridge: Cambridge University Press).

Lebow, Richard Ned (1981) *Between Peace and War: The Nature of International Crisis* (Baltimore, MD: The Johns Hopkins University Press).

Lebow, Richard Ned & Barry S. Strauss (eds.) (1991) *Hegemonic Rivalry: From Thucydides to the Nuclear Age* (Boulder, CO: Westview Press).

Leonhard, Robert (1998) *The Principles of War for the Information Age* (New York: Ballantine Books).

Leonhard, Robert (1994) *Fighting by Minutes: Time and the Art of War* (Westport, CT: Praeger).

Leonhard, Robert (1991) *The Art of Maneuver: Maneuver Warfare Theory and AirLand Battle* (New York: Ballantine Books).

Lewis, John David (2010) *Nothing less than Victory: Decisive Wars and the Lessons of History* (Princeton, NJ: Princeton University Press).

Liberman, Peter (1996) *Does Conquest Pay? The Exploitation of Occupied Industrial Societies* (Princeton, NJ: Princeton University Press).

Libicki, Martin (2012) "Cyberspace is Not a Warfighting Domain," *I/S: A Journal of Law and Policy for the Information Society*, 8(2): 325–40.

Libicki, Martin (2009) *Cyberdeterrence and Cyberwar* (Santa Monica, CA: RAND).

Libicki, Martin (2007) *Conquest in Cyberspace: National Security and Information Warfare* (Cambridge: Cambridge University Press).

Licklider, Roy (1993) "How Civil Wars End: Questions and Method," in Roy Licklider (ed.) *Stopping the Killing: How Civil Wars End* (New York: New York University Press).

Liddell Hart, Basil H. (1991) *Strategy*, 2nd edn. (New York: Meridian).

Liddell Hart, Basil H. (1932) *The British Way in Warfare* (London: Faber).

Liddell Hart, Basil H. (1929) *The Decisive Wars of History* (London: Bell).

Lider, Julian (1983) *Military Theory: Concept, Structure, Problems* (Aldershot: Gower).

Lider, Julian (1980) *Problems of the Classification of Wars* (Stockholm: Utrikespolitiska institutet).

Lind, William S. (1985) *Maneuver Warfare Handbook* (Boulder, CO: Westview Press).

Lindberg, Michael & Daniel Todd (2002) *Brown-, Green- and Blue-Water Fleets: The Influence of Geography on Naval Warfare, 1861 to the Present* (Westport, CT: Praeger).

Lock-Pullan, Richard (2006) *US Intervention Policy and Army Innovation: From Vietnam to Iraq* (London: Routledge).

Lomov, N. A. (2002) *Scientific-Technological Progress and the Revolution in Military Affairs: A Soviet View* (Honolulu, Hawaii: University Press of the Pacific).

Lovering, Tristan (ed.) (2007) *Amphibious Assault: Maneuver from the Sea* (Suffolk: Seafarer Books).

Lowenthal, Mark M. (2011) *Intelligence: From Secrets to Policy*, 5th edn. (Washington DC: CQ Press).

Lukes, Steven (1974) *Power: A Radical View* (London: Macmillan).

Lunde, Henrik (2010) *Hitler's Pre-Emptive War: The Battle for Norway 1940* (Havertown, PA: Casemate Publishers).

Luttwak, Edward N. (1987) *Strategy: The Logic of War and Peace* (Cambridge, MA: Belknap Press).

Luttwak, Edward N. (1975) *The Political Uses of Seapower* (Baltimore, MD: John Hopkins University Press).

Lynn, John A. (2008) *Battle: A History of Combat and Culture* (New York: Basic Books).

Lynn, John A. (ed.) (1993) *Feeding Wars: Logistics in Western Warfare from the Middle Ages to the Present* (Boulder, CO: Westview Press).

Maao, Ole Jorgen (2011) "Mary Kaldor's New Wars: A Critique," in Karl Erik Haug & Ole Jorgen Maao (eds.) *Conceptualizing Modern War* (New York: Columbia University Press).

McInnes, Colin (2002) *Spectator Sport War: The West and Contemporary Conflict* (Boulder, CO: Lynne Rienner).

MacIsaac, David (1986) "Voices from the Central Blue: The Air Power Theorists," in Peter Paret (ed.) *Makers of Modern Strategy* (Princeton, NJ: Princeton University Press).

Mack, Andrew J. R. (1975) "Why Big Nations Lose Small Wars: The Politics of Asymmetric Conflict," *World Politics*, 27(2): 175–200.

Mackinlay, John (2010) *The Insurgent Archipelago* (New York: Columbia University Press).

Mahan, Alfred T. (1999) "The Influence of Sea Power upon History," in David Jablonsky (ed.), *Roots of Strategy*, vol. 4 (Mechanicsburg, PA: Stackpole Books).

Mahan, Alfred T. (1991) *Mahan on Naval Strategy: Selections from the Writings of Rear Admiral Alfred Thayer Mahan* (Annapolis, MD: Naval Institute Press).

Mahan, Alfred T. (1890) *The Influence of Seapower Upon History, 1660–1783* (Boston: Little, Brown and Company).

Mahnken, Thomas G. (2008) *Technology and the American Way of War since 1945* (New York: Columbia University Press).

Mahnken, Thomas G. (2003) "The Future of Strategic Studies," *Journal of Strategic Studies*, 26(1).

Mahnken, Thomas & Joseph A. Maiolo (eds.) (2008) *Strategic Studies – a Reader* (London: Routledge).

Mandel, Robert (2006) *The Meaning of Military Victory* (Boulder, CO: Lynne Rienner).

Mandel, Robert (2002) *Armies without States: The Privatization of Security* (Boulder, CO: Lynne Rienner).

Mansfield, Nick (2008) *Theorizing War: From Hobbes to Badiou* (London: Palgrave Macmillan).

Mansfield, Edward D. & Jack Snyder (2005) *Electing to Fight: Why Emerging Democracies Go to War* (Cambridge, MA: MIT Press).

Mao Tse-tung (1966) *Selected Military Writings* (Peking, China: Foreign Language Press).

Mao Tse-tung (1961) *On Guerrilla Warfare*, translation Samuel B. Griffiths (Chicago: University of Illinois Press).

Marolda, Edward J. & Robert J. Schneller Jr (2001) *Shield and Sword: The United States Navy and the Persian Gulf War* (Annapolis, MD: Naval Institute Press).

Martel, William C. (2007) *Victory in War: Foundations of Modern Military Policy* (Cambridge: Cambridge University Press).

Martin, Laurence (1967) *The Sea in Modern Strategy* (London: Chatto & Windus).

Matheson, Craig (1987) "Weber and the Classification of Forms of Legitimacy," *The British Journal of Sociology*, 38(2): 199–215.

Mearsheimer, John (1983) *Conventional Deterrence* (Ithaca, NY: Cornell University Press).

Meilinger, Philip S. (2003) *Airwar: Theory and Practice* (London: Frank Cass).

Meilinger, Philip S. (2001) *Airmen and Air Theory: A Review of the Sources* (Maxwell, AL: Air University Press).

Meilinger, Philip S. (1997) "Guilio Douhet and the Origins of Airpower Theory," in Philip S. Meilinger (ed.) *The Paths of Heaven* (Maxwell, AL: Air University Press).

Melander, Erik (2005) "Gender Equality and Intrastate Armed Conflict," *International Studies Quarterly*, 49(4): 695–714.

Melander, Erik, Magnus Oberg, & Jonathan Hall (2009) "Are New Wars more Atrocious? Battle Severity, Civilians Killed and Forced Migration before and after the End of the Cold War," *European Journal of International Relations*, 15(3): 505–36.

Menning, Bruce W. (1997) "Operational Art's Origins," *Military Review*, 77(5): 32–47.

Merari, Ariel (1993) "Terrorism as a Strategy of Insurgency," *Terrorism and Political Violence*, 5(4): 213–51.

Mercer, Jonathan (1996) *Reputation and International Politics* (Ithaca, NY: Cornell University Press).

Merom, Gil (2003) *How Democracies Lose Small Wars* (Cambridge: Cambridge University Press).

Mitchell, C. R. (1981) *The Structure of International Conflict* (London: Macmillan).

Mitchell, William (1999) "Winged Defense: The Development and Possibilities of Modern Air Power: Economic and Military', in *Roots of Strategy*, vol. 4 (Mechanicsburg, PA: Stackpole Books).

Mockaitis, Thomas R. (1995) *British Counter-Insurgency in the Post-Imperial Era* (Manchester: Manchester University Press).

Mockaitis, Thomas R. (1990) *British Counter-Insurgency, 1919–1960* (London: Macmillan).

Moorehead, Alan (2007/1956) *Gallipoli* (London: Aurum Press).

Molloy, Ivan (2001) *Rolling Back Revolution: The Emergence of Low Intensity Conflict* (London: Pluto Press).

Moran, Daniel (2001) *Wars of National Liberation* (London: Cassell).

Moreman, Tim R. (1997) "Small Wars and Imperial Policing: The British Army and the Theory and Practice of Colonial Warfare in the British Empire," in Brian Holden Reid (ed.) *Military Power: Land Warfare in Theory and Practice* (London: Frank Cass).

Morgan, John G. & Anthony D. McIvor (2003) "Rethinking the Principles of War," *U.S. Naval Institute Proceedings*, 129(10): 34–8.

Morgan, Patrick (2003) *Deterrence Now* (Cambridge: Cambridge University Press).

Moskos, Charles C. (1976) *Peace Soldiers: The Sociology of a United Nations Military Force* (Chicago: University of Chicago Press).

Mueller, John (2004) *The Remnants of War* (Ithaca, NY: Cornell University Press).

Mueller, Karl P. (1998) "Strategies of Coercion: Denial, Punishment and the Future of Air Power," *Security Studies*, 7(3): 182–228.

Mueller, Karl P. (1997) "Strategic Airpower and Nuclear Strategy: New Theory for a Not-Quite-So-New Apocalypse," in Philip S. Meilinger (ed.) *The Paths of Heaven* (Maxwell, AL: Air University Press).

Mumford, Andrew (2011) *The Counter-Insurgency Myth: The British Experience of Irregular Warfare* (London: Routledge).

Münkler, Herfried (2005) *The New Wars* (London: Polity).

Murray, Williamson (2011) *Military Adaptation in War: With Fear of Change* (Cambridge: Cambridge University Press).

Murray, Williamson (2002) "The Evolution of Joint Warfare," *Joint Forces Quarterly*, 31(2): 30–7.

Murray, Williamson (1994) "The Collapse of Empire: British Strategy, 1919–1945" in Williamson Murray, MacGregor Knox, & Alvin Bernstein (eds.) *The Making of Strategy: Rulers, States, and War* (Cambridge: Cambridge University Press).

Murray, Williamson & Allan R. Millett (eds.) (1996) *Military Innovation in the Interwar Period* (Cambridge: Cambridge University Press).

Murray, Williamson & Mark Grimsley (1994) "Introduction: On strategy," in Williamson Murray, MacGregor Knox, & Alvin Bernstein (eds.), *The Making of Strategy: Rulers, States, and War* (Cambridge: Cambridge University Press).

Nagl, John (2002) *Counterinsurgency Lessons from Malaya and Vietnam: Learning to Eat Soup with a Knife* (New York: Praeger).

Nardulli, Bruce R. Walter L. Perry, & Bruce R. Pirnie (2002) *Disjointed War: Military Operations in Kosovo, 1999* (Santa Monica, CA: Rand).

Naveh, Shimon (1997) *In Pursuit of Military Excellence: Evolution of Operational Theory* (London: Taylor & Francis).

Neumann, Peter & M. L. R. Smith (2007) *The Strategy of Terrorism: How it Works and why it Fails* (London: Routledge).

Newell, Clayton R. (1991) *The Framework of Operational Warfare* (London: Routledge).

Nilsson, Desirée & Mimmi Söderberg Kovacs (2011) "Revisiting an Elusive Concept: A Review of the Debate on Spoilers in Peace Processes," *International Studies Review*, 13(4): 606–26.

Nye, Joseph S. (2004) *Soft Power: The Means to Success in World Politics* (New York: PublicAffairs).

O'Hanlon, Michael (2000) *Technological Change and the Future of Warfare* (Washington DC: Brookings Institution Press).

O'Hara, Vincent (2011) *The German Fleet at War, 1939–1945* (Annapolis, MD: Naval Institute Press).

Olsen, John Andreas (2007) *John Warden and the Renaissance of American Air Power* (Washington DC: Potomac Books).

Olsen, John Andreas (2003) *Strategic Air Power in the Desert Storm* (London: Frank Cass).

Olsen, John Andreas & Martin van Creveld (eds.) (2011) *The Evolution of Operational Art: From Napoleon to the Present* (Oxford: Oxford University Press).

Osinga, Frans P. B. (2007) *Science, Strategy and War: The Strategic Theory of John Boyd* (London: Routledge).

Osinga, Frans P. B. (2002) "Asymmetric Warfare: Rediscovering the Essence of Strategy," in John A. Olsen (ed.) *Asymmetric Warfare* (Trondheim: Luftkrigskolen).

Ostrom, Elinor (1990) *Governing the Commons: The Evolution of Institutions for Collective Action* (Cambridge: Cambridge University Press).

Owens, William A. with Edward Offley (2001) *Lifting the Fog of War* (New York: Farrar, Straus and Giroux).

Oye, Kenneth (ed.) (1985) *Cooperation under Anarchy* (Princeton, NJ: Princeton University Press).

Quine, Willard V. O. (1953) *From a Logical Point of View* (Cambridge, MA: Harvard University Press).

Palmer, Michael A. (2005) *Command at Sea: Naval Command and Control since the Sixteenth Century* (Cambridge, MA: Harvard University Press).

Pape, Robert A. (2005) *Dying to Win: The Strategic Logic Suicide Terrorism* (New York: Random House).

Pape, Robert A. (2004) "The True Worth of Air Power," *Foreign Affairs*, 83(2): 116–30.

Pape, Robert A. (1998) "The Limits of Precision-Guided Air Power," *Security Studies*, 7(2): 93–114.

Pape, Robert A. (1996) *Bombing to Win: Air Power and Coercion in War* (Ithaca, NY: Cornell University Press).

Paret, Peter (ed.) (1986) *Makers of Modern Strategy: From Machiavelli to the Nuclear Age* (Princeton, NJ: Princeton University Press).

Paret, Peter (1976) *Clausewitz and the State* (Oxford: Clarendon Press).

Paris, Roland (2002) "Kosovo and the Metaphor War," *Political Science Quarterly*, 117(3): 423–50.

Parsons, Anthony (1995) *From Cold War to Hot Peace: UN Interventions, 1947–1995* (London: Penguin).

Parsons, Talcott & Edward Shils (eds.) (1951) *Toward a General Theory of Action* (New York: Harper & Row).

Paschall, Rod (1990) *LIC 2010* (Washington DC: Brassey's).

Paul, T. V. (1994) *Asymmetric Conflicts: War Initiation by Weaker Powers* (Cambridge: Cambridge University Press).

Paul, T. V., Patrick Morgan, & James Wirtz (eds.) (2009) *Complex Deterrence: Strategy in a Global Age* (Chicago: Chicago University Press).

Payne, Keith B. (1986) *Strategic Defense: Star Wars in Perspective* (Washington DC: University Press of America).

Peralta, Amanda (1990) *Med andra medel: Från Clausewitz till Guevara – Krig, revolution och politik i marxistisk idétradition* (Göteborg: Daidalos).

Peters, Ralph (2004) "In Praise of Attrition," *Parameters*, 34(2): 24–32.

Pillar, Paul (1983) *Negotiating Peace: War Termination as a Bargaining Process* (Princeton, NJ: Princeton University Press).

Pinker, Steven (2011) *The Better Angels of our Nature* (Cambridge, MA: Harvard University Press).

Popper, Karl R. (2002) *Conjectures and Refutations: The Growth of Scientific Knowledge*, 5th edn. (London: Routledge).

Popper, Karl R. (1970) "Normal Science and Its Dangers," in Imre Lakatos Alan Musgrave (eds.) *Criticism and the Growth of Knowledge* (Cambridge: Cambridge University Press).

Porch, Douglas (1986) "Bugeaud, Galliéni, Lyautey: The Development of French Colonial Warfare," in Peter Paret (ed.) *Makers of Modern Strategy* (Princeton, NJ: Princeton University Press).

Porter, Bruce D. (1994) *War and the Rise of the State: The Military Foundations of Modern Politics* (New York: The Free Press).

Posen, Barry (2003) "Command of the Commons: The Military Foundation of US Hegemony," *International Security*, 28(1): 5–46.

Posen, Barry (1984) *The Sources of Military Doctrine* (Ithaca, NY: Cornell University Press).

Press, Daryl G. (2001) 'The Myth of Air Power in the Persian Gulf War and the Future of Warfare," *International Security*, 26(2): 5–44.

Price, Bryan C. (2012) "Targeting Top Terrorists: How Leadership Decapitation Contributes to Counterterrorism," *International Security*, 36(4): 9–46.

Prunier, Gerard (2009) *Africa's World War: Congo, the Rwandan Genocide, and the Making of Continental Catastrophe* (New York: Oxford University Press).

Prunier, Gerard (2005) *The Rwandan Crisis: History of a Genocide* (New York: Columbia University Press).

Ralston, David B. (1990) *Importing the European Army* (Chicago, IL: University of Chicago Press).

Record, Jeffrey (2007) *Beating Goliath: Why Insurgencies Win* (Washington: Potomac).

Record, Jeffrey & Andrew W. Terrill (2004) *Iraq and Vietnam: Differences, Similarities, and Insights* (Carlisle, PA: Strategic Studies Institute).

Reid, Brian Holden (1998) *Studies in British Military Thought: Debates with Fuller & Liddell Hart* (Lincoln: University of Nebraska Press).

Reid, Brian Holden (1987) *J.F.C. Fuller: Military Thinker* (London: Macmillan).

Reiter, Dan (2009) *How Wars End* (Princeton, NJ: Princeton University Press).

Reiter, Dan (2003) "Exploring the Bargaining Model of War," *Perspectives on Politics*, 1(1): 27–43.

Reiter, Dan & Allan C. Stam (2002) *Democracies at War* (Princeton, NJ: Princeton University Press).

Reno, William (2011) *Warfare in Independent Africa* (Cambridge: Cambridge University Press).

Resende-Santos, Joao (2007) *Neorealism, States, and the Modern Mass Army* (Cambridge: Cambridge University Press).

Rice, Edward E. (1988) *Wars of the Third Kind: Conflict in Underdeveloped Countries* (Berkeley, CA: University of California Press).

Rich, Paul & Isabelle Duyvesteyn (eds.) (2012) *The Routledge Handbook of Insurgency and Counterinsurgency* (London: Routledge).

Rid, Thomas (2013) *Cyber War Will Not Take Place* (Oxford: Oxford University Press).

Ring, Stefan (2005) "Brute Force or Coercion: Two Perspectives of Conflict Management," in Jan Hallenberg & Hakan Karlsson (eds.) *The Iraq War: European Perspectives on Politics, Strategy, and Operations* (London: Routledge), pp. 143–66.

Ringmar, Erik (1996) *Identity, Interest, and Action: A Cultural Explanation of Sweden's Intervention in the Thirty Years War* (Cambridge: Cambridge University Press).

Ritzer, George (2008) *Sociological Theory* (New York: McGraw-Hill).

Robinson, S. S. (1942) *A History of Naval Tactics from 1530 to 1930: The Evolution of Tactical Maxims* (Annapolis, MD: Naval Institute Press).

Rodgers, W. L. (1967) *Naval Warfare under Oars 4ᵗʰ to 16ᵗʰ Centuries: A Study of Strategy, Tactics and Ship Design* (Annapolis, MD: Naval Institute Press).

Röksund, Arne (2007) *The Jeune École: The Strategy of the Weak* (Leiden and Boston, MA: Brill).

Roman, Peter J. (1995) "Strategic Bombers over the Missile Horizon," in John Gooch (ed.) *Airpower: Theory and Practice* (London: Frank Cass).

Rosecrance, Richard (1991) "Albert Wohlstetter," in John Baylis and John Garnett (eds.) *Makers of Nuclear Strategy* (London: Pinter).

Rosecrance, Richard (1973) *International Relations* (New York: McGraw-Hill).

Rosing, Hans (1994) *Vetenskapens logiska grunder*, 9th edn. (Hangö, Finland: Schildts).

Rothenberg, Gunther E. (1985) "Maurice of Nassau, Gustavus Adolphus, Raimondo Montecuccoli, and the 'Military Revolution' of the Seventeenth Century," in Peter Paret (ed.), *Makers of Modern Strategy* (Princeton, NJ: Princeton University Press).

Rueschhoff, Jan L. & Jonathan P. Dunne (2011) "Centers of Gravity from the 'Inside Out',", *Joint Forces Quarterly*, 60(1): 120–5.

Russett, Bruce (1994) *Grasping the Democratic Peace: Principles for a Post-Cold War World* (Princeton, NJ: Princeton University Press).

Samaddar, Ranabir (2004) *Peace Studies* (London: Sage).

Sambanis, Nicholas (2001) "Do Ethnic and Non-Ethnic Civil Wars Have the Same Causes: A Theoretical and Empirical Inquiry, Part 1," *Journal of Conflict Resolution*, 45(3): 259–82.

Sambanis, Nicholas (2004) "What is a Civil War? Conceptual and Empirical Complexities of an Operational Definition," *Journal of Conflict Resolution*, 48(6): 81–58.

Samuels, Martin (1995) *Command or Control? Command, Training and Tactics in the British and German Armies, 1888–1918* (London: Frank Cass).

Schelling, Thomas C. (1966) *Arms and Influence* (New Haven: Yale University Press).

Schelling, Thomas C. (1960) *The Strategy of Conflict* (Cambridge, MA: Harvard University Press).

Schmidt, Brian C. (1994) "The Historiography of Academic International Relations," *Review of International Studies*, 20(4): 349–67.

Schneider, James J. & Lawrence L. Izzo (1987) "Clausewitz's Elusive Center of Gravity," *Parameters*, 17(3): 46–57.

Schurman, Donald M. (1981) *Julian S. Corbett, 1854–1922: Historian of British Maritime Policy from Drake to Jellicoe* (London: Royal Historical Society).

Shamir, Eitan (2011) *Transforming Command: The Pursuit of Mission Command in the U.S., British, and Israeli Armies* (Palo Alto, CA: Stanford University Press).

Shapin, Steven (1995) "Here and Everywhere: Sociology of Scientific Knowledge," *Annual Review of Sociology*, vol. 21: 289–321.

Shapiro, Jacob & David Siegel (2012) "Moral Hazard, Discipline, and the Management of Terrorist Organizations," *World Politics*, 64(1): 39–78.

Shaw, Martin (2003) *War and Genocide: Organized Killing in Modern Society* (Cambridge: Polity Press).

Shearer, David (1998) *Private Armies and Military Intervention*, Adelphi Paper no. 316 (London: IISS).

Shulsky, Abram N. & Gary J. Schmitt (2002) *Silent Warfare: Understanding the World of Intelligence*, 3rd edn. (Washington DC: Brassey's).

Shy, John (1986) "Jomini" in Peter Paret (ed.) *Makers of Modern Strategy from Machiavelli to the Nuclear Age* (Princeton, NJ: Princeton University Press).

Shy, John & Thomas W. Collier (1986) "Revolutionary War," in Peter Paret (ed.) *Makers of Modern Strategy* (Princeton, NJ: Princeton University Press).

Simpkin, Richard E. (1985) *Race to the Swift: Thoughts on Twenty-First Century Warfare* (Oxford: Brassey's).

Simpson, Emile (2012) *War From the Ground Up: Twenty-First Century Combat as Politics* (Oxford: Oxford University Press).

Sinclair, Joseph (1992) *Arteries of War: A History of Military Transportation* (Shrewsbury: Airlife Publishing).

Singer, Peter W. (2004) *Corporate Warriors: The Rise of the Privatized Military Industry* (Ithaca, NY: Cornell University Press).

Sinno, Abdulkader H. (2008) *Organizations at War in Afghanistan and Beyond* (Ithaca, NY: Cornell University Press).

Sjoberg, Laura (2013) *Gendering Global Conflict: Towards a Feminist Theory of War* (New York: Columbia University Press).

Slantchev, Branislav (2012) "Borrowed Power: Debt Finance and the Resort to Arms," *American Political Science Review*, 106(4): 787–809.

Slantchev, Branislav (2011) *Military Threats: The Costs of Coercion and the Prize of Peace* (Cambridge: Cambridge University Press).

Sloan, Elinor C. (2012) *Modern Military Strategy: An Introduction* (London: Routledge).

Smedberg, Marco (2001) *Militär ledning: Från Napoleonkrigen till Bosnienkrisen* (Lund: Historiska Media).

Smedberg, Marco (1998) *Om Luftkriget: Från luftballonger till systemflygplan* (Stockholm: Page One).

Smith, Alastair & Allan C. Stam (2004) "Bargaining and the Nature of War," *Journal of Conflict Resolution*, 48(6): 783–813.

Smith, Mike (2005) Strategy in the Age of 'Low Intensity' Conflict: Why Clausewitz is Still More Relevant than his Critics'", in Jan Angstrom & Isabelle Duyvesteyn (eds.) *Rethinking the Nature of War* (London: Frank Cass).

Smith, Rupert (2005) *The Utility of Force: The Art of War in the Modern World* (London: Allen Lane).

Smith, Steve (2004) "Singing our World into Existence: International Relations Theory and September 11," *International Studies Quarterly*, 48(3): 499–515.

Smith, Steve, Ken Booth, & Marysia Zalewski (1996) "Introduction", in Steve Smith, Ken Booth, & Marysia Zalewski (eds.) *International Theory: Positivism and Beyond* (Cambridge: Cambridge University Press).

Smoke, Richard (1990) *War: Controlling Escalation* (Cambridge, MA: Harvard University Press).

Snyder, Glenn (2007) *Alliance Politics* (Ithaca, NY: Cornell University Press).

Snyder, Glenn (1984) "The Security Dilemma in Alliance Politics," *World Politics*, 36(4): 461–95.

Snyder, Jack (2000) *From Voting to Violence: Democratization and National Conflict* (New York: W. W. Norton).

Snyder, Jack (1984) *The Ideology of the Offensive: Military Decision Making and the Disasters of 1914* (Ithaca, NY: Cornell University Press).

Soeters, Joseph, Patricia Shields, & Bas Rietjens (eds.) (2014) *Routledge Handbook of Research Methods in Military Studies* (London: Routledge).

Sondhaus, Lawrence (2006) *Strategic Culture and Ways of War* (London: Routledge).

Sondhaus, Lawrence (2001) *Naval Warfare 1815–1914* (London: Routledge).

Speller, Ian (2008) "Naval Warfare," in David Jordan, James D. Kiras, David J. Lonsdale, Ian Speller, Christopher Tuck, & C. Dale Walton (eds.), *Understanding Modern Warfare* (Cambridge: Cambridge University Press, 2008), pp. 122–77.

Spykman, Nicholas J. (1942) *America's Strategy in World Politics* (New York: Harcourt, Brace).

Starry, Donn A. (1981) "Extending the Battlefield," *Military Review*, 61(3): 31–50.

Stavridis, James & Willam P. Mack (eds.) (1999) *Command at Sea*, 5th edn. (Annapolis, MD: Naval Institute Press).

Steadman, Stephen J. (1997) "Spoiler Problems in Peace Processes," *International Security*, 22(2): 5–53.

Stern, Maria & Maria Eriksson Baaz (2013) *Sexual Violence as a Weapon of War? Perceptions, Prescriptions, and Problems in the Congo and Beyond* (London: Zed Books).

Stern, Maria & Marysia Zalewski (2009) "Feminist Fatigue(s): Reflections on Feminism and Familiar Fables of Militarism," *Review of International Studies*, 35(3): 611–30.

Stockwell, Richard E. (1956) *Soviet Air Power* (New York: Pageant Press).

Stoecker, Sally (1998) *Forging Stalin's Army: Marshal Tukhachevsky and the Politics of Military Innovation* (Boulder, CO: Westview Press).

Stone, John (2013) "Cyber War Will Take Place!" *Journal of Strategic Studies*, 36(1): 101–8.

Stone, John (2011) *Military Strategy: The Politics and Technique of War* (New York: Continuum).

Strachan, Hew (2011) "Operational Art and Britain, 1909–2009," in John Andreas Olsen & Martin van Creveld (eds.) *The Evolution of Operational Art: From Napoleon to the Present* (Oxford: Oxford University Press).

Strachan, Hew (2007) *Clausewitz's On War: A Biography* (New York: Atlantic Monthly Press).

Strachan, Hew (2003) *The First World War: Volume 1: To Arms* (Oxford: Oxford University Press).

Strachan, Hew (2001) "Manoeuvre and Attrition: A Historical Perspective," in John Andreas Olsen (ed.) *From Manoeuvre Warfare to Kosovo?* Militaerteoretisk skriftserie, no. 2 (The Royal Norwegian Air Force Academy).

Strachan, Hew & Sibylle Scheippers (eds.) (2011) *The Changing Character of War* (Oxford: Oxford University Press).

Strachan, Hew & Andreas Herberg-Rothe (eds.) (2007) *Clausewitz in the Twenty-First Century* (Oxford: Oxford University Press).

Strange, Joe & Richard Iron (2005) *Understanding Centers of Gravity and Critical Vulnerabilities* (Stockholm: Swedish National Defence College).

Sumida, Jon Tetsuro (2008) *Decoding Clausewitz: A New Approach to On War* (Lawrence, Kansas: University Press of Kansas).

Summers, Harry G., Jr (1982) *On Strategy: A Critical Analysis of the Vietnam War* (Novato, CA: Presidio Press).

Sun Tzu (1994) *The Art of War*, translation Ralph D. Sawyer (Boulder, CO: Westview Press).

Swain, Richard M. (1996) "Filling the Void: the Operational Art and the U.S. Army," in B. J. C. McKercher & Michael A. Hennessy (eds.) *The Operational Art: Developments in the Theories of War* (Westport, CT: Praeger).

Taber, Robert (2002) *War of the Flea: The Classic Study of Guerrilla Warfare* (Washington DC: Brassey's).

Tangredi, Sam J. (2002) "Sea Power: Theory and Practice," in John Baylis, James J. Wirtz, & Colin S. Gray (eds.) *Strategy in the Contemporary World: An Introduction to Strategic Studies* (Oxford: Oxford University Press).

Thackrah, John Richard (2004) *Dictionary of Terrorism*, 2nd edn. (London: Routledge).

Themnér, Lotta & Peter Wallensteen (2011) "Armed Conflict, 1946–2010," *Journal of Peace Research*, 48(4): 525–36.

Thompson, Robert (1966) *Defeating Communist Insurgency: Experiences from Malaya and Vietnam* (London: Chatto & Windus).

Thomson, Julian (1991) *Lifeblood of War: Logistics in Armed Conflict* (London: Brassey's).

Thornton, Rod (2007) *Asymmetrical Warfare: Threat and Response in the Twenty-First Century* (Cambridge: Polity Press).

Tickner, J. Ann (2001) *Gendering World Politics* (New York: Columbia University Press).

Till, Geoffrey (2013) *Seapower: A Guide for the Twenty-First Century*, 3rd edn. (London: Routledge).

Tilly, Charles (2003) *The Politics of Collective Violence* (Cambridge: Cambridge University Press).

Tilly, Charles (1992) *Coercion, Capital and European States, AD 990–1992* (Oxford: Blackwells).

Toffler, Alvin & Heidi Toffler (1993) *War and Anti-War: Making Sense of Today's Global Chaos* (New York: Warner Books).

van Tol, Jan, Mark Guzinger, Andrew Krepinevich, & Jim Thomas (2010) *AirSea Battle: A Point-of-Departure Operational Concept* (Washington DC: CSBA).

Triandafillov, V. K. (1994) *The Nature of the Operations of Modern Armies*, translation Jacob W. Kipp (London: Frank Cass).

Trinquier, Roger (1964) *Modern Warfare: The French View of Counterinsurgency* (London: PallMall).

Tuck, Christopher (2008) "Land Warfare," in David Jordan, James D. Kiras, David J. Lonsdale, Ian Speller, Christopher Tuck, & C. Dale Walton (eds.) *Understanding Modern Warfare* (Cambridge: Cambridge University Press).

Ucko, David (2009) *The New Counterinsurgency Era: Transforming the US Military for Modern Wars* (Washington DC: Georgetown University Press).

Ullman, Harlan K. & James P. Wade (1996) *Shock and Awe: Achieving Rapid Dominance* (Washington DC: National Defence University).

Vasquez, John A. (ed.) (2012) *What Do We Know about War?* 2nd edn. (Lanham, MD: Rowman & Littlefield).

Vasquez, John A. (1993) *The War Puzzle* (Cambridge: Cambridge University Press).

Väyrynen, Raimo (ed.) (2006) *The Waning of Major War: Theories and Debates* (London: Routledge).

Vego, Milan (2009) *Joint Operational Warfare: Theory and Practice* (Washington DC: Naval War College Press).

Vego, Milan (2003a) *Naval Strategy and Operations in Narrow Seas*, 2nd edn. (London: Frank Cass).

Vego, Milan (2003b) "Net-Centric is not Decisive," *U.S. Naval Institute Proceedings*, 129(1): 52–7.

Vego, Milan (2000) "Center of Gravity," *Military Review*, 80(2): 23–9.

Vego, Milan (1992) *Soviet Naval Tactics* (Annapolis, MD: Naval Institute Press).

Vennesson, Pascal (1995) "Institution and Airpower: The Making of the French Air Force," in John Gooch (ed.) *Airpower: Theory and Practice* (London: Frank Cass).

Vertzberger, Yacoov (1990) *The World in Their Minds: Information Processing, Cognition and Perception in Foreign Policy Decisionmaking* (Stanford, CA: Stanford University Press).

Vigor, P. H. (1975) *The Soviet View of War, Peace and Neutrality* (London: Routledge).

Vo Nguyen Giap (1970) *The Military Art of People's War: Selected Writings of Vo Nguyen Giap* (New York: Monthly Review Press).

Vo Nguyen Giap (1962) *People's War, People's Army: The Viet Cong Insurrection Manual for Underdeveloped Countries* (New York: Praeger).

Wagner, Robert Harrison (2000) "Bargaining and War," *American Journal of Political Science*, 44(3): 469–84.

Wagner-Pacifici, Robin (2005) *The Art of Surrender: Decomposing Sovereignty at Conflict's End* (Chicago, IL: University of Chicago Press).

Waldman, Thomas (2013) *War, Clausewitz, and the Trinity* (Aldershot: Ashgate).

Wallensteen, Peter (2011) *Understanding Conflict Resolution: War, Peace and the Global System*, 3rd edn. (London: Sage).

Waltz, Kenneth N. (1979) *Theory of International Politics* (New York: McGraw-Hill).

Warden III, John A. (2000) *The Air Campaign: Planning for Combat*, 2nd edn. (New York: ToExcel).

Warden III, John A. (1998) "Success in Modern War: A Response to Robert Pape's *Bombing to Win*," *Security Studies*, 7(2): 172–90.

Warden III, John A. (1995) "The Enemy as a System," *Airpower Journal*, 9(1): 40–55.

Wedin, Lars (2007) *Marianne och Athena: Franskt militärt tänkande från 1700-talet till idag* (Stockholm: Swedish Defence College).

Weigley, Russell F. (1973) *The American Way of War: A History of United States Military Strategy and Policy* (Bloomington, IN: Indiana University Press).

Weinstein, Jeremy (2007) *Inside Rebellion: The Politics of Insurgent Violence* (Cambridge: Cambridge University Press).

Wenger, Andreas & Alex Wilner (2012) *Deterring Terrorism: Theory and Practice* (Stanford, CA: Stanford University Press).

West, Scott D. (1999) *Warden and the Air Corps Tactical School: Déjà Vu?* (Maxwell, AL: Air University Press).

Westad, Odd Arne (ed.) (2000) *Reviewing the Cold War: Approaches, Interpretations, Theory* (London: Frank Cass).

Widen, J. J. (2012) *Theorist of Maritime Strategy: Sir Julian Corbett and his Contribution to Military and Naval Thought* (Farnham: Ashgate).

Widen, J. J. (2011) "Naval Diplomacy: A Theoretical Approach," *Diplomacy & Statecraft*, 22(4): 715–33.

Wight, Martin (1966) "Why is there no International Theory?" in Herbert Butterfield & Martin Wight (eds.) *Diplomatic Investigations: Essays in the Theory of International Politics* (London: Allen & Unwin).

Wilcox, Lauren (2009) "Gendering the Cult of Offense," *Security Studies*, 18(2): 214–40.

Williams, Malcolm & Tim May (1996) *Introduction to the Philosophy of Social Research* (London: UCL Press).

Williams, Phil (1991) "Thomas Schelling," in John Baylis & John Garnett (eds.), *Makers of Nuclear Strategy* (London: Pinter).

Williamson, Murray & Mark Grimsley "Introduction: On Strategy," in Williamson Murray, MacGregor Knox, & Alvin Bernstein (eds.), *The Making of Strategy: Rulers, States, and War* (Cambridge: Cambridge University Press),

Wise, James (2011) *Women at War: Iraq, Afghanistan, and other Conflicts* (Annapolis, MD: Naval Institute Press).

Wohlstetter, Albert (1956) *Protecting US Power to Strike Back in the 1950s and 1960s* (Santa Monica, CA: RAND).

Wolfers, Arnold (1962) *Discord and Collaboration: Essays on International Politics* (Baltimore, MD: The Johns Hopkins Press).

Wood, Jason D. (2008) "Clausewitz in the Caliphate: Center of Gravity in the Post-9/11 Security Environment," *Comparative Strategy*, 27(1): 44–56.

Wright, Quincy (1941) *A Study of War*, vol. (Chicago: University of Illinois Press).

Zetterling, Niklas and Michael Tamelander (2009) *Tirpitz: The Life and Death of Germany's Last Super Battleship* (Havertown, PA: Casemate).

Zuehlke, Mark (2012) *Tragedy at Dieppe: Operation Jubilee, August 19, 1942* (Vancouver: D & M Publishers).

Index

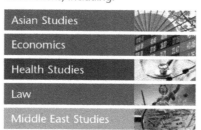